A DISTRIBUTED PI-CALCULUS

Distributed systems are fast becoming the norm in computer science. Formal mathematical models and theories of distributed behaviour are needed in order to understand them. This book proposes a distributed PI-CALCULUS called ADPI, for describing the behaviour of mobile agents in a distributed world. It is based on an existing formal language, the PI-CALCULUS, to which it adds a network layer and a primitive migration construct.

A mathematical theory of the behaviour of these distributed systems is developed, in which the presence of types plays a major role. It is also shown how, in principle, this theory can be used to develop verification techniques for guaranteeing the behaviour of distributed agents.

The text is accessible to computer scientists with a minimal background in discrete mathematics. It contains an elementary account of the PI-CALCULUS, and the associated theory of bisimulations. It also develops the type theory required by ADPI from first principles.

A DISTRIBUTED PI-CALCULUS

MATTHEW HENNESSY

CAMBRIDGE
UNIVERSITY PRESS

CAMBRIDGE
UNIVERSITY PRESS

Shaftesbury Road, Cambridge CB2 8EA, United Kingdom

One Liberty Plaza, 20th Floor, New York, NY 10006, USA

477 Williamstown Road, Port Melbourne, VIC 3207, Australia

314–321, 3rd Floor, Plot 3, Splendor Forum, Jasola District Centre, New Delhi – 110025, India

103 Penang Road, #05–06/07, Visioncrest Commercial, Singapore 238467

Cambridge University Press is part of Cambridge University Press & Assessment, a department of the University of Cambridge.

We share the University's mission to contribute to society through the pursuit of education, learning and research at the highest international levels of excellence.

www.cambridge.org
Information on this title: www.cambridge.org/9780521873307

First published 2007

A catalogue record for this publication is available from the British Library

ISBN 978-0-521-87330-7 Hardback

To the memory of John and Ray

Contents

Preface

From ATM machines dispensing cash from our bank accounts, to online shopping websites, interactive systems permeate our everyday life. The underlying technology to support these systems, both hardware and software, is well advanced. However design principles and techniques for assuring their correct behaviour are at a much more primitive stage.

The provision of solid foundations for such activities, mathematical models of system behaviour and associated reasoning tools, has been a central theme of theoretical computer science over the last two decades. One approach has been the design of *formal calculi* in which the fundamental concepts underlying interactive systems can be described, and studied. The most obvious analogy is the use of the λ-calculus as a simple model for the study of sequential computation, or indeed the study of sequential programming languages. *CCS* (a *C*alculus for *C*ommunicating *S*ystems) [28] was perhaps the first calculus proposed for the study of interactive systems, and was followed by numerous variations. This calculus consists of:

- A simple formal language for describing systems in terms of their structure; how they are constructed from individual, but interconnected, components.
- A semantic theory that seeks to understand the behaviour of systems described in the language, in terms of their ability to interact with users.

Here a system consists of a finite number of independent processes that intercommunicate using a fixed set of named communication channels. This set of channels constitutes a connection topology through which all communication takes place; it includes both communication between system components, and between the system and its users.

Although successful, *CCS* can only describe a very limited range of systems. The most serious restriction is that for any particular system its connection topology is static. However modern interactive systems are highly dynamic, particularly when one considers the proliferation of wide area networks. Here computational entities, or agents, are highly mobile, and as they roam the underlying network they forge new communication links with other entities, and perhaps relinquish existing links.

The PI-CALCULUS [9, 29] is a development from *CCS* that seeks to address at least some dynamic aspects of such agents. Specifically it includes the dynamic generation of communication channels and thus allows the underlying connection topology to vary as systems evolve. Just as importantly it allows private communication links to be established and maintained between agents, which adds considerably to its expressive power. Indeed the PI-CALCULUS very quickly became the focus of intensive research, both in providing for it a semantic understanding, and in its promotion as a suitable foundation for a theory of distributed systems; see [39] for a comprehensive account.

But many concepts fundamental to modern distributed systems, in particular those based on local area networks, are at most implicit in the PI-CALCULUS. Perhaps the most obvious is that of *domain*, to be understood quite generally as a locus for computational activity. Thus one could view a distributed system as consisting of a collection of domains, each capable of hosting computational processes, which in turn can migrate between domains.

The aim of this book is to develop an extension of the PI-CALCULUS in which these domains have an explicit representation. Of course when presented with such a prospect there is a bewildering number of concerns on which we may wish to focus. For example:

- What is the role of these domains?
- How are they to be structured?
- How is interprocess communication to be handled?
- How is agent migration to be described?
- Can agents be trusted upon entry to a *domain*?

Indeed the list is endless. Here our approach is conservative. We wish to develop a minimal extension of the PI-CALCULUS in which the concept of *domain* plays a meaningful, and non-trivial role. However their presence automatically brings a change of focus. The set of communication channels that in the PI-CALCULUS determines the interprocess communication topology now has to be reconciled with the *distribution topology*. Following our minimalistic approach we decide on a very simple distribution topology, namely a set of independent and non-overlapping domains, and only allow communication to happen within individual domains. This makes the communication channels of the PI-CALCULUS into local entities, in the sense that they only have significance relative to a particular domain. Indeed we will view them as a particularly simple form of *local resource*, to be used by migrant agents. Thus we view our extension of the PI-CALCULUS, called ADPI – for ASynchronous Distributed PI-CALCULUS, as a calculus for distributed systems in which

- dynamically created *domains* are hosts to resources, which may be used by *agents*
- agents reside in *domains*, and may migrate between domains for the purpose of using locally defined resources.

Types and type inference systems now form an intrinsic part of computer science. They are traditionally used in programming languages as a form of static analysis to ensure that no runtime errors occur during program execution. Increasingly sophisticated type-theoretic concepts have emerged in order to handle modern programming constructs [36]. However the application of type theory is very diverse. For example types can be used to

- check the correctness of security protocols [12]
- detect deadlocks and livelocks in concurrent programs [26]
- analyse information flow in security systems [22].

In this book we also demonstrate how type systems can be developed to manage access control to resources in distributed systems. In ADPI we can view domains as offering resources, modelled as communication channels, to migrating agents. Moreover a domain may wish to restrict access to certain resources to selected agents. More generally we can think of resources having capabilities associated with them. In our case two natural capabilities spring to mind:

- the ability to *update* a resource, that is write to a communication channel
- the ability to *look up* a resource, that is read from a communication channel.

Then domains may wish to distribute selectively to agents such capabilities on its local resources.

We could develop a version of ADPI in which the principal values manipulated by agents are these capabilities. But this would be a rather complex language, having to explicitly track their generation, management, and distribution. Instead we show that these capabilities can be implicitly managed by using a typed version of ADPI. Moreover the required types are only a mild generalisation of those used in a type inference system for ensuring the absence of runtime errors, when ADPI systems are considered as distributed programs.

The behavioural theory of processes originally developed for *CCS* [28] based on *bisimulations*, has been extended to the PI-CALCULUS, and can be readily extended to ADPI. Indeed the framework is quite general. The behaviour of processes can be described, independently of the syntax, in terms of their ability to *interact* with other processes, or more generally with their computing environment. The form these interactions take depend on the nature of the processes, and in general will depend on the process description language. They can be described mathematically as relations between processes, with

$$P \xrightarrow{l} Q$$

meaning the process P by interacting with its environment can be transformed into the process Q. The label l serves to record the kind of interaction involved, and perhaps some data used in the interaction. For example one can easily imagine the behaviour of an ATM machine being described in this manner, in terms of its internal states, and the evolution between these states depending of the different kinds of interactions with a customer. Such a behavioural description is formalised as a *labelled transition system*, or *lts*, and often refered to as an *operational semantics*.

The theory of bisimulations enables one to take such abstract behavioural descriptions of processes and generate a *behavioural equivalence* between processes. Intuitively

$$P \approx Q \tag{1}$$

will mean that no user, or computing environment, will be able to distinguish between P and Q using the interactions described in their behavioural descriptions.

However the use of types in ADPI has a serious impact on this general behavioural framework, particularly as these types implicitly represent the limited capabilities that agents have over resources. In other words these types limit the ways in which agents can interact with other agents. Consequently whether or not two agents are deemed equivalent will depend on the current distribution of the capabilities on the resources in the system.

The third and final aim of this book is to address this issue. We demonstrate that the general theory of bisimulations can be adapted to take the presence of types into account. We develop a relativised version of *behavioural equivalence* in which judgements such as (1) can never be made in absolute terms, but relative to a description of current capabilities. Moreover we will show that the proof techniques associated with standard bisimulations, based on *coinduction*, can be adapted to this more general framework, at least in principle.

A secondary aim of the book is didactic. Research into the use of formal calculi to model distributed or interactive systems, or even understanding the application of such calculi, requires detailed knowledge of a variety of mathematical concepts. We hope that the book will provide a good introduction to a range of these concepts, and equip the reader with sufficient understanding and familiarity to enable them to pursue independent research in the area. But we do not start from first principles. We assume the reader is at least familiar with elementary discrete mathematics, and in particular *structural induction*. It would also be helpful to have a passing acquaintance with *bisimulations*, as in [28]. Chapter 1 reviews the knowledge assumed in these areas. But other than this, the aim is to be self-contained. In particular we give a detailed exposition of the PI-CALCULUS, and an elementary introduction to types and typing systems.

Structure

As already stated, **Chapter 1: Background** recalls elementary notions of *induction* and *coinduction*, which will be used extensively in all subsequent chapters. However the only form of coinduction to be used is that associated with *bisimulations*, the theory of which is also reviewed.

The PI-CALCULUS, or at least our version of it – called API, for Asynchronous PI-CALCULUS, is explained in **Chapter 2: The asynchronous PI-CALCULUS**. This exposition starts from first principles, giving a detailed account of both syntactic and semantic concerns. We give two semantic accounts. The first, a so-called *reduction* semantics, may be viewed as a description, at a suitable level of abstraction, of a prototypical implementation of the language, explaining how API processes can be executed. The second gives an *lts* for API, explaining how processes can interact, by communicating along channels, with their peers. As we have already indicated this automatically gives us a bisimulation equivalence between processes, and moreover bisimulation theory supplies a very powerful coinductive proof principle for establishing equivalences.

However perhaps the most important topic in this chapter is a discussion of appropriate behavioural equivalences for process description languages in general. On the basis of some simple criteria we give a definition of a behavioural equivalence between processes, called *reduction barbed congruence*, $\cong$, which has the advantage of being applicable, or at least easily adapted to, most process description languages. We will also argue that it is the most natural semantic equivalence between processes; it relies essentially only on the process description language having a reduction semantics, and therefore is widely applicable. The chapter ends by showing how bisimulation equivalence needs to be adapted so as to coincide with $\cong$, thereby providing a complete coinductive proof principle for this natural behavioural equivalence.

In **Chapter 3: Types in API** we turn our attention to types, using a typed version of our language, TYPED API. By focusing on a straightforward notion of runtime error for API, we first explain the use of type systems, the general structure that the types need to take and the associated typechecking system. We then elaborate on the kind of technical results one needs to establish about such a framework. These cumulate to the demonstration of:

- *Subject reduction:* the property of being well-typed is preserved under the reduction semantics.
- *Type safety:* well-typed processes do not give rise to runtime errors.

Next we introduce a more sophisticated capability-based type system, in which a type corresponds to a set of capabilities, or permissions, on a channel or *resource*. By means of examples we show how this type system can be used to manage, or control, access to these resources. Establishing the required technical results in this case is somewhat more challenging.

As we have already indicated, the presence of types affects the perceived behaviour of processes, and consequently the behavioural theories of Chapter 2 need to be adapted to TYPED API. This is the topic of **Chapter 4: Types and behaviour in** API, and is quite a challenge. We need to adapt the standard approach for producing an *lts* from a process description language, explained in detailed in Chapter 2, to generate a more descriptive *lts* in which the actions are parameterised by the environment's knowledge of the current capabilities concerned. Most of this chapter is concerned with technical results, which ensure that the resulting *lts* is, in some sense, self-consistent.

We then go on to show how this parameterised *lts* can be used to generate a parameterised version of bisimulation equivalence between processes. In fact this is relatively straightforward, but we also need to prove that the resulting parameterised equivalence satisfies a range of mathematical properties, which one would intuitively expect from such a framework.

At last, in **Chapter 5: A distributed asynchronous** PI-CALCULUS we give a detailed account of our distributed version of API, called ADPI. The syntax is obtained by adding a new syntactic category, for systems, to that of TYPED API. We obtain a description language in which systems consist of a collection of *domains*, hosting agents, which can autonomously migrate between domains. These domains also host local channels on which agents communicate; but more generally these may be used to model *local resources*, accessible to agents currently located at the host domain. The capability-based type system from Chapter 3 is also extended. One novelty is the use of record types for domains, but the fact that resources are purely local also requires a significant extension to the set of types. Essentially the name of a local resource is useless, without knowledge of its location; for this reason local resources are typed using a primitive kind of *existential* channel type.

We demonstrate the usefulness of the typing system via a sequence of examples, and of course we also prove that it satisfies the standard properties one would expect of any reasonable typing system. The chapter then ends with a detailed

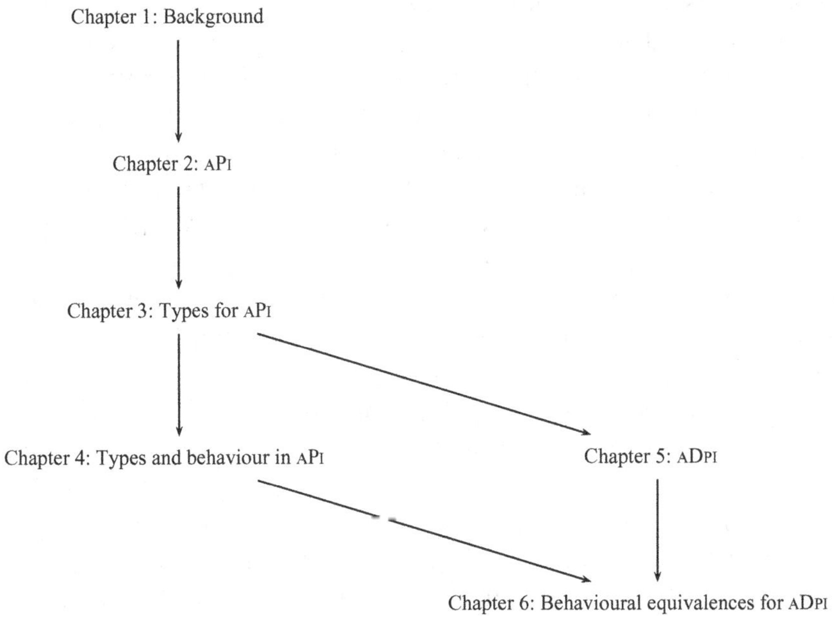

formal account of the role of types in aDpi. This involves defining a version of aDpi, called tagged-aDpi, in which capabilities, rather than values, are the main entities manipulated by agents. This is a rather complicated language as the capabilities, and their propagation, have to be explicitly managed by the reduction semantics. However we demonstrate that in reality, there is no need for such a detailed language; in the presence of the capability-based type system aDpi can be considered as a more abstract, and therefore more manageable, version of tagged-aDpi.

In **Chapter 6: Behavioural equivalences for aDpi** we adapt the parameterised theory of bisimulation equivalence from Chapter 4 to aDpi. In fact we spare the reader most of the technical proofs, as they can easily be adapted from those for aPi. Instead we show, via a number of examples, that at least in theory many of the standard methodologies associated with bisimulation equivalence can be adapted to prove equivalences between aDpi systems.

We also revisit the principal topic of Chapter 2. We justify our parameterised version of bisimulation equivalence by showing that it coincides with a natural intuitively defined behavioural equivalence, a typed version of reduction barbed congruence.

We end with a brief section, entitled **Sources**, with references to the original research papers on which our material is based, together with some pointers to related work.

The book is essentially divided into two parts. After reviewing some required background material in Chapter 2, the following three chapters aim to give a coherent and detailed introduction to the PI-CALCULUS. These chapters could form the basis of a postgraduate course on the PI-CALCULUS. Although they pursue a particular viewpoint, students completing them should be competent in the mathematical techniques underlying the theory of the PI-CALCULUS, and therefore should have no problem absorbing supplementary material, taken for example from [39], [29], or the research literature.

The second part of the book, Chapter 5 and Chapter 6, give a detailed account of the language ADPI, and its behavioural theory. This could form the core of a postgraduate course on *process calculi for distributed systems*, for students familiar with the PI-CALCULUS. However once more this would need to be augmented with additional material from the research literature, to reflect the varied approaches to the subject.

Alternatively, a less theoretical course could be based upon the first four sections of Chapter 2, Chapter 3 and the first three sections of Chapter 5. This foregoes most of the material on behavioural equivalences, concentrating on the basic semantics of the languages (the *reduction semantics*), and typing.

Each chapter ends with a set of exercises, which the reader is encouraged to answer. For the most part these are related directly to the material of the chapter, perhaps extending it in certain directions, or illustrating certain consequences. By and large they should present no difficulties, although a few may be non-trivial.

Acknowledgements

Most of the research reported on here was carried out over the years with a large number of colleagues. The main language of the book, aDpi, was originally developed in conjunction with James Riely, while the behavioural theory, in Chapter 4 and Chapter 6, was developed jointly with Julian Rathke. Other colleagues whose contributions and collaborative efforts I wish to acknowledge include Alberto Ciaffaglione, Adrian Francalanza, Samuel Hym, Massimo Merro and Nobuko Yoshida.

The book was largely written while the author held a Royal Society/Leverhulme Trust Senior Fellowship during the academic year 2005/2006, although some preliminary material on which it was based was presented at the *Bertinoro International Spring School for Graduate Studies in Computer Science* in March 2004.

Finally a number of colleagues read parts of the book in draft form, and made numerous useful suggestions for improvements. These include Adrian Francalanza, Samuel Hym, Sergio Maffeis, Julian Rathke, James Riely and Nobuko Yoshida.

1
Inductive principles

Throughout the book we will make extensive use of both induction and coinduction, and their associated proof techniques. Here we give a brief review of these concepts, and an indication of how we intend to use them.

1.1 Induction

Figure 1.1 contains a definition of the (abstract) syntax of a simple language of machines. Here a ranges over some set of action labels Act, and intuitively a machine can carry out sequences of these actions, and periodically has a choice of which actions to perform. Let $\mathcal{M}$ be the set of all machines defined in Figure 1.1. Formally this is an *inductive* definition of a set, namely the least set S that satisfies

- $\mathsf{stop} \in S$
- $M \in S$ implies $a.M \in S$ for every action label a in Act
- $M_1, M_2 \in S$ implies $M_1 + M_2 \in S$.

The fact that $\mathcal{M}$ is the least set that satisfies these conditions gives us a proof technique for defining and proving properties of machines in $\mathcal{M}$; any other set satisfying the conditions is guaranteed to contain $\mathcal{M}$.

As an example consider the following definition of the *size* of a machine:

- $|\mathsf{stop}| = 0$
- $|a.M| = 1 + |M|$
- $|M_1 + M_2| = |M_1| + |M_2|$.

We know by induction that this function is now defined for every machine. Belabouring the point for emphasis let D be the domain of the size function $|\ \ |$, the set of elements for which it is defined. The three clauses in the definition of $|\ \ |$ above imply that D satisfies the three defining properties of $\mathcal{M}$. So we can conclude that $\mathcal{M} \subseteq D$; that is every machine is in the domain of $|\ \ |$. We refer to

$$M \quad ::= \mathsf{stop} \ \mid a.M \ \mid M + M$$

Figure 1.1 Syntax for finite machines

this form of induction as *structural induction*, as it uses the structure of the language of machines.

We can also use induction to define the intended behaviour of machines. These machines perform sequences of actions, but these sequences can be characterised indirectly by describing what initial action a machine M can perform, and the residual of M after the action, the part of M that subsequently remains to be executed. This is given by defining a ternary relation over $\mathcal{M} \times \mathsf{Act} \times \mathcal{M}$, with

$$M \xrightarrow{a} N \tag{1.1}$$

indicating that the machine M can perform an action labelled a, with N as residual. Formally the relation $M \xrightarrow{a} N$ is defined inductively, as the least relation that satisfies the axiom (M-MOVE), and the rules (M-CHOICE.L) and (M-CHOICE.R) in Figure 1.2. The general form of these rules is

$$\text{(M-RULE)} \quad \frac{\textbf{premise}_1, \ldots \textbf{premise}_n}{\textbf{conclusion}}$$

This consists of a number, possibly zero, of **premises**, and a **conclusion**, meaning that if all of the premises can be established then the **conclusion** is true. When the set of **premises** is empty, we have an axiom, which will be written more simply as

$$\text{(M-AXIOM)} \quad \textbf{conclusion}$$

The nature of these rules ensures that there is always a *least* relation satisfying them. Informally each rule can be viewed as a property of relations; it is true of $\mathcal{R}$ if, whenever each premise is true of $\mathcal{R}$ it follows that the conclusion is also true of $\mathcal{R}$. Now consider a collection of such rules, $\mathcal{C}$. Suppose $\mathcal{R}_i$, $i \in I$, is a family of relations, all of which satisfy each rule in $\mathcal{C}$. Then one can check that $\cap_I \mathcal{R}_i$ also satisfies them. So the least relation satisfying the rules $\mathcal{C}$ can be taken to be the intersection of all the relations satisfying them. In fact we take this least relation to be the relation *defined* by the rules $\mathcal{C}$.

$$\text{(M-MOVE)} \quad a.M \xrightarrow{a} M \qquad \text{(M-CHOICE.L)} \quad \frac{M_1 \xrightarrow{a} N}{M_1 + M_2 \xrightarrow{a} N} \qquad \text{(M-CHOICE.R)} \quad \frac{M_2 \xrightarrow{a} N}{M_1 + M_2 \xrightarrow{a} N}$$

Figure 1.2 An inductive definition of actions

More prosaically one can show this least relation simply consists of all judgements for which there is a proof using the rules from $\mathcal{C}$. As an example of such a $\mathcal{C}$ take those in Figure 1.2, consisting of one axiom and two rules. We can take (1.1) above to be the relation defined by $\mathcal{C}$. Thus if we assert (1.1) for a particular M, N and a, then we have a proof of this fact, using a series of applications of this axiom and of the two rules. For example we can prove

$$a.(b.\,\mathsf{stop} + a.\,\mathsf{stop}) + b.(a.\,\mathsf{stop} + c.b.\,\mathsf{stop}) \xrightarrow{a} (b.\,\mathsf{stop} + a.\,\mathsf{stop}) \tag{1.2}$$

in two steps. The first is an application of the axiom (M-MOVE) to obtain

$$a.(b.\,\mathsf{stop} + a.\,\mathsf{stop}) \xrightarrow{a} (b.\,\mathsf{stop} + a.\,\mathsf{stop})$$

Then an application of (M-CHOICE.L) to this gives (1.2).

So if we want to prove a property of any judgement of the form (1.1) above we can use induction on the length of its proof; that is on the number of applications of rules or axioms, or more generally on the structure of the proof. We call this form of induction *rule induction*.

As an example of its use let us prove the following, rather obvious, fact:

Lemma 1.1 If $M \xrightarrow{a} M'$ *then* $|M'| < |M|$.

Proof: There is an embarrassing number of inductive definitions involved in this statement; the set of machines over which M and M' range, the inductively defined function $|\ |$ and the inductively defined relation $M \xrightarrow{a} N$; for the purposes of exposition we concentrate on this last.

Since $M \xrightarrow{a} M'$ we have a proof of this fact using the rules in Figure 1.2. We prove the statement of the lemma using induction on the structure of this proof; that is we use *rule induction*.

The proof must have non-zero length, and we examine the last rule used in its derivation. There are three possibilities.

- The first is when this last rule is (M-MOVE), in which case the length of the proof is one. Then M and M' are of the form $a.N$ and N respectively, for some machine N. Looking up the definition of the function $|\ |$ we immediately find that $|a.N| = 1 + |N|$, and therefore the required result is true.
- The second possibility is that the rule (M-CHOICE.L) is used. So M has the form $M_1 + M_2$ and we know that $M_1 \xrightarrow{a} M'$. Moreover the derivation of this latter judgement is strictly contained in that of $M \xrightarrow{a} M'$. Therefore we may apply the inductive hypothesis to conclude that $|M'| < |M_1|$. Again looking up the definition of the function we see that $|M| = |M_1| + |M_2|$, and therefore $|M_1| \leq |M|$. The requirement, that $|M'| < |M|$, therefore again follows.
- The third and final possibility is that (M-CHOICE.R) is the last rule used. This is another inductive case, and the argument is identical to the second possibility. ■

Let us end this section by remarking that formally we have defined (1.1) as a ternary relation over $\mathcal{M} \times \mathsf{Act} \times \mathcal{M}$. However we will often view this as a *family* of relations $\xrightarrow{a}$, one for each a in Act.

1.2 Coinduction

Induction is a mathematical argument obtained by virtue of the fact that some relation $\mathcal{R}$ is defined to be the *least* one satisfying certain properties; any other relation satisfying these properties contains $\mathcal{R}$. Coinduction, the dual argument, is obtained by virtue of the fact that a relation $\mathcal{R}$ is defined to be the *largest* one satisfying certain properties; then any other relation satisfying the defining properties is contained in $\mathcal{R}$. To see an example let us first set up the general framework we will use in our behavioural descriptions of languages.

Definition 1.2 (lts) A *labelled transition system*, or more briefly, an *lts*, consists of

- a set of *configurations* or *states*, $\mathcal{S}$
- a set of action labels, Act
- for each action label a, a binary next state relation $R_a \subseteq \mathcal{S} \times \mathcal{S}$.

We will often use suggestive notation such as $P \xrightarrow{a} Q$ to denote the fact that $\langle P, Q\rangle$ is contained in R_a, and refer to Q as a *residual* of P after performing the action a. ♦

The set of states $\mathcal{S}$ will often be simply the set of terms of some language and the relations will define the various ways in which observers or users can interact with programs or processes written in the language. Figures 1.1 and 1.2 give a typical example. Taken together they define the following *lts*:

- The set of states are all terms M that can be defined using the rules in Figure 1.1.
- For each action label a in Act the relation R_a consists of all pairs $\langle M, M'\rangle$ for which the judgement $M \xrightarrow{a} M'$ can be derived using the rules in Figure 1.2.

Indeed this is a proto-typical example of the *operational semantics* of a language. We will see many other examples, but each follow precisely this schema. An lts will be defined using the terms of some language for describing processes, some set of action labels Act appropriate to the language, and for each a in Act an inductively defined relation over process terms. Note that this framework will give us two forms of induction; *structural induction* on process terms, and *rule induction* on the relations.

Now consider an arbitrary lts, $(\mathcal{S}, \mathsf{Act}, \xrightarrow{a})$ and let $\mathcal{R}$ be an arbitrary relation over the set of states $\mathcal{S}$; that is suppose $\mathcal{R} \subseteq \mathcal{S} \times \mathcal{S}$. We say $\mathcal{R}$ is a *strong bisimulation* if it satisfies the following two properties:

(1) $P_1 \mathcal{R} P_2$ and $P_1 \xrightarrow{a} P_1'$ implies $P_2 \xrightarrow{a} P_2'$ for some state P_2' such that $P_1' \mathcal{R} P_2'$
(2) $P_1 \mathcal{R} P_2$ and $P_2 \xrightarrow{a} P_2'$ implies $P_1 \xrightarrow{a} P_1'$ for some state P_1' such that $P_1' \mathcal{R} P_2'$

for every action a in Act. These properties are often written graphically (less precisely); for example the property (1) of $\mathcal{R}$ above can be represented as:

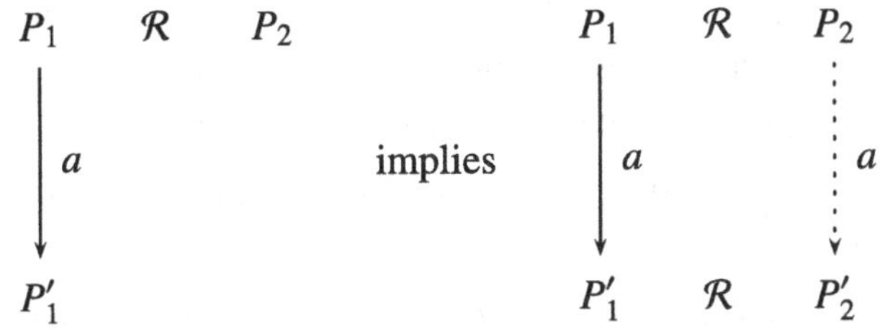

This is often called the *strong transfer property* for $\mathcal{R}$ in the lts in question; in these diagrams the dotted arrow refers to a relation that is required, as opposed to the standard arrow that indicates a given relation. Note that property (2) is equivalent to requiring that the inverse of $\mathcal{R}$, denoted $\mathcal{R}^{-1}$, also satisfies this transfer property. In other words $\mathcal{R}$ is a bisimulation if it, and its inverse, satisfies the transfer property. In general there is no requirement for a bisimulation to be symmetric; but if it happens to be symmetric then checking (2), the transfer property for its inverse, is vacuous.

We use $\sim_{bis}$ to denote the *largest* bisimulation, which is referred to as *strong bisimulation equivalence*. Note that if $\mathcal{R}_i$ is any family of bisimulations, where i ranges over some index set I, then it is easy to check that $\cup_I \mathcal{R}_i$ is also a bisimulation. From this we see that $\sim_{bis}$ exists since we can define it to be the set theoretic union of all bisimulations.

The fact that $\sim_{bis}$ is the *largest* relation satisfying the transfer property gives us a proof technique: any other relation satisfying the transfer property is contained in $\sim_{bis}$. So, for example, to prove that $P \sim_{bis} Q$ for some particular pair of states P, Q, it is sufficient to exhibit *any* bisimulation containing the pair $\langle P, Q \rangle$. For example

$$a.(b.\,\mathsf{stop} + b.\,\mathsf{stop}) + a.b.\,\mathsf{stop} \quad \sim_{bis} \quad a.b.\,\mathsf{stop}$$

because the following is a bisimulation:

$$\begin{array}{rcl} a.(b.\,\mathsf{stop} + b.\,\mathsf{stop}) + a.b.\,\mathsf{stop} & \leftrightarrow & a.b.\,\mathsf{stop} \\ b.\,\mathsf{stop} + b.\,\mathsf{stop} & \leftrightarrow & b.\,\mathsf{stop} \\ b.\,\mathsf{stop} & \leftrightarrow & b.\,\mathsf{stop} \\ \mathsf{stop} & \leftrightarrow & \mathsf{stop} \end{array}$$

Here we have given a graphical representation of a relation $\mathcal{R}$ over machine states by enumerating all its elements; $P \leftrightarrow Q$ signifies that the pair $\langle P, Q \rangle$ is in $\mathcal{R}$.

Demonstrating that $\mathcal{R}$ is indeed a bisimulation requires some checking. But an exhaustive analysis will show that this relation does indeed satisfy the transfer property; each action by a process in the relation can be appropriately matched by an action of its partner.

This form of reasoning, based on the fact that $\sim_{bis}$ is the largest relation satisfying the strong transfer property, is an instance of *coinduction*. We will use it frequently, both to show particular processes equivalent, but also to prove more general properties. As a simple example of the latter let us prove:

Lemma 1.3 In any lts $(\mathcal{S}, \mathsf{Act}, \xrightarrow{a})$ *strong bisimulation equivalence* $\sim_{bis}$ *is an equivalence relation.*

Proof: We have to show that $\sim_{bis}$ is reflexive, symmetric and transitive.

reflexive: The identity relation over states,

$$\{ (P,P) \mid P \in \mathcal{S} \}$$

is easily shown to be a bisimulation, and therefore is contained in strong bisimulation. Consequently $P \sim_{bis} P$ for every element P in $\mathcal{S}$.

symmetric: Individual bisimulations are not necessarily symmetric. But because of the symmetry of the transfer property it is easy to check that the largest bisimulation is symmetric. Let

$$\mathcal{R} = \{ \langle Q,P \rangle \mid P \sim_{bis} Q \}$$

This is easily shown to be a strong bisimulation, from which the symmetry of $\sim_{bis}$ follows.

transitive: Let $\mathcal{R}$ be the set of all pairs $\langle P,Q \rangle$ such that there exists some R such that $P \sim_{bis} R$ and $R \sim_{bis} Q$. Using the symbol $\circ$ to denote the composition of relations, $\mathcal{R}$ could be defined to be $(\sim_{bis}) \circ (\sim_{bis})$. Then one can show that $\mathcal{R}$ is a strong bisimulation. For example suppose $P \mathcal{R} Q$ and $P \xrightarrow{a} P'$; we must find a matching move from Q, that is some $Q \xrightarrow{a} Q'$ such that $P' \mathcal{R} Q'$.
We know that for some R, $P \sim_{bis} R$ and $R \sim_{bis} Q$. So there exists a matching move from R, that is some $R \xrightarrow{a} R'$ such that $P' \sim_{bis} R'$. Furthermore this move from R can be matched by one from Q: there exists some $Q \xrightarrow{a} Q'$ such that $R' \sim_{bis} Q'$. But this is the required matching move, since by definition $P' \mathcal{R} Q'$. ■

1.3 Bisimulation equivalence

The operational behaviour of processes will be described using an lts. In many cases this involves having a special action label in Act, called τ, to represent *unobservable* internal activity; other elements in Act will usually represent some form of *observable* behaviour, that is behaviour that can be seen, or provoked, by external observers. The special nature of the action τ requires a revision of the notion of strong bisimulation.

Example 1.4 Consider the two machines M, N defined by

$$a.b.\mathsf{stop} \qquad a.\tau.b.\mathsf{stop}$$

respectively. According to our definition we have $M \not\sim_{bis} N$, although it is difficult to imagine a scenario in which external users would be able to perceive a difference in their behaviour. ■

We need to revise our definition so as to abstract away from internal actions.

Again we suppose an arbitrary lts $(S, \mathsf{Act}, \xrightarrow{a})$ in which $\mathsf{Act} = \mathsf{eAct} \cup \{\tau\}$. For every sequence $s \in \mathsf{eAct}^*$ we can define the corresponding *weak* action

$$P \overset{s}{\Longrightarrow} Q$$

in which P can evolve to Q performing the visible actions in s, interspersed with arbitrary sequences of internal actions. Formally, if $s = \alpha_1 \alpha_2 \ldots \alpha_n$, $n \geq 0$, where $\alpha_i \in \mathsf{eAct}$, this means that

$$P \xrightarrow{\tau}{}^* \xrightarrow{\alpha_1} \xrightarrow{\tau}{}^* \xrightarrow{\alpha_2} \xrightarrow{\tau}{}^* \ldots \xrightarrow{\tau}{}^* \xrightarrow{\alpha_n} \xrightarrow{\tau}{}^* Q$$

Note that if ε represents the empty sequence then $P \overset{\varepsilon}{\Longrightarrow} Q$ means that $P \xrightarrow{\tau}{}^* Q$.

Now we can revise our definition of bisimulations, using this new notion of action.

Definition 1.5 (bisimulations) A relation $\mathcal{R}$ over the states S of the lts $(S, \mathsf{Act}, \xrightarrow{a})$ is called a *bisimulation* if it satisfies the following transfer property:

- $P_1 \,\mathcal{R}\, P_2$ and $P_1 \overset{s}{\Longrightarrow} P_1'$ implies $P_2 \overset{s}{\Longrightarrow} P_2'$ for some state P_2' such that $P_1' \,\mathcal{R}\, P_2'$
- $P_1 \,\mathcal{R}\, P_2$ and $P_2 \overset{s}{\Longrightarrow} P_2'$ implies $P_1 \overset{s}{\Longrightarrow} P_1'$ for some state P_1' such that $P_1' \,\mathcal{R}\, P_2'$

for every s in eAct^*. Diagrammatically we require both $\mathcal{R}$ and its inverse to satisfy:

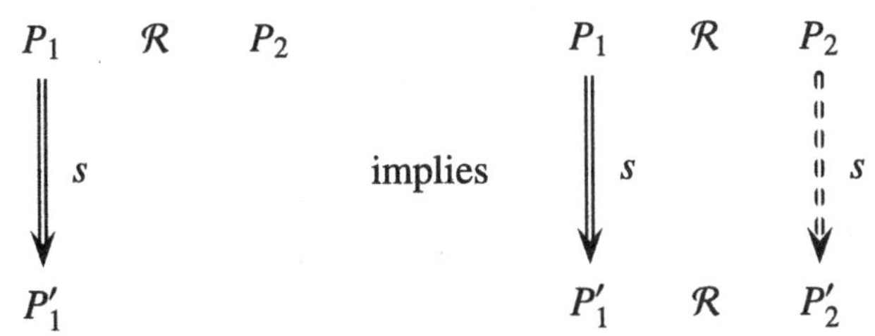

♦

As with strong bisimulations, we know that the largest bisimulation exists and we denote it by $\approx_{bis}$. Moreover it comes with its own form of coinduction: for example to show $P \approx_{bis} Q$ it is sufficient to exhibit a bisimulation containing the pair $\langle P, Q \rangle$. For example $a.b.\,\mathsf{stop} \approx_{bis} a.\tau.b.\,\mathsf{stop}$ because the following is a bisimulation:

$$
\begin{array}{rcl}
a.b.\,\mathsf{stop} & \leftrightarrow & a.\tau.b.\,\mathsf{stop} \\
b.\,\mathsf{stop} & \leftrightarrow & \tau.b.\,\mathsf{stop} \\
b.\,\mathsf{stop} & \leftrightarrow & b.\,\mathsf{stop} \\
\mathsf{stop} & \leftrightarrow & \mathsf{stop}
\end{array}
$$

We can also use coinduction in more general reasoning about the equivalence $\approx_{bis}$; for example we can mimic the arguments given above for $\sim_{bis}$ to prove that $\approx_{bis}$ is an equivalence relation.

To prove that a relation has the transfer property, as currently formulated, is quite onerous; there is a quantification over all sequences s of action labels from eAct^*. It turns out that this can be considerably relaxed; it is sufficient to match strings of length at most one. In fact we can go further and demand only that *strong actions*, $P_1 \xrightarrow{\mu} P'_1$ where μ ranges over Act, be matched; of course this matching may be done by a weak action, one allowing an arbitrary number of interspersed internal actions.

Definition 1.6 (*simple bisimulations*) First some notation. For any $\mu \in \mathsf{Act}$ let $P_1 \stackrel{\hat{\mu}}{\Longrightarrow} P'_1$ mean

- $P_1 \stackrel{\mu}{\Longrightarrow} P'_1$ if μ is an external action label, that is an element of eAct
- $P_1 \xrightarrow{\tau}{}^* P'_1$ if μ is the internal action τ.

Then we say a relation $\mathcal{R}$ over the states of an lts is a *simple bisimulation* if it satisfies the following transfer property, for every μ in Act:

- $P_1 \,\mathcal{R}\, P_2$ and $P_1 \xrightarrow{\mu} P'_1$ implies $P_2 \stackrel{\hat{\mu}}{\Longrightarrow} P'_2$ for some state P'_2 such that $P'_1 \,\mathcal{R}\, P'_2$
- $P_1 \,\mathcal{R}\, P_2$ and $P_2 \xrightarrow{\mu} P'_2$ implies $P_1 \stackrel{\hat{\mu}}{\Longrightarrow} P'_1$ for some state P'_1 such that $P'_1 \,\mathcal{R}\, P'_2$.

Diagrammatically we require $\mathcal{R}$ and its inverse to satisfy:

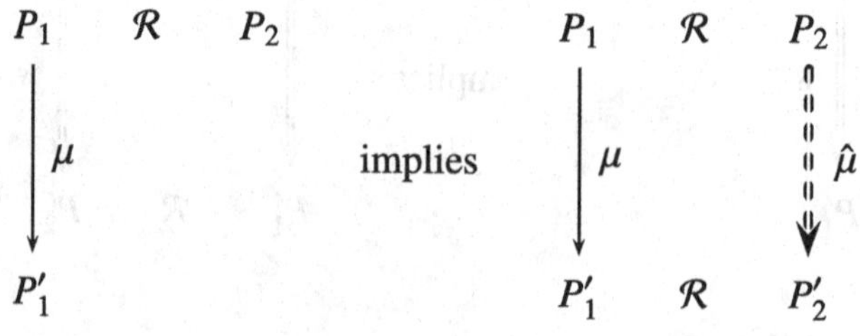

♦

Thus we demand that a strong external action, $P_1 \xrightarrow{\alpha} P'_1$ where $\alpha \in \mathsf{eAct}$, be matched by a weak external action $P_2 \stackrel{\alpha}{\Longrightarrow} P'_2$ but allow single internal actions,

$P_1 \xrightarrow{\tau} P_1'$, to be matched by an action consisting of a series of zero or more internal actions $P_2 \xrightarrow{\tau}{}^* P_2'$.

Theorem 1.7 If $P_1 \mathcal{R} P_2$, where $\mathcal{R}$ is a simple bisimulation, then $P_1 \approx_{bis} P_2$.

Proof: It suffices to show that $\mathcal{R}$ is a bisimulation. Suppose $P_1 \stackrel{s}{\Longrightarrow} P_1'$. We find the matching move by induction on the overall size of the derivation of $P_1 \stackrel{s}{\Longrightarrow} P_1'$. Then there are three possibilities:

- The sequence s is empty ϵ, and indeed the entire derivation sequence is empty, that is $P_1 \stackrel{\epsilon}{\Longrightarrow} P_1'$ because P_1' is P_1.
  In this case the matching move is also the trivial move $P_2 \stackrel{\epsilon}{\Longrightarrow} P_2$.
- The derivation can be deconstructed into $P_1 \xrightarrow{\alpha} Q_1 \stackrel{s'}{\Longrightarrow} P_1'$, where α is an external action. In this case s has the form $\alpha.s'$.
  We can use the fact that $\mathcal{R}$ is a simple bisimulation to find a corresponding weak action $P_2 \stackrel{\alpha}{\Longrightarrow} Q_2$ such that $Q_1 \mathcal{R} Q_2$. But now we can apply induction to the move $Q_1 \stackrel{s'}{\Longrightarrow} P_1'$, to obtain a matching move $Q_2 \stackrel{s'}{\Longrightarrow} P_2'$ such that $P_1' \mathcal{R} P_2'$. These two moves can now be combined to give the required matching move $P_2 \stackrel{\alpha.s'}{\Longrightarrow} P_2'$.
- The derivation can be deconstructed into $P_1 \xrightarrow{\tau} Q_1 \stackrel{s}{\Longrightarrow} P_1'$.
  Here we again apply the definition of simple bisimulations to obtain a move $P_2 \xrightarrow{\tau}{}^* Q_2$ such that $Q_1 \mathcal{R} Q_2$. As in the previous case induction gives a move $Q_2 \stackrel{s'}{\Longrightarrow} P_2'$ such that $P_1' \mathcal{R} P_2'$, and these two moves can be again combined to give the required matching move $P_2 \stackrel{s}{\Longrightarrow} P_2'$. ■

It is this form of bisimulation that we use throughout the book, and we will omit the qualifier *simple*. For the various languages considered we give an operational semantics in the form of an lts. Intuitively

- The states will consist of the collection of *processes* that can be defined using the language; sometimes these will be more general configurations consisting of processes combined with interfaces to external users.
- The action labels, which will always include τ, will be the different ways in which we believe users or observers can interact with processes.
- The next-state relations $\xrightarrow{\mu}$, defined inductively, will represent the manner in which these interactions can change processes.

Given this framework we immediately obtain a behavioural equivalence $\approx_{bis}$ for the processes definable in the language. As we have seen this equivalence automatically comes equipped with powerful coinductive proof techniques. Their properties will be developed, using the notion of simple bisimulations, rather than the original one from Definition 1.5.

2

The asynchronous PI-CALCULUS

Here we describe a simple language in which values are exchanged between concurrent processes via *communication channels*. These channels can be used to model resources and the syntax allows them to be declared as private, for the exclusive shared use of specific processes. The names of these channels/resources can also be transmitted between processes, resulting in a very powerful descriptive language.

We give two different views of the language. The first, via a *reduction semantics*, describes how processes may evolve. This may be seen as a specification of an interpreter for the language and is taken to be the primary semantic definition. The second view is an *action semantics*, which describes how processes can interact with other processes, perhaps as part of a larger system; this describes how processes can behave as part of a larger endeavour. This second view interprets the language as a *labelled transition system* or *lts*, as explained in Definition 1.2, and thus induces automatically a bisimulation equivalence between processes.

2.1 The language API

The syntax of the language API is given in Figure 2.1. It presupposes a set Names of names, ranged over by $n, m, \ldots, a, b, c \ldots$ for communication channels or resources. We also use a set Vars of variables, place-holders for values that can be transmitted via the communication channels. These values will include some unspecified collection of base values such as integers, booleans, strings, etc., ranged over by bv, but more importantly channel names themselves. We will reserve the meta-variable u for *identifiers*, that is either names or variables. The intuitive meaning of each of the syntactic constructs is as follows:

- The simplest possible process, which does nothing, is represented by the term stop.
- The term $c!\langle V\rangle$ represents the next simplest process, which can transmit the *value* V along the channel c. Values V are *structured*, taking the form $(v_1, \ldots, v_k)$, where v_i are

R, S, B ::=	*Process terms*
$u!\langle V\rangle$	Output
$u?(X)\,R$	Input
$(\mathsf{new}\, n)\,R$	Channel name creation
if $v_1 = v_2$ then R_1 else R_2	Matching
$R_1 \mid R_2$	Composition
rec $x.\ B$	Recursive definition
x	Recursion variable
stop	Termination

Figure 2.1 Syntax for aPi

v, w ::=	*Simple values*
n	names
x	variables
bv	basic values
U, V, W ::=	*Values*
$(v_1, \ldots, v_n),\ n \geq 0$	tupling
X, Y ::=	*Patterns*
$(x_1, \ldots, x_n),\ n \geq 0$	tupling

Figure 2.2 Patterns and values in aPi

simple values; these in turn consist of identifiers or basic values. See Figure 2.2 for their syntax. The value $V = (v_1, \ldots, v_k)$ is said to have *arity* k.

- Input from a channel c is represented by the term $c?(X)\,R$, where X is a pattern that may be used to deconstruct the incoming value. Patterns are constructed by the tupling together of variables, as described in Figure 2.2; for simplicity we also assume occurrences of variables in patterns are always unique. The process $c?(X)\,R$ may input a value V along the channel c, deconstruct it using the pattern X and then execute R into which the components of V have been substituted, which we will denote by $R\{\!|{}^{V}\!/\!{}_{X}|\!\}$; see Notation 2.1 below.
- if $v_1 = v_2$ then R_1 else R_2 is a test for the identity of simple values.
- $R_1 \mid R_2$ represents two processes running in parallel; they may exchange values using input/output on channels.
- $(\mathsf{new}\, n)\,R$ is a scoping mechanism for names. For example in the process

$$R_1 \mid (\mathsf{new}\, n)\, R_2$$

the name n is known to R_2 but not to R_1; of course names are values and so in the course of a computation n may be made known to R_1 as the result of a communication; this will be referred to as the *scope extrusion* of the name n.

- $\mathsf{rec}\ x.\ B$ is a mechanism for defining recursive processes. Here B, a process term, represents the *body* of the recursive definition, and occurrences of x within B stand for recursive calls. A more elaborate mechanism would allow these definitions to be parameterised over, for example, values. Note that we do not distinguish between the variables used in recursive definitions, and those used as placeholders for values; this is simply to avoid additional notational complexity.

The term $F_1(b,c)$, defined by

$$F_1(b,c) \Leftarrow \mathsf{rec}\ z.\ b?(x)\ (c!\langle x\rangle \mid z)$$

represents a simple process that repeatedly receives a value on channel b and forwards it along channel c. Note that this *definition* is purely notational. We simply mean that $F_1(b,c)$ is used as a shorthand notation for the process term $\mathsf{rec}\ z.\ b?(x)\ (c!\langle x\rangle \mid z)$; we will use this device extensively. Two such forwarding processes can be run in parallel, as for example in

$$\mathsf{FF}_1 \Leftarrow (\mathsf{new}\, c)(F_1(b,c) \mid F_1(c,d))$$

where $F_1(c,d)$ is given by

$$F_1(c,d) \Leftarrow \mathsf{rec}\ z.\ c?(x)\ (d!\langle x\rangle \mid z)$$

In the system FF_1 the two concurrent processes $F_1(b,c)$ and $F_1(c,d)$ share a common local channel c along which they may communicate. $F_1(b,c)$ can input a value along b and make it available to $F_1(c,d)$ at channel c; $F_1(c,d)$, on receipt of the value, may in turn make it available at d. The restriction operator $(\mathsf{new}\, c)$ ensures that the channel c is private to FF_1; no process other than $F_1(b,c)$ and $F_1(c,d)$ can use it.

Note that in FF_1, $F_1(b,c)$ may input a second value before $F_1(c,d)$ reads the first one from the internal channel c. Consequently FF_1, viewed as a *forwarder* from channel b to d, will not necessarily preserve the order of values transmitted. The basic problem is that outputs are *asynchronous*; having transmitted a value there is no guarantee that the recipient has actually consumed it. However we can use the power of API to transmit channel names to set up a simple communication protocol in which senders await an acknowledgement each time a value is transmitted. Suppose we have at our disposal a channel named ack. Then in

$$c!\langle v, \mathsf{ack}\rangle \mid \mathsf{ack}?()\, R$$

a value v is transmitted on c *together with* the channel ack. The continuation R is then only executed once an acknowledgement has been received on ack. The receiving process is expected to send this acknowledgement, via the simple process $\mathsf{ack}!\langle()\rangle$, whenever a value is received on c. Here the notation $()$ means an *empty tuple* of values; that is no value is sent and the channel ack is simply used for synchronisation. However in future, to avoid the proliferation of brackets, we will render the transmission along these synchronisation channels simply by $\mathsf{ack}!\langle\rangle$. This also explains the input notation. In $\mathsf{ack}?()\,R$ the syntax $()$ represents the *empty pattern*. That is no data is expected on the channel; more correctly this process should be rendered as $\mathsf{ack}?(())\,R$.

This acknowledgement scheme is used in the following revision of the forwarder:

$$F_2(b,c,\mathsf{ack}) \Leftarrow \mathsf{rec}\ z.\ b?(x,y)\ (\ c!\langle x,\mathsf{ack}\rangle \mid \mathsf{ack}?()\ \ (y!\langle\rangle \mid z))$$

Here the input channel b receives from a source client a value to be forwarded, bound to x, and an acknowledgement channel, bound to y. The value is then output to the destination client on the channel c, together with the name of the acknowledgement channel ack. At this point the acknowledgement is awaited on ack; when it is received the original acknowledgement, bound to y, is sent to the source client, and the forwarder is ready for a new input on channel b.

Now consider the revised system

$$\mathsf{FF}_2 \Leftarrow (\mathsf{new}\ c)(F_2(b,c,\mathsf{ack}) \mid F_2(c,d,\mathsf{ack}))$$

where $F_2(c,d,\mathsf{ack})$ is defined by replacing b,c in $F_2(b,c,\mathsf{ack})$ with c,d respectively. Here there is more hope of the order of values forwarded from b to d being preserved. But there is confusion about the use of the channel ack; it is used to arrange acknowledgements internally, between the two internal systems $F_2(b,c,\mathsf{ack})$ and $F_2(c,d,\mathsf{ack})$, and externally, between the system and the destination client. Moreover these two distinct roles can become intertwined.

Instead of the individual components $F_2(b,c,\mathsf{ack})$ and $F_2(c,d,\mathsf{ack})$ relying on a globally available channel ack, an alternative, defensive, strategy would be for these forwarders to generate a new acknowledgement channel for each particular communication, with each acknowledgement channel being used exactly once. Here is how such a forwarder would look:

$$F(b,c) \Leftarrow \mathsf{rec}\ z.\ b?(x,y)\ (\mathsf{new}\,\mathsf{ack})(c!\langle x,\mathsf{ack}\rangle \mid \mathsf{ack}?()\ (y!\langle\rangle \mid z))$$

A system forwarding values from b to d in order using such forwarders would be defined by:

$$\mathsf{FF} \Leftarrow (\mathsf{new}\,c)(F(b,c) \mid F(c,d))$$

where $F(c,d)$ is obtained in the obvious manner from $F(b,c)$.

At this stage, before we give further examples that rely on the transmission of newly generated channels, it is best if we first define a formal semantics that will explain in detail how this mechanism works. Using this formal semantics we can then investigate the actual behaviour of processes such as FF, and see whether this in fact coincides with our intuitive understanding. To do so we need to develop some notation: much, but not all, standard.

Notation 2.1 Terms defined by the grammar in Figure 2.1 in general contain occurrences of *variables*, place-holders for names or processes, and these variables may be bound using the input and recursion constructs; these are called *binders* for variables. If the variable x occurs in the pattern X then all occurrences of x in the sub-term R of $c?(X)\,R$ are said to be *bound*; similarly with all occurrences of x in the sub-term B of $\mathsf{rec}\ x.\ B$. All occurrences of variables that are not bound in a term are said to be *free*. We use $\mathsf{fv}(R)$ to denote the set of variables that occur free in R, and $\mathsf{bv}(R)$ those that occur bound.

Informally we will refer to a *closed term*, a term P such that $\mathsf{fv}(P) = \emptyset$, as a *process*. Intuitively they do not require any instantiation of their variables in order to make sense.

In APi we also have a binder for names; in the term $(\mathsf{new}\, n)\, R$, which may be a process, all occurrences of the name n in R are said to be bound, and we use $\mathsf{fn}(R)$, $\mathsf{bn}(R)$, to denote the set of all names that occur free, bound respectively, in R.

As with any language containing binders we have a modified notion of substitution of simple values into variables. If v is a simple value, then

$$R\{\!|{}^{v}\!/\!{}_{x}|\!\}$$

is the result of substituting v for all free occurrences of x in R, in such a manner that v is not captured by any binding constructs $c?(X)\,(-)$, $\mathsf{rec}\ x.\ -$ or $(\mathsf{new}\, n)(-)$. Note that this result may not be a well-defined term; for example x may be playing the role of a recursion variable in R.

Example 2.2 Substituting n for x in the term $c?(y,z)\ \ (d!\langle y,x\rangle \mid b!\langle z,x\rangle)$ gives the term $c?(y,z)\ \ (d!\langle y,n\rangle \mid b!\langle z,n\rangle)$. In other words

$$(c?(y,z)\ \ (d!\langle y,x\rangle \mid b!\langle z,x\rangle))\{\!|{}^{n}\!/\!{}_{x}|\!\} = c?(y,z)\ \ (d!\langle y,n\rangle \mid b!\langle z,n\rangle)$$

On the other hand

$$(c?(y,z)\ \ (d!\langle y,x\rangle \mid b!\langle z,x\rangle))\{\!|{}^{y}\!/\!{}_{x}|\!\} = c?(w,z)\ \ (d!\langle w,y\rangle \mid b!\langle z,y\rangle)$$

where the new variable w is chosen to be different from the existing free and bound variables. Intuitively the behaviour of a process is independent of the actual identity of bound variables as they are merely place-holders. So here we have renamed the bound variable y so that when the substitution of y for x is made, what was previously a free variable, x, is not transformed into a bound variable. ■

This is generalised to the substitution of a structured value V for a pattern, denoted $R\{\!|{}^{V}\!/\!{}_{X}|\!\}$; again for this to be well-defined we require at least that the structure of V and X match. It is best also to assume that each variable has at most one occurrence in any pattern. So the substitution of V for X in R can be defined, inductively on the structure of X, as a sequence of substitutions of simple values.

In a similar manner we can define $R\{\!|^{n}/_{m}|\!\}$, the capture-avoidance substitution of the name n for free occurrences of the name m in T. These notions of substitution then lead, in the standard manner, to a notion of *α-equivalence* between terms:

$$R_1 \equiv_\alpha R_2$$

Intuitively this means that R_1 and R_2 are the *same* terms except in their use of bound identifiers.

Example 2.3 The process $c?(y,z)\ \ (d!\langle y,x\rangle \mid b!\langle z,x\rangle)$ has the same behaviour as $c?(z,w)\ \ (d!\langle z,x\rangle \mid b!\langle w,x\rangle)$ as only the place-holders for incoming values have been changed. Formally we have

$$c?(y,z)\ \ (d!\langle y,x\rangle \mid b!\langle z,x\rangle) \equiv_\alpha c?(z,w)\ \ (d!\langle z,x\rangle \mid b!\langle w,x\rangle)$$

In a similar manner, assuming m does not appear in P,

$$(\mathsf{new}\, n)(c!\langle n\rangle \mid n?(x)\, P) \equiv_\alpha (\mathsf{new}\, m)(c!\langle m\rangle \mid m?(x)\, (P\{\!|^{m}/_{n}|\!\}))$$

■

We will identify terms up to α-equivalence, or more formally use terms as representatives of their α-equivalence classes.

Convention 2.4 (Barendregt) This identification of terms up to α-equivalence allows us to use a very convenient convention when writing terms. We will always ensure all bound identifiers are distinct, and chosen to be different from all free identifiers. In fact we will go further, ensuring that this *freshness* of bound identifiers is true relative to the context in which the term is being used. We will refer to this as the *Barendregt convention.* ♦

Finally let us consider the most general form of substitution. Let σ be *any* mapping between values. The result of applying this substitution to a term R will be denoted $R\sigma$. It is obtained by systematically replacing all free occurrences of values v, including identifiers, with $\sigma(v)$. Of course bound variables are renamed as necessary to ensure no capture of free names or variables; for example $((\mathsf{new}\, n)\, R)\sigma$ could be defined to be $(\mathsf{new}\, m)(R(\sigma[n \mapsto m])$, where m is chosen to be *fresh*, and $\sigma[n \mapsto m]$ is the renaming that is identical to σ except that it maps n to m. Here *fresh* means distinct from all of $\sigma(n)$, for n in $\mathsf{fn}(R)$. Nevertheless there is no guarantee that the result will be a well-defined term; for example a basic value such as an integer may be substituted for a channel name. However these general substitutions will only ever occur in the questions at the end of chapters. In the body of the text we will only use the forms of substitution already discussed above, $R\{\!|^{m}/_{n}|\!\}$, $R\{\!|^{V}/_{X}|\!\}$, which of course are particular instances of $R\sigma$.

2.2 Reduction semantics for aPi

There are at least two standard methods for giving a formal *operational semantics* to a language such as aPi. One, called *reduction semantics*, describes the allowable computations from individual processes, while the other, which we will refer to as *lts semantics*, describes the possible ways a process may interact with its environment, and the consequences of these interactions. The latter will be discussed in length in Section 2.3, while here we describe the former.

The reduction semantics is defined as a binary relation $\longrightarrow$ between closed terms or processes. The judgement

$$P \longrightarrow Q$$

intuitively means that in one computation step the process P reduces to Q. A computation from P then consists of an arbitrary number of such steps from P; we will use $\longrightarrow^*$ as the reflexive transitive closure of $\longrightarrow$; thus

$$P \longrightarrow^* Q$$

means that a computation from P may lead to Q.

The reduction semantics takes a relaxed view of the syntax of processes, informally interpreting terms spatially. For example intuitively the term

$$P \mid Q$$

represents two computational processes, P and Q, running in parallel. Formally, as a term, it is different from

$$Q \mid P$$

although, intuitively, this term represents exactly the same computational entity; we do not wish to consider it significant that one thread is running at the left, or at the right, of another.

Exactly what terms we consider to represent precisely the same computational entity is to some extent a question of taste. It can be expressed by defining an equivalence relation $\equiv$ between processes, the interpretation being that if $P \equiv Q$ then the terms P and Q are so similar that we do not wish to differentiate between them when viewed as computational entities.

Definition 2.5 (contextual) We say a relation $\mathcal{R}$ over processes is *contextual* if it is preserved by the so-called *static* operators of the language. That is, if $P_1 \;\mathcal{R}\; P_2$ implies

- $P_1 \mid Q \;\mathcal{R}\; P_2 \mid Q$ and $Q \mid P_1 \;\mathcal{R}\; Q \mid P_2$ for every process Q
- $(\mathsf{new}\, n)\, P_1 \;\mathcal{R}\; (\mathsf{new}\, n)\, P_2$ for every name n. ♦

An alternative formulation of *contextual* is obtained by explicitly defining the set of *static contexts*. These are terms with a special marker –, defining a hole into which processes can be placed.

Definition 2.6 (*contexts*) The set of (static) *contexts for* APi is the least set of extended terms such that

- – is a static context
- if $C[-]$ is a static context then so are $C[-] \mid Q$ and $Q \mid C[-]$ for every process Q
- if $C[-]$ is a static context then so is $(\mathsf{new}\, n)\, C[-]$ for every name n.

Note that every static context contains exactly one occurrence of the marker –. ♦

For any process P we let $C[P]$ denote the process that results from syntactically replacing the occurrence of – with P in $C[-]$. Note that this replacement is very different from the notion of substitution defined in Notation 2.1; here names that are free in P may become bound when placed in the context $C[-]$. For example if $C[-]$ is the context $(\mathsf{new}\, b)(- \mid R)$ and P is the process $a!\langle b\rangle$ then $C[P]$ is the process $(\mathsf{new}\, b)(a!\langle b\rangle \mid R)$; the free name b in P has become bound.

Now we can see that a relation $\mathcal{R}$ over processes is *contextual* if and only if it is preserved by (static contexts); that is $P \,\mathcal{R}\, Q$ implies $C[P] \,\mathcal{R}\, C[Q]$ for every static context $C[-]$; see Question 1 at the end of the chapter.

Returning to the discussion on equating certain processes we take $\equiv$, referred to as *structural equivalence*, to be the least relation between processes (i.e. closed terms) that

(i) extends α-equivalence
(ii) is an equivalence relation; that is, is reflexive, symmetric and transitive
(iii) is *contextual*
(iv) and satisfies the axioms in Figure 2.3.

The condition (i) is only mentioned for emphasis; in reality, since we view terms as representing equivalence classes, it is redundant. Condition (ii) means that $\equiv$ acts like an *identity* relation over terms. Condition (iii) just means that the axioms in Figure 2.3 can be applied anywhere in static contexts. The axiom (S-STOP) is a

(S-EXTR)	$(\mathsf{new}\, n)(P \mid Q)$	$=$	$P \mid (\mathsf{new}\, n)\, Q$	if $n \notin \mathsf{fn}(P)$
(S-COM)	$P \mid Q$	$=$	$Q \mid P$	
(S-ASSOC)	$(P \mid Q) \mid R$	$=$	$P \mid (Q \mid R)$	
(S-STOP)	$P \mid \mathsf{stop}$	$=$	P	
	$(\mathsf{new}\, n)\, \mathsf{stop}$	$=$	stop	
(S-FLIP)	$(\mathsf{new}\, n)\, (\mathsf{new}\, m)\, P$	$=$	$(\mathsf{new}\, m)\, (\mathsf{new}\, n)\, P$	

Figure 2.3 Structural equivalence for APi

(R-COMM)
$$c!\langle V\rangle \mid c?(X)\,R \longrightarrow R\{\!|^{V}/_{X}|\!\}$$

(R-UNWIND)
$$\text{rec } x.\,B \longrightarrow B\{\!|^{\text{rec } x.\,B}/_{x}|\!\}$$

(R-EQ)
$$\text{if } v = v \text{ then } P \text{ else } Q \longrightarrow P$$

(R-NEQ)
$$\text{if } v_1 = v_2 \text{ then } P \text{ else } Q \longrightarrow Q \quad v_1 \neq v_2$$

(R-STRUCT)
$$\frac{P \equiv P',\ P \longrightarrow Q,\ Q \equiv Q'}{P' \longrightarrow Q'}$$

Figure 2.4 Reduction semantics for API

form of garbage collection; it is possible to derive a more general form of garbage collection, namely

$$(\text{new } n)\,P \quad \equiv \quad P \quad \text{if } n \notin \text{fn}(P)$$

See Question 6 at the end of the chapter. The axiom (S-FLIP) says that the order in which new names are generated is not important. The most significant rule is (S-EXTR); as we shall see it is this rule that underlies the formal definition of *scope extrusion*.

Note that this definition of structural equivalence is an example of an inductive definition, as outlined in Section 1.1. Consequently there is a form of *rule induction* associated with $\equiv$, which can be used to prove properties of it; the first application of this proof method will be in the proof of Lemma 2.13 below.

Formally the reduction semantics $\longrightarrow$ is defined to be the least *contextual* relation that satisfies the rules given in Figure 2.4. There are three axioms. The most important is (R-COMM), which states that a computation step can occur by the transmission of a value V along a channel c. Of course in general the resulting substitution $R\{\!|^{V}/_{X}|\!\}$ may not be meaningful because the structure of V and the pattern X may not match. So these rules should be interpreted as giving axioms only when all terms involved are well-defined. In the next chapter we will develop type systems that will ensure that such ill-defined substitutions will never occur. The axiom (R-UNWIND) dictates that the reductions of a recursively defined process are determined by those of its body and again is subject to the substitution being well-defined. The axioms (R-EQ) and (R-NEQ) allow the testing for equality between values. Finally the rule (R-STRUCT) effectively says that reduction is defined up to structural equivalence. As we shall see it is this rule that gives much of the power to the reduction semantics.

Let us now look at some examples to see how these rules can be used to infer computations of processes.

Example 2.7 Consider the process FF_1 discussed above:

$$\mathsf{FF}_1 \Leftarrow (\mathsf{new}\, c)(F_1(b,c) \mid F_1(c,d))$$

The only possible reduction from this process is an unwinding of one of these recursive definitions. It is instructive to see how such a step can be inferred from the definition of the reduction relation $\longrightarrow$. Recall that $F_1(b,c)$ represents the recursive process $\mathsf{rec}\, z.\, b?(x)\,(c!\langle x\rangle \mid z)$, and therefore an instance of the reduction rule (R-UNWIND) gives

$$F_1(b,c) \longrightarrow b?(x)\,(c!\langle x\rangle \mid z)\{\!|^{F_1(b,c)}/_z|\!\}$$

since $b?(x)\,(c!\langle x\rangle \mid z)$ is the body of the recursive definition. Performing the substitution this equates to

$$F_1(b,c) \longrightarrow b?(x)\,(c!\langle x\rangle \mid F_1(b,c))$$

For notational convenience let us use $B(b,c)$ to denote the residual of this judgement, namely $b?(x)\,(c!\langle x\rangle \mid F_1(b,c))$. So in summary one application of (R-UNWIND) gives

$$F_1(b,c) \longrightarrow B(b,c)$$

Let us now see how this reduction can take place as part of the larger system FF_1. The fact that $\longrightarrow$ is *contextual* means that it satisfies two inference rules, which essentially say that the rules in Figure 2.4 may be applied anywhere under occurrences of the static operators $\mid$ and $(\mathsf{new}\, n)$:

(R-PAR)
$$\frac{P \longrightarrow P'}{\begin{array}{l} P \mid Q \longrightarrow P' \mid Q \\ Q \mid P \longrightarrow Q \mid P' \end{array}}$$

(R-NEW)
$$\frac{P \longrightarrow P'}{(\mathsf{new}\, n)\, P \longrightarrow (\mathsf{new}\, n)\, P'}$$

So we have the following formal derivation, where the inferences are justified by the rules used:

1	$F_1(b,c) \longrightarrow B(b,c)$	(R-UNWIND)
2	$F_1(b,c) \mid F_1(c,d) \longrightarrow B(b,c) \mid F_1(c,d)$	(R-PAR) to 1
3	$\mathsf{FF}_1 \longrightarrow (\mathsf{new}\, c)(B(b,c) \mid F_1(c,d))$	(R-NEW) to 2

In other words one possible computation step from the system FF_1 is given by

$$\mathsf{FF}_1 \longrightarrow (\mathsf{new}\, c)(B(b,c) \mid F_1(c,d))$$

Nevertheless these unwindings, even within static contexts, do not lead to interesting computations. After the second unwinding, via an application of

(R-UNWIND) to the other recursive process $F_1(c,d)$, no more reductions are possible; the system is in a stable state awaiting input on c:

$$(\mathsf{new}\, c)(B(b,c) \mid B(c,d))$$

However we can place FF_1 in a context in which the channels b and d are used:

$$b!\langle v\rangle \mid \mathsf{FF}_1 \mid d?(x)\,\mathsf{print}!\langle x\rangle \tag{2.1}$$

Note that here we are implicitly using the structural equivalence; formally we should write

$$(b!\langle v\rangle \mid \mathsf{FF}_1) \mid d?(x)\,\mathsf{print}!\langle x\rangle \quad \text{or} \quad b!\langle v\rangle \mid (\mathsf{FF}_1 \mid d?(x)\,\mathsf{print}!\langle x\rangle)$$

But these terms are structurally equivalent and because of the rule (R-STRUCT) it does not actually matter which we use. Consequently when writing down a number of processes in parallel we omit the bracketing. Let us refer to this initial process, (2.1) above, as Sys_1.

Here once more the only possible initial moves are these unwindings of the recursive definitions, which gives

$$\mathsf{Sys}_1 \longrightarrow^* \quad b!\langle v\rangle \quad \mid \quad (\mathsf{new}\, c)(B(b,c) \mid B(c,d)) \quad \mid \quad d?(x)\,\mathsf{print}!\langle x\rangle \tag{Sys_2}$$

and let us refer to this latter process as Sys_2. At this point, to obtain a reduction, we will need to use the rule (R-STRUCT), using the fact that

$$b!\langle v\rangle \quad \mid \quad (\mathsf{new}\, c)(B(b,c) \mid B(c,d)) \equiv (\mathsf{new}\, c)(b!\langle v\rangle \mid B(b,c) \quad \mid B(c,d)) \tag{2.2}$$

Here the private channel c has been *extruded*, using the structural rule (S-EXTR), to allow the inference of the communication along the channel b. This inference uses the axiom (R-COMM), followed by an application of the rule (R-PAR) and then (R-NEW), to give the reduction

$$(\mathsf{new}\, c)(b!\langle v\rangle \mid B(b,c) \mid B(c,d)) \longrightarrow (\mathsf{new}\, c)(c!\langle v\rangle \mid F_1(b,c) \mid B(c,d)) \tag{2.3}$$

Thus an application of (R-STRUCT) to (2.2) and (2.3), followed by (R-PAR), gives the reduction

$$\mathsf{Sys}_2 \longrightarrow (\mathsf{new}\, c)(c!\langle v\rangle \mid F_1(b,c) \mid B(c,d)) \quad \mid d?(x)\,\mathsf{print}!\langle x\rangle \tag{Sys_3}$$

At this point, in Sys_3, communication is possible along the channel c, at least intuitively, but to formally derive it we again need various applications of the rules. The basic axiom used is

$$c!\langle v\rangle \mid B(c,d) \longrightarrow d!\langle v\rangle \mid F_1(c,d)$$

an instance of (R-COMM). An application of (R-PAR), then (R-STRUCT), then (R-NEW), then (R-PAR), gives:

$$\mathsf{Sys}_3 \longrightarrow \quad \mathsf{FF}_1 \quad \mid d!\langle v\rangle \mid d?(x)\,\mathsf{print}!\langle x\rangle \tag{Sys_4}$$

In a similar manner the communication of v on d can be derived, cumulating in the overall derivation

$$\mathsf{Sys}_1 \longrightarrow^* \mathsf{FF}_1 \mid \mathsf{print}!\langle v\rangle$$

Such a sequence of individual reductions, each derivable from the defining rules of the reduction semantics, is called a *computation*. The initial state of this computation is Sys_1, and the terminal state is the process $\mathsf{FF}_1 \mid \mathsf{print}!\langle v\rangle$. Note that this terminal state is *stable*; there is no further reduction that can be made from it.

There are slight variations in the possible computations starting from the initial state Sys_1, essentially caused by the unwinding of recursive definitions. But it is possible to prove that

- all are finite; they must end in a stable state, from which no further reductions are possible
- all these stable states are structurally equivalent to $(\mathsf{FF}_1 \mid \mathsf{print}!\langle v\rangle)$. ■

Convention 2.8 (syntactic abbreviations) When writing processes we assume that the input and restriction operator binds more strongly than parallel composition. We will also use brackets to help disambiguate terms where necessary and freely use Barendregt's convention to ensure bound names and variables are unique.

We will often abbreviate $(\mathsf{new}\, n_1)\ldots(\mathsf{new}\, n_k)\, P$ to $(\mathsf{new}\, \tilde{n})\, P$ and render $c?()\, T$, $c!\langle\rangle$ as $c?T$, $c!$ respectively. Finally trailing occurrences stop will sometimes be omitted. ♦

In the next example we see how the reduction semantics correctly handles dynamically created channels, and their scoping.

Example 2.9 Consider the forwarder from b to c, defined by

$$F(b,c) \Leftarrow \mathsf{rec}\ z.\ b?(x,y)\ (\mathsf{new}\,\mathsf{ack})(c!\langle x,\mathsf{ack}\rangle \mid \mathsf{ack}?(y! \mid z))$$

Such forwarders can be combined together as in the previous example but their use requires that an implicit protocol be followed. Consider the new system Sys defined by

$$\mathsf{Sys} \Leftarrow \mathsf{User} \mid \mathsf{FF} \mid \mathsf{Print}$$

The composite forwarder FF, defined in Section 2.1, consists of two forwarders linked together:

$$\mathsf{FF} \Leftarrow (\mathsf{new}\, c)(F(b,c) \mid F(c,d))$$

The User sequentially supplies two values to the system,

$$\mathsf{User} \Leftarrow (\mathsf{new}\,\mathsf{ack}_1)(b!\langle v_1,\mathsf{ack}_1\rangle \mid \mathsf{ack}_1?\,(\mathsf{new}\,\mathsf{ack}_2)\ b!\langle v_2,\mathsf{ack}_2\rangle)$$

and the process Print inputs two values sequentially from channel d and prints the second one,

$$\mathsf{Print} \Leftarrow d?(x_1, x_2)\,(x_2! \mid d?(y_1, y_2)\,(y_2! \mid \mathsf{print}!\langle y_1\rangle))$$

In Sys the only possible initial reductions are, once more, the unwindings of the recursive definitions, giving

$$\mathsf{Sys} \longrightarrow^{*} \mathsf{User} \mid (\mathsf{new}\, c)(B(b,c) \mid B(c,d)) \mid \mathsf{Print} \quad (\mathsf{Sys}_1)$$

Here we use $B(-,-)$ to denote the result of unwinding the definition of a forwarder; for example $B(b,c)$ represents $b?(x,y)\,(\mathsf{new\,ack})(c!\langle x, \mathsf{ack}\rangle \mid \mathsf{ack}?(y! \mid F(b,c)))$.

At this stage, intuitively, communication is possible along the channel b between User and FF. However the axiom (R-COMM) can only be applied if c and also ack_1, part of the value being communicated, is first *extruded* using (S-EXTR). One possible rearrangement using the structural rules is given by

$$\mathsf{Sys}_1 \equiv (\mathsf{new}\, c, \mathsf{ack}_1)(\mathsf{User} \mid (B(b,c) \mid B(c,d))) \mid \mathsf{Print}$$

because c and ack_1 do not occur in User. Now the axiom (R-COMM) can be applied to $\mathsf{User} \mid B(b,c)$, and subsequently using (R-PAR) and (R-NEW) we obtain

$$(\mathsf{new}\, c, \mathsf{ack}_1)(\mathsf{User} \mid (B(b,c) \mid B(c,d))) \longrightarrow (\mathsf{new}\, c, \mathsf{ack}_1)(\mathsf{User}_1 \mid (B_1(b,c) \mid B(c,d)))$$

where User_1 and $B_1(b,c)$ represent the obvious processes,

$$\mathsf{ack}_1?\,(\mathsf{new\,ack}_2)\, b!\langle v_2, \mathsf{ack}_2\rangle \quad \text{and} \quad (\mathsf{new\,ack})(c!\langle v_1, \mathsf{ack}\rangle \mid \mathsf{ack}?(\mathsf{ack}_1! \mid F(b,c)))$$

respectively. So an application of (R-PAR) and (R-STRUCT), gives

$$\mathsf{Sys}_1 \longrightarrow (\mathsf{new}\, c, \mathsf{ack}_1)(\mathsf{User}_1 \mid B_1(b,c) \mid B(c,d)) \mid \mathsf{Print} \quad (\mathsf{Sys}_2)$$

Note that *a priori*, from the syntactic form of Sys_2, it may seem that c is actually shared between the user and the composite forwarder. However Sys_2 is structurally equivalent to

$$(\mathsf{new\,ack}_1)(\mathsf{User}_1 \mid (\mathsf{new}\, c)(B_1(b,c) \mid B(c,d))) \mid \mathsf{Print}$$

a term that gives a truer picture of the sharing of resources.

In Sys_2 an internal communication within the forwarder, of the value v_1 along the channel c, is now possible. This leads to the reduction from Sys_2 to

$$(\mathsf{new}\, c, \mathsf{ack}_1)(\mathsf{User}_1 \mid (\mathsf{new\,ack})(\mathsf{ack}?(\mathsf{ack}_1! \mid F(b,c)) \mid B_1(c,d))) \mid \mathsf{Print} \quad (\mathsf{Sys}_3)$$

where $B_1(c,d)$ represents $(\mathsf{new\,ack}_2)(d!\langle v_1, \mathsf{ack}_2\rangle \mid \mathsf{ack}_2?(\mathsf{ack}! \mid F(c,d)))$; for the sake of clarity, and to comply with Barengregt's convention, we have used

α-conversion to rename the second acknowledgement used in the forwarder, from ack to ack_2. In Sys_3 there are now two acknowledgements awaiting reception and there is a possible communication between the forwarder and the print process along the channel d. However, to formally deduce this communication as a reduction, we need to use (S-EXTR) to *extrude* the new acknowledgement channel ack_2 to the surrounding system. This in turn requires the extrusion of the local channels c, ack and ack_1, or the use of (S-FLIP), and, after the application of many rules we obtain the reduction

$$\mathsf{Sys}_3 \longrightarrow \mathsf{Sys}_4$$

where Sys_4 represents the process

$$\begin{aligned}&(\mathsf{new}\, c, \mathsf{ack}_1, \mathsf{ack}, \mathsf{ack}_2)(\mathsf{User}_1 \mid (\mathsf{ack}?(\mathsf{ack}_1! \mid F(b,c))\\&\quad \mid \mathsf{ack}_2?(\mathsf{ack}! \mid F(c,d)) \mid \mathsf{Print}_1)\end{aligned}$$

Here Print_1 is shorthand for the process

$$\mathsf{ack}_2! \mid d?(y_1, y_2)\ y_2! \mid \mathsf{print}!\langle y_1\rangle$$

At this point there are three acknowledgements awaiting reception and no further communications along b, c or d are possible until at least some are delivered. In fact progress depends on the acknowledgement ack_2 from the printer being delivered to the second forwarder; this will liberate the acknowledgement ack, which when delivered will in turn liberate ack_1, on which User_1 is waiting. This leads to the series of reductions

$$\mathsf{Sys}_4 \longrightarrow^* (\mathsf{new}\, c, \mathsf{ack}_1, \mathsf{ack}, \mathsf{ack}_2)(\mathsf{User}_2 \mid F(b,c) \mid F(c,d) \mid \mathsf{Print}_2) \qquad (2.4)$$

where User_2 represents

$$(\mathsf{new}\, \mathsf{ack}_2)\, b!\langle v_2, \mathsf{ack}_2\rangle$$

and Print_2 the process

$$d?(y_1, y_2) y_2! \mid \mathsf{print}!\langle y_1\rangle$$

However the current term can be simplified considerably using the derived structural equation already mentioned:

$$(\mathsf{new}\, n)\, P \;\equiv\; P \quad \text{if } n \notin \mathsf{fn}(P)$$

The channels ack_1, ack and ack_2 do not occur freely in the residual process in (2.4) and therefore applying this rule we obtain

$$\begin{aligned}&(\mathsf{new}\, c, \mathsf{ack}_1, \mathsf{ack}, \mathsf{ack}_2)(\mathsf{User}_2 \mid F(b,c) \mid F(c,d) \mid \mathsf{Print}_2)\\&\quad \equiv (\mathsf{new}\, c)(\mathsf{User}_2 \mid F(b,c) \mid F(c,d) \mid \mathsf{Print}_2)\end{aligned}$$

and since c does not appear freely in User_2 and Print_2 we can apply (S-EXTR) to obtain

$$(\mathsf{new}\, c)(\mathsf{User}_2 \mid F(b,c) \mid F(c,d) \mid \mathsf{Print}_2) \equiv \mathsf{User}_2 \mid \mathsf{FF} \mid \mathsf{Print}_2$$

Thus an application of (R-STRUCT) to (2.4) above gives

$$\mathsf{Sys}_4 \longrightarrow^* (\mathsf{User}_2 \mid \mathsf{FF} \mid \mathsf{Print}_2) \qquad (\mathsf{Sys}_5)$$

In Sys_5 the user may send the second value, which eventually makes its way through the system, followed by a series of acknowledgements travelling in the opposite direction. ■

We have just seen one possible computation from the system

$$\mathsf{User} \mid \mathsf{FF} \mid \mathsf{Print}$$

Again there are possible variations, depending on recursive unwindings. But again it is possible to prove that all must terminate and the resulting stable process must be structurally equivalent to $\mathsf{FF} \mid \mathsf{print}!\langle v_2 \rangle$. This shows that the values are forwarded through the composite forwarder in a sequential manner. This should be contrasted with the possible computations from

$$\mathsf{User} \mid \mathsf{FF}_1 \mid \mathsf{Print}$$

where FF_1 is the simple composite forwarder, which uses no acknowledgements. This system can indeed evolve to a stable state, similar to the one above, namely $\mathsf{FF}_1 \mid \mathsf{print}!\langle v_2 \rangle$. But it may also evolve to the very different stable state $\mathsf{FF}_1 \mid \mathsf{print}!\langle v_1 \rangle$, in which the first value sent is actually printed. These two possibilities constitute a formal demonstration that the first composite forwarder does not necessarily forward values in sequence.

In the next example we see a very powerful use of the dynamic creation of channels. With them we can give a very simple definition of *compute servers*, which can service an arbitrary number of independent clients, even clients who are not known when the servers are originally installed.

Example 2.10 [*A Compute Server*] A *compute server*, when given some appropriate data, performs a specific computation on the data and returns the result. We will abstract from the details of the actual computation, representing it as an operation on values. To be specific let us assume an operation *isprime* that takes an integer and returns **true** or **false**, depending on whether the input is prime. Then the corresponding *compute server* is defined by

$$\mathsf{primeS} \Leftarrow \mathsf{rec}\; z.\; \mathsf{in}_p?(x,y)\; (z \mid y!\langle \mathit{isprime}(x) \rangle)$$

At the service point in_p a pair of values is received, the first of which should be an integer and the second a channel. The integer is tested for primality and the result is returned on the received channel. The recursive definition ensures that the service is always available and can handle an arbitrary number of calls. The use of *isprime* is meant to signify some auxiliary computation, the details of which are not of interest. However in a more expressive language the body of the server would be better written as

$$\mathsf{in}_p?(x,y)\,(z \mid \mathsf{let}\ a = \mathit{isprime}(x)\ \mathsf{in}\ y!\langle a\rangle)$$

emphasising that the auxiliary computation is performed eagerly by the server.

The interest in sending a *reply channel* with the data is to ensure that different calls to the service are not confused. For example if Client_1 sends the value 27 and, more or less at the same time, Client_2 sends 29 then we have to ensure that the first receives the answer **false** and the second **true**, and not vice-versa. To make this clear let us define these clients:

$$\mathsf{Client}_i(v) \Leftarrow (\mathsf{new}\ r)(\mathsf{in}_p!\langle v, r\rangle \mid r?(x)\,\mathsf{print}_i!\langle x\rangle)$$

The client generates a new return channel r, sends it together with an integer v, awaits the result on the reply channel, and prints it. Now consider the system

$$\mathsf{Sys} \Leftarrow \mathsf{Client}_1(27) \mid \mathsf{Client}_2(29) \mid \mathsf{primeS}$$

Each client can access the service in any order, and their respective interactions with the service can even overlap. But we are assured that only **false** will be available at print_1 and only **true** at print_2. In particular if

$$\mathsf{Sys} \longrightarrow^* Q$$

where Q is a stable process, then it is structurally equivalent to the process

$$\mathsf{print}_1!\langle \mathbf{false}\rangle \mid \mathsf{print}_2!\langle \mathbf{true}\rangle \mid \mathsf{primeS}$$

■

We give one more example of the power of communication channels, showing how they can be used to implement a notion of *state* or *memory*.

Example 2.11 [*A Memory*] A channel may be viewed as a very restricted form of memory cell, where, unlike a normal memory cell the value it contains disappears once it is read. However we can use it to mimic a standard memory cell if we ensure that the current value is reinstated each time it is read. This is the idea behind the following process, which uses a private resource s in which to store the current value:

$$\begin{aligned}\mathsf{Mem} \Leftarrow (\mathsf{new}\ s)(s!\langle 0\rangle \\ &\mid \mathsf{rec}\ g.\ \mathsf{get}?(y)\ s?(z)\ (y!\langle z\rangle \mid s!\langle z\rangle \mid g) \\ &\mid \mathsf{rec}\ p.\ \mathsf{put}?(x,y)\ s?(z)\ (y! \mid s!\langle x\rangle \mid p))\end{aligned}$$

The initial value is set to 0. There are then two *methods* for accessing the cell:

- To obtain the current value the user must send along the access channel get a return channel that is bound to the variable y. The current value is read from s and sent to the user along the return channel. In addition the value is *reinstated* in the local store s.
- To change the value of the cell a user must send the new value, which will be bound to x, and an acknowledgement channel, to be bound to y. The current value is read from s and ignored. The new value is installed and the user is sent an acknowledgement.

A typical client of Mem is defined as follows:

$$\mathsf{Client} \Leftarrow (\mathsf{new}\, a)(\mathsf{put}!\langle 4, a\rangle \mid a?\,(\mathsf{new}\, r)(\mathsf{get}!\langle r\rangle \mid r?(x)\,\mathsf{print}!\langle x\rangle))$$

The value 4 is sent together with a newly declared acknowledgement channel a. When the acknowledgement has been received the value in the store is obtained, using a newly declared return channel, and printed.

Using the reduction semantics one can show that the composite system

$$\mathsf{Client} \mid \mathsf{Mem}$$

will reduce to a term that is structurally equivalent to

$$\mathsf{print}!\langle 4\rangle \mid \mathsf{Mem}$$

Indeed up to structural equivalence this is the only stable term to which it can reduce.

Consider a client that puts in two values, and then retrieves the current state of the memory:

$$\begin{aligned}\mathsf{Client}_2 \Leftarrow (\mathsf{new}\, a)(\mathsf{put}!\langle 4, a\rangle \mid a?\,(\mathsf{new}\, b)(\mathsf{put}!\langle 6, b\rangle \mid\\ b?\,(\mathsf{new}\, r)(\mathsf{get}!\langle r\rangle \mid r?(x)\,\mathsf{print}!\langle x\rangle)))\end{aligned}$$

One can show that the composite system

$$\mathsf{Client}_2 \mid \mathsf{Mem}$$

will reduce to essentially one stable state, namely

$$\mathsf{print}!\langle 6\rangle \mid \mathsf{Mem}$$

■

In all of the examples seen so far systems have been described in terms of their components, together with communication channels, between them. However this *connectivity* between the system components, such as users and servers, has been relatively static, although various acknowledgement and reply channels are generated dynamically on demand. But APi can also describe systems in which the *connectivity*, that is the sharing of communication channels between processes, can vary arbitrarily. For example consider the following server, for providing forwarders between channels:

$$\mathsf{GenF} \Leftarrow \mathsf{rec}\ w.\ \mathsf{for}?(\mathsf{f},\mathsf{t})(w \mid F(\mathsf{f},\mathsf{t}))$$

where $F(\mathsf{f},\mathsf{t})$ is shorthand for the recursive code

$$\mathsf{rec}\ z.\ \mathsf{f}?(x,y)\ (\mathsf{new\,ack})(\mathsf{t}!\langle x,\mathsf{ack}\rangle \mid \mathsf{ack}?(y! \mid z))$$

The process GenF when it receives a pair of channels at for, say b, c, spawns off the forwarder $F(b,c)$ and concurrently awaits another request on for. Repeated use of this server will lead to many different communication linkages being established, some of which may subsequently disappear. So dynamically changing communication topologies are very easy to program in APi.

2.3 An action semantics for APi

Here we give a different, more general, view of a process, describing how it would behave when placed within a larger computational environment, consisting of other processes. The possible interactions between a process and this larger environment consist of the exchange of messages along channels common to both, although the process may also decide to ignore the environment. Consequently this view of a process may be given in terms of an lts, as defined in Definition 1.2, where the actions represent its ability to send and receive values along channels, or to compute internally.

We will define three judgements:

- $P \xrightarrow{c?V} Q$: the ability of the process P to receive the value V along the channel c, with the residual Q representing the resulting change in the process.
- $P \xrightarrow{(\tilde{b})c!V} Q$, where $(\tilde{b}) \subseteq \mathsf{fn}(V)$ and $c \notin (\tilde{b})$: the ability of P to send a value V along c, simultaneously exporting the set of names $(\tilde{b})$; that is we do not differentiate between different orderings of the exported names. Again Q represents the residual of P after this action has been performed.
- $P \xrightarrow{\tau} Q$: the reduction of P to Q by some internal activity. This will be defined in terms of the first two judgements, and hopefully will be related to the reduction semantics in Section 2.2.

Notation 2.12 The symbol α_i will be used to range over all input action labels, those of the form $c?V$, while α_o will refer to an arbitrary output label, $(\tilde{b})c!V$. We will use α to represent an arbitrary external action label, input or output, while μ will range over all possible actions; that is it may also include τ. We use $\mathsf{bn}(\mu)$ to denote the set of *bound* names in the action μ: if this is an input action then $\mathsf{bn}(\alpha)$

(L-IN)
$$c?(X)R \xrightarrow{c?V} R\{^V/_x\}$$

(L-OUT)
$$c!\langle V\rangle \xrightarrow{c!V} \mathsf{stop}$$

(L-COMM)
$$\frac{P \xrightarrow{c?V} P',\quad Q \xrightarrow{(\tilde{b})c!V} Q'}{P \mid Q \xrightarrow{\tau} (\mathsf{new}\,\tilde{b})(P' \mid Q')}\quad (\tilde{b}) \cap \mathsf{fn}(Q) = \emptyset \qquad \frac{P \xrightarrow{(\tilde{b})c!V} P',\quad Q \xrightarrow{c?V} Q'}{P \mid Q \xrightarrow{\tau} (\mathsf{new}\,\tilde{b})(P' \mid Q')}\quad (\tilde{b}) \cap \mathsf{fn}(Q) = \emptyset$$

(L-OPEN)
$$\frac{P \xrightarrow{\alpha_o} P'}{(\mathsf{new}\,n)\,P \xrightarrow{(n)\alpha_o} P'}$$

(L-UNWIND)
$$\mathsf{rec}\ x.\ B \xrightarrow{\tau} B\{^{\mathsf{rec}\ x.\ B}/_x\}$$

(L-NEQ)
$$\mathsf{if}\ v_1 = v_2\ \mathsf{then}\ P\ \mathsf{else}\ Q \xrightarrow{\tau} Q \quad v_1 \neq v_2$$

(L-EQ)
$$\mathsf{if}\ v = v\ \mathsf{then}\ P\ \mathsf{else}\ Q \xrightarrow{\tau} P$$

(L-CNTX)
$$\frac{P \xrightarrow{\mu} P'}{\begin{array}{l}P|Q \xrightarrow{\mu} P' \mid Q\\ Q \mid P \xrightarrow{\mu} Q \mid P'\end{array}}\quad \mathsf{bn}(\mu) \notin \mathsf{fn}(Q)$$

(L-CNTX)
$$\frac{P \xrightarrow{\mu} P'}{(\mathsf{new}\,b)\,P \xrightarrow{\mu} (\mathsf{new}\,b)\,P'}\quad b \notin \mathsf{n}(\mu)$$

Figure 2.5 An action semantics for API

is empty, while if it is the output action $(\tilde{b})c!V$ then it is the set $\{\tilde{b}\}$. Finally $\mathsf{n}(\mu)$ denotes the set of names that appear anywhere in μ, while $\mathsf{fn}(\mu)$, the free names in μ, are those in $\mathsf{n}(\mu)$ that are not in $\mathsf{bn}(\mu)$. ∎

It is worth emphasising that here we are not concerned with any external view of these actions. We are simply defining, very intentionally, the ability of processes to perform these actions rather than the ability of some observer to discern that these actions have taken place. This more subtle viewpoint will be discussed in Section 2.6.

These relations are defined to be the least relations between *processes*, that is closed terms in API, which satisfy the inference rules in Figure 2.5. The first two axioms, (L-IN) and (L-OUT), are straightforward but note that the input move is only possible when the substitution of V for X in R is well-defined.

The output axiom (L-OUT) needs no explanation. The rule (L-OPEN) allows new names to be *exported*. For example using this rule, and (L-OUT), we may deduce that the process $(\mathsf{new}\,b)\ c!\langle b\rangle$ can export the new name b along the channel c:

$$(\mathsf{new}\,b)\ c!\langle b\rangle \xrightarrow{(b)c!b} \mathsf{stop}$$

However it is essential to note that (L-OPEN) can only be applied when the resulting action label $(n)\alpha_o$ is well-defined; for example if α is $c!V$ then this demands that n is different from c, and that it appears in the value V.

The rule (L-COMM), consisting of two symmetric rules, defines the action $\xrightarrow{\tau}$ as the simultaneous occurrence of input and output actions. For example we have the action

$$c?(x)\,R \mid c!\langle v\rangle \xrightarrow{\tau} R\{\!|^{v}/_{x}|\!\} \mid \mathsf{stop}$$

The rule (L-COMM) also implements *scope extrusion*. For example it can be used to deduce

$$c?(x)\,x!\langle v\rangle \mid (\mathsf{new}\,b)\,c!\langle b\rangle \xrightarrow{\tau} (\mathsf{new}\,b)(b!\langle v\rangle \mid \mathsf{stop})$$

from the two prior judgements

$$c?(x)\,x!\langle v\rangle \xrightarrow{c?b} b!\langle v\rangle \quad \text{and} \quad (\mathsf{new}\,b)\,c!\langle b\rangle \xrightarrow{(b)c!b} \mathsf{stop}$$

A more interesting example is

$$c?(x)\,(x!\langle v\rangle \mid P) \mid (\mathsf{new}\,b)(c!\langle b\rangle \mid b?(x)\,R) \xrightarrow{\tau} (\mathsf{new}\,b)(b!\langle v\rangle \mid P \mid \mathsf{stop} \mid b?(x)\,R)$$

where we assume x does not occur in P. Here the process $(\mathsf{new}\,b)(c!\langle b\rangle \mid b?(x)\,R)$ uses the channel c to send a *private* channel b to its partner, on which it, and only it, can receive data. Its partner uses this newly acquired private channel to send some private data, say v, resulting in the system

$$(\mathsf{new}\,b)(\mathsf{stop} \mid P \mid \mathsf{stop} \mid R\{\!|^{v}/_{x}|\!\})$$

Since b is guaranteed not to occur in P this term is effectively the same as

$$P \mid R\{\!|^{v}/_{x}|\!\}$$

For example these two terms can be shown to be structurally equivalent. They represent a system in which the original process has successfully obtained the private data from its partner, and the private link between them used for the transfer of this data has disappeared.

Note the side conditions in the rule (L-COMM); the extruded names $(\tilde{b})$ should not occur free in Q or otherwise those free occurrences would be captured in the residual. So for example we can **not** deduce

$$(c?(x)\,x!\langle b\rangle) \mid (\mathsf{new}\,b)(c!\langle b\rangle) \xrightarrow{\tau} (\mathsf{new}\,b)(b!\langle b\rangle \mid \mathsf{stop}) \tag{2.5}$$

Intuitively the process $(\mathsf{new}\,b)(c!\langle b\rangle)$ is exporting some *arbitrary but fresh* name along c and consequently it cannot be the same as the existing name b belonging to its partner. However recall that processes are identified up to α-equivalence and therefore we can take a different representative for $(\mathsf{new}\,b)\,c!\langle b\rangle$, for example $(\mathsf{new}\,d)\,c!\langle d\rangle$. Then with applications of (L-IN) and (L-OUT), followed by a valid application of (L-COMM), since d is chosen not to occur freely in $c?(x)\,x!\langle b\rangle$, we may deduce

$$c?(x)\,x!\langle b\rangle \;\mid\; (\mathsf{new}\,b)(c!\langle b\rangle) \;\xrightarrow{\tau}\; (\mathsf{new}\,d)(d!\langle b\rangle \mid \mathsf{stop})$$

Note that this implicit method of working up to α-equivalence could be made explicit by adding the inference rule:

$$\text{(L-}\alpha\text{)}\quad \frac{P \xrightarrow{\mu} P' \qquad P \equiv_\alpha Q}{Q \xrightarrow{\mu} P'}$$

to Figure 2.5. An alternative view is to say that (2.5) cannot be deduced because of Barendregt's convention, given on page 15. The process $(c?(x)\,x!\langle b\rangle) \mid (\mathsf{new}\,b)$ $c!\langle b\rangle$ should not be written because a bound name b is also free. Consequently it should be replaced by an equivalent one respecting the convention, such as the one we have used above.

The remaining rules in Figure 2.5 are straightforward; (L-UNWIND), (L-EQ), (L-EQ) and (L-NEQ) are taken from the reduction semantics, while (L-CNTX) allows actions to be deduced in static contexts; again the side conditions ensure that no free names inadvertently become bound.

It is interesting to compare the definition of $\xrightarrow{\tau}$ with that of the reduction relation $\longrightarrow$ of the previous section. The judgement $P \xrightarrow{\tau} Q$ is defined purely in terms of the auxiliary input and output relations applied to P, and does not explicitly use the structure of the process P. On the other hand the reduction judgement $P \longrightarrow Q$ relies heavily on the structure of P, and the use of the structural equivalence $\equiv$ in order to rearrange P so that the structure required for making a reduction may be made explicit. This use of structural equivalence makes reduction $\longrightarrow$ a much larger relation; it will relate many more processes than $\xrightarrow{\tau}$. Revisiting Example 2.9 of the previous section we can derive

$$\mathsf{User} \mid (\mathsf{new}\,c)(B(b,c) \mid B(c,d)) \longrightarrow (\mathsf{new}\,c, \mathsf{ack}_1)(\mathsf{User}_1 \mid (B_1(b,c) \mid B(c,d)))$$

It is easy to see that the corresponding judgement

$$\mathsf{User} \mid (\mathsf{new}\,c)(B(b,c) \mid B(c,d)) \xrightarrow{\tau} (\mathsf{new}\,c, \mathsf{ack}_1)(\mathsf{User}_1 \mid (B_1(b,c) \mid B(c,d)))$$

cannot be derived. But the reader should be able to infer

$$\mathsf{User} \mid (\mathsf{new}\,c)(B(b,c) \mid B(c,d)) \xrightarrow{\tau} (\mathsf{new}\,\mathsf{ack}_1)(\mathsf{User}_1 \mid (\mathsf{new}\,c)\,(B_1(b,c) \mid B(c,d)))$$

and this latter process is structurally equivalent to $(\mathsf{new}\,c, \mathsf{ack}_1)(\mathsf{User}_1 \mid (B_1(b,c) \mid B(c,d)))$.

This is a general phenomenon. The internal action relation $\xrightarrow{\tau}$ is able to mimic reduction, $\longrightarrow$, up to structural equivalence. However the proof is not straightforward. The difficulty lies in the use of the rule (R-STRUCT) in the definition of reduction, which uses the structural equivalence of Figure 2.3. We need the follow lemma:

Lemma 2.13 If $P \equiv Q$ and $P \xrightarrow{\mu} P'$ then there exists some Q' such that $Q \xrightarrow{\mu} Q'$ such that $P' \equiv Q'$.

Proof: Structural equivalence is the smallest equivalence relation that satisfies the six axioms given in Figure 2.3, and the two (implicit) rules, associated with the requirement that it is *contextual*. Now let the relation $\mathcal{R}$ be defined by saying $P \mathcal{R} Q$ if whenever $P \xrightarrow{\mu} P'$ there exists some Q' such that $Q \xrightarrow{\mu} Q'$, and $P' \equiv Q'$. Since $\equiv$ is an equivalence relation it is straightforward to show that $\mathcal{R}$ is also an equivalence relation. Therefore the result will follow, if we show $\mathcal{R}$ also satisfies these six axioms, and the two (implicit) rules. In effect this is a proof by rule induction, as explained in Chapter 1, on the derivation of $P \equiv Q$.

As an example we look at the axiom (S-EXTR); since it is an axiom the induction hypothesis will not be of any use. One possibility is that P has the form $(\mathsf{new}\, n)(P_1 \mid P_2)$ and Q is $P_1 \mid (\mathsf{new}\, n)\, P_2$, where $n \notin \mathsf{fn}(P_1)$. We must show that there is a move from Q that matches the action $P \xrightarrow{\mu} P'$. Because of the structure of P there are only two possible rules that can be used to infer this action:

(L-OPEN): In this case the structure of the label μ must be of the form $(n)\alpha_o$, where α_o is an output label and n must appear in the value being sent. Because of the condition that n cannot appear in $\mathsf{fn}(P_1)$ we can conclude that the action is performed by P_2. That is it has the form

$$(\mathsf{new}\, n)(P_1 \mid P_2) \xrightarrow{(n)\alpha_o} P_1 \mid P_2'$$

where $P_2 \xrightarrow{\alpha_o} P_2'$. Note that this implies that the bound names in α_o do not occur free in P_1.

We have now accumulated enough information to infer

$$(\mathsf{new}\, n)\, P_2 \xrightarrow{(n)\alpha_o} P_2'$$

using (L-OPEN). Then (L-CNTX) gives the required matching move

$$P_1 \mid (\mathsf{new}\, n)\, P_2 \xrightarrow{(n)\alpha_o} P_1 \mid P_2'$$

in which the residual processes match exactly.

(L-CNTX): Here the μ-move must occur within the $(\mathsf{new}\, n)$ – construct and there are many possibilities for the derivation of this μ-move from $P_1 \mid P_2$. It may be performed by P_1 alone, by P_2 alone, or it may be an internal action in which both participate. This last possibility is the most interesting and we look at one case, where there is an output from P_2 to P_1. The interest here is that n may form part of the value being

sent, which is freely allowed under the occurrence of $(\mathsf{new}\, n)$ in P, whereas in Q it would have to be *extruded* from $(\mathsf{new}\, n)\, P_1$ to P_2.
So we are in the situation where $P \xrightarrow{\tau} P'$ and P' has the form

$$(\mathsf{new}\, n)\, (\mathsf{new}\, \tilde{b})(P_1' \mid P_2')$$

where $P_1 \xrightarrow{c?V} P_1'$, $P_2 \xrightarrow{(\tilde{b})c!V} P_2'$. First suppose n is not free in the output label. Then we can ensure, using α-conversion if necessary, that it does not appear anywhere in the label and so (L-CNTX) can be used to infer $(\mathsf{new}\, n)\, P_2 \xrightarrow{(\tilde{b})c!V} (\mathsf{new}\, n)\, P_2'$ and (L-COMM) then gives the move

$$P_1 \mid (\mathsf{new}\, n)\, P_2 \xrightarrow{\tau} (\mathsf{new}\, \tilde{b})(P_1' \mid (\mathsf{new}\, n)\, P_2')$$

We claim that this is a required matching move. For, since $n \notin \mathsf{fn}(P_1)$, $P_1 \xrightarrow{c?V} P_1'$ and we are assuming that n does not appear in the label $c?V$, we know that $n \notin \mathsf{fn}(P_1')$. Thus (S-EXTR) (and (S-FLIP)) can be applied to give

$$(\mathsf{new}\, n)\, (\mathsf{new}\, \tilde{b})(P_1' \mid P_2') \equiv (\mathsf{new}\, \tilde{b})(P_1' \mid (\mathsf{new}\, n)\, P_2')$$

On the other hand if n is free in the output label then (L-OPEN) gives $(\mathsf{new}\, n)\, P_2 \xrightarrow{(n)(\tilde{b})c!V} P_2'$ and we get the slightly different move

$$P_1 \mid (\mathsf{new}\, n)\, P_2 \xrightarrow{\tau} (\mathsf{new}\, n)\, (\mathsf{new}\, \tilde{b})(P_1' \mid P_2')$$

which matches exactly.

The symmetric case, when P has the form $P_1 \mid (\mathsf{new}\, n)\, P_2$, and Q is $(\mathsf{new}\, n)(P_1 \mid P_2)$ is equally delicate. Again a careful analysis of the derivation of the action $P \xrightarrow{\mu} P'$ is required in order to find the corresponding action from Q. For example the action could be a communication from $(\mathsf{new}\, n)\, P_2$ to P_1 in which n is exported. In this case P' will have the form $(\mathsf{new}\, n)(P_1' \mid P_2')$ and one can show that $P_1 \mid P_2 \xrightarrow{\tau} P_1' \mid P_2'$, thereby providing the required move from Q.

This completes our examination of the one axiom (S-EXTR). Luckily, all the other axioms are completely straightforward as indeed are the two inductive cases in the definition of $\equiv$. ■

Proposition 2.14 $P \longrightarrow Q$ *implies* $P \xrightarrow{\tau} Q'$ *for some* Q' *such that* $Q \equiv Q'$.

Proof: This is proved by rule induction on the definition of the relation $P \longrightarrow Q$. In other words we have to show that the relation $\xrightarrow{\tau}$ satisfies all the defining axioms and rules of $\longrightarrow$, given in Figure 2.4.

All the axioms are straightforward and the one explicit inductive rule (S-STRUCT) is covered by the previous lemma. The implicit inductive rules, present because $\longrightarrow$ is defined to be *contextual*, are also straightforward because of (L-CNTX). ■

The converse is much more straightforward. In fact the reduction relation can mimic precisely internal actions. However, since $P \xrightarrow{\tau} Q$ is defined in terms of the external actions $P \xrightarrow{\alpha} Q$, when giving the proof of this fact we also require auxiliary properties of these more general actions.

Proposition 2.15

- *If* $P \xrightarrow{(\tilde{b})c!\langle V\rangle} Q$ *then* P *is structurally equivalent to* $(\mathsf{new}\,\tilde{b})(c!\langle V\rangle \mid Q)$.
- *If* $P \xrightarrow{c?V} Q$ *then* P *is structurally equivalent to a term of the form* $(\mathsf{new}\,\tilde{b})(P' \mid c?(X)\,R)$. *where* $(\tilde{b}) \cap \mathsf{n}(V) = \emptyset$, *and* Q *is structurally equivalent to* $(\mathsf{new}\,\tilde{b})(P' \mid R\{\!|^V/_X|\!\})$.
- $P \xrightarrow{\tau} Q$ *implies* $P \longrightarrow Q$.

Proof: The proofs of the first two statements are simple rule inductions, on the inference of the actions $P \xrightarrow{(\tilde{b})c!V} Q$ and $P \xrightarrow{c?V} Q$.

The final statement, which is the most interesting, is also by induction on the inference of $P \xrightarrow{\tau} Q$. If this is an instance of the axioms (L-EQ), (L-NEQ) or (L-UNWIND) then the result is immediate since these axioms are also used in the definition of reduction. So suppose (L-COMM) is used. Without loss of generality we can assume the internal action has the form

$$P_1 \mid P_2 \xrightarrow{\tau} (\mathsf{new}\,\tilde{b})(P_1' \mid P_2')$$

where $P_1 \xrightarrow{c?V} P_1'$ and $P_2 \xrightarrow{(\tilde{b})c!V} P_2'$; that is P has the form $P_1 \mid P_2$ and Q is $(\mathsf{new}\,\tilde{b})(P_1' \mid P_2')$. Here we can use the first two parts of the proposition to give the structure of the processes involved, up to structural equivalence. We have

$$P_2 \equiv (\mathsf{new}\,\tilde{b})(P_2' \mid c!\langle V\rangle)$$

and

$$P_1 \equiv (\mathsf{new}\,\tilde{n})(P_1'' \mid c?(X)\,R)$$

Moreover, using α-conversion if necessary, we can choose the bound names $(\tilde{n})$ and $(\tilde{b})$ so that they are different from each other and also different from all the free names in both P_1 and P_2; this will be useful when manipulating the terms up to structural equivalence. The second part of this proposition also gives the structure of the residual P_1':

$$P_1' \equiv (\mathsf{new}\,\tilde{n})(P_1'' \mid R\{\!|^V/_X|\!\})$$

Therefore using the structural manipulation rules, including (S-EXTR), we can rearrange $P_1 \mid P_2$, the initial process, into the form

$$(\mathsf{new}\,\tilde{b},\tilde{n})(P_1'' \mid P_2' \quad \mid c!\langle V\rangle \mid c?(X)\,R)$$

This has been constructed so that it can be easily seen to reduce to

$$(\mathsf{new}\,\tilde{n},\tilde{b})(P_1'' \mid P_2' \quad \mid R\{\!|^V/_X|\!\})$$

using the reduction rules from Figure 2.4. But, since $(\tilde{n})$ do not occur free in P_2', this term is structurally equivalent to $(\mathsf{new}\,\tilde{b})(P_1' \mid P_2')$. So an application of (R-STRUCT) gives the required

$$P_1 \mid P_2 \longrightarrow (\mathsf{new}\,\tilde{b})(P_1' \mid P_2')$$

There are two more cases to consider in the possible derivations for $P \xrightarrow{\tau} Q$. These are the inductive cases, where the instances of the rule (L-CNTX) are used. However they are straightforward and left to the reader. ■

We can now sum up the relationship between the two relations $\longrightarrow$ and $\xrightarrow{\tau}$.

Corollary 2.16 $P \longrightarrow Q$ *if and only if* $P \xrightarrow{\tau} Q'$ *for some* Q' *such that* $Q \equiv Q'$. ■

2.4 A coinductive behavioural equivalence for API

At this stage we have an interpretation of API as an lts, as given in Definition 1.2:

- The states or configurations are all API processes, that is all the closed terms in API.
- The relations over the configurations are given by the actions $\xrightarrow{\mu}$, the least relations that can be deduced from inference rules in Figure 2.5.

This is turn means that we have a bisimulation equivalence, denoted $P \approx_{bis} Q$, between API processes. However we must be a little careful in applying the general definition to this lts generated by API, because of the use of bound variables in actions. For example if $P \xrightarrow{(b)c!b} P'$ where b has a free occurrence in Q then we would not expect Q to be able to perform an exact matching move $Q \overset{(b)c!b}{\Longrightarrow} Q'$. Instead we apply Barendregt's convention, which dictates that this action should not be considered as b is not fresh to its context, since it appears free in Q. Thus the convention dictates that when the definition of bisimulation is applied to the processes P, Q, only actions whose bound names do not occur freely in P and Q are expected to be matched.

We have already discussed in Chapter 1 the attractiveness of this semantic equivalence. For example to show that two processes are equivalent it is sufficient to exhibit a bisimulation containing them. In fact Lemma 2.13 provides us with a method of working with bisimulations *up to structural equivalence*. First a simple consequence:

Corollary 2.17 In API, $P \equiv Q$ *implies* $P \approx_{bis} Q$. ■

Proof: Since $\equiv$ is symmetric, Lemma 2.13 immediately implies that $\equiv$ is a weak bisimulation, and the result therefore follows from the definition of $\approx_{bis}$, as the largest bisimulation. ■

Definition 2.18 (*bisimulation equivalence up to structural equivalence*) A relation $\mathcal{R}$ over processes is called a *bisimulation up to structural equivalence* if both it and its inverse satisfies the transfer property:

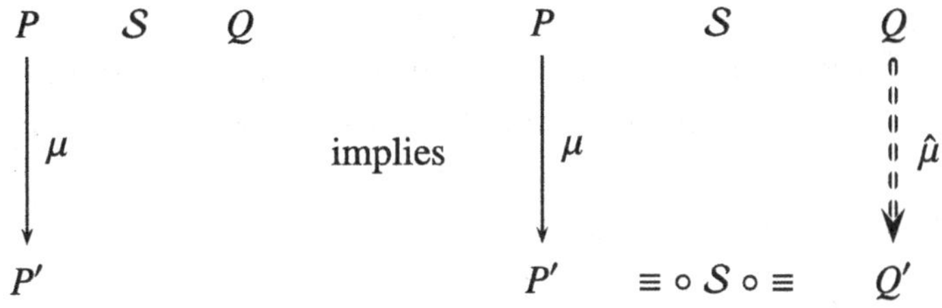

In other words when matching the residuals of actions it is sufficient to work up to structural equivalence.

Proposition 2.19 If $P \; \mathcal{R} \; Q$, where $\mathcal{R}$ is a bisimulation up to structural equivalence, then $P \approx_{bis} Q$.

Proof: The result will follow if we can show that the relation $\equiv \circ \mathcal{R} \circ \equiv$, which we abbreviate to $\mathcal{S}$, is a bisimulation since trivially the identity relation is contained in $\equiv$ and therefore $\mathcal{R} \subseteq \mathcal{S}$.

So suppose $P \; \mathcal{S} \; Q$ and $P \xrightarrow{\mu} P'$; we must find a matching move from Q. Let $P_1, \; Q_1$ be such that

$$P \equiv P_1 \; \mathcal{R} \; Q_1 \equiv Q$$

Using Lemma 2.13 we can find a move $P_1 \xrightarrow{\mu} P_1'$ such that $P' \equiv P_1'$. Using the supposed transfer property of $\mathcal{R}$ we can find a move $Q_1 \overset{\hat{\mu}}{\Longrightarrow} Q_1'$ such that $P_1' \; \mathcal{S} \; Q_1'$. Again using Lemma 2.13, possibly a number of times, we can find a move $Q \overset{\hat{\mu}}{\Longrightarrow} Q'$ such that $Q_1' \equiv Q'$. This is in fact the required matching move since we have

$$P' \equiv P_1' \; \mathcal{S} \; Q_1' \equiv Q'$$

from which it follows that $P' \; \mathcal{S} \; Q'$.

We also have to show that $\mathcal{S}^{-1}$ satisfies the transfer property; however the proof is practically identical to that for $\mathcal{S}$. ■

Bisimulation equivalence also interacts coherently with the operators of aPi; they are *contextual*. Here we outline the proof of two results that, together, show that it is contextual.

Proposition 2.20 In aPi, *$P \approx_{bis} Q$ implies $(\mathsf{new}\, n)\, P \approx_{bis} (\mathsf{new}\, n)\, Q$.*

Proof: Let $\mathcal{S}$ be the set of all pairs $\langle (\mathsf{new}\, n)\, P_1, (\mathsf{new}\, n)\, P_2 \rangle$ such that $P_1 \approx_{bis} P_2$ and let $\mathcal{R}$ be $\mathcal{S} \cup \approx_{bis}$. The result follows if we can show that $\mathcal{R}$ is a bisimulation. This however is not very difficult as every action from $(\mathsf{new}\, n)\, P$ is determined by an action from P.

Note however that $\mathcal{R}$ must include $\approx_{bis}$. This is because processes of the form $(\mathsf{new}\, n)\, R$ may *extrude* n as part of an output action. For example one possible action from $(\mathsf{new}\, n)\, P_1$ is $(\mathsf{new}\, n)\, P_1 \xrightarrow{(n)\alpha_o} P_1'$, where α_o is an output action $P_1 \xrightarrow{\alpha_o} P_1'$. This latter can be matched by a partner process, one such that $(\mathsf{new}\, n)\, P_1 \;\mathcal{S}\; (\mathsf{new}\, n)\, P_2$, because $P_1 \approx_{bis} P_2$. Because of this equivalence there is an action $P_2 \stackrel{\hat{\alpha_o}}{\Longrightarrow} P_2'$ such that $P_1' \approx_{bis} P_2'$; this in turn can be transformed into an action matching the original one from $(\mathsf{new}\, n)\, P_1$, $(\mathsf{new}\, n)\, P_2 \stackrel{(n)\hat{\alpha_o}}{\Longrightarrow} P_2'$. But note that the resulting pair $\langle P_1', P_2' \rangle$ is not in $\mathcal{S}$; however it is in $\mathcal{R}$, which is all that is required for the proof to go through. ■

Proposition 2.21 In API*,* $P_1 \approx_{bis} P_2$ *implies* $P_1 \mid Q \approx_{bis} P_2 \mid Q$.

Proof: This proof is somewhat more complicated. The relation consisting of all pairs of the form $\langle P_1 \mid Q, P_2 \mid Q \rangle$ such that $P_1 \approx_{bis} P_2$ is not in general a bisimulation. We have to construct a more sophisticated one. Let $\mathcal{R}$ be the least relation that satisfies

- $P_1 \approx_{bis} P_2$ implies $\langle P_1, P_2 \rangle \in \mathcal{R}$
- $\langle P_1, P_2 \rangle \in \mathcal{R}$ implies $\langle P_1 \mid Q, P_2 \mid Q \rangle \in \mathcal{R}$ for every process Q
- $\langle P_1, P_2 \rangle \in \mathcal{R}$ implies $\langle (\mathsf{new}\, n)\, P_1, (\mathsf{new}\, n)\, P_2 \rangle \in \mathcal{R}$ for every name n.

We show $\mathcal{R}$ is a bisimulation from which the result will follow because of the second clause. Note that by definition $\mathcal{R}$ is symmetric and therefore we need only prove the transfer property in one direction.

Let $\langle P, Q \rangle \in \mathcal{R}$ and $P \xrightarrow{\mu} P'$. We must find a matching move from Q, a move $Q \stackrel{\hat{\mu}}{\Longrightarrow} Q'$ such that $\langle P', Q' \rangle \in \mathcal{R}$. How we find this matching move depends on the structure of P and Q. To discover this structure we do an induction on the proof that the pair is in $\mathcal{R}$. There are three possibilities:

- $\langle P, Q \rangle \in \mathcal{R}$ because $P \approx_{bis} Q$. The fact that $\approx_{bis}$ is a bisimulation immediately gives the required matching move.
- P, Q have the form $P_1 \mid Q'$, $P_2 \mid Q'$, respectively, and $\langle P_1, P_2 \rangle \in \mathcal{R}$. Here induction will ensure that every move from P_1 can be matched by a move from P_2.
  The proof proceeds by rule induction on the derivation of the action $P \xrightarrow{\mu} P'$. There are numerous cases and we only examine one, when μ is τ because of an output from P_1 to Q'. So we have actions
  $$P_1 \xrightarrow{(\tilde{b})\alpha_o} P_1' \qquad Q' \xrightarrow{\alpha_i} Q''$$
  where P' is $(\mathsf{new}\, \tilde{b})(P_1' \mid Q'')$; here α_o is some simple output action $a!V$ and α_i the *complementary* input action $a?V$.
  Induction now gives a matching move from P_2, an action $P_2 \stackrel{(\tilde{b})\alpha_o}{\Longrightarrow} P_2'$ such that $\langle P_1', P_2' \rangle \in \mathcal{R}$. We can combine this matching move with the complementary action from Q' to give $Q \xrightarrow{\tau}{}^{*} (\mathsf{new}\, \tilde{b})(P_2' \mid Q'')$. This is the required matching move; the second, and more particularly the third, clause in the definition of $\mathcal{R}$, ensures that $\langle P', (\mathsf{new}\, \tilde{b})(P_2' \mid Q'') \rangle \in \mathcal{R}$.

- The final possibility is handled in a similar manner. Here P, Q have the form $(\mathsf{new}\,n)\,P_1$ and $(\mathsf{new}\,n)\,P_2$, respectively, for some n, and $\langle P_1, P_2\rangle \in \mathcal{R}$. The move from P is determined by a move from P_1, induction gives a matching move from P_2, which in turn gives the required matching move from Q. ■

Thus the equivalence relation $\approx_{bis}$ is *contextual*; an argument completely symmetric to that of Proposition 2.21 will show $P_1 \approx_{bis} P_2$ implies $Q \mid P_1 \approx_{bis} Q \mid P_2$. With some more work we could also prove that it is also preserved by the other constructs in the language. But the *static* operators are sufficient for our purposes.

2.5 Contextual equivalences

We have seen that $\approx_{bis}$ is an excellent behavioural equivalence for aPi:

- it is bisimulation based, and therefore has associated with it powerful coinductive proof techniques
- it is *contextual*, and therefore appropriate for a compositional approach to process verification.

In this section we step back and examine the extent to which it is the most appropriate semantic equivalence for aPi, despite these favourable properties.

From the most general point of view, processes should only be considered to be *semantically* different if a user can observe a difference in their behaviour. The difficulty is in formalising how users interact with processes and how they can come to discern differences. In aPi users can only interact with processes by communicating on channels, and these interactions form the basis of the definition of $\approx_{bis}$. Consequently we would expect that bisimulation equivalence will imply whatever semantic equivalence based on user interaction that emerges. Nevertheless, there is still room for discussion on what this more basic notion of equivalence should be.

As a first attempt we could say that two processes are distinguishable only if there is some action that one can perform and the other cannot; *a priori* a user could then discern a difference by asking for this action to be performed. But this is easily seen to be much too weak a notion. Defined in the following manner P_1 and Q_1 would be considered to be semantically equivalent, as they both offer the same interaction on channel a:

$$P_1 \Leftarrow (\mathsf{new}\,n)(a!\langle n\rangle \mid n?b!) \qquad Q_1 \Leftarrow (\mathsf{new}\,n)(a!\langle n\rangle \mid n?c!) \tag{2.6}$$

But they obviously should be considered semantically different and the difference can be discerned by subsequent interaction. An observer that inputs on the channel received on a, will receive either a or b, depending on whether they are observing P_1

or Q_1. In other words our semantic equivalence should take into account repeated, or more complex, methods for interacting with, or observing processes.

The literature is littered with various attempts at formalising what it means to observe processes, many of which are difficult to justify. Here we take a different approach; we define our semantic equivalence in terms of desirable, and reasonable, properties we would like it to enjoy. The approach is straightforward. We list desirable properties $\mathcal{P}_1, \ldots, \ldots, \mathcal{P}_n$ and define our semantic equivalence to be the *largest* equivalence relation between processes that satisfies all of them. In other words processes will be distinguished only if it is required by one of our desirable properties.

The first property is purely observational:

Definition 2.22 (observations) Let $P \Downarrow^{\mathsf{barb}} c$ if $P \stackrel{(\tilde{b})c!V}{\Longrightarrow} P'$, for some P', $(\tilde{b})$ and value V.
We say a relation $\mathcal{R}$ over processes *preserves observations* if

$$\langle P, Q\rangle \in \mathcal{R} \text{ implies } P \Downarrow^{\mathsf{barb}} c \text{ if and only if } Q \Downarrow^{\mathsf{barb}} c$$

for every name c. ♦

This notion of observation is easy to justify. We can design a simple test that will determine if a process can perform such an observation. For example let $C_c[-]$ be the context given by

$$[-] \,|\, c?(x)\mathsf{eureka!}$$

Then the overall system $C_c[P]$ will be able to report eureka if and only if $P \stackrel{(\tilde{b})c!v}{\Longrightarrow} P'$, for some P', for some simple value v.

Nevertheless we have already seen that this property alone is not sufficient to determine a good semantic equivalence; for example P_1 and Q_1 defined above in (2.6) would not be distinguished.

Another desirable property is *preservation by contexts*; as we have already mentioned this means that the equivalence could be used in the compositional construction and analysis of systems. To keep life simple we will concentrate on *static* contexts. So as a second attempt we could use these two properties:

Definition 2.23 (a contextual equivalence) Let $\simeq$ be the largest equivalence relation over processes that

- preserves observations
- is *contextual*. ♦

This is a considerable improvement on our first attempt. For example, this satisfies the property

$$P \simeq Q \text{ implies } C[P] \simeq C[Q]$$

for any static context $C[\ ]$. Indeed this property enables us to show that $P_1 \not\simeq Q_1$, where these processes are defined in (2.6). To see this it is sufficient to observe them in a static context, which examines the further actions they perform. Let $C_{ab}[-]$ be the context

$$[-] \mid a?(x)\, x! \mid b?\mathsf{eureka}!$$

Then $C_{ab}[P_1] \Downarrow^{\mathsf{barb}} \mathsf{eureka}$ whereas $C_{ab}[Q_1] \not\Downarrow^{\mathsf{barb}} \mathsf{eureka}$. Consequently $C_{ab}[P_1] \not\simeq C_{ab}[Q_1]$, and therefore $P \not\simeq Q$.

This is the standard method for showing that two processes are *not* related via $\simeq$; find a static context and an observation that will distinguish them when placed in that context. But proving that two processes *are* equivalent is far less straightforward. In the following example we use

$$P \oplus Q \tag{2.7}$$

as an abbreviation for

$$(\mathsf{new}\, n)(n! \mid n?P \mid n?Q)$$

where n is chosen so that it does not occur in either of P, Q. This is called the *internal choice* between P and Q because it may non-deterministically choose to execute either of these processes. Consider

$$P_2 \Leftarrow b?c! \qquad Q_2 \Leftarrow b?c! \oplus \mathsf{stop} \tag{2.8}$$

P_2 can output on c after having received an input on b. Q_2 also has this behaviour but it may, in addition, evolve into the deadlocked state stop; in other words Q_2 may (randomly) decide either to act like P_2, or become deadlocked. It turns out that $P_2 \simeq Q_2$ but how do we prove it?

We could construct a relation $\mathcal{R}$ that

- contains the pair $\langle P_2, Q_2 \rangle$
- is *contextual*
- preserves observations.

Since $\simeq$ is the largest relation with the last two properties it will follow that $\mathcal{R} \subseteq \simeq$ and therefore that $P_2 \simeq Q_2$. However constructing such as $\mathcal{R}$ turns out to be a non-trivial task. The obvious candidate $\mathcal{R}_1$, given (up to structural congruence) by

$$\begin{array}{ccc} P_2 & \longleftrightarrow & Q_2 \\ c!\langle\rangle & \longleftrightarrow & c!\langle\rangle \mid (\mathsf{new}\, n)(n?\,\mathsf{stop}) \\ \mathsf{stop} & \longleftrightarrow & (\mathsf{new}\, n)(n?\,\mathsf{stop}) \end{array}$$

is not *contextual*. We could force it to be *contextual*, by considering the least relation $\mathcal{R}_2$ that contains $\mathcal{R}_1$ and is closed under static contexts. But is $\mathcal{R}_2$ now closed under *observations*?

It turns out that this is indeed true although the proof is not straightforward. But it does emphasise that although our approach to defining semantic equivalences may be reasonable, in general it leads to relations that are very difficult to handle mathematically.

Nevertheless this example also shows that $\simeq$ must be rejected as a behavioural equivalence, as it does not detect possible deadlocks in processes. Although the deadlock in question is internal to Q_2 its existence will have an effect on observers of the system. For example if Q' is the process $b! \mid c?\,\mathsf{print}!$ then $(P_2 \mid Q')$ will always result in a print, whereas $(Q_2 \mid Q')$ may become deadlocked, depending on the internal choice made by Q_2.

The more basic problem with $\simeq$ is that it does not take into account in any way the *internal branching structure* of processes; Q_2 has a primitive branching structure not present in P_2, and one of the possible choices leads to problematic behaviour not present in P_2. So we must add to our list of desirable properties something that will take this *internal branching structure* of processes into account. There is no obvious candidate and here we rely on a reduced version of bisimulation, which demands that the internal reductions of related processes should in turn be related. This property is very discerning and it is probably the most refined manner in which one might want to distinguish the internal potential branchings of processes.

Definition 2.24 (*reduction-closure*) The relation $\mathcal{R}$ over processes is said to be *reduction-closed* if, whenever $\mathcal{S}$ is either $\mathcal{R}$ or its inverse $\mathcal{R}^{-1}$, it satisfies the transfer property:

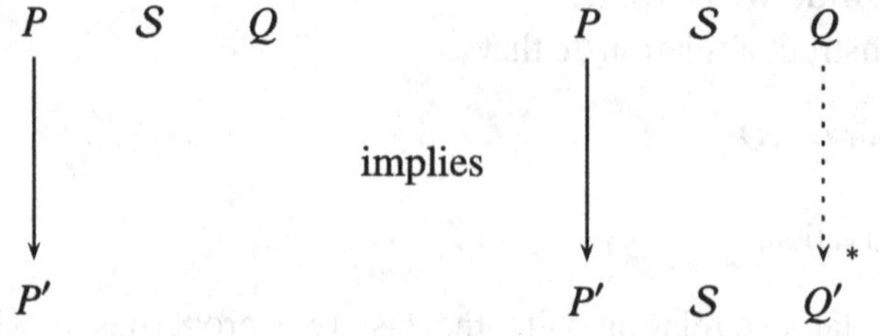

Formally we require that if $\langle P, Q\rangle \in \mathcal{R}$ and $P \longrightarrow P'$ then there exists some process Q' such that $Q \longrightarrow^* Q'$ and $\langle P', Q'\rangle \in \mathcal{R}$, and similarly for reductions from Q. ♦

We add this to our list of desirable properties, to give us our third, and final property based semantic equivalence:

Definition 2.25 (reduction barbed congruence) Let $\cong$ be the largest relation over processes that

- preserves observations
- is *contextual*
- is reduction-closed. ♦

Proposition 2.26 The relation $\cong$ is an equivalence relation.

Proof: See Question 3 at the end of the chapter. ■

With this new equivalence we can distinguish between the processes P_2, Q_2 defined above in (2.8). We can prove that if $\mathcal{R}$ is *any* equivalence relation that has these desirable properties it is not possible for it to contain the pair $\langle P_2, Q_2\rangle$. For if it did, it would also have to contain the pair $\langle C_{bc}[P_2], C_{bc}[Q_2]\rangle$, where $C_{bc}[-]$ is the context $[-] \mid b! \mid c?\mathsf{eureka}!$. But since $\mathcal{R}$ is reduction-closed and $C_{bc}[Q_2] \longrightarrow Q'$, where Q' is the deadlocked process $C_{bc}[\mathsf{stop}]$, this would require a reduction $C_{bc}[P_2] \longrightarrow^* Q''$ for some Q'' such that $\langle Q', Q''\rangle \in \mathcal{R}$. But it is straightforward to see that $Q'' \Downarrow^{\mathsf{barb}} \mathsf{eureka}$ for all Q'' such that $C_{bc}[P_2] \longrightarrow^* Q''$; there are in fact only three possibilities, up to structural equivalence, $C_{bc}[P_2]$ itself, $c! \mid c?\mathsf{eureka}!$ and $\mathsf{eureka}!$. Now, since $\mathcal{R}$ preserves observations, this would require $Q' \Downarrow^{\mathsf{barb}} \mathsf{eureka}$, which is obviously not true.

We take $\cong$ to be our *touchstone* equivalence, motivated by a minimal set of desirable properties one might require of a semantic equivalence. The reasoning just carried out provides a general strategy, based on these properties, for showing that two processes are *not* equivalent. It is also possible to use the definition of $\cong$ in order to develop properties of it. For example structural equivalence has its three defining properties, that is, it is contextual, reduction-closed and preserves observations. Since $\cong$ is the largest such relation it follows that $P \equiv Q$ implies $P \cong Q$.

However, as we have already demonstrated with $\simeq$, this form of definition often makes it difficult to show that a pair of processes *are* equivalent. In general it is necessary to construct a relation containing them that has the three defining properties, something that is not always easy. Another trivial example emphasises the point.

Example 2.27 Let P_3, Q_3 be the processes

$$(b! \oplus b!) \quad b!$$

respectively, where the internal choice operator $\oplus$ is defined in (2.7) above. To show $P_3 \cong Q_3$ we need to construct a relation $\mathcal{R}$ that contains the pair $\langle P_3, Q_3 \rangle$ and has the three desirable properties. The obvious candidate

$$\mathcal{R}_1 = \{\langle P_3, Q_3 \rangle\} \cup \mathsf{Id}$$

where Id is the identity relation, is reduction-closed (trivially) but fails to be *contextual*. Another possibility would be to let $\mathcal{R}_2$ be the closure of $\mathcal{R}_1$ under static contexts, as in the proof of Proposition 2.21. But now one has to show that $\mathcal{R}_2$ is reduction-closed. This involves an inductive proof on the inductive closure, together with an analysis of b residuals of processes. The argument is not involved but it does seem overly complicated for such a simple pair of processes. ■

This provides a good raison d'être for bisimulation equivalence:

Proposition 2.28 $P \approx_{bis} Q$ *implies* $P \cong Q$.

Proof: From Proposition 2.21 and Proposition 2.20 we know that $\approx_{bis}$ is *contextual* and it obviously preserves *observations*. Let us prove that it is also *reduction-closed*.

Suppose $P \approx_{bis} Q$ and $P \longrightarrow P'$; we must find a matching move $Q \longrightarrow^* Q'$. By Proposition 2.14 we know $P \xrightarrow{\tau} P''$ for some P'' such that $P' \equiv P''$. We can therefore find a derivation $Q \xrightarrow{\tau}{}^* Q'$ for some Q' such that $P'' \approx_{bis} Q'$. Applying Proposition 2.15, we know $Q \longrightarrow^* Q'$ and this is the required matching move; since $\equiv$ is contained in $\approx_{bis}$ (see Corollary 2.17), it follows that $P' \approx_{bis} Q'$.

So bisimulation equivalence has all the defining properties of $\cong$. Since $\cong$ is the largest such equivalence it follows that $\approx_{bis} \subseteq \cong$. ■

Thus bisimulation equivalence may be viewed as providing a convenient methodology for proving processes semantically equivalent. For example to show P_3 and Q_3, from Example 2.27 are equivalent, it is sufficient to show that $\mathcal{R}_1$ is a bisimulation (up to structural equivalence), a simple task. Essentially we are replacing the need to analyse $\mathcal{R}_2$, the closure of $\mathcal{R}_1$ under static contexts, with an analysis of $\mathcal{R}_1$ with respect to arbitrary actions.

Can we always use this proof method to demonstrate the equivalence of processes? The answer is **no**.

Example 2.29 It is trivial to see that $c?c! \not\approx_{bis} \mathsf{stop}$ but it turns out that $c?c! \cong \mathsf{stop}$. To see this let $\mathcal{R}$ denote the set of all pairs $\langle P_1, P_2 \rangle$ such that

$$P_1 \equiv (\mathsf{new}\,\tilde{n})(P \mid c?c!)$$
$$P_2 \equiv (\mathsf{new}\,\tilde{n})\,P$$

for some P. It is possible to show that $\mathcal{R}$ satisfies the defining properties of $\cong$; Corollary 2.16 is useful in proving that it is reduction-closed. Then since $\mathcal{R}$ contains the pair $\langle c?c!, \mathsf{stop}\rangle$ it follows that $c?c! \cong \mathsf{stop}$. ■

Intuitively the reason for not being able to distinguish between $c?c!$ and stop is that, regardless of the context in which these are placed, it is difficult to conceive of an observation that can distinguish them. One can send a message along c to the former, but since output is *asynchronous*, that is no behaviour can depend on its receipt, an observation can also not depend on it. Another more general example is given by

$$c?(x)\,(c!\langle x\rangle \mid c?(x)\,R) \cong c?(x)\,R$$

Bisimulation equivalence is defined in terms of the ability of processes to *perform* input and output actions whereas $\cong$ is defined on the ability of contexts to *observe* these actions. Thus Proposition 2.28 is understandable; but underlying these counter-examples to the converse implication is the fact that certain actions cannot be *observed.*

2.6 An observational lts for API

Here we take as basic the reduction semantics of Section 2.2 and discuss the extent to which *observers can see* the actions being performed by processes.

Consider the context $C_{out}[-]$ given by the term

$$[-] \mid c?(x)\,R$$

Placing the process P in this context may be viewed as testing if P can output a simple value on the channel c. Indeed if we define the residual R to be the term

$$\mathsf{if}\ x = n\ \mathsf{then}\ \mathsf{eureka!}\ \mathsf{else}\ \mathsf{stop}$$

for a particular name n, then we can determine if P can output n on c. For the testing harness

$$C_{out}[P]$$

will be able to report eureka if and only if P can output the name n on the channel c. Consequently, we can give a stronger interpretation to the judgement

$$P \xrightarrow{c!n} Q$$

taking it to mean

- the process P has the ability to output the value n on c, thereby being transformed into Q
- moreover *the surrounding environment can observe that P has indeed performed the output of n along c.*

(A-CON)

$$c?(X)\,R \xrightarrow{c?V}_a R\{V/x\}$$

(A-DELV)

$$P \xrightarrow{c?V}_a P \mid c!\langle V\rangle$$

(A-CNTX)

$$\frac{P \xrightarrow{\mu}_a P'}{\begin{array}{l} P|Q \xrightarrow{\mu}_a P' \mid Q \\ Q \mid P \xrightarrow{\mu}_a Q \mid P' \end{array}}\ \mathsf{bn}(\mu) \notin \mathsf{fn}(Q)$$

$$\frac{P \xrightarrow{\mu}_a P'}{(\mathsf{new}\, b)\, P \xrightarrow{\mu}_a (\mathsf{new}\, b)\, P'}\ b \notin \mathsf{n}(\mu)$$

Figure 2.6 Asynchronous input rules for API

Turning to input, the situation is quite different. How can we determine if a process has actually input n on c ? The context $C_{in}[-]$ defined by

$$[-] \mid (c!\langle n\rangle \mid \mathsf{eureka!}\,)$$

is certainly not good enough, as $C_{in}[P]$ can report eureka regardless of the properties of P. In fact it is not possible to come up with a context $C_{in}[-]$ with the property that P inputs n on c if and only if $C_{in}[P]$ can report eureka.

So if we wish to define relations that represent the manner in which a user can *observe* a process, we have to replace $P \xrightarrow{c?V} Q$ with a weaker relation; we have to weaken the input rules used in Figure 2.5.

Let $P \xrightarrow{c?V}_a Q$ be the least relation satisfying the rules given in Figure 2.6. The first rule (A-CON), also used for $P \xrightarrow{c?V} Q$, now represents the fact that when V is made available for input along c then the proffered value may be *consumed* by a process of the form $c?(X)\,P$. However since the observer, providing the input, has no way of confirming its reception, it is also possible that the offered value remains unconsumed. Thus we also allow the rule (A-DEL)

$$P \xrightarrow{c?V}_a P \mid c!\langle V\rangle$$

for any process P. Intuitively this means that, when an observer proffers the value V along c, the value may just remain there waiting for the process to consume it; the value is *delivered* to the process P, but it awaits consumption. The final rules are borrowed directly from Figure 2.5 and simply allow the axioms to occur appropriately under static contexts.

The properties of the new asynchronous input action are very close to those of the standard (synchronous) version:

Lemma 2.30

- $P \xrightarrow{c?V} P'$ *implies* $P \xrightarrow{c?V}_a P'$.
- $P_1 \xrightarrow{c?V}_a P_1'$ *and* $P_2 \xrightarrow{(\tilde{b})c!V} P_2'$ *implies* $P_1 \mid P_2 \xrightarrow{\tau}{}^* Q$ *for some* Q *structurally equivalent to* $(\mathsf{new}\,\tilde{b})(P_1' \mid P_2')$.

Proof: The proof of the first statement is straightforward, as all the defining rules for $P \xrightarrow{c?V} P'$ are included in those of $P \xrightarrow{c?V}_a P'$.

The second is proved by induction on why $P_1 \xrightarrow{c?V}_a P'_1$. If this is inferred by the axiom (A-CON) the result is immediate since we have $P_1 \xrightarrow{c?V} P'_1$. The non-trivial case is when it is inferred by the axiom (A-DELV). In this case P'_1 is $P_1 \mid c!\langle V\rangle$ and from Proposition 2.15 we know P_2 is structurally equivalent to $(\mathsf{new}\,\tilde{b})(c!\langle V\rangle \mid P'_2)$. So, via applications of (S-EXTR), $(\mathsf{new}\,\tilde{b})(P'_1 \mid P'_2)$ is structurally equivalent to $P_1 \mid P_2$; the bound variables can be chosen fresh to P_1. And so trivially, up to structural equivalence, $P_1 \mid P_2 \xrightarrow{\tau}{}^* (\mathsf{new}\,\tilde{b})(P'_1 \mid P'_2)$, in zero steps.

The inductive cases, when $P_1 \xrightarrow{c?V}_a P'_1$ is inferred by the rules in (A-CNTX), are routine. For example suppose P_1, P'_1 have the form $(\mathsf{new}\,d)\,P$, $(\mathsf{new}\,d)\,P'$, where $P \xrightarrow{c?V}_a P'$; let us choose the bound name d so that it is new to P_2. Then by induction we have

$$P \mid P_2 \xrightarrow{\tau}{}^* Q'$$

such that $Q' \equiv (\mathsf{new}\,\tilde{b})(P' \mid P'_2)$. An application of (L-CNTX) gives

$$(\mathsf{new}\,d)(P \mid P_2) \xrightarrow{\tau}{}^* (\mathsf{new}\,d)\,Q'$$

Note that $P_1 \mid P_2$ is structurally equivalent to $(\mathsf{new}\,d)(P \mid P_2)$ and therefore an application of Lemma 2.13 then gives

$$P_1 \mid P_2 \xrightarrow{\tau}{}^* Q$$

for some $Q \equiv (\mathsf{new}\,d)\,Q'$. This is the required matching move, because, since d is chosen to be fresh, we have $(\mathsf{new}\,d)\,Q' \equiv (\mathsf{new}\,\tilde{b})(P'_1 \mid P'_2)$. ■

With these inference rules we now have a new interpretation of API as an lts:

- the configurations are, as before, the closed terms in API
- the relations over the configurations are given by the actions
  - $P \xrightarrow{c?V}_a Q$
  - $P \xrightarrow{(\tilde{b})c!V} Q$
  - $P \xrightarrow{\tau} Q$.

We refer to this as the *asynchronous* lts for API, or the *asynchronous* interpretation of API. For notational convenience an arbitrary action in this lts will be denoted by $P \xrightarrow{\mu}_a P'$, although for output and internal actions this will coincide with the standard actions $P \xrightarrow{\mu} P'$. In particular, it is worth remembering that the internal action $P \xrightarrow{\tau}_a P$ is *still* defined in terms of the standard (synchronous) input and output actions.

Definition 2.31 (asynchronous bisimulations for API) Any relation that satisfies the transfer properties in the *asynchronous* lts for API is called an *asynchronous* bisimulation. Let $P \approx_a Q$ denote the corresponding weak bisimulation equivalence. We refer to this relation as *asynchronous bisimilarity*. ♦

This new semantic equivalence enjoys many of the properties of that defined in Section 2.4. For example it is straightforward to adapt Definition 2.18, to asynchronous bisimulations, to obtain *asynchronous bisimulations up to structural equivalence*, and we have the following adaptation of Proposition 2.19:

Proposition 2.32 If $P \mathcal{R} Q$, where $\mathcal{R}$ is an asynchronous bisimulation up to structural equivalence, then $P \approx_u Q$.

Proof: The proof is very similar to that of Proposition 2.19. However we need to generalise Lemma 2.13 to the asynchronous actions. We need to show that if $P \equiv Q$ and $P \xrightarrow{c?V}_a P'$ then there exists some Q' such that $Q \xrightarrow{c?V}_a Q'$ such that $P' \equiv Q'$. This is straightforward by induction on the derivation of the action $P \xrightarrow{c?V}_a P'$; See Question 5 at the end of the chapter.

With this result the proof now follows as in Proposition 2.19. ■

Example 2.33 Here we show that $c?c! \approx_a \mathsf{stop}$.

Let $\mathcal{R}$ be the least relation that satisfies

(i) $\mathsf{stop}\, \mathcal{R}\, \mathsf{stop}$
(ii) $c?c!\, \mathcal{R}\, \mathsf{stop}$
(iii) $P \mathcal{R} Q$ implies $P \mid d!\langle V\rangle \mathcal{R} Q \mid d!\langle V\rangle$ for every name d and value V.

We show that $\mathcal{R}$ is an asynchronous bisimulation up to structural induction, from which it will follow that $c?c! \approx_a \mathsf{stop}$. Because of the novelty of asynchronous actions it is worthwhile going into some detail here.

Suppose $P \mathcal{R} Q$ and $P \xrightarrow{\mu}_a P'$; we must find a matching move from Q. This is found by induction on the proof that $P \mathcal{R} Q$. There are three cases. The first, when both P and Q are stop is vacuously true.

The second is when P is $c?c!$ and Q is again stop. Here there are two possible moves from P, namely $P \xrightarrow{c?}_a c!$ and $P \xrightarrow{c?}_a c?c! \mid c!$. Both are matched, up to structural induction, by the asynchronous action $Q \xrightarrow{c?}_a \mathsf{stop} \mid c!$. For example, to see the first match note that $c! \equiv \mathsf{stop} \mid c!$, and therefore by (i), followed by an instance of (iii) we have $\mathsf{stop} \mid c!\ \mathcal{R}\ \mathsf{stop} \mid c!$.

The third is when P, Q have the form $P' \mid d!\langle V\rangle$, $Q' \mid d!\langle V\rangle$, respectively, and we know $P' \mathcal{R} Q'$. Here there are numerous possibilities for the move from P. If it is performed by P' we may use induction to find the corresponding move from Q' and therefore from Q. If it is performed by the right component $d!\langle V\rangle$ then it is straightforward. The only remaining possibility is a communication between P' and this component, namely $P' \mid d!\langle V\rangle \xrightarrow{\tau}_a P'' \mid \mathsf{stop}$ because $P' \xrightarrow{d?V} P''$.

By the first part of Lemma 2.30 we know $P' \xrightarrow{d?V}_a P''$, which has, by induction, a matching move $Q' \xrightarrow{d?V}_a Q''$; the second part of the same lemma gives the required

matching move from Q, namely $Q \xrightarrow{\tau}_a^* Q'' \mid \mathsf{stop}$.
Incidentally it is possible to show that in this case d must be c and the value V the empty pattern. But this is not actually needed in the proof.

We also have to show the corresponding result for Q; that is if $P \mathrel{\mathcal{R}} Q$ then every move from Q can be matched by a move from Q. Fortunately, because of the manner in which $\mathcal{R}$ is defined, this is straightforward. ■

This example demonstrates that constructing asynchronous bisimulations is not quite as easy as standard bisimulations; one must always take into account possible input moves generated by the rule (A-DELV). Nevertheless they are much easier to handle than contextual relations. Moreover there are slightly easier formulations, at the expense of changing the definition of *bisimulation*; see Question 16. However it is also possible to show that $\approx_{bis} \subseteq \approx_a$ (see Question 12), which in turn means that we can also demonstrate that $P \approx_{bis} Q$ by exhibiting a (standard) bisimulation $\mathcal{R}$ that contains the pair (P, Q).

However asynchronous bisimulations have the advantage of providing a complete proof methodology for $\cong$; if $P \cong Q$ then there is an asynchronous bisimulation that relates them. This is the topic of the next section.

2.7 Justifying bisimulation equivalence contextually

First let us show that $\approx_a$ satisfies all the desirable properties that are used to define $\cong$. Since $\approx_a$ is itself an asynchronous bisimulation, it is obviously reduction-closed; it is also straightforward to prove that it preserves observations.

Proposition 2.34 The relation $\approx_a$ *is* contextual.

Proof: We use a slight adjustment to the proof of of Proposition 2.21. Let $\mathcal{R}$ be the least relation containing $\approx_a$, with the property that if $\langle P_1, P_2\rangle \in \mathcal{R}$ then

- $\langle P_1 \mid Q, P_2 \mid Q\rangle \in \mathcal{R}$ for every process Q
- $\langle (\mathsf{new}\, n)\, P_1, (\mathsf{new}\, n)\, P_2\rangle \in \mathcal{R}$ for every name n.

We prove that $\mathcal{R}$ is a weak bisimulation up to structural equivalence. From this it will follow that $\approx_a$ is preserved by both parallel and name binding contexts.

As in the proof of Proposition 2.21 it is sufficient to show that whenever $\langle P, Q\rangle \in \mathcal{R}$ every move $P \xrightarrow{\mu}_a P'$ has a matching move $Q \xRightarrow{\hat{\mu}}_a Q'$. The proof proceeds by induction on why $\langle P, Q\rangle \in \mathcal{R}$, but here the matching is up to structural equivalence. Most cases are identical. There is only one complication, when $\mu = \tau$ and the move is an internal communication. Here P, Q are of the form $P_1|Q'$, $P_2|Q'$ and we know by induction that $\langle P_1, P_2\rangle \in \mathcal{R}$. Suppose the move we are trying to match is $P_1 \mid Q' \xrightarrow{\tau} (\mathsf{new}\,\tilde{b})(P_1' \mid Q'')$ because $P_1 \xrightarrow{c?V} P_1'$ and $Q' \xrightarrow{(\tilde{b})c!V} Q''$.

Here we employ Lemma 2.30. Using the first part we know $P_1 \xrightarrow{c?V}_a P_1'$ and therefore by induction this can be matched by a move $P_2 \overset{c?V}{\Longrightarrow}_a P_2'$. Now employing the second part of the same lemma we have, up to structural induction, a required matching move $P_2 \mid Q' \xrightarrow{\tau}{}^* (\mathsf{new}\,\tilde{b})(P_2' \mid Q'')$. ■

Corollary 2.35 If $P \approx_a Q$ then $P \eqsim Q$.

Proof: Follows from the fact that $\approx_a$ has all the defining properties of $\eqsim$. ■

Thus asynchronous bisimulation equivalence is as least as good as the standard version, in that it provides a proof method for establishing that processes are reduction barbed congruent. The key to the converse of this result is the fact that for every *asynchronous* action there is a specific context, or test, which can *observe* it. We have already alluded informally to these contexts in the discussion of Section 2.6.

Definition 2.36 (*definability of actions*) We say the external action α (in the asynchronous lts) is *definable* if for every finite set of names N, and every pair of actions names succ, fail, not contained in N, there is a *testing* process $T(N, \mathsf{succ}, \mathsf{fail}, \alpha)$ with the property that, for every process P such that $\mathsf{fn}(P) \subseteq N$,

- $P \xrightarrow{\alpha}_a P'$ implies that $T(N, \mathsf{succ}, \mathsf{fail}, \alpha) \mid P \longrightarrow^* (\mathsf{new}\,\mathsf{bn}(\alpha))(\mathsf{succ}!\langle \mathsf{bn}(\alpha)\rangle \mid P')$
- $T(N, \mathsf{succ}, \mathsf{fail}, \alpha) \mid P \longrightarrow^* Q$, where $Q \Downarrow^{\mathsf{barb}} \mathsf{succ}$, $Q \not\Downarrow^{\mathsf{barb}} \mathsf{fail}$, implies that $Q \equiv (\mathsf{new}\,\mathsf{bn}(\alpha))(\mathsf{succ}!\langle \mathsf{bn}(\alpha)\rangle \mid P')$ for some P' such that $P \overset{\alpha}{\Longrightarrow}_a P'$. ♦

Note that there is a subtlety here with the bound names in actions; these can only occur in output actions. The tests cannot provoke exactly the same reaction from a process P as these actions. For example if $P \xrightarrow{(b)c!\langle a,b\rangle}_a P'$ then running P in parallel with the associated test $T(N, \mathsf{succ}, \mathsf{fail}, \alpha)$ will not result in $\mathsf{succ}! \mid P'$ but only in the more restricted term $(\mathsf{new}\,b)(\mathsf{succ}!\langle b\rangle \mid P')$, in which the subsequent behaviour on b is not immediately available.

Theorem 2.37 (*actions are definable*) *Every external action in the asynchronous lts of* aPI *is definable.*

Proof: The input case is now straightforward, because of asynchrony. If α is $c?\langle V\rangle$, in which case $\mathsf{bn}(\alpha)$ is empty, let $T(N, \mathsf{succ}, \mathsf{fail}, \alpha)$ be the term

$$c!\langle V\rangle \mid \mathsf{succ}!$$

which does not use fail; for convenience we abbreviate this to T. Then a simple proof, by induction on why $P \xrightarrow{c?V}_a P'$, will show that, up to structural equivalence, $T \mid P \xrightarrow{\tau}{}^* \mathsf{succ}! \mid P'$. It follows from the third part of Proposition 2.15 that $T \mid P \longrightarrow^* \mathsf{succ}! \mid P'$.

To prove the converse first suppose $T \mid P \xrightarrow{\tau}{}^* Q$. It is easy to see that Q has either the form $T \mid P''$ where $P \xrightarrow{\tau}{}^* P''$ or it has the form $\mathsf{succ}! \mid P'$ where $P \overset{\alpha}{\Longrightarrow} P'$.

But in either case Q may be written, up to structural equivalence, as $\mathsf{succ}! \mid P'$ where $P \overset{\alpha}{\Longrightarrow}_a P'$, because of the first part of Lemma 2.30. Therefore, again by Corollary 2.16, if $T \mid P \longrightarrow^* Q$, where $Q \Downarrow^{\mathsf{barb}} \mathsf{succ}$, then Q must be structurally equivalent to a term of the form $\mathsf{succ}! \mid P'$, where $P \overset{\alpha}{\Longrightarrow}_a P'$.

In the output case, when α has the form $(\tilde{b})c!V$, we have already given the essential idea of the context in the discussion in Section 2.3. The precise details are quite complicated because in API we have allowed values V to be tuples of simple values. We will give the proof of the case when $\alpha = (b)c!(b, v)$; from this it should be clear that a proof can also be constructed in the more general case, for an arbitrary V.

Here $T(N, \mathsf{succ}, \mathsf{fail}, \alpha)$, which again we abbreviate to T, has the structure

$$\mathsf{fail}! \mid c?(x, y)\, Q$$

where Q tests the incoming values to ensure

- the value bound to y is v
- that bound to x is a *new* channel.

The first requirement is easy to code using a construct of the form $\mathsf{if}\ x = v\ \mathsf{then}\ Q'\ \mathsf{else\ stop}$. We also know that a channel is new if it is different from all the names in N, which by the hypothesis includes all those occurring free in the processes we are testing. So our context takes the form

$$\begin{aligned} \mathsf{fail}! \mid c?(x, y)\mathsf{if}\ y = v\ \mathsf{then}\ & \\ & \mathsf{if}\ x \in N\ \mathsf{then\ stop} \\ & \mathsf{else\ fail}?\,\mathsf{succ}!\langle x\rangle\ \mathsf{else\ stop} \end{aligned}$$

where $\mathsf{if}\ y \in N\ \mathsf{then}\ P\ \mathsf{else}\ P'$ is an abbreviation for the obvious sequence of nested tests for equality for membership of N.

We leave the reader to check the requirements in this case; because of Corollary 2.16 these may be simplified to:

- $P \xrightarrow{\alpha} P'$ implies $T \mid P \xrightarrow{\tau}{}^* Q$ for some Q structurally equivalent to $(\mathsf{new}\, b)(\mathsf{succ}!\langle b\rangle \mid P')$
- $T \mid P \xrightarrow{\tau}{}^* Q$, where $Q \Downarrow^{\mathsf{barb}} \mathsf{succ}$ and $Q \not\Downarrow^{\mathsf{barb}} \mathsf{fail}$ implies Q is structurally equivalent to $(\mathsf{new}\, b)(\mathsf{succ}!\langle b\rangle \mid P'$, where $P \overset{\alpha}{\Longrightarrow} P'$.

Note that the use of fail in the test ensures that if $Q \not\Downarrow^{\mathsf{barb}} \mathsf{fail}$ then the process being tested has to have performed the output action. ■

The next lemma enables us to recover the full use of the residuals obtained by using these tests to provoke actions, essentially stripping off the bound names inherited from output actions.

Lemma 2.38 (extrusion) Suppose $(\tilde{n}) \subseteq (\tilde{m})$, *where both are sequences of distinct names.*
Then $(\mathsf{new}\,\tilde{n})\,(P \mid \mathsf{succ}!\langle\tilde{m}\rangle) \;\cong\; (\mathsf{new}\,\tilde{n})\,(Q \mid \mathsf{succ}!\langle\tilde{m}\rangle)$ *implies* $P \cong Q$, *provided* succ *is fresh.*

Proof: We define a relation $\mathcal{R}$ by letting $P\,\mathcal{R}\,Q$ if there is some succ fresh to P and Q and some $(\tilde{n}) \subseteq (\tilde{m})$ such that

$$(\mathsf{new}\,\tilde{n})(P \mid \mathsf{succ}!\langle\tilde{m}\rangle) \cong (\mathsf{new}\,\tilde{n})(Q \mid \mathsf{succ}!\langle\tilde{m}\rangle) \tag{2.9}$$

The result follows if we can show that $\mathcal{R}$ satisfies the defining properties of $\cong$. Note that because of Question 10, the actual fresh name used here, succ, is not actually important; for if succ' is another fresh name then (2.9) also implies, by applying an injective substitution, that

$$(\mathsf{new}\,\tilde{n})(P \mid \mathsf{succ}'!\langle\tilde{m}\rangle) \cong (\mathsf{new}\,\tilde{n})(Q \mid \mathsf{succ}'!\langle\tilde{m}\rangle)$$

The freshness of succ ensures that $\mathcal{R}$ is obviously reduction-closed. Let us see why it also preserves observations. So suppose $P \Downarrow^{\mathsf{barb}} b$ where $P\,\mathcal{R}\,Q$, that is

$$(\mathsf{new}\,\tilde{n})(P \mid \mathsf{succ}!\langle\tilde{m}\rangle) \cong (\mathsf{new}\,\tilde{n})(Q \mid \mathsf{succ}!\langle\tilde{m}\rangle)$$

for some $(\tilde{n}) \subseteq (\tilde{m})$. We have to show $Q \Downarrow^{\mathsf{barb}} b$.

If b does not occur in $(\tilde{n})$ then this is obvious, since $(\mathsf{new}\,\tilde{n})(P \mid \mathsf{succ}!\langle\tilde{m}\rangle) \Downarrow^{\mathsf{barb}} b$. So suppose it does. We no longer have $(\mathsf{new}\,\tilde{n})(P \mid \mathsf{succ}!\langle\tilde{m}\rangle) \Downarrow^{\mathsf{barb}} b$ but b can be extruded via succ. Suppose b is the ith element in the list $(\tilde{m})$. Then let T denote the process

$$\mathsf{succ}?(X)\,x_i?\mathsf{eureka}!$$

where eureka is some fresh name, and the pattern X is chosen to match $(\tilde{m})$. Then because $P \Downarrow^{\mathsf{barb}} b$ we also have

$$T \mid (\mathsf{new}\,\tilde{n})(P \mid \mathsf{succ}!\langle\tilde{m}\rangle) \;\Downarrow^{\mathsf{barb}}\; \mathsf{eureka}$$

Since

$$T \mid (\mathsf{new}\,\tilde{n})(P \mid \mathsf{succ}!\langle\tilde{m}\rangle) \;\cong T \mid (\mathsf{new}\,\tilde{n})(Q \mid \mathsf{succ}!\langle\tilde{m}\rangle)$$

it must be that

$$T \mid (\mathsf{new}\,\tilde{n})(Q \mid \mathsf{succ}!\langle\tilde{m}\rangle) \;\Downarrow^{\mathsf{barb}}\; \mathsf{eureka}$$

But this is only possible if $Q \Downarrow^{\mathsf{barb}} b$.

Now let us show that $\mathcal{R}$ is *contextual*. As an example we show that it is preserved by parallel contexts; the case of name binding is even simpler.

Assuming $P_1 \mathcal{R} P_2$ we have to show that $(P_1 \mid Q) \mathcal{R} (P_2 \mid Q)$ for an arbitrary process Q; that is

$$(\mathsf{new}\,\tilde{n})(P_1 \mid Q \mid \mathsf{succ}'!\langle\tilde{m}\rangle) \cong (\mathsf{new}\,\tilde{n})(P_2 \mid Q \mid \mathsf{succ}'!\langle\tilde{m}\rangle) \tag{2.10}$$

for some $(\tilde{n}) \subseteq (\tilde{m})$, and for some name succ' fresh to P_1, P_2, Q and $(\tilde{m})$. We know that for some succ not occurring in P_1, P_2 and $(\tilde{m})$,

$$(\mathsf{new}\,\tilde{n})(P_1 \mid \mathsf{succ}!\langle\tilde{m}\rangle) \cong (\mathsf{new}\,\tilde{n})(P_2 \mid \mathsf{succ}!\langle\tilde{m}\rangle) \tag{2.11}$$

for some $(\tilde{n}) \subseteq (\tilde{m})$. *A priori* succ may occur in Q; but Question 10 may be applied to ensure that this is not the case. However some names in $(\tilde{n})$ may be used in Q, which precludes the straightforward application of (2.11) to achieve (2.10).

However we may proceed as above, when proving that $\mathcal{R}$ preserves observations. Let X be a pattern that matches $\tilde{m}$, and Q_X an open term such that $Q_X \{\!|^{\tilde{m}}/_X|\!\}$ evaluates to the process Q; it is obtained by replacing each occurrence of m_i in Q by x_i. Then (2.11) implies

$$(\mathsf{new}\,\mathsf{succ})((\mathsf{new}\,\tilde{n})(P_1 \mid \mathsf{succ}!\langle\tilde{m}\rangle) \mid O) \cong (\mathsf{new}\,\mathsf{succ})((\mathsf{new}\,\tilde{n})$$
$$(P_2 \mid \mathsf{succ}!\langle\tilde{m}\rangle) \mid O)$$

where O is the process

$$\mathsf{succ}?(X)\,(Q_X \mid \mathsf{succ}'!\langle X\rangle)$$

This takes all the values in V, including those scoped by $(\tilde{n})$, and makes then available both to Q and on the new fresh channel succ'. However it is easy to check that

$$(\mathsf{new}\,\mathsf{succ})((\mathsf{new}\,\tilde{n})(P \mid \mathsf{succ}!\langle\tilde{m}\rangle) \mid O) \approx_{bis} (\mathsf{new}\,\tilde{n})(P \mid Q \mid \mathsf{succ}'!\langle\tilde{m}\rangle)$$

for any process P, by constructing an explicit bisimulation. The required result, (2.10), now follows by Proposition 2.28. ■

We are now ready to prove that asynchronous bisimulation equivalence completely characterises our touchstone equivalence:

Theorem 2.39 (full-abstraction) $P_1 \approx_a P_2$ *if and only if* $P_1 \cong P_2$.

Proof: We already know, from Corollary 2.35, that $\approx_a \subseteq \cong$. So the result will follow if we can show that $\cong$ is an *asynchronous* bisimulation, up to structural equivalence.

So suppose $P_1 \cong P_2$ and $P_1 \xrightarrow{\mu}_a P_1'$. We must find a matching weak move from P_2. If μ is τ we obtain it from the fact that $\cong$ is reduction-closed. So let us assume that it is an external action α. We now use the test for α given by the definability result, choosing N to contain all the free names in both P_1 and P_2 and choosing succ and fail to be fresh to both P_1 and P_2; for convenience we denote it by T.

Because $\approxeq$ is *contextual* we know that

$$T \mid P_1 \approxeq T \mid P_2$$

We also know that

$$T \mid P_1 \longrightarrow^* (\mathsf{new}\,\mathsf{bn}(\alpha))(\mathsf{succ}!\langle\mathsf{bn}(\alpha)\rangle \mid P_1')$$

and therefore $T \mid P_2 \longrightarrow^* Q$ for some Q such that

$$(\mathsf{new}\,\mathsf{bn}(\alpha))(\mathsf{succ}!\langle\mathsf{bn}(\alpha)\rangle \mid P_1') \approxeq Q$$

This means that $Q \Downarrow^{\mathsf{barb}} \mathsf{succ}$ and $Q \not\Downarrow^{\mathsf{barb}} \mathsf{fail}$ and so the second part of definability gives that Q is structurally equivalent to some process $(\mathsf{new}\,\mathsf{bn}(\alpha))(\mathsf{succ}!\langle\mathsf{bn}(\alpha)\rangle \mid P_2')$, where $P_2 \stackrel{\alpha}{\Longrightarrow}_a P_2'$. Since structural equivalence is contained in $\approxeq$ we know

$$(\mathsf{new}\,\mathsf{bn}(\alpha))(\mathsf{succ}!\langle\mathsf{bn}(\alpha)\rangle \mid P_1') \approxeq (\mathsf{new}\,\mathsf{bn}(\alpha))(\mathsf{succ}!\langle\mathsf{bn}(\alpha)\rangle \mid P_2')$$

to which the extrusion lemma can be applied to obtain the required $P_1' \approxeq P_2'$. ■

This completes our exposition of our version of the PI-CALCULUS, API. The primary semantics of the language is expressed as a reduction semantics, which describes how in principle processes perform computations. This reduction semantics is in turn the main ingredient in the behavioural equivalence between processes, $\approxeq$, which is designed to capture how processes behave as components in larger systems. We then established that bisimulations provide a proof methodology for establishing such behavioural equivalences. Finally we showed how the definition of bisimulations could be adjusted, so that the result, asynchronous bisimulations, provides a complete proof methodology for $\approxeq$; if two processes are behaviourally indistinguishable there is an asynchronous bisimulation that relates them.

2.8 Questions

1. Prove that a relation $\mathcal{R}$ over API processes is contextual, according to Definition 2.5, if and only if $P\,\mathcal{R}\,Q$ implies $C[P]\,\mathcal{R}\,C[Q]$ for every static context $C[-]$.
2. If the axiom (S-FLIP) from Figure 2.3 is dropped from the definition of structural equivalence does Corollary 2.16 still remain true?
   What about when either of the axioms in (S-STOP) are dropped?
3. Prove that $\approxeq$ is an equivalence relation.
4. Show that $P \equiv Q$ implies $P \approxeq Q$.
5. Prove that $\equiv \circ \xrightarrow{\mu}_a \;\subseteq\; \xrightarrow{\mu}_a \circ \equiv$.
6. If n does not appear in the free names of P show that $(\mathsf{new}\,n)\,P \equiv P$.
7. Prove that an asynchronous bisimulation up to $\equiv$ for API is also an asynchronous bisimulation.
8. Show that $b?c! \simeq b?c! \oplus \mathsf{stop}$ where $\simeq$ is defined in Definition 2.23.

9. Complete Example 2.29, to show that $c?c! \cong \mathsf{stop}$.
10. Let us say the mapping σ over Names is injective for a subset N of Names whenever $\sigma(n) = \sigma(m)$ implies $n = m$, for all n, m in N.
    - Suppose σ is injective for $\mathsf{fn}(P)$, and $P \longrightarrow Q$. Prove $P\sigma \longrightarrow Q\sigma$.
    - Prove that if σ is injective for $\mathsf{fn}(P) \cup \mathsf{fn}(Q)$ then $P \cong Q$ implies $P\sigma \cong Q\sigma$.

    Here $R\sigma$ denotes the result of substituting every occurrence of n in R by $\sigma(n)$, renaming bound names as necessary in order to avoid the capture of bound names.

    Give a counter-example to both statements, when σ is not injective.
11. Suppose $\mathcal{A}_l$ and $\mathcal{A}_r$ are two relations over APi processes. Then we say that $\mathcal{R}$ is a bisimulation up to $(\mathcal{A}_l, \mathcal{A}_r)$ if both it and its inverse satisfy the transfer property:

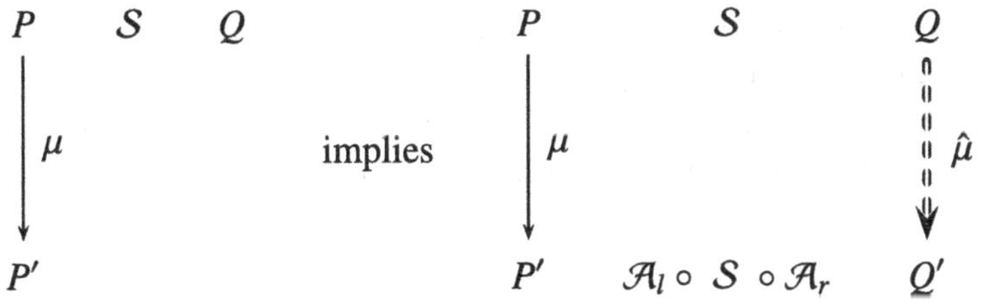

    - Suppose $\mathcal{R}$ is a bisimulation up to $(\sim_{bis}, \approx_{bis})$. Show that $P \,\mathcal{R}\, Q$ implies $P \approx_{bis} Q$.
    - On the other hand show that $P \,\mathcal{R}\, Q$ does not necessarily imply $P \approx_{bis} Q$ when $\mathcal{R}$ is a bisimulation up to $(\approx_{bis}, \approx_{bis})$.
12. (i) Show that $P \overset{c?V}{\Longrightarrow}_a Q$ if and only if there exists some Q' structurally equivalent to Q such that $P \mid c!\langle V\rangle \longrightarrow^* Q'$.

    (ii) Use part (i) to prove that $P \approx_{bis} Q$ implies $P \approx_a Q$.
13. Let Pi be the language obtained by replacing the asynchronous output $c!\langle V\rangle$ in APi with $c!\langle V\rangle.P$. The reduction semantics for the new language is obtained by replacing the rule (R-COMM) in Figure 2.4, with

    (R-SYN.COMM)
    $$c!\langle V\rangle.P \mid c?(X)\,R \longrightarrow P \mid R\{\!|^{V}\!/\!_{X}|\!\}$$

    Give a characterisation of reduction barbed congruence, $\cong$, for Pi, in analogy with Theorem 2.39.
14. Give a characterisation of the equivalence $\simeq$, defined in Definition 2.23, for the language Pi.
15. Adapt the characterisation of $\simeq$ for Pi given in the previous question to the language APi.
16. A relation $\mathcal{R}$ over APi is called an *acs-bisimulation* if it and its inverse satisfy the following transfer property: whenever $P \,\mathcal{R}\, Q$ and $P \xrightarrow{\mu} P'$ then
    - if μ is an output action, or τ, then $Q \overset{\hat{\mu}}{\Longrightarrow} Q'$ for some Q' such that $P' \,\mathcal{R}\, Q'$
    - otherwise if μ is an input action $c?V$ then

– either it is again matched in the standard way, by $Q \stackrel{\hat{\mu}}{\Longrightarrow} Q'$ such that $P' \mathcal{R} Q'$
– or $Q \xrightarrow{\tau}{}^* Q'$ for some Q' such that $P' \mathcal{R} (Q' \mid c!\langle V \rangle)$.

It is argued in [2] that these forms of bisimulation are more convenient than the standard bisimulations in the asynchronous lts given on page 45.
Prove that $P \approx_a Q$ if and only if there is an *acs-bisimulation* $\mathcal{R}$ such that $P \mathcal{R} Q$.

17. Prove $c?(x)\,(c!\langle x\rangle \mid c?(x)\,R) \cong c?(x)\,R$ for any term R whose free variables include at most x.
18. Let E_{ab} denote the process $\mathsf{rec}\ z.\ (a?(x)\,b!\langle x\rangle|z) \ \mid \mathsf{rec}\ z.\ (b?(y)\,a!\langle y\rangle|z)$. Show $E_{ab} \cong \mathsf{stop}$.
19. Let us say a relation $\mathcal{R}$ over API processes is *pcontextual* if it satisfies the first clause of Definition 2.5: $P_1 \ \mathcal{R}\ P_2$ implies $P_1 \mid Q \ \ \mathcal{R}\ \ P_2 \mid Q$ and $Q \mid P_1 \ \ \mathcal{R}\ \ Q \mid P_2$ for every process Q. Then let $\cong_p$ be the largest relation over processes that is reduction-closed, preserves observations, and is *pcontextual*.
Prove $P \cong Q$ if and only $P \cong_p Q$.
20. Let API_l be the language obtained by omitting the construct (if then $v_1 = v_2$ then R_1 else R_2) from API. Show that (full-abstraction), Theorem 2.39, no longer holds for API_l.

3
Types for API

In this chapter we look at type systems for the language API. The traditional view of types is that they provide an aid to programmers to avoid runtime errors during the execution of programs. We start with this view, explaining what runtime errors might occur during the execution of API processes, and design a type system that eliminates the possibility of such errors.

We then modify the set of types, so that they implement a more subtle notion of *resource access control*. Here the resources are simply channels, and the more subtle type system enables access to these resources to be managed; that is read and write accesses can be controlled. The view taken is that one no longer programs directly with resource names. Instead programming is in terms of *capabilities* on these names, the ability to read to or write from a particular resource. These *capabilities* are managed by the owners of resources and may be selectively distributed to be used by other processes.

3.1 Runtime errors

The traditional use of types and type checking is to eliminate *runtime errors* in high-level programs. Specifically types are annotations inserted into the program text by the program designer, or inferred automatically by a type inference system, which indicate the intended use of various resources. Then prior to execution the annotated program is *typechecked*, that is syntactically analysed, to ensure that the behaviour of the program will indeed respect the intended use of these resources. This static analysis is such that when a program successfully passes it cannot produce a runtime error. In general the analysis required will depend on the kind of runtime errors that one wishes to avoid. To focus the discussion let us consider some simple errors that can occur during the computation, or reduction, of an API process.

There are base values in API, such as integers and booleans, and suppose we also had in the language some operators for manipulating base values, such as a successor function succ for integers or not on booleans. Then we may have processes in which a value of one type finds itself in a context where a value of a different type is expected:

$$c!\langle 0\rangle \mid c?(x)\, d!\langle \mathsf{not}(x)\rangle$$

This obviously leads to a runtime error that we would like to avoid.

Without these operators on data the existence of base values can still lead to problems; they may be accidentally mistaken for channels. For example in

$$c?(x)\, x!\langle v\rangle$$

the channel c is obviously expecting to receive a channel. But as part of the larger system

$$c!\langle \mathbf{true}\rangle \mid c?(x)\, x!\langle v\rangle \tag{3.1}$$

it will actually receive the boolean value **true**. This is another kind of error we would like to eliminate.

Even ignoring base values, there are also errors that can arise because of the *shape* of values being transmitted through channels, so-called *arity mismatches*. For example the process

$$c?(x,y)\, x!\langle y\rangle \tag{3.2}$$

expects a *pair* of values, the first of which incidentally should be a channel. But in

$$c!\langle v\rangle \mid c?(x,y) y!\langle x\rangle \tag{3.3}$$

it is only sent a single entity.

In the previous chapter we have also indiscriminately used the same variables as place-holders for values and for recursively defined processes. This imprecision can also lead to problems. In the process

$$\mathsf{rec}\, x.\ (a?(y)\, x!\langle y\rangle \mid x) \tag{3.4}$$

there is obviously a misunderstanding with respect to the role of the variable x; it is used both as a place-holder for channels and for processes. A similar misunderstanding occurs in

$$c?(x)\, (x!\langle v\rangle \mid x)$$

Our static analysis should also preclude such misunderstandings about variables.

We formalise the notion of runtime error as a predicate on processes, that is closed terms. One such definition is the least contextual relation satisfying the rules given in Figure 3.1. The three axioms (ERR-CHAN), (ERR-COMM) and (ERR-REC) are defined precisely with the three different examples above, (3.1), (3.3) and (3.4), in

(ERR-CHAN)
$v?(X)\,R \longrightarrow^{\text{err}}$
$v!\langle V\rangle \longrightarrow^{\text{err}}$ *if* v not a name

(ERR-COMM)
$a?(X)\,R \mid a!\langle V\rangle \longrightarrow^{\text{err}}$
if $X,\ V$ do not match

(ERR-REC)
$\mathsf{rec}\ x.\ B \longrightarrow^{\text{err}}$ if $B\{^{\mathsf{rec}\ x.\ B}/_{x}\}$ not defined

(ERR-STR)
$$\frac{P \equiv P',\ P \longrightarrow^{\text{err}}}{P' \longrightarrow^{\text{err}}}$$

Figure 3.1 Runtime errors in APi

mind, while the rule (ERR-STR) and the implicit contextual rules give more contexts in which these errors might occur.

So the object of our analysis is to ensure that if a process P passes then it will never give rise to a term Q such that $Q \longrightarrow^{\text{err}}$; that is for every Q such that $P \longrightarrow^{*} Q$ we should have $Q \not\longrightarrow^{\text{err}}$.

Let us now investigate briefly what form this static analysis should take. If we look at example (3.1) above it is not clear which sub-process, the sender or the receiver, is at fault. It actually depends on the *intended* use of the channel c, either to transmit boolean values, or to transmit channels. In the current description of the process there is no indication of this intention. In fact we need to augment the language with a facility for indicating the intended use of channels. When a new channel is declared it must have associated with it a *declaration type*, indicating the valid uses to which it may be put. Thus in

$$(\mathsf{new}\, c : \mathsf{D})(c!\langle \mathbf{true}\rangle \mid c?(x)\, x!\langle v\rangle) \tag{3.5}$$

if the declaration type D indicates a boolean channel, that is a channel for carrying boolean values, then the right-hand process is misusing c, while if it indicates a channel that carries channels the fault lies with the left-hand one.

In general the declaration type of a channel should indicate the kind of values that it can handle. These could be integer values, boolean values, or in turn channels. But looking at the example (3.3) above the type should also indicate the *structure* of the value. Here one process thinks it is receiving a *pair* of values while the other is sending a single identifier.

We also need to differentiate between the different kinds of channels that can be transmitted. In

$$c?(x)\, x!\langle a\rangle$$

we can deduce that c carries channels but a priori there are no constraints on the transmitted value a. However in

$$(c!\langle d\rangle \mid d?(y)\, y!\langle 0\rangle) \mid c?(x)\, x!\langle a\rangle \tag{3.6}$$

Channel types:	$\mathsf{C} ::= \mathsf{rw}\langle \mathsf{T} \rangle$
Base Types:	$\mathsf{base} ::= \mathsf{int} \mid \mathsf{bool} \mid \mathsf{unit} \mid \mathsf{str} \mid \ldots$
Declaration types:	$\mathsf{D} ::= \mathsf{C}$
Value Types:	$\mathsf{A} ::= \mathsf{base} \mid \mathsf{C}$
Transmission Types:	$\mathsf{T} ::= (\mathsf{A}_1, \ldots, \mathsf{A}_n), n \geq 0$

Figure 3.2 Simple types for APi

we see that it is further constrained to only carry channels that in turn can carry integer channels. If the value output on y were changed to **true** then the declaration type of c would have to indicate that it transmits channels that in turn transmit boolean channels.

The precise definition of the types, called *simple types*, is given in Figure 3.2, where they are classified into different *kinds*. The most important is that of channel type, $\mathsf{rw}\langle \mathsf{T} \rangle$, where T denotes the type of values that can be transmitted. Thus, following our discussion, in (3.6) the channel c should have the declaration type $\mathsf{rw}\langle \mathsf{rw}\langle \mathsf{rw}\langle \mathsf{int} \rangle\rangle\rangle$ while in (3.2) we would expect it to have a declaration type of the form $\mathsf{rw}\langle(\mathsf{rw}\langle \mathsf{T} \rangle, \mathsf{T})\rangle$ for some type T.

Note that we have introduced a separate class of declaration types, D, although the only allowed declaration types are channel types. This redundancy is convenient for future developments, and we will tend to confine the use of declaration types to the process language.

Notation 3.1 We use

$$\vdash^{s} \mathsf{T} : \mathbf{ty}$$

to indicate that T is a well-formed type; again this is notation that will be more significant in later developments. Also if C is the type $\mathsf{rw}\langle \mathsf{A} \rangle$ then A is referred to as the *object type* of C. ■

So the static analysis of a process will be relative to a collection of associations from channel names to their declaration types, indicating their intended use. This will be called a *type environment*. Moreover as the analysis proceeds this environment will be augmented. For example if we are analysing the process in (3.5) above in a given environment we will end up analysing the sub-process

$$c!\langle \mathbf{true} \rangle \mid c?(x)\, x!\langle v \rangle$$

in the environment augmented by the association of c with its declaration type D. This in turn will lead to the analysis of

$$c?(x)\, x!\langle v \rangle$$

(E-EMPTY)
$$\frac{}{\vdash^{s} \mathbf{env}}$$

(E-NEW.ID)
$$\frac{\vdash^{s} \mathsf{C} : \mathbf{ty} \quad \Gamma \vdash^{s} \mathbf{env}}{\Gamma, u : \mathsf{C} \vdash^{s} \mathbf{env}} \quad u \notin \mathsf{dom}(\Gamma)$$

(E-NEW.BASE)
$$\frac{\Gamma \vdash^{s} \mathbf{env}}{\Gamma, x : \mathsf{base} \vdash^{s} \mathbf{env}} \quad x \notin \mathsf{dom}(\Gamma)$$

(E-PROC)
$$\frac{\Gamma \vdash^{s} \mathbf{env}}{\Gamma, x : \mathsf{proc} \vdash^{s} \mathbf{env}} \quad x \notin \mathsf{dom}(\Gamma)$$

Figure 3.3 Simple type environments for API

and hence that of the open term

$$x!\langle v\rangle$$

where now the environment will need a type to associate with the variable x; this will be the object type of D. But what this latter point also implies is that type environments need to associate types not only with names but also with variables.

Essentially type environments are finite lists of type associations, pairs of the form $u : \mathsf{A}$. But in order to check the correct use of recursion variables we also need to include type associations of the form $x : \mathsf{proc}$. This will indicate that x is only to be used for the purpose of a recursive definition; it is important to realise that this special proc will only play a role in the construction of type environments, and will not be used, for example, to type values. So let us introduce a further meta-variable for the class of types that can appear in environments:

$$\mathsf{E} ::= \mathsf{A} \mid \mathsf{proc} \tag{3.7}$$

Then an environment will have the form

$$u_1 : \mathsf{E}_1,\ u_2 : \mathsf{E}_2,\ \ldots, u_n : \mathsf{E}_n,\ n \geq 0$$

subject to some mild restrictions. Rather than impose these restrictions globally let us give a formal definition of what it means to have a *valid* type environment.

In Figure 3.3 we give rules for inferring valid environments, using judgements of the form

$$\Gamma \vdash^{s} \mathbf{env}$$

The first rule, an axiom, says that the empty association list is a valid type environment while the second says that an existing environment may be augmented by adding a *new* identifier, a name or a variable, and an associated channel type C; here $\mathsf{dom}(\Gamma)$ is the set of identifiers that have an associated type in Γ. We are also allowed to add new variables assigned to base types, with (E-NEW.BASE) and new recursion variables, with (E-PROC); here base ranges over the collection of

(STY-ID)
$$\frac{\Gamma, u : \mathsf{A}, \Gamma' \vDash^{s} \mathbf{env}}{\Gamma, u : \mathsf{A}, \Gamma' \vDash^{s} u : \mathsf{A}}$$

(STY-PROC)
$$\frac{\Gamma, x : \mathsf{proc}, \Gamma' \vDash^{s} \mathbf{env}}{\Gamma, x : \mathsf{proc}, \Gamma' \vDash^{s} x : \mathsf{proc}}$$

(STY-BASE)
$$\frac{\mathsf{bv} \in \mathsf{base} \quad \Gamma \vDash^{s} \mathbf{env}}{\Gamma \vDash^{s} \mathsf{bv} : \mathsf{base}}$$

(STY-TUP)
$$\frac{\Gamma \vDash^{s} v_i : \mathsf{A}_i \quad (\forall i)}{\Gamma \vDash^{s} (v_1, \ldots, v_k) : (\mathsf{A}_1, \ldots, \mathsf{A}_k)}$$

Figure 3.4 Typing values in API

base types, which we leave unspecified. This is perhaps being overly formalistic, as basically a valid type environment is a finite type association list, a list of pairs $u : \mathsf{C}$, $x : \mathsf{base}$ or $x : \mathsf{proc}$, where each identifier has a unique entry. But later we will see that the formation of type environments will get non-trivial, and thus we will make a distinction between an association list and a valid type environment. We will also use the notation Γ, Γ' to denote the association list obtained by adding on the associations in Γ' to those in Γ; of course there is no guarantee that the resulting association list is a valid type environment.

The association between identifiers and types determined by an environment can be generalised to arbitrary values V, by structural induction, and the rules for making the judgements

$$\Gamma \vDash^{s} V : \mathsf{T}$$

are given in Figure 3.4. The intuition behind $\Gamma \vDash^{s} V : \mathsf{T}$ is that relative to the environment Γ the value V may be used anywhere a value of type T is required. To deal with base values we assume base types are actually sets of base values; for example int and bool are the set of integers, booleans respectively. Then the rule (STY-BASE) assigns to the base values the type to which they belong.

3.2 Typechecking with simple types

Rather than giving an algorithm for analysing processes and their correct use of channels, we will give a *typechecking* system, a set of inference rules for establishing that a process term is *well-typed* relative to a given type environment Γ; that is we check it uses identifiers according to the constraints laid down by Γ. *Type inference* would then consist of an algorithm that given a process term P constructs, if possible, a valid type environment relative to which P is well-typed.

As explained in the previous section, the process terms will come from an embellished version of API, called TYPED API, in which bound names have associated with them a declaration type. Formally the language is obtained by replacing the name creation construct

$$(\mathsf{new}\, n)\, T \tag{3.8}$$

in Figure 2.1 with

$$(\mathsf{new}\, n : \mathsf{D})\, T \tag{3.9}$$

We can still view the reduction semantics of Chapter 2 as applying to TYPED API, simply by viewing the unannotated term (3.8) as standing for *any* term of the form (3.9). Indeed it is appropriate that the reduction semantics should not refer to the types of any of the names involved. Moreover we will continue with this view, omitting the declaration types in terms unless they are directly relevant to the discussion. However formally we must define structural equivalence, an important component of the reduction semantics, as a relation over typed processes. So the defining axioms, in Figure 2.3, must be interpreted as acting on typed processes. For example (S-EXTR) now means that for every type D,

$$\text{(S-EXTR)} \quad (\mathsf{new}\, n : \mathsf{D})(P \mid Q) = P \mid (\mathsf{new}\, n : \mathsf{D})\, Q \quad \text{if } n \notin \mathsf{fn}(P)$$

and the second part of (S-STOP) reads

$$\text{(S-EXTR)} \quad (\mathsf{new}\, n : \mathsf{D})\, \mathsf{stop} = \mathsf{stop}$$

There is a more significant change to (S-FLIP), which now must read

$$\text{(S-FLIP)}\ (\mathsf{new}\, n : \mathsf{D}_n)\, (\mathsf{new}\, m : \mathsf{D}_m)\, P = (\mathsf{new}\, m : \mathsf{D}_m)\ (\mathsf{new}\, n : \mathsf{D}_n)\, P \text{ if } n \neq m$$

Declarations can only be flipped if the names involved are different.

The inference rules for typechecking are given in Figure 3.5 where the judgements are of the form

$$\Gamma \vdash^{s} R : \mathsf{proc}$$

where R is an arbitrary, possibly open, process term. There is one rule for each construct in the language. Most of the rules are straightforward. (STY-STOP) says that term stop represents a well-typed process relative to any valid type environment. To typecheck $R_1 \,|\, R_2$ it is sufficient to typecheck the components R_1 and R_2 individually, (STY-PAR), while to typecheck $(\mathsf{new}\, n : \mathsf{D})\, R$ relative to the environment Γ we need to check the term R relative to the augmented environment $\Gamma, n : \mathsf{D}$. The treatment of if $v_1 = v_2$ then R_1 else R_2 also uses induction. Γ must know the values v_1, v_2 and in turn the terms R_1 and R_2 must be typechecked.

$$\frac{\Gamma \vdash^{s} u : \mathsf{rw}\langle \mathsf{T}\rangle \quad \Gamma, \langle X{:}\mathsf{T}\rangle \vdash^{s} R : \mathsf{proc}}{\Gamma \vdash^{s} u?(X)\,R : \mathsf{proc}}\ (\text{STY-IN}) \qquad \frac{\Gamma \vdash^{s} u : \mathsf{rw}\langle \mathsf{T}\rangle \quad \Gamma \vdash^{s} V : \mathsf{T}}{\Gamma \vdash^{s} u!\langle V\rangle : \mathsf{proc}}\ (\text{STY-OUT})$$

$$\frac{\Gamma \vdash^{s} v_1 : \mathsf{A}_1, v_2 : \mathsf{A}_2 \quad \Gamma \vdash^{s} R_1 : \mathsf{proc} \quad \Gamma \vdash^{s} R_2 : \mathsf{proc}}{\Gamma \vdash^{s} \mathsf{if}\ v_1 = v_2\ \mathsf{then}\ R_1\ \mathsf{else}\ R_2 : \mathsf{proc}}\ (\text{STY-EQ})$$

$$\frac{\Gamma \vdash^{s} \mathbf{env}}{\Gamma \vdash^{s} \mathsf{stop} : \mathsf{proc}}\ (\text{STY-STOP}) \qquad \frac{\Gamma, x : \mathsf{proc} \vdash^{s} B : \mathsf{proc}}{\Gamma \vdash^{s} \mathsf{rec}\ x.\ B : \mathsf{proc}}\ (\text{STY-REC})$$

$$\frac{\Gamma, n : \mathsf{D} \vdash^{s} R : \mathsf{proc}}{\Gamma \vdash^{s} (\mathsf{new}\, n : \mathsf{D})\, R : \mathsf{proc}}\ (\text{STY-NEW}) \qquad \frac{\Gamma \vdash^{s} R_1 : \mathsf{proc},\ R_2 : \mathsf{proc}}{\Gamma \vdash^{s} R_1 \mid R_2 : \mathsf{proc}}\ (\text{STY-PAR})$$

Figure 3.5 Inference of simple types in APi

The only non-trivial rules are for input and output, which in turn refer to the judgements in Figure 3.4 for assigning types to values. The term $u!\langle V\rangle$ is well-typed relative to Γ if

- Γ can assign to u a channel type
- Γ can assign to the value being sent, V, the object type of that assigned to u.

The input rule (STY-IN) says that for $u?(X)\,R$ to be well-typed relative to Γ

- u must have a channel type of the form $\mathsf{rw}\langle\mathsf{T}\rangle$ in Γ
- the residual R must be well-typed in an augmented type environment.

This new environment is formed by adding appropriate associations between the variables in the pattern X and the components of the type T. Formally the extension $\Gamma, \langle X{:}\mathsf{T}\rangle$ should be viewed as the result of appending to the environment Γ a list obtained by structural induction from the pattern X and the type T. It will be convenient, for later use, to have a more general construction for these association lists.

Definition 3.2 (constructing environments) The association list $\langle V{:}\mathsf{T}\rangle$ is defined by induction on the structure of the value V. Note this is a partial operation; for example it will not give a result if the structure of V does not match that of T.

- If V is a base value bv then T must be the base type of bv and in this case the result is the empty list.
- If V is a variable x and T is a base type base then the result, $\langle x{:}\mathsf{base}\rangle$, is the singleton list $x : \mathsf{base}$.
- If V is an identifier u and T is a channel type C the result, $\langle u{:}\mathsf{C}\rangle$, is the singleton list $u : \mathsf{C}$.

- If V is $(v_1, \ldots, \ldots, v_n)$, for some $n \geq 0$, the new list is only defined if T has a corresponding structure $(\mathsf{A}_1, \ldots, \mathsf{A}_n)$. The new list is then constructed by induction:

$$\langle v_1 {:} \mathsf{A}_1 \rangle, \ldots, \langle v_n {:} \mathsf{A}_n \rangle$$

Because variables have unique occurrences in patterns we are assured that $\langle X{:}\mathsf{T}\rangle$ is a valid environment, whenever it is defined. But this is not always true of the more general construction $\langle V{:}\mathsf{T}\rangle$. ♦

Referring once more to the rule (STY-IN), one consequence of this definition is that there is no possibility of typechecking a term of the form $u?(X)\, R$ relative to an environment unless the object type of u in that environment matches the pattern X.

Before looking at some examples it is worth emphasising the way in which we treat bound variables in typing judgements. Throughout we make the restriction that typing rules can only be applied to judgements

$$\Gamma \vdash^{s} R : \mathbf{proc}$$

when the domain of Γ does not contain any bound name in R; indeed this is another application of the Barendregt convention, Convention 2.4. So for example in the rule (STY-NEW) we know that n is new to Γ and therefore the extended environment $\Gamma, n : \mathsf{D}$ is well-formed, assuming Γ is. Similarly in (STY-IN) we know that all the variables in the pattern X are new to Γ and therefore $\Gamma, \langle X{:}\mathsf{T}\rangle$ will be a valid environment, assuming X matches T. But there may be times, for example when generating the proof of a typing judgement, when we are required to form a sub-judgement of the form

$$\Gamma \vdash^{s} (\mathsf{new}\, n : \mathsf{D})\, R : \mathbf{proc} \tag{3.10}$$

where n already appears in Γ. In such cases we recall the fact that terms actually denote equivalence classes under α-conversion, and we interpret rules involving bound variables, such as (STY-NEW), as saying that to infer (3.10) above it is sufficient to infer

$$\Gamma \vdash^{s} (\mathsf{new}\, m : \mathsf{D})\, R' : \mathbf{proc}$$

for some m not in the domain of Γ, such that

$$(\mathsf{new}\, m : \mathsf{D})\, R' \equiv_{\alpha} (\mathsf{new}\, n : \mathsf{D})\, R$$

In the sequel we will say a term R is *well-typed* if it can be typechecked, that is if there is some environment Γ such that $\Gamma \vdash^{s} R : \mathsf{proc}$ can be inferred from the rules in Figure 3.10. It will also often be convenient to drop these occurrences of proc, rendering typing judgements simply as $\Gamma \vdash^{s} R$.

Example 3.3 Consider the typechecking of the process

$$(\mathsf{new}\, d : \mathsf{D})(c!\langle d\rangle \mid d?(y)\, y!\langle 0\rangle) \;\mid\; c?(x)\, x!\langle b\rangle$$

a slight modification of that in (3.6) above. Let Γ_d be the type environment

$$d : \mathsf{rw}\langle \mathsf{rw}\langle \mathsf{int}\rangle\rangle$$

Then an application of (STY-OUT) followed by (STY-IN) gives

$$\Gamma_d \vdash^{s} d?(y)\, y!\langle 0\rangle$$

Let $\Gamma_{c,d}$ denote the environment

$$c : \mathsf{rw}\langle \mathsf{rw}\langle \mathsf{rw}\langle \mathsf{int}\rangle\rangle\rangle,\ d : \mathsf{rw}\langle \mathsf{rw}\langle \mathsf{int}\rangle\rangle$$

Since this is an extension of Γ_d we also have

$$\Gamma_{c,d} \vdash^{s} d?(y)\, y!\langle 0\rangle$$

and using (STY-OUT) again, followed by (STY-PAR), we obtain

$$\Gamma_{c,d} \vdash^{s} c!\langle d\rangle \mid d?(y)\, y!\langle 0\rangle$$

Now provided D is exactly the type $\mathsf{rw}\langle \mathsf{rw}\langle \mathsf{int}\rangle\rangle$ an application of (STY-NEW) gives

$$\Gamma_c \vdash^{s} (\mathsf{new}\, d : \mathsf{D})(c!\langle d\rangle \mid d?(y)\, y!\langle 0\rangle)$$

where Γ_c is the list $c : \mathsf{rw}\langle \mathsf{rw}\langle \mathsf{rw}\langle \mathsf{int}\rangle\rangle\rangle$. Finally let $\Gamma_{c,b}$ denote

$$\Gamma_c,\ b : \mathsf{rw}\langle \mathsf{int}\rangle$$

Then another application of (STY-OUT), (STY-IN) and (STY-PAR) gives

$$\Gamma_{c,b} \vdash^{s} (\mathsf{new}\, d : \mathsf{D})(c!\langle d\rangle \mid d?(y)\, y!\langle 0\rangle) \mid c?(x)\, x!\langle b\rangle$$

It is easy to see that for the process to be well-typed the form of the type D is determined by that of c. Also all the entries in $\Gamma_{c,b}$ are necessary to type this process in the sense that if Γ is any other environment for which

$$\Gamma \vdash^{s} (\mathsf{new}\, d : \mathsf{D})(c!\langle d\rangle \mid d?(y)\, y!\langle 0\rangle) \mid c?(x)\, x!\langle b\rangle$$

can be derived, then $\mathsf{dom}(\Gamma)$ must include at least b, c and Γ must coincide with $\Gamma_{c,b}$ on these names. ■

Example 3.4 [*Typing the Compute Server*] Recall from Example 2.10 that this is defined by

$$\mathsf{primeS} \Leftarrow \mathsf{rec}\ z.\ (z \mid \mathsf{in}?(x, y)\, y!\langle isprime(x)\rangle)$$

where *isprime* represents some test for primality. The only free name occurring in primeS is in and therefore we should be able to type it relative to some environment Γ_s that simply maps in to some type S. This channel expects two pieces of data, an integer and a channel; moreover the channel will be used to return a boolean value. So S has to be

$$\mathsf{rw}\langle (\mathsf{int}, \mathsf{rw}\langle \mathsf{bool}\rangle)\rangle$$

However to formally derive the judgement

$$\Gamma_s \vdash^{s} \mathsf{primeS} \tag{3.11}$$

we need to add a rule for handling the operation *isprime*:

$$\text{(STY-OP)}\quad \frac{\Gamma \vdash^{s} u : \mathsf{int}}{\Gamma \vdash^{s} isprime(u) : \mathsf{bool}} \tag{3.12}$$

With this new rule the derivation of (3.11) is straightforward. It relies on establishing two judgements:

$$\Gamma, z : \mathsf{proc} \vdash^{s} z : \mathsf{proc}$$

$$\Gamma, z : \mathsf{proc} \vdash^{s} \mathsf{in}?(x, y)\, y!\langle isprime(x)\rangle$$

The second uses an application of (STY-IN), followed by (STY-OUT), and the above (STY-OP). The former requires an instance of a value judgement, (STY-ID).

Now consider the typed version of the clients:

$$\mathsf{Client}_i(v) \Leftarrow (\mathsf{new}\, r : \mathsf{D}_r)\, \mathsf{in}!\langle v, r\rangle \mid r?(x)\, \mathsf{print}_i!\langle x\rangle$$

The declaration type of the reply channel D_r is determined by that of in; it has to be $\mathsf{rw}\langle\mathsf{bool}\rangle$. Assuming that v is an integer one can infer

$$\Gamma_s,\ \mathsf{print}_i : \mathsf{rw}\langle\mathsf{bool}\rangle \vdash^{s} \mathsf{Client}_i(v)$$

Summing up, we can type the overall system

$$\mathsf{Sys} \Leftarrow \mathsf{Client}_1(27) \mid \mathsf{Client}_2(29) \mid \mathsf{primeS}$$

relative to any type environment Γ_s such that

$$\Gamma_s \vdash^{s} \mathsf{in} : \mathsf{S},\ \ \mathsf{print}_i : \mathsf{rw}\langle\mathsf{bool}\rangle$$ ■

3.3 Properties of typechecking

The object of this section is to prove that typechecking provides a successful static analysis for the avoidance of runtime errors. Specifically, we prove that if there exists a type environment Γ such that $\Gamma \vdash^{s} P$ then whenever $P \longrightarrow^{*} Q$ we are assured that $Q \not\longrightarrow^{err}$. The proof strategy is divided into two steps:

(i) Show that well-typed processes do not contain runtime errors. That is $\Gamma \vdash^{s} Q$ implies $Q \not\longrightarrow^{err}$. This is referred to as *type safety*; see Theorem 3.13.
(ii) Show that being well-typed with respect to a type environment is an invariant under reduction. That is $\Gamma \vdash^{s} P$ and $P \longrightarrow Q$ implies $\Gamma \vdash^{s} Q$. This is often referred to as *subject reduction*; see Theorem 3.12.

Type safety is usually a straightforward inductive proof, but subject reduction depends on a *substitution* result, which roughly says that variables in typing judgements can be substituted by appropriately typed values. To prove this result we need, in turn, to develop a series of properties of the formal systems for making typing judgements. Although we are only interested in the typing of processes, this depends on the type system for values, and even the system for constructing valid environments; see the rule (STY-STOP) in Figure 3.5. So properties of all three formal systems have to be considered. The vast majority of these properties have straightforward proofs, usually by rule induction on typing judgements. But these proofs are usually long, being tedious case analyses on the derivation of judgements. Consequently we concentrate on elaborating the precise properties required, leaving many of the details in the proofs to the reader.

First let us look at some of the many natural properties one would expect of the formal system defined in Figure 3.5. Perhaps the simplest is:

Lemma 3.5 (*sanity checks*)

(i) $\Gamma, \Gamma' \vdash_s \mathbf{env}$ *implies* $\Gamma \vdash_s \mathbf{env}$
(ii) *If* $\Gamma \vdash_s u : \mathsf{E}$ *then* $\Gamma \vdash_s \mathbf{env}$
(iii) *If* $\Gamma \vdash_s R : \mathsf{proc}$ *then* $\Gamma \vdash_s \mathbf{env}$.

Proof: The first statement is proved by induction on the size of Γ'. The base case is when this is empty, which is trivial. Otherwise it has the form $\Gamma'', u : \mathsf{E}$ and the judgement

$$\Gamma, \Gamma'', u : \mathsf{E} \vdash_s \mathbf{env}$$

must have been inferred from one of the three rules (E-NEW.ID), (E-NEW.BASE) or (E-PROC). But the premise in each rule allows us to conclude that $\Gamma, \Gamma'' \vdash_s \mathbf{env}$. We can now apply induction to this statement to obtain the required $\Gamma \vdash_s \mathbf{env}$.

The proofs of the second and third statements are by induction on the derivation of the judgement in question; it is sufficient to carry out a case analysis on the last rule used. Thus the proof of the second statement has four cases, since the proof of the judgement could end in any of the four rules in Figure 3.4, while the proof of the third has eight cases, arising from the seven rules in Figure 3.5, and the trivial possibility of an application of (STY-ID), when R is a variable. Note that some of these cases, for example the rule (STY-NEW), rely on part (i), while others, such as (STY-IN), rely on part (ii). ■

One minor, but crucial, property of the typing system in Figure 3.4 is that, relative to a given environment, it assigns *unique* types to values; however the reader should be warned that this will not be true of later typing systems.

Proposition 3.6 $\Gamma \vdash^{s} V : \mathsf{T}_1$ *and* $\Gamma \vdash^{s} V : \mathsf{T}_2$ *implies that* T_1 *and* T_2 *are identical.*

Proof: An easy proof by induction on the structure of V; for each possible case there is only one applicable typechecking rule, depending on the type T. ■

This result means that we can view a type environment Γ as a function that maps identifiers in its domain $\mathsf{dom}(\Gamma)$ to types. We use $\Gamma(u)$ to denote the type associated with the identifier u.

Although we have been careful in the construction of environments, it turns out that the order in which type associations are added does not really matter:

Proposition 3.7 (interchange) Let Γ *and* Γ' *denote the lists* $\Gamma_1, u : \mathsf{E}, u' : \mathsf{E}', \Gamma_2$ *and* $\Gamma_1, u' : \mathsf{E}', u : \mathsf{E}, \Gamma_2$ *respectively. Then*

- $\Gamma \vdash^{s} \mathbf{env}$ *implies* $\Gamma' \vdash^{s} \mathbf{env}$
- $\Gamma \vdash^{s} V : \mathsf{T}$ *implies* $\Gamma' \vdash^{s} V : \mathsf{T}$
- $\Gamma \vdash^{s} R$ *implies* $\Gamma' \vdash^{s} R$.

Proof: The first statement is proved by induction on the size of Γ', with the only non-trivial case being when it is empty where a case analysis is required on the forms of u, u'; the inductive case is taken care of by Lemma 3.5(i).

The other two statements are proved by rule induction, and an analysis of the last rule used. The essential fact underlying these results is that any derivation of a judgement using Γ can be replaced by one using Γ'; environments have unique entries for identifiers and in typechecking they are essentially only used as look-up tables. ■

The following are more substantial, but the structure of the proofs are similar; they also require the property (interchange).

Proposition 3.8

- ***(Weakening)*** *Suppose* $\Gamma, \Gamma' \vdash^{s} \mathbf{env}$*. Then*
  - $\Gamma \vdash^{s} V : \mathsf{T}$ *implies* $\Gamma, \Gamma' \vdash^{s} V : \mathsf{T}$
  - $\Gamma \vdash^{s} R$ *implies* $\Gamma, \Gamma' \vdash^{s} R$.
- ***(Strengthening)***
  - *If* $\Gamma,\ u : \mathsf{E} \vdash^{s} V : \mathsf{T}$ *where* u *does not occur in* V*, then* $\Gamma \vdash^{s} V : \mathsf{T}$.
  - *If* $\Gamma,\ u : \mathsf{E} \vdash^{s} R$ *where* u *does not occur in* R*, then* $\Gamma \vdash^{s} R$.

Proof: The proof details, which are considerable but mundane, are left to the reader; here we only give their structure, and some typical example cases.

- (Weakening): Both cases are proved by rule induction, and an analysis of the last rule used in the derivation. For example if $\Gamma \vdash^{s} V : \mathsf{T}$ is proved by an instance of (STY-ID), then exactly the same rule can be applied to the extended environment Γ, Γ', to conclude $\Gamma, \Gamma' \vdash^{s} V : \mathsf{T}$.

Similarly suppose $\Gamma \vDash_s R$ because of an application of (STY-NEW). Then R must be of the form $(\mathsf{new}\, n : \mathsf{D})\, R_1$, where by Barendregt's convention we can assume that n is new to both Γ and Γ'. Moreover because of the application of (STY-NEW) we know $\Gamma, n : \mathsf{D} \vDash_s R_1$. But the type formation rules, specifically (E-NEW.ID), ensure that $\Gamma, \Gamma', n : \mathsf{D} \vDash_s \mathbf{env}$, and a sequence of applications of (interchange) therefore gives $\Gamma, n : \mathsf{D}, \Gamma' \vDash_s \mathbf{env}$. So induction can be applied, to give $\Gamma, n : \mathsf{D}, \Gamma' \vDash_s R_1$. Another sequence of applications of (interchange) leads to $\Gamma, \Gamma', n : \mathsf{D} \vDash_s R_1$. Now (STY-NEW) gives the required $\Gamma, \Gamma' \vDash_s R$.

- (Strengthening): Here the structure of the proof is identical, using rule induction and an analysis of the last rule used. Because of the side conditions, each application of a rule using the environment $\Gamma, u : \mathsf{E}$ can be replaced by an application of the same rule using Γ. But once more the case (STY-NEW) requires the property (interchange). ■

The most important technical property of the type inference system is that in some sense typing is preserved by the substitution of values into variables, provided the types assigned to these values and variables coincide.

Proposition 3.9 (*substitution*)

(i) (values) *Suppose* $\Gamma \vDash_s v : \mathsf{A}$ *and* $\Gamma, x : \mathsf{A} \vDash_s V : \mathsf{T}$. *Then* $\Gamma \vDash_s V\{\!|^{v}/_{x}|\!\} : \mathsf{T}$.

(ii) (processes) *Suppose* $\Gamma \vDash_s v : \mathsf{A}$ *and* $\Gamma, x : \mathsf{A} \vDash_s R$. *Then* $R\{\!|^{v}/_{x}|\!\}$ *is well-defined and* $\Gamma \vDash_s R\{\!|^{v}/_{x}|\!\}$.

(iii) (recursion) *Suppose* $\Gamma \vDash_s R_1$ *and* $\Gamma, x : \mathsf{proc} \vDash_s R_2$. *Then* $R_2\{\!|^{R_1}/_{x}|\!\}$ *is well-defined and* $\Gamma \vDash_s R_2\{\!|^{R_1}/_{x}|\!\}$.

Proof: The first result is a straightforward induction on the derivation of $\Gamma, x : \mathsf{A} \vDash_s V : \mathsf{T}$ from the rules in Figure 3.4. The only delicate case is the use of the axiom (STY-ID), where a case analysis is required on whether or not v is the variable x.

Let us consider the second result, for processes. Under the assumption that $\Gamma \vDash_s v : \mathsf{A}$, suppose $\Gamma, x : \mathsf{A} \vDash_s R$. We show, by rule induction, that this can be transformed into a derivation of $\Gamma \vDash_s R\{\!|^{v}/_{x}|\!\}$. We examine the last rule used in the derivation of $\Gamma, x : \mathsf{A} \vDash_s R$, which is either from Figure 3.5, or an application of (STY-ID) from Figure 3.4 to infer a variable. For simplicity we use J' to denote $J\{\!|^{v}/_{x}|\!\}$ for any syntactic object J. Using this notation we have to show $\Gamma \vDash_s R'$. There are eight possibilities.

- (STY-OUT): Here the term R has the form $u!\langle V\rangle$ and we must have

$$\Gamma, x : \mathsf{A} \vDash_s u : \mathsf{rw}\langle\mathsf{T}\rangle$$
$$\Gamma, x : \mathsf{A} \vDash_s V : \mathsf{T}$$

for some transmission type T. We can apply part (i) of the proposition to both judgements to obtain $\Gamma \vDash_s u' : \mathsf{rw}\langle\mathsf{T}\rangle$ and $\Gamma \vDash_s V' : \mathsf{T}$. An application of (STY-OUT) now gives the required $\Gamma \vDash_s u'!\langle V'\rangle$.

- (STY-IN): Here the term R is $u?(Y)\,S$ and we know

$$\Gamma, x : \mathsf{A} \vDash^{s} u : \mathsf{rw}\langle\mathsf{T}\rangle$$
$$\Gamma, x : \mathsf{A}, \langle Y{:}\mathsf{T}\rangle \vDash^{s} S$$

for some transmission type T. Note that the ability to apply (STY-IN) means that x cannot be in the pattern Y. This time we apply part (i) of the proposition to the first judgement to obtain

$$\Gamma \vDash^{s} u' : \mathsf{rw}\langle\mathsf{T}\rangle$$

To the second we need to apply (interchange), Proposition 3.7, possibly a number of times, to obtain

$$\Gamma, \langle Y{:}\mathsf{T}\rangle, x : \mathsf{A} \vDash^{s} S$$

Also (weakening), from Proposition 3.8, applied to the hypothesis $\Gamma \vDash^{s} v : \mathsf{A}$, gives $\Gamma, \langle Y{:}\mathsf{T}\rangle \vDash^{s} v : \mathsf{A}$. So induction may be applied, to obtain

$$\Gamma, \langle Y{:}\mathsf{T}\rangle \vDash^{s} S'$$

Now (STY-IN) gives the required

$$\Gamma \vDash^{s} u'?(Y)\,S' \quad \text{that is} \quad \Gamma \vDash^{s} R'$$

All other cases are similar, using the part (i) of the proposition or induction. But note that the cases (STY-REC) and (STY-NEW) also require an application of (interchange), while that of (STY-ZERO) needs (weakening).

The final result, for recursion, is proved in a similar manner, by rule induction on the inference $\Gamma, x : \mathsf{proc} \vDash^{s} R_2$. Let us examine two cases.

- (STY-PROC): Here R_2 is some variable y, and $\Gamma, x : \mathsf{proc} \vDash^{s} R_2$ is true because somewhere in $\Gamma, x : \mathsf{proc}$ there is the entry $y : \mathsf{proc}$. There are two cases. In the first x and y coincide, and the required result is immediate, since $R_2\{\!|{}^{R_1}\!/\!_x|\!\}$ unravels to R_1. In the second $x \neq y$, and so the entry must appear somewhere in Γ; in other words $\Gamma \vDash^{s} y$. So the result is again immediate, since $R_2\{\!|{}^{R_1}\!/\!_x|\!\}$ is y.
- (STY-NEW): Here R_2 has the form $(\mathsf{new}\, n : \mathsf{D})\,R$ and $\Gamma, x : \mathsf{proc} \vDash^{s} R_2$ because $\Gamma, x : \mathsf{proc}, n : \mathsf{D} \vDash^{s} R$. Using (interchange), Proposition 3.7, this can be rewritten as $\Gamma, n : \mathsf{D}, x : \mathsf{proc} \vDash^{s} R$. Also (weakening), from Proposition 3.8, applied to the hypothesis $\Gamma \vDash^{s} R_1$ gives $\Gamma, n : \mathsf{D} \vDash^{s} R_1$.

  Now we can apply induction, to obtain $\Gamma, n : \mathsf{D} \vDash^{s} R\{\!|{}^{R_1}\!/\!_x|\!\}$. Then an application of (STY-NEW) gives $\Gamma \vDash^{s} (\mathsf{new}\, n : \mathsf{D})((R)\{\!|{}^{R_1}\!/\!_x|\!\})$. However using α-conversion if necessary, or invoking Barendregt's convention, we can ensure that the bound variable n does not appear in R_1, and therefore the term we have just typed with respect to Γ is $((\mathsf{new}\, n : \mathsf{D})\,R)\{\!|{}^{R_1}\!/\!_x|\!\}$, that is the required $R_2\{\!|{}^{R_1}\!/\!_x|\!\}$. ■

There is a simple generalisation of the substitution result for processes to patterns:

Corollary 3.10 Suppose $\Gamma \vDash^s V : \mathsf{T}$. *Then* $\Gamma, \langle X{:}T\rangle \vDash^s R$ *implies* $R\{\!\!\{^V\!/\!_X\}\!\!\}$ *is well-defined and* $\Gamma \vDash^s R\{\!\!\{^V\!/\!_X\}\!\!\}$.

Proof: By induction on the structure of the pattern X. ■

We are now nearly ready to prove subject reduction. Recall that the structural equivalence plays a large role in the reduction semantics. So let us first factor this out.

Proposition 3.11 Suppose $P \equiv Q$. *Then* $\Gamma \vDash^s P$ *implies* $\Gamma \vDash^s Q$.

Proof: This is proved by induction on the proof of $P \equiv Q$. The contextual rules in the definition of $\equiv$ pose no problem. For example suppose P, Q have the form $(\mathsf{new}\, n : \mathsf{D})\, P'$, $(\mathsf{new}\, n : \mathsf{D})\, Q'$ and they are structurally equivalent because $P' \equiv Q'$. Because $\Gamma \vDash^s P$ we know $\Gamma, n : \mathsf{D} \vDash^s P'$ and therefore by induction we have that $\Gamma, n : \mathsf{D} \vDash^s Q'$. An application of (STY-NEW) then gives the required $\Gamma \vDash^s Q$.

So we need only consider the axioms in the definition of structural equivalence, the typed versions of those in Figure 2.3. Most are straightforward, but note that one part of (S-STOP) requires (strengthening).

The only non-trivial axiom is (S-EXTR), which might be expected. So suppose $P \vDash^s (\mathsf{new}\, n : \mathsf{D})(P \mid Q)$, where n does not occur free in P. This could only have been derived by an application of (STY-NEW) preceded by one of (STY-PAR) and therefore we must have

$$\Gamma,\ n : \mathsf{D} \vDash^s P$$
$$\Gamma,\ n : \mathsf{D} \vDash^s Q$$

We can apply (strengthening) to the former to obtain $\Gamma \vDash^s P$. Now an application of (STY-NEW) followed by (STY-PAR) gives the required

$$\Gamma \vDash^s P \mid (\mathsf{new}\, n : \mathsf{D})\, Q$$

The converse is similar but requires an application of (weakening). ■

Theorem 3.12 (subject reduction for simple types) Suppose $\Gamma \vDash^s P$. *Then* $P \longrightarrow Q$ *implies* $\Gamma \vDash^s Q$.

Proof: The proof is by induction on the derivation of the judgement $P \longrightarrow Q$, from the rules in Figure 2.4 and those obtained from the contextuality of reduction. The latter are handled routinely by induction and the troublesome rule (R-STR) follows from the previous lemma. So we need only consider the axioms. Both (R-EQ) and (R-NEQ) are trivial. So let us consider the first two axioms.

- Suppose $\Gamma \vdash^{s} c!\langle V \rangle \mid c?(X) R$. We have to show $\Gamma \vdash^{s} R\{\!|^{V}\!/x|\!\}$, which will follow from Corollary 3.10 if we can show that for some type T

$$\Gamma, \langle X : \mathsf{T} \rangle \vdash^{s} R \quad \text{and} \quad \Gamma \vdash^{s} V : \mathsf{T} \tag{3.13}$$

But we know $\Gamma \vdash^{s} c!\langle V \rangle$ from which we can obtain $\Gamma \vdash^{s} V : \mathsf{T}_1$ for some type T_1. In fact this is a type for which we also know $\Gamma \vdash^{s} c : \mathsf{rw}\langle \mathsf{T}_1 \rangle$. In addition from $\Gamma \vdash^{s} c?(X) R$ we obtain $\Gamma, \langle X : \mathsf{T}_2 \rangle \vdash^{s} R$ for some type T_2, a type for which we can deduce $\Gamma \vdash^{s} c : \mathsf{rw}\langle \mathsf{T}_2 \rangle$. But inferred channel types are unique – see Proposition 3.6, and therefore $\mathsf{T}_1 = \mathsf{T}_2$. The result therefore follows from (3.13).

- Suppose $\Gamma \vdash^{s} \mathsf{rec}\ x.\ B$. This could only have been derived using (STY-REC) and therefore we know $\Gamma, x : \mathsf{proc} \vdash^{s} B$. We can now immediately apply Proposition 3.9 (processes) to obtain the required $\Gamma \vdash^{s} B\{\!|^{\mathsf{rec}\ x.\ B}\!/x|\!\}$. ∎

Theorem 3.13 (type safety) For any process P, $\Gamma \vdash^{s} P$ implies $P \not\longrightarrow^{err}$.

Proof: The proof is straightforward, which is not surprising since the typechecking system was designed with the particular definition of $\longrightarrow^{err}$ in mind.

We prove, by rule induction, that if $P \longrightarrow^{err}$ then there is no Γ for which $\Gamma \vdash^{s} P$ can be derived. Looking at the definition in Figure 3.1 we see that seven possibilities have to be considered.

- (ERR-CHAN): Obvious. For example if v is not a name then there is no way to infer a type for $v!\langle V \rangle$ using (STY-OUT).
- (ERR-COMM): This is the only case that is not completely trivial. Here P has the form $a?(X) R \mid a!\langle V \rangle$ and the pattern X and value V do not match. Suppose that for some environment Γ we were able to type at least $a!\langle V \rangle$. This would mean that there is a type T, the object type of a in Γ, such that $\Gamma \vdash^{s} V : \mathsf{T}$. But such an inference is only possible if V matches the type T, which means that T does not match the pattern X. So the list extension $\Gamma, \langle X : \mathsf{T} \rangle$ is not defined and therefore (STY-IN) cannot be used to complete the typing of R.
- (ERR-REC): Here P has the form $\mathsf{rec}\ x.\ B$ and the substitution $B\{\!|^{\mathsf{rec}\ x.\ B}\!/x|\!\}$ is not defined. For any Γ we can apply Proposition 3.9 (recursion), with R_1 and R_2 instantiated to $\mathsf{rec}\ x.\ B$, B respectively. This implies that either $\Gamma \not\vdash^{s} \mathsf{rec}\ x.\ B$ or $\Gamma, x : \mathsf{proc} \not\vdash^{s} B$. But the latter possibility also means that $\Gamma \not\vdash^{s} \mathsf{rec}\ x.\ B$ as the only way to infer the well-typing of a recursive definition is with (STY-REC).

All the other possibilities follow by induction. Suppose, for example, that $(\mathsf{new}\ n : \mathsf{D}) P \longrightarrow^{err}$ because $P \longrightarrow^{err}$. By induction P is not typeable and therefore we cannot use (STY-NEW), the only possible rule, to infer that $(\mathsf{new}\ n : \mathsf{D}) P$ is well-typed. ∎

Combining these two results we can now conclude that being well-typed precludes the possibility of runtime errors.

Corollary 3.14 Suppose $\Gamma \vdash^{s} P$. *Then* $Q \not\longrightarrow^{err}$ *for every process* Q *such that* $P \longrightarrow^{*} Q$.

Proof: Subject reduction implies that $\Gamma \vdash^{s} Q$ and therefore we can apply type safety to obtain $Q \not\longrightarrow^{\text{err}}$. ■

3.4 Types as capabilities

Channels are resources that are shared among processes for communication purposes. But so far when a process gains knowledge of a channel it may make use of it in any manner it wishes. The language API allows three valid uses of a channel c:

- values, of the appropriate type, may be *read* from c
- values, again of the appropriate type, may be *written* to c
- c may be *compared* with other identifiers for identity.

Each of these may be viewed as *capabilities* on the channel c and currently knowledge of c provides all three capabilities. But in many situations it may be advantageous to be more discriminating in their distribution. A simple example is provided by the memory cell Mem in Example 2.11. For the integrity of the memory to be maintained it is important that Mem is the only process in its environment that has read permission on the two access methods get and put. Otherwise a rogue process could set up a rival memory cell with the same access methods but giving spurious results; this is discussed in more depth in Example 3.15 below. In this section we show how the typing rules in Figure 3.5 can be modified in a simple manner so as to implement this more refined view of types. Moreover we show that all the properties of typechecking derived in the previous section remain valid.

The previous monolithic view of channel types, in Figure 3.2 is broken down into three separate capability types:

read: A channel name at the type $\mathsf{r}\langle \mathsf{T} \rangle$ can only be used to read values, and use them with *at most* the capabilities given by T.

write: Similarly at the type $\mathsf{w}\langle \mathsf{T} \rangle$ it can only be used to write values, and use them with *at least* the capabilities in T.

read and write: The more general type $\mathsf{rw}\langle \mathsf{T}_r, \mathsf{T}_w \rangle$ allows the reading of values with *at most* the capabilities of T_r and *at least* those of T_w.

This last type is often abbreviated to $\mathsf{rw}\langle \mathsf{T} \rangle$ when both the read and write capabilities are the same, namely $\mathsf{T} = \mathsf{T}_r = \mathsf{T}_w$; however we shall see that the more general form will be technically convenient.

The idea now is that processes no longer transmit values among themselves, but rather transmit certain *capabilities* on those values. The precise capabilities transferred in a given communication are determined by the type of the channel responsible for that communication. Referring back to Example 2.11, at some point in its history the client obtains the names of the channels put, get, and it is the type at which they are obtained that determines how they can be used. To discuss this further consider an extension of that example.

Example 3.15 [*A Memory Server*] Consider the following definition of a *memory service* memSERV, which receives a request for a memory on the channel s, generates a new *memory*, with the associated access methods put and get, and sends them back on the reply channel, bound to x:

$$\mathsf{memSERV} \Leftarrow \mathsf{rec}\ w.\ s?(x)\ (w \mid (\mathsf{new\,put} : \mathsf{D}_p, \mathsf{get} : \mathsf{D}_g)(x!\langle \mathsf{put}, \mathsf{get}\rangle \mid \mathsf{Mem}))$$

Here Mem is the code for a memory, given in Example 2.11. However there the methods put and get were free; here they are bound, and in effect each time the service is called on s a new memory, with new put and get methods, is generated; a priori a client can have no knowledge of these yet to be created access methods. But the *client* mClient, defined below, sends a request to the server, obtains the newly created access methods and uses them as in Example 2.11:

$$\mathsf{mClient} \Leftarrow (\mathsf{new}\, r : \mathsf{D}_r)(s!\langle r\rangle \mid r?(x,y)\ \mathsf{Client}_{x,y})$$

$$\mathsf{Client}_{x,y} \Leftarrow (\mathsf{new}\, a : \mathsf{D}_a)(x!\langle 4, a\rangle \mid a?\,(\mathsf{new}\, b : \mathsf{D}_b)(y!\langle b\rangle \mid b?(z)\ \mathsf{print}!\langle z\rangle))$$

The various declaration types can easily be instantiated so that the combined system

$$\mathsf{memSERV} \mid \mathsf{mClient}$$

can be typed using the type inference of the previous section. But so can the system

$$\mathsf{memSERV} \mid \mathsf{badClient}$$

that contains a rogue client badClient:

$$\begin{aligned} \mathsf{badClient} &\Leftarrow (\mathsf{new}\, r : \mathsf{D}_r)(s!\langle r\rangle \mid r?(z,w)\ \mathsf{badMem}) \\ \mathsf{badMem} &\Leftarrow \mathsf{rec}\ p.\ z?(x,y)\ (y! \mid p) \mid \\ &\quad\ \ \mathsf{rec}\ g.\ w?(y)\ (y!\langle 27\rangle \mid g) \end{aligned}$$

This client also obtains the two new access methods but sets up a rival service on both, effectively pretending to be a memory cell that always contains the arbitrary number 27; updates to this rogue memory cell leave the contents unchanged. ■

With capability types we can guard against such rogue clients by ensuring that when memSERV exports the names of the new access methods the client only obtains *write* permission on them. The export type of these names is determined by the *write capability* on the variable x in the definition of memSERV

$$\ldots (x!\langle \mathsf{put}, \mathsf{get}\rangle \mid \ldots$$

that, as we shall see, is determined in turn by that of the access point to the service *s*.

3.4.1 Capability types and environments

Intuitively a channel at the type $\mathsf{rw}\langle \mathsf{T}\rangle$ can be used both for reading and for writing, that is, in the same manner as a channel at the type $\mathsf{r}\langle \mathsf{T}\rangle$ or at the type $\mathsf{w}\langle \mathsf{T}\rangle$. For this reason it is convenient to introduce a *subtyping* relation between these capability types. The judgement

$$\mathsf{T}_1 <: \mathsf{T}_2 \tag{3.14}$$

means that any value that a process has at type T_1 may be used in an occurrence where the type T_2 is required. For example we will have

$$\mathsf{rw}\langle \mathsf{T}\rangle <: \mathsf{w}\langle \mathsf{T}\rangle$$

because if a process has a value, say *c*, at the type $\mathsf{rw}\langle \mathsf{int}\rangle$ then that process may use the code

$$\ldots c!\langle 1\rangle \ldots$$

because this is a use of *c* at the ***supertype*** $\mathsf{w}\langle \mathsf{int}\rangle$. In (3.14) above we say T_1 is a *subtype* of T_2, or T_2 is a *supertype* of T_1. This ordering $<:$ is reasonable if we interpret a type (informally) as the *set* of identifiers that can be assigned that type.

There is another informal view of a type as a *set* of capabilities. For example the type $\mathsf{rw}\langle \mathsf{int}\rangle$ represents the set of capabilities $\{\mathsf{r}\langle \mathsf{int}\rangle, \mathsf{w}\langle \mathsf{int}\rangle\}$ while $\mathsf{w}\langle \mathsf{int}\rangle$ is the singleton set $\{\mathsf{w}\langle \mathsf{int}\rangle\}$. Under this view, to which we will often refer, (3.14) above means that the set of capabilities T_2 is a *subset* of T_1; that is T_1 has *at least* the capabilities of T_2, and possibly more.

The informal description of capability types in Figure 3.6 has a side condition that uses the subtyping relation on types of the form $\mathsf{rw}\langle \mathsf{T}_r, \mathsf{T}_w\rangle$; here the subscripts $_r$, $_w$ are simply an informal indication of the role of the types concerned. Intuitively if a channel *c* is known at this type one would expect that values read from *c* would have *at most* the capabilities of values written to *c*; otherwise capabilities could be manufactured spontaneously. This requirement is enforced by demanding that $\mathsf{T}_w <: \mathsf{T}_r$. See Example 3.33 for more discussion on this point.

However formally we make no use of Figure 3.6; instead we concentrate on the formal system determined by the rules in Figure 3.7. In this system the judgements take the form

$$\mathsf{T}_1 <: \mathsf{T}_2$$

where of course the entities T_1 and T_2 are similar in structure to those described informally in Figure 3.6. The main rule is (SUB-CHAN.A), which is in effect

Channel types:	$\mathsf{C} ::= \mathsf{r}\langle\mathsf{T}\rangle \mid \mathsf{w}\langle\mathsf{T}\rangle \mid \mathsf{rw}\langle\mathsf{T}_r, \mathsf{T}_w\rangle$ provided $\mathsf{T}_w <: \mathsf{T}_r$
Base types:	$\mathsf{base} ::= \mathsf{int} \mid \mathsf{bool} \mid \mathsf{unit} \mid \mathsf{str} \mid \ldots$
Declaration types:	$\mathsf{D} ::= \mathsf{C}$
Value Types:	$\mathsf{A} ::= \mathsf{base} \mid \mathsf{C}$
Transmission Types:	$\mathsf{T} ::= (\mathsf{A}_1, \ldots, \mathsf{A}_n),\ n \geq 0$

Figure 3.6 Capability types for APi – informal

(SUB-TUPLE)
$$\frac{\mathsf{A}_i <: \mathsf{A}'_i \quad (\forall i)}{(\mathsf{A}_1 \ldots \mathsf{A}_n) <: (\mathsf{A}'_1 \ldots \mathsf{A}'_n)}$$

(SUB-BASE)
$$\mathsf{base} <: \mathsf{base}$$

(SUB-PROC)
$$\mathsf{proc} <: \mathsf{proc}$$

(SUB-CHAN.A)
$$\frac{\mathsf{T}^1_r <: \mathsf{T}^2_r, \mathsf{T}^2_w <: \mathsf{T}^1_w \quad \mathsf{T}^1_w <: \mathsf{T}^1_r}{\mathsf{w}\langle\mathsf{T}^1_w\rangle <: \mathsf{w}\langle\mathsf{T}^2_w\rangle \quad \mathsf{r}\langle\mathsf{T}^1_r\rangle <: \mathsf{r}\langle\mathsf{T}^2_r\rangle \quad \mathsf{rw}\langle\mathsf{T}^1_r, \mathsf{T}^1_w\rangle <: \mathsf{rw}\langle\mathsf{T}^2_r, \mathsf{T}^2_w\rangle}$$

(SUB-CHAN.B)
$$\frac{\mathsf{T}_w <: \mathsf{T}_r}{\mathsf{rw}\langle\mathsf{T}_r, \mathsf{T}_w\rangle <: \mathsf{w}\langle\mathsf{T}_w\rangle \quad \mathsf{rw}\langle\mathsf{T}_r, \mathsf{T}_w\rangle <: \mathsf{r}\langle\mathsf{T}_r\rangle}$$

Figure 3.7 Subtyping for APi

three different homomorphic rules, for types of the form $\mathsf{r}\langle-\rangle$, $\mathsf{w}\langle-\rangle$ and $\mathsf{rw}\langle-\rangle$ respectively. Note that $<:$ is *co-variant* in $\mathsf{r}\langle-\rangle$, as might be expected, but *contra-variant* in $\mathsf{w}\langle-\rangle$. To see why the latter is necessary suppose we allowed $\mathsf{w}\langle\mathsf{T}_1\rangle <: \mathsf{w}\langle\mathsf{T}_2\rangle$, where $\mathsf{T}_1 <: \mathsf{T}_2$, that is where a value at type T_2 may have *fewer* capabilities than required by T_1. This would allow the typing of

$$\ldots a!\langle v\rangle \ldots$$

for such a value v, where a reader on a may be expecting values with all the capabilities of the type T_1. Again this is discussed further in Example 3.32.

We now use the rules of Figure 3.7 to give a formal definition of the set of capability types, and the subtyping relation between them.

Definition 3.16 (*capability types*) Let us write $\vdash \mathsf{T} : \mathbf{ty}$ to mean that the judgement $\mathsf{T} <: \mathsf{T}$ can be derived using the rules in Figure 3.7. We use **Types** to denote the set of all such T. Note that we have now dropped the superscript ^{s}, indicating that we are no longer dealing with simple types.

We also have a *subtyping* relation between members of **Types**; for $\mathsf{T}_1,\ \mathsf{T}_2 \in$ **Types** let $\mathsf{T}_1 <: \mathsf{T}_2$ whenever the judgement $\mathsf{T}_1 <: \mathsf{T}_2$ can be derived from the rules. ♦

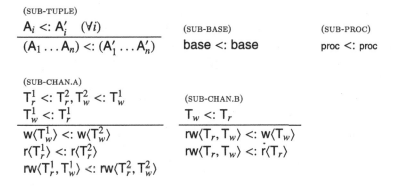

It is worthwhile noting that this formal definition implements the informal constraint on the construction on channel types given in Figure 3.6:

Lemma 3.17

(i) *If* $\vdash \mathsf{rw}\langle \mathsf{T}_r, \mathsf{T}_w\rangle : \mathbf{ty}$ *then* $\mathsf{T}_w <: \mathsf{T}_r$.
(ii) *If the judgement* $\mathsf{T}_1 <: \mathsf{T}_2$ *can be derived then* $\vdash \mathsf{T}_1 : \mathbf{ty}$ *and* $\vdash \mathsf{T}_2 : \mathbf{ty}$.

Proof:

(i) $\vdash \mathsf{rw}\langle \mathsf{T}_r, \mathsf{T}_w\rangle : \mathbf{ty}$ means that we can derive $\vdash \mathsf{rw}\langle \mathsf{T}_r, \mathsf{T}_w\rangle <: \mathsf{rw}\langle \mathsf{T}_r, \mathsf{T}_w\rangle$. The only rule for doing so is (SUB-CHAN.A), the premise of which ensures the required result.
(ii) A simple proof by induction on the derivation of the judgement $\mathsf{T}_1 <: \mathsf{T}_2$. For example suppose these are $\mathsf{rw}\langle \mathsf{T}_r^1, \mathsf{T}_w^1\rangle$, $\mathsf{rw}\langle \mathsf{T}_r^2, \mathsf{T}_w^2\rangle$ respectively, and the judgement was inferred via an application of (SUB-CHAN.A). This means we already have the judgements $\mathsf{T}_r^1 <: \mathsf{T}_r^2$, $\mathsf{T}_w^2 <: \mathsf{T}_w^1$ and $\mathsf{T}_w^1 <: \mathsf{T}_r^1$, to all of which we can apply induction. So for example this gives $\mathsf{T}_r^1 <: \mathsf{T}_r^1$, $\mathsf{T}_w^1 <: \mathsf{T}_w^1$, and therefore, because we already know that $\mathsf{T}_w^1 <: \mathsf{T}_r^1$, we can apply the same rule to establish $\vdash \mathsf{rw}\langle \mathsf{T}_r^1, \mathsf{T}_w^1\rangle : \mathbf{ty}$. Establishing $\vdash \mathsf{rw}\langle \mathsf{T}_r^2, \mathsf{T}_w^2\rangle : \mathbf{ty}$ is equally straightforward, since $\mathsf{T}_w^2 <: \mathsf{T}_w^1 <: \mathsf{T}_r^1 <: \mathsf{T}_r^2$. ■

Lemma 3.18 **Types** *ordered by* $<:$ *is a pre-order.*

Proof: Reflexivity is trivial since T is in **Types** only if we can derive $\mathsf{T} <: \mathsf{T}$. Suppose $\mathsf{T}_1 <: \mathsf{T}_2$ and $\mathsf{T}_2 <: \mathsf{T}_3$. One can prove by induction on the derivation of the latter that $\mathsf{T}_1 <: \mathsf{T}_3$. The proof proceeds by a case analysis on the last rule applied. As an example suppose this rule is (SUB-CHAN.A) with the conclusion

$$\mathsf{rw}\langle \mathsf{T}_r^2, \mathsf{T}_w^2\rangle <: \mathsf{rw}\langle \mathsf{T}_r^3, \mathsf{T}_w^3\rangle \qquad (3.15)$$

So T_2, T_3 are of the form $\mathsf{rw}\langle \mathsf{T}_r^2, \mathsf{T}_w^2\rangle$, $\mathsf{rw}\langle \mathsf{T}_r^3, \mathsf{T}_w^3\rangle$ respectively. We know, because (SUB-CHAN.A) was applied, that $\mathsf{T}_r^2 <: \mathsf{T}_r^3$ and $\mathsf{T}_w^3 <: \mathsf{T}_w^2$.

Because $\mathsf{T}_1 <: \mathsf{rw}\langle \mathsf{T}_r^2, \mathsf{T}_w^2\rangle$, one can show that T_1 must also be of the form $\mathsf{rw}\langle \mathsf{T}_r^1, \mathsf{T}_w^1\rangle$, and, because (SUB-CHAN.A) is the only rule that could be used to make this inference, we must also have $\mathsf{T}_r^1 <: \mathsf{T}_r^2$ and $\mathsf{T}_w^2 <: \mathsf{T}_w^1$.

Induction now gives $\mathsf{T}_r^1 <: \mathsf{T}_r^3$ and $\mathsf{T}_w^3 <: \mathsf{T}_w^1$. Also by Lemma 3.17(ii) we know $\mathsf{rw}\langle \mathsf{T}_r^1, \mathsf{T}_w^1\rangle$ is a valid type, and therefore by part (i) that $\mathsf{T}_w^1 <: \mathsf{T}_r^1$. So we have all the information required to use (SUB-CHAN.A) to deduce $\mathsf{T}_1 <: \mathsf{T}_3$.

There are many other possibilities for the conclusion (3.15) to the application of (SUB-CHAN.A), and there are the three other rules in Figure 3.7 to consider. But in each case similar inductive reasoning can be used to conclude $\mathsf{T}_1 <: \mathsf{T}_3$. The case analysis can be helped by a so-called *inversion of subtyping* result, which, given $\mathsf{T}_2 <: \mathsf{T}_3$ and the structure of T_3, determines the structure of T_2; see Question 6 at the end of the chapter. ■

In fact we can easily show that this pre-order is actually a partial order, that is $<:$ is anti-symmetric over capability types. However we will not use this property.

Intuitively a type represents a *set* of capabilities, and the combining of capabilities has the informal counterpart at the level of types as a *greatest lower bound* operation. However only certain forms of capabilities, those that are in some sense *consistent*, may be combined together. For example the types $\mathsf{r}\langle\mathsf{int}\rangle$ and $\mathsf{w}\langle\mathsf{bool}\rangle$ cannot be combined as in a well-typed process one cannot have an identifier with both these types. But $\mathsf{r}\langle\mathsf{int}\rangle$ and $\mathsf{w}\langle\mathsf{int}\rangle$ can be combined to obtain $\mathsf{rw}\langle\mathsf{int}\rangle$; this is the *greatest lower bound* of $\mathsf{r}\langle\mathsf{int}\rangle$ and $\mathsf{w}\langle\mathsf{int}\rangle$ with respect to $<:$.

Definition 3.19 (partially complete pre-orders) In a pre-order $\langle A, <\rangle$ let us write $a \downarrow b$ to mean that there is some element c such that $c < a$ and $c < b$; in other words a and b have a *lower bound*. Similarly we write $a \uparrow b$ to mean they have an upper bound.

Then $\langle A, <\rangle$ is said to be *partially complete* or *pc* if for every pair of elements a, b in A

- $a \downarrow b$ implies a and b have a *greatest lower bound* (glb), denoted $a \sqcap b$; this element is also a lower bound and it dominates all other lower bounds. Thus $a \sqcap b < a$, $a \sqcap b < b$, and $c < a \sqcap b$ whenever $c < a$ and $c < b$
- if they have an upper bound, $a \uparrow b$, then they have a *least upper bound* (lub), denoted $a \sqcup b$.

Note that *lubs* and *glbs* need not be unique, although they will be whenever $\langle A, <\rangle$ is a partial order. Nevertheless we still use the standard notation $a \sqcup b$ and $a \sqcap b$ for arbitrarily chosen instances. ♦

This definition of upper and lower bounds can be generalised from pairs of elements to subsets of a pre-order A. For example if $S \subseteq A$ we will write $S\downarrow$ to mean that there is some element c in A with the property that $c < a$ for every a in S. One can show that if A is partially complete then for every non-empty finite subset S, $S\downarrow$ implies S has a greatest lower bound, which we will denote as $\sqcap S$; see Question 5 at the end of the chapter.

*Proposition 3.20 The pre-order $\langle$**Types**$, <:\rangle$ is partially complete.*

Proof: The proof proceeds in three steps. First we define two symmetric partial operations on types, $\mathsf{T}_1 \sqcap \mathsf{T}_2$ and $\mathsf{T}_1 \sqcup \mathsf{T}_2$, by simultaneous structural induction. The base case is when both T_1 and T_2 are base types, where we have the obvious clauses:

$$\mathsf{int} \sqcap \mathsf{int} = \mathsf{int} \qquad \mathsf{int} \sqcup \mathsf{int} = \sqcup$$

$$\mathsf{bool} \sqcap \mathsf{bool} = \mathsf{bool} \qquad \mathsf{bool} \sqcup \mathsf{bool} = \mathsf{bool}$$

Other base types would have similar clauses.

For channel types $\mathsf{T}_1 \sqcap \mathsf{T}_2$ may be read off from the following schema, where now superscripts ^{r,w} are used to indicate the role of the type expressions to which they are applied:

$$\begin{array}{rll}
\mathsf{w}\langle \mathsf{T}_1^w\rangle \sqcap \mathsf{w}\langle \mathsf{T}_2^w\rangle &= \mathsf{w}\langle \mathsf{T}_1^w \sqcup \mathsf{T}_2^w\rangle & \\
\mathsf{r}\langle \mathsf{T}_1^r\rangle \sqcap \mathsf{r}\langle \mathsf{T}_2^r\rangle &= \mathsf{r}\langle \mathsf{T}_1^r \sqcap \mathsf{T}_2^r\rangle & \\
\mathsf{r}\langle \mathsf{T}_1^r\rangle \sqcap \mathsf{w}\langle \mathsf{T}_2^w\rangle &= \mathsf{rw}\langle \mathsf{T}_1^r, \mathsf{T}_2^w\rangle & \text{provided } \mathsf{T}_2^w <: \mathsf{T}_1^r \\
\mathsf{r}\langle \mathsf{T}_1^r\rangle \sqcap \mathsf{rw}\langle \mathsf{T}_2^r, \mathsf{T}_2^w\rangle &= \mathsf{rw}\langle \mathsf{T}_1^r \sqcap \mathsf{T}_2^r, \mathsf{T}_2^w\rangle & \text{provided } \mathsf{T}_2^w <: \mathsf{T}_1^r \\
\mathsf{w}\langle \mathsf{T}_1^w\rangle \sqcap \mathsf{rw}\langle \mathsf{T}_2^r, \mathsf{T}_2^w\rangle &= \mathsf{rw}\langle \mathsf{T}_2^r, \mathsf{T}_1^w \sqcup \mathsf{T}_2^w\rangle & \text{provided } \mathsf{T}_1^w <: \mathsf{T}_2^r \\
\mathsf{rw}\langle \mathsf{T}_1^r, \mathsf{T}_1^w\rangle \sqcap \mathsf{rw}\langle \mathsf{T}_2^r, \mathsf{T}_2^w\rangle &= \mathsf{rw}\langle \mathsf{T}_1^r \sqcap \mathsf{T}_2^r, \mathsf{T}_1^w \sqcup \mathsf{T}_2^w\rangle & \text{provided } \mathsf{T}_1^w <: \mathsf{T}_2^r,\ \ \mathsf{T}_2^w <: \mathsf{T}_1^r
\end{array}$$

This is interpreted as saying that if the right-hand side is defined then so is the left-hand side; moreover symmetric instances, such as $\mathsf{w}\langle \mathsf{T}_1^w\rangle \sqcap \mathsf{r}\langle \mathsf{T}_2^r\rangle$, have been omitted.

There is a similar, but more restricted, schema for calculating $\mathsf{T}_1 \sqcup \mathsf{T}_2$:

$$\begin{array}{rl}
\mathsf{w}\langle \mathsf{T}_1^w\rangle \sqcup \mathsf{w}\langle \mathsf{T}_2^w\rangle &= \mathsf{w}\langle \mathsf{T}_1^w \sqcap \mathsf{T}_2^w\rangle \\
\mathsf{r}\langle \mathsf{T}_1^r\rangle \sqcup \mathsf{r}\langle \mathsf{T}_2^r\rangle &= \mathsf{r}\langle \mathsf{T}_1^r \sqcup \mathsf{T}_2^r\rangle \\
\mathsf{r}\langle \mathsf{T}_1^r\rangle \sqcup \mathsf{rw}\langle \mathsf{T}_2^r, \mathsf{T}_2^w\rangle &= \mathsf{rw}\langle \mathsf{T}_1^r \sqcup \mathsf{T}_2^r, \mathsf{T}_2^w\rangle \\
\mathsf{w}\langle \mathsf{T}_1^w\rangle \sqcup \mathsf{rw}\langle \mathsf{T}_2^r, \mathsf{T}_2^w\rangle &= \mathsf{rw}\langle \mathsf{T}_2^r, \mathsf{T}_1^w \sqcap \mathsf{T}_2^w\rangle \\
\mathsf{rw}\langle \mathsf{T}_1^r, \mathsf{T}_1^w\rangle \sqcup \mathsf{rw}\langle \mathsf{T}_2^r, \mathsf{T}_2^w\rangle &= \mathsf{rw}\langle \mathsf{T}_1^r \sqcup \mathsf{T}_2^r, \mathsf{T}_1^w \sqcap \mathsf{T}_2^w\rangle
\end{array}$$

Finally the definitions are extended to tuple types in the obvious manner:

$$(\mathsf{T}_1, \ldots, \mathsf{T}_n) \sqcap (\mathsf{T}_1', \ldots, \mathsf{T}_n') = (\mathsf{T}_1 \sqcap \mathsf{T}_1', \ldots, \mathsf{T}_n \sqcap \mathsf{T}_n')$$
$$(\mathsf{T}_1, \ldots, \mathsf{T}_n) \sqcup (\mathsf{T}_1', \ldots, \mathsf{T}_n') = (\mathsf{T}_1 \sqcup \mathsf{T}_1', \ldots, \mathsf{T}_n \sqcup \mathsf{T}_n')$$

The second step is to establish:

- if there is a T_l such that $\mathsf{T}_l <: \mathsf{T}_1$ and $\mathsf{T}_l <: \mathsf{T}_2$ then $\mathsf{T}_1 \sqcap \mathsf{T}_2$ exists
- if there is a T_h such that $\mathsf{T}_1 <: \mathsf{T}_h$ and $\mathsf{T}_2 <: \mathsf{T}_h$ then $\mathsf{T}_1 \sqcup \mathsf{T}_2$ exists.

The proof is by simultaneous induction on the structure of T_l and T_h, and essentially proceeds by case analysis. For example if T_l has the form $\mathsf{rw}\langle \mathsf{T}_l^r, \mathsf{T}_l^w\rangle$ then T_1 and T_2 can take many forms. Let us look at one possibility, when T_1 is $\mathsf{rw}\langle \mathsf{T}_1^r, \mathsf{T}_1^w\rangle$ and T_2 is $\mathsf{w}\langle \mathsf{T}_2^w\rangle$. According to the above schema, to show $\mathsf{T}_1 \sqcap \mathsf{T}_2$ exists we need to establish

(1) $\mathsf{T}_1^w \sqcup \mathsf{T}_2^w$ exists
(2) $\mathsf{T}_2^w <: \mathsf{T}_1^r$.

However because of the rules of subtyping, in Figure 3.7, we know that $\mathsf{T}_1^w <: \mathsf{T}_l^w$ and $\mathsf{T}_2^w <: \mathsf{T}_l^w$, and so by induction we have (1). The subtyping rules also give $\mathsf{T}_l^r <: \mathsf{T}_1^r$. Moreover they enforce the invariant $\mathsf{T}_l^w <: \mathsf{T}_l^r$, from which (2) follows.

Note incidentally that these two conditions ensure that $\mathsf{T}_1 \sqcap \mathsf{T}_2$, that is $\mathsf{rw}\langle \mathsf{T}_1^r, \mathsf{T}_1^w \sqcup \mathsf{T}_2^w\rangle$, is a valid type; since T_1 is a valid type we know $\mathsf{T}_1^w <: \mathsf{T}_1^r$, and so using (2) we obtain the consistency requirement $\mathsf{T}_1^w \sqcup \mathsf{T}_2^w <: \mathsf{T}_1^r$.

(E-EXT)

$$\frac{\vdash \mathsf{C} : \mathbf{ty} \quad \Gamma \vdash \mathbf{env}}{\Gamma, u : \mathsf{C} \vdash \mathbf{env}} \ \Gamma \downarrow u : \mathsf{C}$$

(E-BASE)

$$\frac{\Gamma \vdash \mathbf{env}}{\Gamma, x : \mathsf{base} \vdash \mathbf{env}} \ \Gamma \downarrow x : \mathsf{base}$$

(E-EMPTY) (E-PROC) as in Figure 3.3

$\Gamma \downarrow u : \mathsf{A}$ means: $\Gamma \vdash u : \mathsf{A}'$ implies $\mathsf{A} \downarrow \mathsf{A}'$

Figure 3.8 Capability type environment for APi

The final step is to show that whenever these operations are defined the resulting types have the required properties:

- $\mathsf{T}_l <: \mathsf{T}_1 \sqcap \mathsf{T}_2$ for every T_l such that $\mathsf{T}_l <: \mathsf{T}_1$ and $\mathsf{T}_l <: \mathsf{T}_2$
- $\mathsf{T}_1 \sqcup \mathsf{T}_2 <: \mathsf{T}_h$ for every T_h such that $\mathsf{T}_1 <: T_h$ and $\mathsf{T}_2 <: \mathsf{T}_h$.

Again the proof is by simultaneous induction on T_l and T_h and proceeds by case analysis. ■

The partial meet operation on types enables us to combine capabilities that a process may gradually accumulate on a given resource. In fact it will be technically convenient to generalise the notion of type environments to take this gradual accumulation of capabilities into account. The revised definition is given in Figure 3.8, where now an environment Γ may be extended by an entry $u : \mathsf{A}$, provided this information is *consistent with* Γ; this is written $\Gamma \downarrow u : \mathsf{E}$ and means that E has a lower bound with any E' such that $\Gamma \vdash u : \mathsf{E}'$. That is, to extend Γ with $u : \mathsf{E}$ the identifier u no longer needs to be new to Γ; but the capability E cannot contradict any knowledge Γ already has of u. Note that the new rule, (E-EXT), subsumes the original rule (E-NEW.ID) in Figure 3.3, as $\Gamma \downarrow u : \mathsf{E}$ is vacuously true whenever u is new to Γ; similarly with (E-BASE).

So for example

$$\ldots c : \mathsf{r}\langle\mathsf{int}\rangle, \ldots, c : \mathsf{w}\langle\mathsf{int}\rangle \tag{3.16}$$

is now a valid environment, as the final entry $c : \mathsf{w}\langle\mathsf{int}\rangle$ is consistent with the environment $\ldots, c : \mathsf{r}\langle\mathsf{int}\rangle, \ldots$, assuming these are the only entries for c, whereas

$$\ldots c : \mathsf{r}\langle\mathsf{int}\rangle, \ldots, c : \mathsf{w}\langle\mathsf{bool}\rangle \vdash \mathbf{env}$$

cannot be derived because $c : \mathsf{w}\langle\mathsf{bool}\rangle$ is not consistent with it. The environment (3.16) above will occur when typechecking a process that first receives the resource c with the capability $\mathsf{r}\langle\mathsf{int}\rangle$ and subsequently receives the extra capability $\mathsf{w}\langle\mathsf{int}\rangle$ on it. It is also worth pointing out that the addition of this side-condition means that

$$\frac{\Gamma, u : \mathsf{A}, \Gamma' \vdash \mathbf{env}}{\Gamma, u : \mathsf{A}, \Gamma' \vdash u : \mathsf{A}'} \;\mathsf{A} <: \mathsf{A}' \quad \text{(TY-SUB)}$$

$$\frac{\Gamma \vdash v : \mathsf{T} \quad \Gamma \vdash v : \mathsf{T}'}{\Gamma \vdash v : (\mathsf{T} \sqcap \mathsf{T}')} \quad \text{(TY-MEET)}$$

(TY-BASE) (TY-PROC) (TY-TUP) as in Figure 3.4

Figure 3.9 Typing values with capability types aPi

formally the judgements for valid type environment formation and for assigning types to values need to be defined by simultaneous induction.

This assignment of types to values also needs to be adjusted; the new rules are given in Figure 3.9. The first (new) one, (TY-SUB), merely says that any name known at a type A, may be used at any supertype A' of it; this is perfectly understandable via the (informal) intuition of a type being a set of capabilities and $\mathsf{A} <: \mathsf{A}'$ meaning A' *is a subset of* A. The second (new) rule (TY-MEET) allows us to combine known capabilities of a given name. Thus if Γ denotes the environment (3.16) above, (TY-MEET) enables us to deduce $\Gamma \vdash c : \mathsf{rw}\langle\mathsf{int}\rangle$. As stated, this rule has a slight lacuna as *a priori* we do not necessarily know if the meet $\mathsf{A} \sqcap \mathsf{A}'$ exists. So for the moment let us say that this rule can only be applied whenever we know it exists. But as we shall see, in Proposition 3.26 below, the premises actually always guarantee its existence.

3.4.2 Type checking

Having discussed the subtyping structure on the capability types we now describe the rules governing typechecking for processes. There are three modifications, given in Figure 3.10, two of which are very natural. The new rule (TY-IN) is a minor variation of (STY-IN). To infer $\Gamma \vdash u?(X)\,R$ it is now sufficient to have only the *read* capability on u; that is $\Gamma \vdash u : \mathsf{r}\langle\mathsf{T}\rangle$ for an appropriate type T, rather than as in Figure 3.5 $\Gamma \vdash u : \mathsf{rw}\langle\mathsf{T}\rangle$. Similarly in the new rule (TY-OUT) it is sufficient to have the output capability on the channel concerned.

It is worthwhile examining the effect of subtyping on these two rules. As an example suppose $\mathsf{rw}\langle\mathsf{T}_r, \mathsf{T}_w\rangle$ is the only entry for c in Γ. At what type is it necessary to have a value v in order for the output

$$c!\langle v\rangle$$

to be well-typed? Suppose T_v is the only entry for v in Γ. Then (TY-OUT) and (TY-SUB) demand the existence of a type T such that

$$\mathsf{T}_v <: \mathsf{T} \text{ and } \mathsf{rw}\langle\mathsf{T}_r, \mathsf{T}_w\rangle <: \mathsf{w}\langle\mathsf{T}\rangle$$

(TY-IN)
$$\frac{\Gamma \vdash u : \mathsf{r}\langle \mathsf{T}\rangle \quad \Gamma, \langle X{:}\mathsf{T}\rangle \vdash R : \mathsf{proc}}{\Gamma \vdash u?(X)\,R \ : \mathsf{proc}}$$

(TY-OUT)
$$\frac{\Gamma \vdash u : \mathsf{w}\langle \mathsf{T}\rangle \quad \Gamma \vdash V : \mathsf{T}}{\Gamma \vdash u!\langle V\rangle : \mathsf{proc}}$$

(TY-STOP) (TY-REC)
(TY-NEW) (TY-PAR) as in Figure 3.5

(TY-MATCH)
$$\frac{\Gamma \vdash v_1 : \mathsf{A}_1, v_2 : \mathsf{A}_2 \quad \Gamma \vdash R_2 : \mathsf{proc} \quad \Gamma, \langle v_1{:}\mathsf{A}_2\rangle, \langle v_2{:}\mathsf{A}_1\rangle \vdash R_1 : \mathsf{proc}}{\Gamma \vdash \mathsf{if}\ v_1 = v_2\ \mathsf{then}\ R_1\ \mathsf{else}\ R_2 \ : \mathsf{proc}}$$

(TY-MIS.MATCH)
$$\frac{\Gamma \vdash v_1 : \mathsf{A}_1, v_2 : \mathsf{A}_2 \quad \Gamma \vdash R_2 : \mathsf{proc}}{\Gamma \vdash \mathsf{if}\ v_1 = v_2\ \mathsf{then}\ R_1\ \mathsf{else}\ R_2 \ : \mathsf{proc}} \quad \mathsf{A}_1 \not\downarrow \mathsf{A}_2$$

Figure 3.10 Inference of capability types in API

Because of the contra-variance of $\mathsf{w}\langle - \rangle$ this amounts to the constraint that

$$\mathsf{T}_v <: \mathsf{T}_w$$

In other words to send a value on the channel c the value must have *at least* all the capabilities required by the output type T_w.

A similar analysis will show that $c?(x)\,R(x)$ is well-typed if the residual $R(x)$ uses x with *at most* the capabilities required by the input type T_r. That is we must be able to infer

$$\Gamma, x : \mathsf{T}_x \vdash R(x)$$

for some type T_x such that $\mathsf{T}_r <: \mathsf{T}_x$. However there is a further implicit constraint. In the type entry for c, $\mathsf{rw}\langle \mathsf{T}_r, \mathsf{T}_w\rangle$, there is the constraint $\mathsf{T}_w <: \mathsf{T}_r$; T_r can have *at most* the capabilities of T_w. Effectively the constraint on T_x is $\mathsf{T}_w <: \mathsf{T}_r <: \mathsf{T}_x$. So in the best possible world the receiving code $R(x)$ can use the incoming value, bound to x, with at most the capabilities allowed by the *write* capability of the channel used in the communication.

The third new rule (TY-MATCH) in Figure 3.5 takes advantage of the extra structure of types and is particularly relevant for capability based typing systems. However it does require some motivation. In capability based type systems, as we have already noted, a process only receives values with some specific capabilities. Subsequently it may receive some further capabilities on that value and it should be able to accumulate these for future use. For example the process

$$\mathsf{in}_A?(x)\ \ \mathsf{in}_B?(y)\ \ \mathsf{if}\ x = y\ \mathsf{then}\ R_1\ \mathsf{else}\ R_2$$

receives two values from the resources in_A and in_B, presumably with certain capabilities. When executing the code R_1 it is known that these two values are in fact the same and therefore within R_1 that actual value should be available at both the capabilities received along in_A and along in_B. This is the purpose of the rule (TY-MATCH). It says we can assume $\mathsf{if}\ v_1 = v_2\ \mathsf{then}\ R_1\ \mathsf{else}\ R_2$ is well-typed relative to Γ if

- R_2 is well-typed relative to Γ
- v_1 and v_2 have associated with them some capabilities, given by A_1 and A_2 respectively
- R_1 is well-typed in an environment where v_1 has in addition the capabilities of v_2, namely the type A_2, and vice-versa for v_2.

The precise environment for checking R_1 is obtained by adding to Γ

- the knowledge that v_1 has the capabilities of v_2, that is adding $\langle v_1{:}\mathsf{A}_2\rangle$
- symmetrically, adding the knowledge that v_2 has the capabilities of v_1, adding $\langle v_2{:}\mathsf{A}_1\rangle$.

Of course this extra information may render the environment inconsistent; that is $\Gamma, \langle v_1{:}\mathsf{A}_2\rangle, \langle v_2{:}\mathsf{A}_1\rangle$ is not a valid type environment. In this case the rule (TY-MATCH) cannot be successfully applied, as our type system will have a property similar to the (sanity checks), Lemma 3.5: whenever the judgement $\Gamma' \vdash P$ can be inferred we will be assured that $\Gamma' \vdash \mathbf{env}$. But for this case we have the alternative rule (TY-MIS.MATCH), from Figure 3.10. It turns out that whenever value terms v_1 and v_2 can be assigned incompatible types they can never be made identical using any well-typed substitution. Consequently here we know that the true branch will never be executed, and only R_2 needs to be checked.

Example 3.21 [*Typing the Memory Server*] Let us now reconsider the *memory server* from Example 3.15, which in turn uses the memory code Mem from Example 2.11. First let us decide on the declaration types of the get and put methods. Since they are read by the memory and written to by clients they need to be declared with both read and write capabilities. But the channels transmitted are only ever used for writing. Therefore appropriate definitions are

$$\mathsf{D}_g = \mathsf{rw}\langle \mathsf{w}\langle \mathsf{int}\rangle\rangle$$

$$\mathsf{D}_p = \mathsf{rw}\langle (\mathsf{int}, \mathsf{w}\langle\rangle)\rangle$$

If $\Gamma_{p,g}$ is an environment that assigns put, get to $\mathsf{D}_g, \mathsf{D}_p$ respectively, then it is easy to establish

$$\Gamma_{p,g} \vdash \mathsf{Mem}$$

Turning now to the server memSERV its only free name is s and therefore it should be possible to type it with respect to some simple environment Γ_s that maps

s to a type of the form $\mathsf{rw}\langle \mathsf{S} \rangle$. Note again that we need to give s a read and write capability; it will be read by the server and written to by clients.

However the channels transmitted on s are only ever used by the server to send the access methods; therefore S should take the form

$$\mathsf{w}\langle (\mathsf{S}_p, \mathsf{S}_g) \rangle$$

where S_p, S_g are the types at which the server wishes clients to have access to the put and get methods, respectively. Since it wishes to retain read capability for itself these are released with the write capability only:

$$\mathsf{S}_p = \mathsf{w}\langle (\mathsf{int}, \mathsf{w}\langle \rangle) \rangle$$
$$\mathsf{S}_g = \mathsf{w}\langle \mathsf{w}\langle \mathsf{int} \rangle \rangle$$

Note that these in turn allow the memory to only use the write capability on the return channels sent via these methods.

To sum up, Γ_s assigns to s the type

$$\mathsf{rw}\langle\ \mathsf{w}\langle\ (\mathsf{w}\langle (\mathsf{int}, \mathsf{w}\langle \rangle) \rangle,\ \mathsf{w}\langle \mathsf{w}\langle \mathsf{int} \rangle \rangle)\ \rangle\ \rangle$$

One can now check that

$$\Gamma_s \vdash \mathsf{memSERV}$$

The ability to type the client mClient depends on the declaration types of the bound names r, a, b. Suppose we define these by

$$\mathsf{D}_r = \mathsf{rw}\langle (\mathsf{S}_p, \mathsf{S}_g) \rangle$$
$$\mathsf{D}_a = \mathsf{rw}\langle \rangle$$
$$\mathsf{D}_b = \mathsf{rw}\langle \mathsf{int} \rangle$$

Then one can establish the judgement

$$\Gamma_s \vdash \mathsf{mClient}$$

Note also that again these bound names must be declared with both a read and write capability, typically the former being transmitted to the memory and the latter exercised by the client itself.

However the important point of the example is that there is no possible type D_r for which

$$\Gamma_s \vdash \mathsf{badClient}$$

For the sake of argument suppose D_r has the form $\mathsf{rw}\langle \mathsf{C}_p, \mathsf{C}_g \rangle$; it must take this form in order to have any chance of typing the process. Then in order to derive

$$\Gamma_s,\ r : \mathsf{D}_r \vdash r?(z, w)\,\mathsf{badMem}$$

it would be necessary to derive

$$\Gamma_s,\ r : \mathsf{D}_r,\ z : \mathsf{C}_p, w : \mathsf{C}_g \vdash \mathsf{badMem}$$

But because of the definition of badMem this is obviously only possible if C_p is a read capability; that is it is a subtype of some type of the form $\mathsf{r}\langle\mathsf{T}\rangle$. But, as we now argue, the further constraint that $s!\langle r\rangle$ be well-typed does not allow this.

The typing requirement

$$\Gamma_s,\ r : \mathsf{D}_r \vdash s!\langle r\rangle$$

requires that

$$\mathsf{D}_r <: \mathsf{S},\ \text{that is } \mathsf{rw}\langle \mathsf{C}_p, \mathsf{C}_g\rangle <: \mathsf{w}\langle \mathsf{S}_p, \mathsf{S}_g\rangle$$

This in turn implies, among other things, that

$$\mathsf{S}_p <: \mathsf{C}_p$$

However the form of S_p, $\mathsf{w}\langle\ldots\rangle$ – a write only capability, means that C_p cannot be a read capability.

The essence of this example is that the type of the request channel of the memory server ensures that clients only obtain the write capability on the put and get methods of the newly generated memory cell. The type system ensures a capability-based approach to programming, in which predefined access control decisions can be enforced. ■

Example 3.22 [*Using the Rule* (TY-MATCH)] Consider the process OOI

$$(\mathsf{new}\ s : \mathsf{rw})(\mathsf{out}_r!\langle s\rangle \mid \mathsf{out}_w!\langle s\rangle \mid R)$$

where R is the recursive process

$$\mathsf{rec}\ x.\ \mathsf{in}?(y)\ (\mathsf{if}\ y = s\ \mathsf{then}\ (\mathsf{give}!\langle\mathsf{gold}\rangle \mid x)\ \mathsf{else}\ (\mathsf{give}!\langle\mathsf{brass}\rangle \mid x))$$

Here we use rw as an abbreviation for the type of a synchronisation channel, one that can send and receive the empty tuple, $\mathsf{rw}\langle()\rangle$; in a similar manner we use r, w to represent $\mathsf{r}\langle()\rangle$, $\mathsf{w}\langle()\rangle$ respectively.

The process R accepts a value on the port in and only if this is the newly created resource s does it give out gold; in other cases it gives out brass.

Suppose Γ has the following entries:

$$\begin{aligned}
\mathsf{out}_r &\to \mathsf{rw}\langle\mathsf{r}\rangle\\
\mathsf{out}_w &\to \mathsf{rw}\langle\mathsf{w}\rangle\\
\mathsf{in} &\to \mathsf{rw}\langle\mathsf{rw}\rangle\\
\mathsf{give}, \mathsf{spend} &\to \mathsf{rw}\langle\mathsf{str}\rangle
\end{aligned}$$

Then it is straightforward to infer

$$\Gamma \vdash \mathsf{OOI}$$

But is it possible to type a process that can successfully obtain the treasured gold? The important point is that in will only accept values that have both the read and write capabilities, and these are distributed separately via the ports out_r, out_w respectively.

Let Probe be defined by

$$\mathsf{out}_r?(x)\,\mathsf{out}_w?(y)\ \mathsf{if}\ x = y\ \mathsf{then}\ (\ \mathsf{in}!\langle x\rangle \mid \mathsf{give}?(z)\,\mathsf{spend}!\langle z\rangle\ )\ \mathsf{else}\ \mathsf{stop}$$

When Probe is run in parallel with OOI the sought after gold will be spent. Moreover

$$\Gamma \vdash \mathsf{Probe}$$

But the rule (TY-MATCH), from Figure 3.10, is essential to the inference. The crucial step is the inference of

$$\Gamma,\ x : \mathsf{r},\ y : \mathsf{w} \vdash \mathsf{if}\ x = y\ \mathsf{then}\ (\mathsf{in}!\langle x\rangle \mid \mathsf{give}?(z)\,\mathsf{spend}!\langle z\rangle)\ \mathsf{else}\ \mathsf{stop}$$

Using (TY-MATCH) this follows from

$$\Gamma,\ x : \mathsf{r},\ y : \mathsf{w},\ x : \mathsf{w},\ y : \mathsf{r} \vdash \mathsf{in}!\langle x\rangle \mid \mathsf{give}?(z)\,\mathsf{print}!\langle z\rangle$$

Here x has the capabilities required for the typing of $\mathsf{in}!\langle x\rangle$; we have

$$\Gamma \vdash \mathsf{in} : \mathsf{w}\langle \mathsf{rw}\rangle$$
$$\Gamma \vdash x : \mathsf{rw}$$

where the last judgement is inferred via an instance of (TY-MEET) from Figure 3.9.

It is easy to see that the rule (STY-EQ), from Figure 3.5, is not sufficient to type Probe; with this rule the capabilities on x can never be augmented to satisfy the requirements of in. ■

Example 3.23 [*Using the Rule* (TY-MIS.MATCH)] Suppose Γ is an environment such that

$$a \rightarrow \mathsf{rw}\langle \mathsf{int}\rangle$$
$$\mathsf{in} \rightarrow \mathsf{rw}\langle \mathsf{rw}\langle \mathsf{bool}\rangle\rangle$$

and consider the process P defined by

$$\mathsf{in}?(x)\ \mathsf{if}\ x = a\ \mathsf{then}\ a!\langle \mathbf{false}\rangle\ \mathsf{else}\ \mathsf{stop}$$

Then obviously the sub-term $a!\langle\mathbf{false}\rangle$ cannot be typed with respect to Γ. Nevertheless we have

$$\Gamma \vdash P$$

This follows from the rule (TY-MISMATCH) because

$$\Gamma, x : \mathsf{rw}\langle\mathsf{int}\rangle \vdash x : \mathsf{rw}\langle\mathsf{int}\rangle$$

$$\Gamma, x : \mathsf{rw}\langle\mathsf{int}\rangle \vdash a : \mathsf{rw}\langle\mathsf{bool}\rangle$$

and $\mathsf{rw}\langle\mathsf{int}\rangle \not<: \mathsf{rw}\langle\mathsf{bool}\rangle$.

In other words the conditional nature of (TY-MATCH) leads to occurrences of untyped sub-terms within well-typed processes. However these untyped sub-terms can never be executed. One may be tempted to add an extra premise to the rule (TY-MIS.MATCH), requiring that R_1 be well-typed with respect to Γ, despite the fact that it will never be executed. However for the effect of this see Question 15 at the end of the chapter. ■

3.4.3 Subject reduction

Despite the fact that environments may have multiple entries many of the properties of typechecking capability types are inherited directly from Section 3.3, or are mild generalisations thereof; but there are complications in the proofs, due both to these multiple entries and to the presence of subtyping.

We leave it to the reader to check that the sanity checks in Lemma 3.5 remain true. Perhaps the most important difference between the two typing systems is that values no longer have unique types; Proposition 3.6 is obviously no longer true. Nevertheless we now outline how an environment Γ can still be considered as a function from its domain $\mathsf{dom}(\Gamma)$, that is the set of identifiers for which it has an entry, to types. For any $u \in \mathsf{dom}(\Gamma)$ let $\Gamma\{u\}$ be the non-empty set of types E for which there is an entry $u : \mathsf{E}$ in Γ.

Lemma 3.24 Suppose $\Gamma \vdash \mathbf{env}$ *and* $u \in \mathsf{dom}(\Gamma)$. *Then*

(1) $\Gamma\{u\}\downarrow$

(2) $\Gamma \vdash u : \sqcap(\Gamma\{u\})$.

Proof: We prove both statements simultaneously by induction on the derivation of $\Gamma \vdash \mathbf{env}$, and an analysis of the last rule used. If this is (E-EMPTY) then the results are true vacuously, as u cannot be in $\mathsf{dom}(\Gamma)$.

So we can assume it has the structure $\Gamma', u' : \mathsf{E}'$ and $\Gamma \vdash \mathbf{env}$ is inferred by one of the rules (E-BASE), (E-PROC) or (E-EXT); as an example we consider the last.

Here if u does not appear in Γ' both required statements (1) and (2) are immediate; for if u is in the domain of Γ it must be that u and u' coincide, and therefore $\Gamma\{u\}$ is the singleton set $\{\mathsf{E}'\}$.

So we may assume that u is in the domain of Γ'. Then induction applied to (2) gives $\Gamma' \vdash u : \sqcap(\Gamma'\{u\})$, and using a simple argument on value judgements this can be extended to

$$\Gamma \vdash u : \sqcap(\Gamma'\{u\}) \tag{3.17}$$

Now if u' is different from u then $\Gamma\{u\}$ is the same as $\Gamma'\{u\}$; so (1) follows by induction, and (2) coincides with (3.17). So we may assume that $u' = u$, and therefore that $\Gamma\{u\} = \Gamma'\{u\} \cup \{\mathsf{E}'\}$.

1. As we have already seen, induction applied to (2) gives $\Gamma' \vdash u : \sqcap(\Gamma'\{u\})$. Therefore the side condition on the formation rule (E-EXT) ensures that $(\sqcap(\Gamma'\{u\})) \downarrow \mathsf{E}'$, which is enough to ensure that $\Gamma\{u\} \downarrow$.
2. We now know from (1) that $(\sqcap(\Gamma'\{u\})) \sqcap \mathsf{E}'$ exists, and it is easy to see that it is a greatest lower bound for the set $\Gamma\{u\}$. So we need only establish $\Gamma \vdash (\sqcap(\Gamma'\{u\})) \sqcap \mathsf{E}'$. But this follows from an application of (TY-MEET), to (3.17) and $\Gamma \vdash u : \mathsf{E}'$. ■

With this lemma we can now easily interpret well-formed environments as partial functions.

Definition 3.25 (environments as partial functions) For every u in $\mathsf{dom}(\Gamma)$ let $\Gamma(u)$ denote $\sqcap(\Gamma\{u\})$.

We also use Γ^r and Γ^w for the related partial functions for looking up the read or write capabilities on a given identifier. For example $\Gamma^r(u)$ is only defined if $\Gamma(u)$ is defined and has one of the forms $\mathsf{r}\langle \mathsf{T}_r\rangle$ or $\mathsf{rw}\langle \mathsf{T}_w, \mathsf{T}_r\rangle$, in which case it returns the type T_r. We will also use the notation $\Gamma(u)\downarrow_{\mathsf{def}}$, $\Gamma^r(u)\downarrow_{\mathsf{def}}$, etc. to indicate that these partial functions are defined for a particular element, u. The properties of these functions are pursued in Question 9. ♦

Thus we can consider, as with simple types in Section 3.2, an environment as mapping identifiers in its domain to types, with many of the expected properties. For example the second part of Lemma 3.24 may now be read as saying $\Gamma \vdash u : \Gamma(u)$ whenever u is in the domain of Γ.

The main properties of value typing, replacing Proposition 3.6, may now be stated.

Proposition 3.26

(i) $\Gamma \vdash u : \mathsf{A}$ *implies* $\Gamma(u)$ *exists, and* $\Gamma(u) <: \mathsf{A}$.
(ii) $\Gamma \vdash u : \mathsf{r}\langle \mathsf{T}_1\rangle$ *and* $\Gamma \vdash u : \mathsf{w}\langle \mathsf{T}_2\rangle$ *implies* $\mathsf{T}_2 <: \mathsf{T}_1$.
(iii) $\Gamma \vdash V : \mathsf{T}_1$ *and* $\Gamma \vdash V : \mathsf{T}_2$ *implies* $\mathsf{T}_1 \sqcap \mathsf{T}_2$ *exists and* $\Gamma \vdash V : (\mathsf{T}_1 \sqcap \mathsf{T}_2)$.
(iv) ***(subsumption)*** $\Gamma \vdash V : \mathsf{T}_1$ *and* $\mathsf{T}_1 <: \mathsf{T}_2$ *implies* $\Gamma \vdash V : \mathsf{T}_2$.

Proof: First consider statement (i). $\Gamma \vdash u : \mathsf{A}$ means that u is in the domain of Γ, and therefore by Definition 3.25 $\Gamma(u)$ exists. Moreover it is defined to be $\sqcap(\Gamma\{u\})$, and so obviously $\Gamma(u) <: \mathsf{A}$.

The second statement is a consequence of the first. For if $\Gamma \vdash u : \mathsf{r}\langle \mathsf{T}_1\rangle$ we are assured that $\Gamma(u)$ exists, and therefore $\Gamma(u) <: \mathsf{r}\langle \mathsf{T}_1\rangle$ and $\Gamma(u) <: \mathsf{w}\langle \mathsf{T}_2\rangle$. So $\Gamma(u)$ must have the form $\mathsf{rw}\langle \mathsf{T}_r, \mathsf{T}_w\rangle$. Then the subtyping rules, and the first part of Lemma 3.17 give the required

$$\mathsf{T}_2 <: \mathsf{T}_w <: \mathsf{T}_r <: \mathsf{T}_1$$

The third statement is also a corollary of the first, at least when V is a simple identifier u. In this case $\Gamma(u)$ exists, and we know $\Gamma(u) <: \mathsf{T}_i$. So $\mathsf{T}_1 \sqcap \mathsf{T}_2$ exists and therefore $\Gamma \vdash u : \mathsf{T}_1 \sqcap \mathsf{T}_2$ follows by an application of (TY-MEET). If V is a base value then T_1 and T_2 must be identical, since base values belong to only one base type. Otherwise, when V is a vector, say $(v_1, \ldots, v_n)$, the two types T_1, T_2 take the form $(\mathsf{A}_1^1, \ldots, \mathsf{A}_n^1)$, $(\mathsf{A}_1^2, \ldots, \mathsf{A}_n^2)$ respectively. Here we know $\Gamma \vdash v_i : \mathsf{A}_i^1, \mathsf{A}_i^2$, and by induction we obtain $\Gamma \vdash v_i : (\mathsf{A}_i^1 \sqcap \mathsf{A}_i^2)$, and an application of (TY-TUP) gives $\Gamma \vdash (v_1, \ldots, v_n) : (\mathsf{A}_1^1 \sqcap \mathsf{A}_1^2, \ldots, \mathsf{A}_n^1 \sqcap \mathsf{A}_n^2)$. But this amounts to the required $\Gamma \vdash V : (\mathsf{T}_1 \sqcap \mathsf{T}_2)$, since by definition $(\mathsf{A}_1^1, \ldots, \mathsf{A}_n^1) \sqcap (\mathsf{A}_1^2, \ldots, \mathsf{A}_n^2) = (\mathsf{A}_1^1 \sqcap \mathsf{A}_1^2, \ldots, \mathsf{A}_n^1 \sqcap \mathsf{A}_n^2)$.

The proof of the final statement is a simple induction on the derivation of $\Gamma \vdash V : \mathsf{T}_1$, with the base case being provided by the rule (TY-SUB) from Figure 3.9. ■

Now let us reconsider the properties in Proposition 3.8. These can be generalised by lifting the subtyping relation to environments:

Definition 3.27 (comparing environments) For valid type environments let $\Gamma_1 <: \Gamma_2$ if $\Gamma_2 \vdash u : \mathsf{E}$ implies $\Gamma_1 \vdash u : \mathsf{E}$. ♦

This makes the set of all type environments into a pre-order, and it is worth noting that it is not a partial order. For example with

$$\Gamma_1 = c : \mathsf{r}\langle \mathsf{int}\rangle, c : \mathsf{w}\langle \mathsf{int}\rangle \quad \text{and} \quad \Gamma_2 = c : \mathsf{rw}\langle \mathsf{int}\rangle$$

we have $\Gamma_1 <: \Gamma_2$ and $\Gamma_2 <: \Gamma_1$ although they are different. We will write $\Gamma_1 \equiv \Gamma_2$ to mean that both $\Gamma_1 <: \Gamma_2$ and $\Gamma_2 <: \Gamma_1$ are true; we say the environments Γ_1 and Γ_2 are *equivalent*.

Proposition 3.28 (weakening) Suppose $\Gamma' <: \Gamma$. *Then*

- $\Gamma \vdash V : \mathsf{T}$ *implies* $\Gamma' \vdash V : \mathsf{T}$
- $\Gamma \vdash R$ *implies* $\Gamma' \vdash R$.

Proof: By induction on the derivations of $\Gamma \vdash V : \mathsf{T}$ and $\Gamma \vdash R$ respectively, and an analysis of the last rule applied. So the proof is similar to (weakening) in Proposition 3.8, but there are more cases. Here we examine two instances.

As a first example suppose $\Gamma \vdash (\mathsf{new}\, n : \mathsf{D})\, R$, because of an application of (TY-NEW) to $\Gamma, n : \mathsf{D} \vdash R$. Again we can assume that n is fresh to both Γ and Γ'. It is therefore easy to check that $\Gamma', n : \mathsf{D}$ is also a well-defined environment, and that $\Gamma, n : \mathsf{D} <: \Gamma', n : \mathsf{D}$. So we can apply induction to obtain $\Gamma', n : \mathsf{D} \vdash R_1$ from which the required $\Gamma' \vdash (\mathsf{new}\, n : \mathsf{D})\, R$ follows by (TY-NEW).

As a second example suppose $\Gamma \vdash \mathsf{if}\ v_1 = v_2\ \mathsf{then}\ R_1\ \mathsf{else}\ R_2$ because of an application of (TY-MATCH) to

(1) $\Gamma \vdash v_1 : \mathsf{A}_1$
(2) $\Gamma \vdash v_2 : \mathsf{A}_2$
(3) $\Gamma \vdash R_2$
(4) $\Gamma, \langle v_1{:}\mathsf{A}_2\rangle, \langle v_2{:}\mathsf{A}_1\rangle \vdash R_1$.

We can apply induction to the first three statements to obtain

(1') $\Gamma' \vdash v_1 : \mathsf{A}_1$
(2') $\Gamma' \vdash v_2 : \mathsf{A}_2$
(3') $\Gamma' \vdash R_2$.

Now suppose that $\Gamma', \langle v_1{:}\mathsf{A}_2\rangle, \langle v_2{:}\mathsf{A}_1\rangle$ happens to be a valid environment. Then it is dominated by $\Gamma, \langle v_1{:}\mathsf{A}_2\rangle, \langle v_2{:}\mathsf{A}_1\rangle$ and so we can also apply induction to (iv) to obtain

(4') $\Gamma', \langle v_1{:}\mathsf{A}_2\rangle, \langle v_2{:}\mathsf{A}_1\rangle \vdash R_1$

and then the required result will follow by an application of (TY-MATCH).

So the possibility remains that $\Gamma', \langle v_1{:}\mathsf{A}_2\rangle, \langle v_2{:}\mathsf{A}_1\rangle$ is not a valid environment. In fact the third part of Proposition 3.26 ensures that this can only happen when v_1 is different from v_2. An analysis of the environment construction rules, in Figure 3.8 will reveal that this is only possible if a type A exists such that either

(a) $\Gamma' \vdash v_1 : \mathsf{A}$ and $\mathsf{A} \not\downarrow \mathsf{A}_2$ or
(b) $\Gamma' \vdash v_2 : \mathsf{A}$ and $\mathsf{A} \not\downarrow \mathsf{A}_1$.

But in both cases we have enough information to apply (TY-MIS.MATCH) to obtain the required result $\Gamma' \vdash \mathsf{if}\ v_1 = v_2\ \mathsf{then}\ R_1\ \mathsf{else}\ R_2$. ■

It is worth pointing out that this proof of (weakening) does not rely on the property (interchange), unlike the corresponding proof for simple types, that of Proposition 3.8.

This last result says that equivalent environments are equally powerful, from the point of view of typechecking. Despite not using (interchange) in the previous proof it remains true in this new typechecking system, and provides an important example of equivalent environments:

Lemma 3.29 (interchange) Suppose $\Gamma_1, u : \mathsf{E}, u' : \mathsf{E}', \Gamma_2 \vdash \mathbf{env}$. *Then*

- $\Gamma_1, u' : \mathsf{E}', u : \mathsf{E}, \Gamma_2 \vdash \mathbf{env}$
- $\Gamma_1, u : \mathsf{E}, u' : \mathsf{E}', \Gamma_2 \;\equiv\; \Gamma_1, u' : \mathsf{E}', u : \mathsf{E}, \Gamma_2$.

Proof: See Question 8 at the end of the chapter. ■

Note that the more restricted version of (interchange) used in Proposition 3.7 is an immediate corollary of the two results we have just given. Finally (strengthening) from Proposition 3.8 also remains true. The proof we give here relies on (interchange), but a more general version may be found in Question 12.

Proposition 3.30 (strengthening)

- $\Gamma, u : \mathsf{E} \vdash V : \mathsf{T}$ *implies* $\Gamma \vdash V : \mathsf{T}$, *provided* u *does not occur in* V.
- $\Gamma, u : \mathsf{E} \vdash R$ *implies* $\Gamma \vdash R$, *provided* u *does not occur in* R.

Proof: In each case the proof proceeds by induction on the derivation involved, and a case analysis on the last rule used in the derivation. Let us consider a typical case, for the second statement, when R has the form if $v_1 = v_2$ then R_1 else R_2 and the rule used is (TY-MATCH). Then we have

(1) $\Gamma, u : \mathsf{E} \vdash v_1 : \mathsf{A}_1,\ v_2 : \mathsf{A}_2$
(2) $\Gamma, u : \mathsf{E} \vdash R_2$
(3) $\Gamma, u : \mathsf{E}, \langle v_1{:}\mathsf{A}_2\rangle, \langle v_2{:}\mathsf{A}_1\rangle \vdash R_1$.

Since v_1 and v_2 cannot be u, the corresponding result for value judgements, and induction, give

(1') $\Gamma \vdash v_1 : \mathsf{A}_1,\ v_2 : \mathsf{A}_2$
(2') $\Gamma \vdash R_2$.

A number of applications of (interchange), from the previous lemma, gives

$$\Gamma, u : \mathsf{E}, \langle v_1{:}\mathsf{A}_2\rangle, \langle v_2{:}\mathsf{A}_1\rangle \;\equiv\; \Gamma, \langle v_1{:}\mathsf{A}_2\rangle, \langle v_2{:}\mathsf{A}_1\rangle, u : \mathsf{E}$$

So (3) can be replaced by

(3') $\Gamma, \langle v_1{:}\mathsf{A}_2\rangle, \langle v_2{:}\mathsf{A}_1\rangle, u : \mathsf{E} \vdash R_1$

to which induction can be applied to obtain

(3") $\Gamma, \langle v_1{:}\mathsf{A}_2\rangle, \langle v_2{:}\mathsf{A}_1\rangle \vdash R_1$.

Now (TY-MATCH), applied to (1'), (2'), (3") gives the required result. ■

At this stage we have developed for capability types all of the properties of the proof inference system that underlie both the substitution result and subject reduction for simple types.

Theorem 3.31 (*subject reduction for capability types*) *Suppose* $\Gamma \vdash P$ *and* $P \longrightarrow Q$. *Then* $\Gamma \vdash Q$.

Proof: As in the case of simple types subject reduction relies essentially on developing corresponding substitution results, along the lines of those in Proposition 3.9, the main one being:

$$\Gamma \vdash v : \mathsf{A} \text{ and } \Gamma, x : \mathsf{A} \vdash R \text{ implies } \Gamma \vdash R\{\!|^v/_x|\!\} \qquad (3.18)$$

However despite having accumulated all the necessary properties used in the proof of Proposition 3.9, these are not sufficient to establish (3.18) for capability types. With simple types, the proof of (3.18) in the case when R has the form $\mathsf{if}\ v_1 = v_2\ \mathsf{then}\ R_1\ \mathsf{else}\ R_2$ is handled in a straightforward manner by induction, because of the purely inductive nature of the corresponding typing rule, (STY-EQ) in Figure 3.5. With capability types the corresponding rule, (TY-MATCH) in Figure 3.10 is more complicated, and it turns out we need to formulate a more general substitution result than (3.18).

We refrain from doing so here. The details will be spelt out in a more sophisticated setting in Chapter 5; see the proof of Proposition 5.31. However having established (3.18), the proof of subject reduction itself is a minor extension to the proof of the corresponding result for simple types, Theorem 3.12; again the details are spelt out in the more sophisticated setting of Chapter 5, in Theorem 5.34.

For those wishing to complete the theorem directly for TYPED API, see Question 17 at the end of the chapter. ■

Instead let us look at some examples that re-enforce the various requirements we have made on the subtyping relation for capability types.

Example 3.32 [*Contra-variance of Write*] We work with an environment Γ_1 such that $\Gamma_1(a) = \mathsf{rw}\langle\mathsf{rw}\rangle$, $\Gamma_1(c) = \mathsf{r}$, where, as in Example 3.22, rw, r stand for $\mathsf{rw}\langle()\rangle$, $\mathsf{r}\langle()\rangle$ respectively. Note $\mathsf{rw} <: \mathsf{r}$.

Suppose on the contrary we allowed subtyping to be co-variant on write capabilities, with the rule

$$\frac{\mathsf{T}_1 <: \mathsf{T}_2}{\mathsf{w}\langle\mathsf{T}_1\rangle <: \mathsf{w}\langle\mathsf{T}_2\rangle} \qquad (3.19)$$

So we would have $\mathsf{w}\langle\mathsf{rw}\rangle <: \mathsf{w}\langle\mathsf{r}\rangle$. Note that this would allow us to infer

$$\Gamma \vdash a!\langle c\rangle$$

because of the rule (TY-SUB), in Figure 3.9. This spells trouble; a *reader* on a, with type $\mathsf{rw}\langle\mathsf{rw}\rangle$, may be expecting a value with both read and write capabilities, while c, in the environment Γ_1, has only the read capability. Such a reader is defined by

$$a?(y)\,(y?\mid y!)$$

With (3.19) it would be straightforward to infer

$$\Gamma_1 \vdash a!\langle c\rangle \mid a?(y)\,(y?\mid y!)$$

Yet

$$a!\langle c\rangle \mid a?(y)\,(y?\mid y!) \quad\longrightarrow\quad c?\mid c!$$

and $\Gamma_1 \not\vdash c?\mid c!$. ■

Example 3.33 [Constraint on Read Write/Types] Here we show that the constraint $\mathsf{T}_w <: \mathsf{T}_r$ is required when forming the type $\mathsf{rw}\langle\mathsf{T}_r,\mathsf{T}_w\rangle$ in Figure 3.7. Suppose this were dropped. Then $\mathsf{F} = \mathsf{rw}\langle\mathsf{rw},\mathsf{r}\rangle$ would be a valid type and

$$\Gamma_2 \vdash a!\langle c\rangle \mid a?(y)\,(\mathsf{new}\,b:\mathsf{F})(b!\langle y\rangle \mid b?(x)\,x!\mid x?)$$

where Γ_2 is such that $\Gamma_2(a)$ and $\Gamma_2(c)$ are $\mathsf{rw}\langle\mathsf{r}\rangle$, r respectively. Here again trouble brews; c is sent on channel a, which only transmits read capabilities. It is passed through b, which can magically fabricate new capabilities. We have

$$a!\langle c\rangle \mid a?(y)\,(\mathsf{new}\,b:\mathsf{F})(b!\langle y\rangle \mid b?(x)\,x!\mid x?) \longrightarrow^{*} (\mathsf{new}\,b:\mathsf{F})(c!\mid c?)$$

and this latter process cannot be typed by Γ_2.

Example 3.34 [Co-variance of Read] Now suppose we demanded that subtyping was contra-variant in read; that is we had the typing rule

$$\frac{\mathsf{T}_1 <: \mathsf{T}_2}{\mathsf{r}\langle\mathsf{T}_2\rangle <: \mathsf{r}\langle\mathsf{T}_1\rangle}$$

Then we would have $\mathsf{r}\langle\mathsf{r}\rangle <: \mathsf{r}\langle\mathsf{rw}\rangle$, thereby allowing the inference of

$$\Gamma_2 \vdash a?(y)\,(y?\mid y!)$$

again because of the rule (TY-IN) and (TY-SUB). This now leads to a failure of subject reduction because $\Gamma_2 \not\vdash c?\mid c!$ while

$$\Gamma_2 \vdash a!\langle c\rangle \;\mid\; a?(y)\,(y?\mid y!)$$

and

$$a!\langle c\rangle \;\mid\; a?(y)\,(y?\mid y!) \quad\longrightarrow\quad c?\mid c!$$

■

We started this chapter by remarking that a type checking system is best justified by a clear definition of the *runtime errors* it eliminates. But for the type system in Figure 3.10 we have no corresponding definition of runtime error. For example we have managed to show that badClient cannot be typechecked, relative to Γ_s, but we have no formal statement of what exactly badClient violates. Intuitively it receives the methods get, put, with a restricted set of capabilities and seeks to use them with capabilities it has not been granted. But what exactly does it mean to *receive a value with a set of capabilities*? Or for a process to *use a value at a capability it has not been granted*? Similarly with the counter-examples to subject reduction just discussed in Example 3.33. There is some reasonable sense in which they misuse granted capabilities but this misuse has not been elaborated.

This can be formalised, using a *tagged* version of APi, where each occurrence of a value is tagged according to the capabilities with which it can be exercised. The tags on a value are then changed during transmission in accordance with the type of the transmitting channel. However the formalisation is non-trivial and is postponed until Section 5.4.

3.5 Questions

1. Prove $\Gamma \vdash^{s} R$ implies $\Gamma \vdash R$.
2. Prove the following more general form of (strengthening) for simple types:

   (i) $\Gamma,\ u : \mathsf{E},\ \Gamma' \vdash^{s} \mathbf{env}$ implies $\Gamma,\ \Gamma' \vdash^{s} \mathbf{env}$.
   (ii) If $\Gamma,\ u : \mathsf{E},\ \Gamma' \vdash^{s} V : \mathsf{T}$ where u does not occur in V, then $\Gamma,\ \Gamma' \vdash^{s} V : \mathsf{T}$.
   (iii) If $\Gamma,\ u : \mathsf{E},\ \Gamma' \vdash^{s} R$ where u does not occur free in R, then $\Gamma,\ \Gamma' \vdash^{s} R$.

   Your proof should not rely on (interchange), Proposition 3.7.
3. Show that the processes memSERV, mClient and badClient from Example 3.15 can all be typed relative to some simple type environment, as defined in Section 3.2. You should also instantiate the declaration types used by these processes with simple types.
4. Show that $\Gamma \vdash (\mathsf{new}\, n : \mathsf{D})\, R$ implies that D has to be a channel type.
5. Suppose $\langle A, < \rangle$ is a partially complete pre-order.

   - Prove that $S \downarrow$ implies S has a greatest lower bound, whenever S is a finite non-empty subset of A.
   - Prove a similar result for upper bounds; that is, providing S is finite and non-empty, $S \uparrow$ implies S has a least upper bound.
   - Show that if a and b are both greatest lower bounds for a subset S of A then $a < b$ and $b < a$.

6. Prove the following *inversion* properties of subtyping:

   (i) For any base type, $\mathsf{T} <: \mathsf{base}$ implies $\mathsf{T} = \mathsf{base}$.
   (ii) If $\mathsf{S} <: (\mathsf{T}_1, \ldots \mathsf{T}_n)$ then $\mathsf{S} = (\mathsf{S}_1, \ldots, \mathsf{S}_n)$, where $\mathsf{S}_i <: \mathsf{T}_i$.
   (iii) If $\mathsf{S} <: \mathsf{r}\langle \mathsf{T}_r \rangle$ then

   - either $\mathsf{S} = \mathsf{r}\langle \mathsf{S}_r \rangle$, where $\mathsf{S}_r <: \mathsf{T}_r$
   - or $\mathsf{S} = \mathsf{rw}\langle \mathsf{S}_r, \mathsf{S}_w \rangle$, where $\mathsf{S}_r <: \mathsf{T}_r$.

(iv) If $\mathsf{S} <: \mathsf{w}\langle \mathsf{T}_w \rangle$ then

- either $\mathsf{S} = \mathsf{w}\langle \mathsf{S}_w \rangle$, where $\mathsf{T}_w <: \mathsf{S}_w$
- or $\mathsf{S} = \mathsf{rw}\langle \mathsf{S}_r, \mathsf{S}_w \rangle$, where $\mathsf{T}_w <: \mathsf{S}_w$.

(v) If $\mathsf{S} <: \mathsf{rw}\langle \mathsf{T}_r, \mathsf{T}_w \rangle$ then $\mathsf{S} = \mathsf{rw}\langle \mathsf{S}_r, \mathsf{T}_w \rangle$, where $\mathsf{S}_r <: \mathsf{T}_r$ and $\mathsf{T}_w <: \mathsf{S}_r$.

7. In a similar vein show how the structure of T is determined by that of S, whenever $\mathsf{S} <: \mathsf{T}$.
8. (Interchange) for capability types. Prove that $\Gamma_1, u : \mathsf{E}, u' : \mathsf{E}', \Gamma_2 \vdash \mathbf{env}$ implies
   (i) $\Gamma_1, u' : \mathsf{E}', u : \mathsf{E}, \Gamma_2 \vdash \mathbf{env}$
   (ii) $\Gamma_1, u : \mathsf{E}, u' : \mathsf{E}', \Gamma_2 \equiv \Gamma_1, u' : \mathsf{E}', u : \mathsf{E}, \Gamma_2$.
9. Suppose u is in the domain of the capability type environment Γ. Prove
   (i) $\Gamma \vdash u : \mathsf{r}\langle \mathsf{T}_r \rangle$ implies $\Gamma^r(u)$ is defined and $\Gamma^r(u) <: \mathsf{T}_r$
   (ii) $\Gamma \vdash u : \mathsf{w}\langle \mathsf{T}_w \rangle$ implies $\Gamma^w(u)$ is defined and $\mathsf{T}_w <: \Gamma^r(u)$.
10. Let $\langle A, < \rangle$ be a partially complete pre-order. $S \subseteq A$ is said to be *pairwise consistent* if $a \downarrow b$ for every pair $a, b \in S$.
    (i) Prove that in $\langle \mathbf{Types}, <: \rangle$, every finite non-empty pairwise consistent subset of **Types** has a greatest lower bound.
    (ii) Is this true for an arbitrary partially complete pre-order?
11. Suppose σ is a mapping over $\mathsf{Names} \cup \mathsf{Vars}$ that maps names to names and variables to variables. For such a σ let $\Gamma\sigma$ be the type association list obtained by replacing each $u : \mathsf{E}$ in Γ by $\sigma(u) : \mathsf{E}$.
    Assuming σ is injective on the domain of Γ, prove:
    (i) $\Gamma \vdash \mathbf{ty}$ implies $\Gamma\sigma \vdash \mathbf{ty}$
    (ii) $\Gamma \vdash V : \mathsf{T}$ implies $\Gamma\sigma \vdash \sigma(V) : \mathsf{T}$
    (iii) $\Gamma \vdash R$ implies $\Gamma\sigma \vdash R\sigma$.
    Show that these are not generally true when σ is not injective.
12. Without using (interchange) prove the following more general form of (strengthening): $\Gamma, u : \mathsf{E}, \Gamma' \vdash R$ implies $\Gamma, \Gamma' \vdash R$, whenever u does not occur in R.
13. Let $\mathbf{Types}_{ps}$ be the subset of capability types of the form $\mathsf{r}\langle \mathsf{T}_r \rangle$, $\mathsf{w}\langle \mathsf{T}_w \rangle$ or $\mathsf{rw}\langle \mathsf{T} \rangle$. Show that the pre-order $\langle \mathbf{Types}_{ps}, <: \rangle$ is not partially complete.
14. Show that well-defined type environments are not necessarily preserved by well-typed substitutions. That is, if $\Gamma \vdash v : \mathsf{A}$ then $\Gamma, \Delta\{\!|^v/_x|\!\} \vdash \mathbf{env}$ does not necessarily follow from $\Gamma, x; \mathsf{A}, \Delta \vdash \mathbf{env}$.
15. Suppose we replace the rule (TY-MIS.MATCH) with

(TY-MIS.MATCH.BIS)

$$\frac{\Gamma \vdash v_1 : \mathsf{A}_1, v_2 : \mathsf{A}_2 \quad \Gamma \vdash R_1 : \mathsf{proc} \quad \Gamma \vdash R_2 : \mathsf{proc}}{\Gamma \vdash \mathsf{if}\ v_1 = v_2\ \mathsf{then}\ R_1\ \mathsf{else}\ R_2 : \mathsf{proc}} \quad \mathsf{A}_1 \not\downarrow \mathsf{A}_2$$

Show that subject reduction no longer holds for the revised typing system.

16. Without using (interchange) prove the following substitution property for the capability typechecking system: suppose $\Gamma \vdash v : \mathsf{A}$ and x is new to Γ, and $\Gamma, \Delta\{\!|^{v}\!/\!_{x}|\!\} \vdash \mathbf{env}$. Then $\Gamma, x : \mathsf{A}, \Delta \vdash R$ implies $\Gamma, \Delta\{\!|^{v}\!/\!_{x}|\!\} \vdash R\{\!|^{v}\!/\!_{x}|\!\}$.
17. Use the result of the previous question to prove Theorem 3.31, subject reduction for capability types. There should be no need to use (interchange).

4
Types and behaviour in APi

One component of the behavioural equivalences in Chapter 2 is the ability of users to interact with processes. We have just developed, in Chapter 3, a capability-based view of processes, where interaction depends on knowledge of these capabilities; moreover these capabilities can change over time. Thus the behaviour of processes, or the perceived behaviour from a user's point of view, depends on current capabilities. The purpose of this chapter is to modify the behavioural theories of Chapter 2 so as to take these capabilities into account.

As a simple illustration consider the memory server $\mathsf{memSERV}$ of Example 2.11, which was typed in Example 3.21 using the environment Γ_s; this maps the entry point to the server, s, to the type $\mathsf{rw}\langle \mathsf{S} \rangle$. The ability of a client to use this server depends on it having the output capability, $\mathsf{w}\langle \mathsf{S} \rangle$, on the channel s. If Client is a process that does not have this capability then the server effectively behaves like the empty process stop, *from* Client*'s point of view*.

The client's point of view is captured by a type environment, say Γ_{client}, which encapsulates its capabilities. So what we need is a form of behavioural equivalence parameterised on type environments,

$$\Gamma \models P \approx Q \tag{4.1}$$

indicating that P and Q are equivalent from the point of view of any user typeable by Γ. Then if Γ_{client} is such that $\Gamma_{client} \nvdash s : \mathsf{w}\langle \mathsf{S} \rangle$ we would expect

$$\Gamma_{client} \models \mathsf{memSERV} \approx \mathsf{stop} \tag{4.2}$$

Moreover we would like to be able to reason using the following **compositionality principle**:

$$\text{from } \Gamma \vdash R \text{ and } \Gamma \models P \approx Q \text{ it follows that } \Gamma \models R \mid P \approx R \mid Q \tag{4.3}$$

Using this principle we would then be able to deduce from $\Gamma_{client} \vdash \mathsf{Client}$ and (4.2) above that

$$\Gamma_{client} \models \mathsf{Client} \mid \mathsf{memSERV} \approx \mathsf{Client} \tag{4.4}$$

under the reasonable assumption that the parameterised equivalence, as yet undefined, satisfies the general property $\Gamma \models P \approx P \mid \mathsf{stop}$, whenever $\Gamma \vdash P$. This statement, (4.4), would then be a formalisation of the fact that the server cannot be used by the client, whenever $\Gamma_{client} \not\vdash s : \mathsf{w}\langle \mathsf{S} \rangle$.

In this chapter we will restrict our interest to bisimulation equivalence, developing a version of it parameterised on type environments, representing the context's capabilities on the available resources. However before embarking on this, it is worthwhile to develop more intuition about the intent of the judgements of the form (4.1) above. Intuitively the type environment Γ constrains both the processes being observed, P and Q, and the surrounding environment, the context, or processes trying to use, or observe, P and Q. Unfortunately, because capabilities can be generated dynamically, the type environment of the observed processes, and that of the observing processes may diverge.

Example 4.1 Consider the two processes

$$P \Leftarrow (\mathsf{new}\, c : \mathsf{rw})(a!\langle c \rangle \mid c?P')$$

$$Q \Leftarrow (\mathsf{new}\, c : \mathsf{rw})(a!\langle c \rangle \mid \mathsf{stop})$$

and suppose that they are typeable with respect to an environment Γ whose only entry for a is $\mathsf{rw}\langle \mathsf{r} \rangle$; in other words, a can only be used to transmit channel names that themselves in turn can only be used for at most read access.

We would expect

$$\Gamma \models P \approx Q$$

because no observing process can exercise the $c?P'$ component of P. This follows since the observing process can only gain knowledge of the new channel c by receiving it on the channel a; but this method of transmission ensures that it can never obtain write access on c, because of the type of a in Γ, and therefore can never activate the $c?P'$ component.

More importantly this example demonstrates that the observing environment can evolve to be different from that of the observed processes. Here, after the transmission of c on a, the residuals of the observed processes P and Q are working in an environment in which c has both read and write capabilities, while the observing environment only has write access. If we call the former Γ_i, the *internal* environment, and the latter Γ_e, the *external* environment, we have in this example $\Gamma_i <: \Gamma_e$. ■

Life can get even more complicated; situations may arise in which the external environment knows more than the internal environment.

Example 4.2 Consider the two processes

$$P \Leftarrow a(x)?R_1$$
$$Q \Leftarrow a(x)?R_2$$

and an observer trying to decide on the judgement

$$\Gamma \models P \approx Q$$

where Γ allows a to read/write identifiers with write capability only. Here, a priori, Γ is both the internal and external environment.

As part of the investigation an observer may generate a completely new name n, new to Γ, with both read and write capabilities, and transmit it along a to the observed processes, P and Q. The result now is that the external environment has n with both read and write capabilities, while the internal environment only has it with the write capability. We have $\Gamma_e <: \Gamma_i$. ■

These two examples indicate that to be completely general we need to develop a theory of judgements of the form

$$\Gamma_e; \Gamma_i \models P \approx Q$$

where Γ_e and Γ_i are two *consistent* type environments constraining the observing and the observed respectively. This is a rather daunting prospect. Instead we make a choice and we make a choice to use one environment only. Moreover this lies somewhere between Γ_e and Γ_i. We develop judgements of the form

$$\mathcal{I} \models P \approx Q \tag{4.5}$$

where $\mathcal{I}$ is a type environment representing the observer's current knowledge of the declared capabilities of P and Q. We ignore everything else in the observer's environment, while the internal type environment Γ_i, will remain implicit; it will periodically play a role. When making judgements of the form (4.5) it will for the most part be assumed that there is some, unspecified, type environment Γ_i that types P and Q. Moreover by careful development of the theory we will be able to assume $\Gamma_i <: \mathcal{I}$; that is, despite Example 4.2, the observer's knowledge is always **contained** in that of the observed.

4.1 Actions-in-context for aPi

Here we revisit the ideas of Section 2.3 to develop an lts for TYPED aPi. The ability of a process P to perform actions is constrained by a type environment $\mathcal{I}$, representing the current capabilities a user has of the channels of P. Following the above discussion we change our focus from processes to *configurations*. These consist of processes paired with type environments, representing an observer's current knowledge.

Definition 4.3 (configurations) A configuration is a pair

$$\mathcal{I} \triangleright P$$

where P is a process from TYPED APi and $\mathcal{I}$ is a type environment such that $\Gamma_i \vdash P$ for some other type environment Γ_i such that $\Gamma_i <: \mathcal{I}$; we say $\mathcal{I}$ is *compatible* with Γ_i. Since P is a closed term we can assume that both Γ_i and $\mathcal{I}$ do not contain any variables. ♦

Thus we define the judgements, called *actions-in-context*, which take the form

$$\mathcal{I} \triangleright P \xrightarrow{\mu} \mathcal{I}' \triangleright P' \tag{4.6}$$

where $\mathcal{I} \triangleright P$ and $\mathcal{I}' \triangleright P'$ are both configurations. Intuitively this indicates that

- P has the ability to perform the typed action μ, an input, output or internal move as described in Section 2.3
- the knowledge $\mathcal{I}$ allows the environment to participate in this action.

Thus, for example, if μ is an output on a channel a then $\mathcal{I}$ requires the input capability on a. Note that actions-in-context may change not only the process performing them but also the user's knowledge. For example an output action may increase the user's knowledge, by either sending new names or sending new capabilities on known names. The typed action labels μ can take one of three forms:

$\alpha_i = (\tilde{c} : \tilde{\mathsf{D}})a?V$: The input of the value V along the channel a, which contains the new names $(\tilde{c})$, declared by the observer at the types $(\tilde{\mathsf{D}})$. These labels are only defined when a does not occur in $(\tilde{c})$, which in turn is a distinct sequence of names; we also insist that all these bound names c_i have to appear somewhere in the imported value V.

$\alpha_o = (\tilde{c} : \tilde{\mathsf{D}})a!V$: the output of the value V along the channel a, simultaneously exporting the new names in the set $(\tilde{c})$. Again this label is only defined if the names $(\tilde{c})$ are all distinct, different from a, and we insist that all the bound names c_i appear somewhere in the exported value V. These new names are declared by the observed process at the types $(\tilde{\mathsf{D}})$.

$\mu = \tau$: this indicates, as usual, some internal activity, and should more or less coincide with the reduction semantics.

(L-IN)

$$\frac{\mathcal{I}^w(a)\downarrow_{\mathsf{def}} \qquad \mathcal{I} \vdash V : \mathcal{I}^w(a)}{\mathcal{I} \triangleright a?(X)\,R \xrightarrow{a?V} \mathcal{I} \triangleright R\{\!|V/X|\!\}}$$

(L-WEAK)

$$\frac{\mathcal{I}, n : \mathsf{D} \triangleright P \xrightarrow{\alpha_i} \mathcal{I}' \triangleright P'}{\mathcal{I} \triangleright P \xrightarrow{(n:\mathsf{D})\,\alpha_i} \mathcal{I}' \triangleright P'} \quad n \textit{ fresh}$$

(L-OUT)

$$\frac{\mathcal{I}^r(a)\downarrow_{\mathsf{def}}}{\mathcal{I} \triangleright a!\langle V\rangle \xrightarrow{a!V} \mathcal{I}, \langle V{:}\mathcal{I}^r(a)\rangle \triangleright \mathsf{stop}}$$

(L-OPEN)

$$\frac{\mathcal{I} \triangleright P \xrightarrow{\alpha_o} \mathcal{I}' \triangleright P'}{\mathcal{I} \triangleright (\mathsf{new}\, n : \mathsf{D})\, P \xrightarrow{(n:\mathsf{D})\,\alpha_o} \mathcal{I}' \triangleright P'}$$

(L-CTXT)

$$\frac{\mathcal{I} \triangleright P \xrightarrow{\mu} \mathcal{I}' \triangleright P'}{\begin{array}{l}\mathcal{I} \triangleright P \mid Q \xrightarrow{\mu} \mathcal{I}' \triangleright P' \mid Q\\ \mathcal{I} \triangleright Q \mid P \xrightarrow{\mu} \mathcal{I}' \triangleright Q \mid P'\end{array}} \quad \mathsf{bn}(\mu) \cap \mathsf{fn}(Q) = \emptyset$$

$$\frac{\mathcal{I} \triangleright P \xrightarrow{\mu} \mathcal{I}' \triangleright P'}{\mathcal{I} \triangleright (\mathsf{new}\, n : \mathsf{D})\, P \xrightarrow{\mu} \mathcal{I}' \triangleright (\mathsf{new}\, n : \mathsf{D})\, P'} \quad n \notin \mu$$

Figure 4.1 External actions-in-context for TYPED API

Notation 4.4

- We will use the complementary notation, $\overline{\mu}$ introduced briefly in the proof of Proposition 2.21, on these actions; as usual $\overline{\tau}$ is τ itself, while $(\tilde{c} : \tilde{\mathsf{D}})a?V$ is $(\tilde{c} : \tilde{\mathsf{D}})a!V$, and $(\tilde{c} : \tilde{\mathsf{D}})a!V$ is $(\tilde{c} : \tilde{\mathsf{D}})a?V$.
- If μ is an external action, $(\tilde{c} : \tilde{\mathsf{D}})a!V$ or $(\tilde{c} : \tilde{\mathsf{D}})a?V$, then $(\tilde{c})$ are the *bound* names of μ, denoted $\mathsf{bn}(\mu)$, while $\mathsf{ch}(\mu)$ denotes the channel used in μ, namely a.
- As in Notation 2.12 we use α_i, α_o to range over all valid input and output labels respectively. ■

The rules for generating these judgements are formally defined in Figure 4.1, for the input and output actions, and in Figure 4.2 for internal actions. The first rule, (L-IN), allows the process $a?(X)\,R$ to input the value V, assuming the environment

(L-COMM)
$$\frac{\mathcal{I}_1 \rhd P \xrightarrow{(\tilde{c}:\tilde{\mathsf{D}}')a?V} \mathcal{I}'_1 \rhd P' \quad \mathcal{I}_2 \rhd Q \xrightarrow{(\tilde{c}:\tilde{\mathsf{D}})a!V} \mathcal{I}'_2 \rhd Q'}{\mathcal{I} \rhd P \mid Q \xrightarrow{\tau} \mathcal{I} \rhd (\mathsf{new}\,\tilde{c} : \tilde{\mathsf{D}})(P' \mid Q')}$$

(L-COMM)
$$\frac{\mathcal{I}_1 \rhd P \xrightarrow{(\tilde{c}:\tilde{\mathsf{D}})a!V} \mathcal{I}'_1 \rhd P' \quad \mathcal{I}_2 \rhd Q \xrightarrow{(\tilde{c}:\tilde{\mathsf{D}}')a?V} \mathcal{I}'_2 \rhd Q'}{\mathcal{I} \rhd P \mid Q \xrightarrow{\tau} \mathcal{I} \rhd (\mathsf{new}\,\tilde{c} : \tilde{\mathsf{D}})(P' \mid Q')}$$

(L-EQ)
$$\mathcal{I} \rhd \mathsf{if}\ v = v\ \mathsf{then}\ P\ \mathsf{else}\ Q \xrightarrow{\tau} \mathcal{I} \rhd P$$

(L-REC)
$$\mathcal{I} \rhd \mathsf{rec}\ x.\ B \xrightarrow{\tau} \mathcal{I} \rhd B\{\!|^{\mathsf{rec}\ x.\ B}/_{x}|\!\}$$

(L-NEQ)
$$\mathcal{I} \rhd \mathsf{if}\ v_1 = v_2\ \mathsf{then}\ P\ \mathsf{else}\ Q \xrightarrow{\tau} \mathcal{I} \rhd Q \quad v_1 \neq v_2$$

Figure 4.2 Internal actions-in-context for TYPED APi

has write permission on the channel a, that is the type $\mathcal{I}^w(a)$ is defined, and the value V is already known to the environment at a type suitable to be sent on a, that is $\mathcal{I} \vdash V : \mathcal{I}^w(a)$; as indicated in Definition 3.25, we use $\mathcal{I}^w(a)\downarrow_{\mathsf{def}}$ to say that the partial function $\mathcal{I}^w$ is defined for a. The next rule, (L-WEAK), allows the environment to invent new names to send to the observed process. For example suppose n is a fresh name. Then this rule means

$$\mathcal{I} \rhd a?(x)\,R \xrightarrow{(n:\mathsf{D})a?n} \mathcal{I}, n : \mathsf{D} \rhd R\{\!|^{n}/_{x}|\!\}$$

for any type D satisfying $\mathsf{D} <: \mathcal{I}^w(a)$, because

$$\mathcal{I}, n : \mathsf{D} \rhd a?(x)\,R \xrightarrow{a?n} \mathcal{I}, n : \mathsf{D} \rhd R\{\!|^{n}/_{x}|\!\}$$

can be inferred from (L-IN). Note that there are implicit side conditions in the rule (L-WEAK), enforced by insisting that the rule can only be applied when the action label in question, $(n : \mathsf{D})\alpha_i$ is well-formed. For example if α_i is $(\tilde{c} : \tilde{\mathsf{D}})a?V$, in order for the action label $(n : \mathsf{D})\alpha_i$ to be well-defined, n must be different from a and all the names in $(\tilde{c})$, and it must appear somewhere in V. So the rule can only be applied in these circumstances. The explicit side-condition, that n be *fresh*, might be automatically inferred from Barendregt's principle but just to be safe we mention it as part of the rule.

There are also two rules governing output. If $\mathcal{I}$ has read capability on the channel a then (L-OUT) allows the process $a!\langle V\rangle$ to output the value V on a; moreover the observer obtains on V the capabilities determined by its read capabilities on a. The extra knowledge gained is captured by extending the type environment with $\langle V{:}\mathcal{I}^r(a)\rangle$. Note that the fact that $\mathcal{I} \rhd a!\langle V\rangle$ is a configuration ensures that the augmented association list, $\mathcal{I}, \langle V{:}\mathcal{I}^r(a)\rangle$, is a valid environment; see Question 3 at the end of the chapter.

The second output rule, (L-OPEN), allows the observed process to export new names. For example suppose the channel a is known to the environment as one from which values may be read at some type C_r, that is $\mathcal{I}^r(a)$ is C_r. Then (L-OPEN) allows us to deduce

$$\mathcal{I} \triangleright (\mathsf{new}\, b : \mathsf{D})(a!\langle b\rangle \mid b?(x)\, R) \xrightarrow{(b:\mathsf{D})a!b} \mathcal{I},\, b : \mathsf{C}_r \triangleright \mathsf{stop} \mid b?(x)\, R$$

because (L-OUT) gives

$$\mathcal{I} \triangleright a!\langle b\rangle \mid b?(x)\, R \xrightarrow{a!b} \mathcal{I}, b : \mathsf{C}_r \triangleright \mathsf{stop} \mid b?(x)\, R$$

Note that the observer gains the new name b not at the declaration type D but at its read type on the export channel a, namely C_r. Barendregt's convention ensures that b does not occur in $\mathcal{I}$ and therefore this action represents the export of a new name to the environment.

Also, as with (L-WEAK), the rule (L-OPEN) has extra implicit side-conditions. If α_o is the label $(\tilde{c} : \tilde{\mathsf{D}})a!V$, then to ensure that the resulting label is well-defined n must be different from a and all of $(\tilde{c})$, and must occur somewhere in V; in addition Barendregt's convention ensures that n does not occur in $\mathcal{I}$.

Finally in Figure 4.1 there is a straightforward contextual rule, with some explicit side-conditions to ensure the proper functioning of free and bound names.

The rules for internal actions-in-context, in Figure 4.2 are also for the most part straightforward; (L-REC), (L-EQ) and (L-NEQ) are all borrowed from the reduction semantics in Figure 2.4. So we concentrate on explaining the communication rule (L-COMM). Intuitively a τ action represents some internal communication, which is therefore independent of the ability of an observer to see it happen. However to make the definition of actions-in-context inductive in character we need to define these in terms of observable input and output actions-in-context. For this reason, in (L-COMM) we allow the input and complementary output actions to occur relative to *arbitrary* knowledge environments, $\mathcal{I}_1$ and $\mathcal{I}_2$ respectively. Note however that in the conclusion the observer's environment $\mathcal{I}$ does not change after the internal action has occurred. This is in agreement with the intuition that internal actions are independent of the observer; the rule is constructed so that if a process can perform a τ action-in-context with respect to some environment $\mathcal{I}$ it can do so with respect to *any* environment; see Corollary 4.13. Note also that the sender and receiver do not a priori have to agree on the declaration types of the newly generated channels.

Finally let us point out that there are some alternative formulations we could have used in the presentation of these rules. For example instead of (L-IN) we could have:

(L-IN′)

$$\frac{\mathcal{I} \vdash a : \mathsf{w}\langle\mathsf{T}\rangle \qquad \mathcal{I} \vdash V : \mathsf{T}}{\mathcal{I} \triangleright a?(X)\, R \xrightarrow{a?V} \mathcal{I} \triangleright R\{\!|V/X|\!\}}$$

However this is an equivalent rule. For $\mathcal{I} \vdash a : \mathsf{w}\langle\mathsf{T}\rangle$ if and only if $\mathcal{I}^w(a)$ exists and $\mathsf{T} <: \mathcal{I}^w(a)$; this means that if $\mathcal{I} \vdash V : \mathsf{T}$ and $\mathcal{I} \vdash a : \mathsf{w}\langle\mathsf{T}\rangle$ then $\mathcal{I} \vdash V : \mathcal{I}^w(a)$.

Similarly instead of (L-OUT) we could have

$$\frac{\text{(L-OUT}')\quad \mathcal{I} \vdash a : \mathsf{r}\langle\mathsf{T}\rangle}{\mathcal{I} \triangleright a!\langle V\rangle \xrightarrow{a!V} \mathcal{I},\ \langle V{:}\mathsf{T}\rangle \triangleright \mathsf{stop}}$$

This of course implies (L-OUT) as the type T may be chosen to be $\mathcal{I}^r(a)$ but in general allows many more actions to be derivable. However the extra actions are not of great interest as they simply consist in exporting V at supertypes of $\mathcal{I}^r(a)$.

The remainder of this section is devoted to a detailed analysis of actions-in-context, and their properties. For example, although we have given rules for the deducing actions-in-context (4.6) as of yet we have no guarantee that the residual $\mathcal{I}' \triangleright P'$ is a valid configuration, even if $\mathcal{I} \triangleright P$ is; indeed we need to develop a considerable number of consistency results about these judgements before being able to prove so. In order to give the material some structure we divide it into three convenient subsections. Throughout these it will be very convenient to have a simple criteria for ensuring that an extension of a valid environment is again a valid environment; if $\mathcal{I} \vdash \mathbf{env}$, when can we be sure that $\mathcal{I}, \langle V{:}\mathsf{T}\rangle$ is also a valid environment? A sufficient condition is given in the following:

Lemma 4.5 Suppose $\Gamma <: \mathcal{I}$ *are two valid environments, and* $(\tilde{n})$ *are fresh names. Then* $\Gamma, \langle \tilde{n}{:}\tilde{\mathsf{D}}\rangle \vdash V : \mathsf{T}$ *implies* $\mathcal{I}, \langle V{:}\mathsf{T}\rangle \vdash \mathbf{env}$.

Proof: See Question 2 at the end of the chapter. ■

4.1.1 The role of type environments

The most significant aspect of actions-in-context (4.6) is that the resulting knowledge of the environment, $\mathcal{I}'$ is completely determined by the initial knowledge, $\mathcal{I}$, and the action μ.

Definition 4.6 (action residuals) The partial function after from type environments and typed action labels to type environments is defined as follows:

- $\mathcal{I}$ after τ is always defined to be $\mathcal{I}$
- if μ is the input label $(\tilde{c} : \tilde{\mathsf{D}})a?V$ then $\mathcal{I}$ after μ is always defined to be $\mathcal{I}, \langle \tilde{c}{:}\tilde{\mathsf{D}}\rangle$, where each c_i is new to $\mathcal{I}$
- if μ is the output label $(\tilde{c} : \tilde{\mathsf{D}})a!V$ then $\mathcal{I}$ after μ is defined to be $\mathcal{I}, \langle V{:}\mathcal{I}^r(a)\rangle$, whenever this is a valid environment; again here we assume that each c_i is new to $\mathcal{I}$. ♦

Proposition 4.7 Suppose $\mathcal{I} \triangleright P \xrightarrow{\mu} \mathcal{I}' \triangleright P'$ is an action-in-context. Then $(\mathcal{I}\ \mathsf{after}\ \mu)$ is a well-defined environment and coincides with $\mathcal{I}'$.

Proof: By induction on the inference of $\mathcal{I} \triangleright P \xrightarrow{\mu} \mathcal{I}' \triangleright P'$, and an examination of the last rule used. Note that we can ignore the case when μ is τ, as the result is trivial.

As an example suppose the last rule used is (L-OUT). Then $\mathcal{I} \triangleright a!\langle V\rangle$ is a configuration and $\mathcal{I}^r(a)\downarrow_{\mathsf{def}}$; we have to show that $\mathcal{I}, \ \langle V{:}\mathcal{I}^r(a)\rangle \vdash \mathbf{env}$. This will follow from Lemma 4.5 if we can find a valid type environment $\Gamma <: \mathcal{I}$ such that $\Gamma \vdash V : \mathcal{I}^r(a)$.

Since $\mathcal{I} \triangleright a!\langle V\rangle$ is a configuration we know there is some type environment $\Gamma_i <: \mathcal{I}$ such that $\Gamma_i \vdash a!\langle V\rangle$; this is the required Γ. For we know there is some type T such that $\Gamma_i \vdash V : \mathsf{T}$ and $\Gamma_i \vdash a : \mathsf{w}\langle\mathsf{T}\rangle$. Also $\Gamma_i <: \mathcal{I}$ implies that $\Gamma_i \vdash a : \mathsf{r}\langle\mathcal{I}^r(a)\rangle$. So from part (ii) of Proposition 3.26 we have that $\mathsf{T} <: \Gamma_i^r(a)$. Therefore (subsumption) from the same proposition gives the required $\Gamma_i \vdash V : \mathcal{I}^r(a)$.

All other cases are considerably simpler, and left to the reader. ■

It is worth emphasising that the new environment after an action is actually independent of the process being observed. If

$$\mathcal{I} \triangleright P \xrightarrow{\mu} \mathcal{I}_1 \triangleright P'$$
$$\mathcal{I} \triangleright Q \xrightarrow{\mu} \mathcal{I}_2 \triangleright Q'$$

then $\mathcal{I}_1$ is the same as $\mathcal{I}_2$; they both coincide with $\mathcal{I}\ \mathsf{after}\ \mu$.

Notation 4.8 To emphasise the determinacy of the effect of actions-in-context on the environment's knowledge, in future we often abbreviate

$$\mathcal{I} \triangleright P \xrightarrow{\mu} (\mathcal{I}\ \mathsf{after}\ \mu) \triangleright Q$$

to simply

$$\mathcal{I} \triangleright P \xrightarrow{\mu} Q$$

Further we will write $P \xrightarrow{\mu} Q$ to mean that there exists some $\mathcal{I}$ such that $\mathcal{I} \triangleright P \xrightarrow{\mu} Q$. ■

The notation $P \xrightarrow{\mu} Q$ may seem like odd notation but it simply indicates that P, under the right external circumstances, has the ability to perform the action μ. The *right external circumstances*, necessary to allow the action μ to happen, is also easy to define.

Definition 4.9 (allowing actions) We define the partial predicate allows between environments and action labels as follows:

- $\mathcal{I}$ allows τ is always true
- $\mathcal{I}$ allows $(\tilde{c} : \tilde{\mathsf{D}})a?V$ is true whenever $\mathcal{I}^w(a)$ is defined and $\mathcal{I}, \langle \tilde{c}{:}\tilde{\mathsf{D}} \rangle \vdash V : \mathcal{I}^w(a)$
- $\mathcal{I}$ allows $(\tilde{c} : \tilde{\mathsf{D}})a!V$ is true whenever $\mathcal{I}^r(a)$ is defined.

As usual here, as we view c_i as bound variables, the implicit assumption is that they are new to $\mathcal{I}$. ♦

The next result states that if a process P has the ability to perform an action and the environment $\mathcal{I}$ allows the action to happen, then the action can occur in the configuration $\mathcal{I} \triangleright P$:

Proposition 4.10 Suppose $\mathcal{I}_1 \triangleright P \xrightarrow{\mu} Q$. Then

- $\mathcal{I}_1$ allows μ
- *if $\mathcal{I}_2$ allows μ then $\mathcal{I}_2 \triangleright P \xrightarrow{\mu} Q$, whenever $\mathcal{I}_2 \triangleright P$ is a configuration.*

Proof: The first result is again a simple proof by induction on the derivation of the judgement $\mathcal{I}_1 \triangleright P \xrightarrow{\mu} Q$. So we concentrate on the second. Suppose

$$\mathcal{I}_1 \triangleright P \xrightarrow{\mu} Q \tag{4.7}$$

We show that $\mathcal{I}_2$ allows μ enables us to transform the derivation of (4.7) into a derivation of $\mathcal{I}_2 \triangleright P \xrightarrow{\mu} Q$. The proof proceeds by induction on the derivation of (4.7). We examine some of the more interesting cases; note that the case when (L-COMM) is used is trivial.

- Suppose (4.7) is inferred using (L-IN). This case is straightforward. We know μ has the simple form $a?V$, and the hypothesis, $\mathcal{I}_2$ allows μ, means that $\mathcal{I}_2^w(a)$ is defined and $\mathcal{I}_2 \vdash V : \mathcal{I}_2^w(a)$ is precisely the premise required to apply (L-IN) to obtain the required
$$\mathcal{I}_2 \triangleright P \xrightarrow{\mu} Q$$
- Suppose (4.7) is inferred using (L-OUT). Here μ has the form $a!V$, P is $a!\langle V \rangle$ and the hypothesis is that $\mathcal{I}_2^r(a)$ is defined. The crucial point here is that $\mathcal{I} \triangleright a!\langle V \rangle$ is a configuration, and we repeat the argument already used in the proof of Proposition 4.7. There is a type environment $\Gamma_i <: \mathcal{I}$ such that $\Gamma_i \vdash a!\langle V \rangle$. From the former we can deduce that $\Gamma_i \vdash a : \mathsf{r}\langle \mathcal{I}^r(a) \rangle$, and from the latter we have $\Gamma_i \vdash a : \mathsf{w}\langle \mathsf{T} \rangle$ for some T such that $\Gamma_i \vdash V : \mathsf{T}$. The second part of Proposition 3.26 ensures that $\mathsf{T} <: \mathcal{I}^r(a)$, and then (subsumption) gives $\Gamma_i \vdash V : \mathcal{I}^r(a)$. Once more Lemma 4.5 ensures that $\mathcal{I}, \langle V{:}\mathcal{I}^r(a) \rangle$ is a valid type environment. This means that (L-OUT) can be applied to deduce the required
$$\mathcal{I}_2 \triangleright P \xrightarrow{\mu} Q$$

- All of the inductive cases are straightforward. We examine one instance, when (4.7) is inferred using (L-WEAK). Here μ has the form $(n : \mathsf{D})\alpha_i$ where α_i is an input action label $(\tilde{c} : \tilde{\mathsf{D}})a?V$ and the action has the form

$$\mathcal{I}_1 \rhd P \xrightarrow{\mu} Q$$

because

$$\mathcal{I}_1, n : \mathsf{D} \rhd P \xrightarrow{\alpha_i} Q \tag{4.8}$$

The hypothesis, $\mathcal{I}_2$ allows μ unravels to the assumption that $\mathcal{I}_2^w(a)$ is defined and $\mathcal{I}_2, n : \mathsf{D}, \langle\tilde{c}{:}\tilde{\mathsf{D}}\rangle \vdash V : \mathcal{I}_2^w(a)$.

We turn this hypothesis into a statement about the environment $(\mathcal{I}_2, n : \mathsf{D})$. Since the action label is well-defined n must be different from a and so $(\mathcal{I}_2, n : \mathsf{D})^w(a)$ is exactly the same as $\mathcal{I}_2^w(a)$. In other words we have that $(\mathcal{I}_2, n : \mathsf{D})^w(a)$ is well-defined and $(\mathcal{I}_2, n : \mathsf{D}), \langle\tilde{c}{:}\tilde{\mathsf{D}}\rangle \vdash V : (\mathcal{I}_2, n : \mathsf{D})^w(a)$; that is $(\mathcal{I}_2, n : \mathsf{D})$ allows α_i. So we can apply induction to (4.8) to obtain

$$\mathcal{I}_2, n : \mathsf{D} \rhd P \xrightarrow{\alpha_i} Q$$

An application of (L-WEAK) now gives the required conclusion. ■

The fact that the derivation of the actions-in-context $\mathcal{I} \rhd P \xrightarrow{\mu} Q$ depends on specific information present in $\mathcal{I}$ means that they are preserved by various manipulations on $\mathcal{I}$. We give two examples in the next result.

Lemma 4.11 (sanity checks)

(Weakening): *Suppose* $\mathcal{I} \rhd P \xrightarrow{\mu} P'$. *Then* $\mathcal{I}_m <: \mathcal{I}$ *implies* $\mathcal{I}_m \rhd P \xrightarrow{\mu} P'$, *whenever* $\mathcal{I}_m \rhd P$ *is a configuration.*

(Fresh strengthening): *Suppose* $\mathcal{I}, n : \mathsf{D} \rhd P \xrightarrow{\mu} P'$, *where* n *does not occur in the action label* μ. *If* $\mathcal{I} \rhd P$ *is a configuration then* $\mathcal{I} \rhd P \xrightarrow{\mu} P'$.

Proof: Weakening is proved by derivation induction on $\mathcal{I} \rhd P \xrightarrow{\mu} P'$. The type environment is only used in two rules, (L-IN) and (L-OUT), where $\mathcal{I}_m$ can be used in place of $\mathcal{I}$. For example suppose the derivation is a result of an application of the rule (L-IN); that is $\mathcal{I} \rhd a?(X)\,R \xrightarrow{a?V} R\{\!|V/X|\!\}$ because $\mathcal{I}^w(a)\downarrow_{\mathsf{def}}$ and $\mathcal{I} \vdash V : \mathcal{I}^w(a)$. Since $\mathcal{I}_m <: \mathcal{I}$ this means that $\mathcal{I}_m^w(a)$ is also defined. Moreover the contra-variance of $\mathsf{w}\langle-\rangle$ means that $\mathcal{I}^w(a) <: \mathcal{I}_m^w(a)$ and by (weakening) in the type system, and (subsumption) we therefore have $\mathcal{I}_m \vdash V : \mathcal{I}_m^w(a)$. So we have established the two premises necessary to derive $\mathcal{I}_m \rhd a?(X)\,R \xrightarrow{a?V} R\{\!|V/X|\!\}$ via an application of (L-IN).

Fresh strengthening is a simple corollary of the previous result, Proposition 4.10. For if n does not appear in μ then one can show that $(\mathcal{I}, n : \mathsf{D})$ allows μ implies $\mathcal{I}$ allows μ. In the input case this inference relies on both (interchange) and (strengthening) for the typing system, Proposition 3.7 and Proposition 3.30. ■

4.1.2 Subject reduction

We would expect, in analogy with Theorem 3.31 for the reduction semantics, that internal moves preserve well-typing:

$$\Gamma \vdash P \text{ and } \mathcal{I} \rhd P \xrightarrow{\tau} P' \ \text{ implies } \ \Gamma \vdash P' \tag{4.9}$$

However, unlike the reduction semantics, internal moves are defined in terms of input and output actions and therefore we have to develop appropriate results on how these interact with well-typedness. Unfortunately, because the environments used to type processes in actions-in-context are implicit, the statement of these results is somewhat complex. Even worse these implicit environments play a limited role in the proof of (4.9). For although we know there is some $\Gamma_i <: \mathcal{I}$ such that $\Gamma_i \vdash P$, a priori there need be no relationship between the implicit Γ_i and the explicit Γ.

Theorem 4.12 (subject reduction) Suppose $\mathcal{I} \rhd P \xrightarrow{\mu} Q$ *and* $\Gamma \vdash P$.

- *If* μ *is* τ *then* $\Gamma \vdash Q$.
- *If* μ *is an output action then* $\Gamma^w(\mathsf{ch}(\mu)))\downarrow_{\mathsf{def}}$ *and* $(\Gamma \ \mathsf{after}\ \overline{\mu}) \vdash Q, \ \ V : \Gamma^w(a)$.
- *If* μ *is the input action then* $\Gamma^r(\mathsf{ch}(\mu))\downarrow_{\mathsf{def}}$ *and* $(\Gamma\ \mathsf{after}\ \mu) \vdash_{\mathbf{env}}$ *implies* $(\Gamma\ \mathsf{after}\ \overline{\mu}) \vdash Q$.

Proof: The proof is by induction on the derivation of the judgement

$$\mathcal{I} \rhd P \xrightarrow{\mu} P' \tag{4.10}$$

and analysis of the last rule used.

Suppose it is the axiom (L-IN). So the action is

$$\mathcal{I} \rhd a?(X)\,R \xrightarrow{a?V} \mathcal{I} \rhd R\{\!|^{V}\!/\!_{X}|\!\}$$

The typing rule (TY-IN) from Figure 3.10 gives some T_r such that $\Gamma \vdash a : \mathsf{r}\langle \mathsf{T}_r\rangle$ and $\Gamma, \langle X{:}\mathsf{T}_r\rangle \vdash R$; the former gives our first requirement, that $\Gamma^r(a)\downarrow_{\mathsf{def}}$.

Here $(\Gamma\ \mathsf{after}\ \overline{\mu})$ unravels to $\Gamma, \langle V{:}\Gamma^r(a)\rangle$ and so let us assume that this is a well-defined environment. Since $\Gamma^r(a) <: \mathsf{T}_r$ this means $(\Gamma\ \mathsf{after}\ \overline{\mu}) \vdash V : \mathsf{T}_r$. Then by (weakening) we have $\Gamma\ \mathsf{after}\ \overline{\mu}, \langle X{:}\mathsf{T}_r\rangle \vdash R$ and so the substitution result, Proposition 3.9 adapted to capability types, gives the required Γ after $\overline{\mu} \vdash R\{\!|^{V}\!/\!_{X}|\!\}$.

Suppose (L-OUT) is the last rule used in the derivation of (4.10). So the action is

$$\mathcal{I} \rhd a!\langle V\rangle \xrightarrow{a!V} \mathcal{I}, \ \langle V{:}\mathcal{I}^r(a)\rangle \rhd \mathsf{stop}$$

The typing rule (TY-OUT) from Figure 3.10 gives a type T_w such that $\Gamma \vdash a : \mathsf{w}\langle\mathsf{T}_w\rangle, \ V : \mathsf{T}_w$; again the first part implies $\Gamma^w(a)\downarrow_{\mathsf{def}}$. Here $(\Gamma\ \mathsf{after}\ \overline{\mu})$ is simply Γ and the contra-variance of $\mathsf{w}\langle - \rangle$, together with the second part of Proposition 3.26, therefore gives $(\Gamma\ \mathsf{after}\ \overline{\mu}) \vdash V : \Gamma^w(a)$, and we are finished, since trivially $(\Gamma\ \mathsf{after}\ \overline{\mu}) \vdash \mathsf{stop}$.

Suppose (4.10) is inferred using (L-COMM). Here we have

$$\mathcal{I} \triangleright P \mid Q \xrightarrow{\tau} \mathcal{I} \triangleright (\mathsf{new}\,\tilde{c} : \tilde{\mathsf{D}})(P' \mid Q')$$

because

$$\begin{aligned} \mathcal{I}_1 \triangleright P &\xrightarrow{(\tilde{c}:\tilde{\mathsf{D}}')a?V} \mathcal{I}_1' \triangleright P' \\ \text{and } \mathcal{I}_2 \triangleright Q &\xrightarrow{(\tilde{c}:\tilde{\mathsf{D}})a!V} \mathcal{I}_2' \triangleright Q' \end{aligned} \tag{4.11}$$

for some $\mathcal{I}_1$, $\mathcal{I}_2$. From $\Gamma \vdash P \mid Q$ we have to prove $\Gamma \vdash (\mathsf{new}\,\tilde{c} : \tilde{\mathsf{D}})(P' \mid Q')$; in fact we establish $\Gamma, \langle\tilde{c}{:}\tilde{\mathsf{D}}\rangle \vdash P' \mid Q'$.

We can apply induction to the input and output moves in (4.11) because our assumption means $\Gamma \vdash P$ and $\Gamma \vdash Q$. The output move gives

$$\Gamma \vdash a : \mathsf{w}\langle\Gamma^w(a)\rangle$$

$$\Gamma, \langle\tilde{c}{:}\mathsf{D}\rangle \vdash Q',\ V : \Gamma^w(a)$$

while the input move gives

$$\Gamma \vdash a : \mathsf{r}\langle\Gamma^r(a)\rangle$$

$$\Gamma,\ \langle V{:}\Gamma^r(a)\rangle \vdash P', \text{ provided } \Gamma,\ \langle V{:}\Gamma^r(a)\rangle \vdash \mathbf{env}$$

So it remains to show that $\Gamma, \langle\tilde{c}{:}\tilde{\mathsf{D}}\rangle \vdash P'$. Note that the fact that the types of the bound names in the input and output actions in (4.11) may be different has not hindered the progress of the proof.

By Proposition 3.26 we know that $\Gamma^w(a) <: \Gamma^r(a)$ and therefore that $\Gamma, \langle\tilde{c}{:}\mathsf{D}\rangle \vdash V : \Gamma^r(a)$; by Lemma 4.5 this is sufficient to ensure that $\Gamma,\ \langle V{:}\Gamma^r(a)\rangle$ is a well-defined environment. Moreover this means that $\Gamma, \langle\tilde{c}{:}\mathsf{D}\rangle <: \Gamma,\ \langle V{:}\Gamma^r(a)\rangle$ and the required typing of P' therefore follows by (weakening), Proposition 3.28.

The remaining axioms, (L-REC), (L-EQ) and (L-NEQ) are straightforward, as is the inductive case (L-CTXT). This leaves (L-OPEN) and (L-WEAK) to consider; we examine the latter and leave the former to the reader. So we have

$$\mathcal{I} \triangleright P \xrightarrow{(b:\mathsf{D}\tilde{c}:\tilde{\mathsf{D}})a?V} \mathcal{I}' \triangleright Q$$

because

$$\mathcal{I}, b : \mathsf{D} \triangleright P \xrightarrow{(\tilde{c}:\tilde{\mathsf{D}})a?V} \mathcal{I}' \triangleright Q \tag{4.12}$$

The inductive hypothesis applied to (4.12) gives the existence of $(\mathcal{I}, b : \mathsf{D})^r(a)$. But since a and b must be different this must coincide with $\mathcal{I}^r(a)$.

Now suppose $\Gamma,\ \langle V{:}\mathcal{I}^r(a)\rangle$ is a well-defined environment. Once more, since $\mathcal{I}^r(a)$ coincides with $(\mathcal{I}, b : \mathsf{D})^r(a)$, we can apply the inductive hypothesis to (4.12) to obtain the required $\Gamma,\ \langle V{:}\mathcal{I}^r(a)\rangle \vdash Q$. ■

Subject reduction will be a particularly useful tool when developing further properties of actions-in-context. Our first example is to show that these are actually defined over configurations.

Corollary 4.13 Suppose $\mathcal{I} \triangleright P$ is a configuration and $\mathcal{I} \triangleright P \xrightarrow{\mu} \mathcal{I}' \triangleright Q$. Then $\mathcal{I}' \triangleright Q$ is also a configuration.

Proof: We know that some Γ_i exists, with $\Gamma_i <: \mathcal{I}$, such that $\Gamma_i \vdash P$; and that $\mathcal{I}'$ is $(\mathcal{I}\ \mathsf{after}\ \mu)$. We must find a type environment $\Gamma_i' <: (\mathcal{I}\ \mathsf{after}\ \mu)$ such that $\Gamma_i' \vdash Q$. If μ is the internal action τ then the required Γ_i' is obviously Γ_i itself, from subject reduction. Otherwise it is $\Gamma_i, \langle \tilde{c}{:}\tilde{\mathsf{D}}\rangle$, where $(\tilde{c} : \tilde{\mathsf{D}})$ are the newly created names in μ.

To see this first suppose μ is the output action $(\tilde{c} : \tilde{\mathsf{D}})a!V$. Then subject reduction gives $(\Gamma_i\ \mathsf{after}\ \overline{\mu}) \vdash Q$, that is $\Gamma_i, \langle \tilde{c}{:}\tilde{\mathsf{D}}\rangle \vdash Q$, which is one of our requirements. We also have to show $\Gamma_i, \langle \tilde{c}{:}\tilde{\mathsf{D}}\rangle <: \mathcal{I}\ \mathsf{after}\ \mu$, that is $\Gamma_i, \langle \tilde{c}{:}\tilde{\mathsf{D}}\rangle <: \mathcal{I}, \langle V{:}\mathcal{I}^r(a)\rangle$.

From the fact that $\Gamma_i <: \mathcal{I}$ one can show that $\Gamma_i^w(a) <: \mathcal{I}^r(a)$. Moreover by subject reduction we also have $\Gamma_i, \langle \tilde{c}{:}\tilde{\mathsf{D}}\rangle \vdash V : \Gamma_i^w(a)$, which via (subsumption) gives $\Gamma_i, \langle \tilde{c}{:}\tilde{\mathsf{D}}\rangle \vdash V : \mathcal{I}^r(a)$. The required $\Gamma_i, \langle \tilde{c}{:}\tilde{\mathsf{D}}\rangle <: \mathcal{I}\ \mathsf{after}\ \mu$ now follows by an application of Lemma 4.5.

On the other hand if μ is the input label $(\tilde{c} : \tilde{\mathsf{D}})a?V$ then $(\mathcal{I}\ \mathsf{after}\ \mu)$ is $\mathcal{I}, \langle \tilde{c}{:}\tilde{\mathsf{D}}\rangle$ and obviously $\Gamma_i, \langle \tilde{c}{:}\tilde{\mathsf{D}}\rangle <: \mathcal{I}, \langle \tilde{c}{:}\tilde{\mathsf{D}}\rangle$. But we have to establish

$$\Gamma_i, \langle \tilde{c}{:}\tilde{\mathsf{D}}\rangle \vdash Q \tag{4.13}$$

To do so we use the fact that $\mathcal{I}\ \mathsf{allows}\ \mu$ is well-defined, which unravels to $\mathcal{I}, \langle \tilde{c}{:}\tilde{\mathsf{D}}\rangle \vdash V : \mathcal{I}^w(a)$. Since $\mathcal{I}^w(a) <: \Gamma^w(a) <: \Gamma^r(a)$, and $\Gamma_i <: \mathcal{I}$ this means $\Gamma_i, \langle \tilde{c}{:}\tilde{\mathsf{D}}\rangle \vdash V : \Gamma_i^r(a)$. This is enough to ensure that $\Gamma_i \mathsf{after} \overline{\mu} \vdash \mathbf{env}$, and therefore by subject reduction, that $\Gamma_i\ \mathsf{after}\ \overline{\mu} \vdash Q$. Since $\Gamma_i, \langle \tilde{c}{:}\tilde{\mathsf{D}}\rangle <: (\Gamma_i\ \mathsf{after}\ \overline{\mu})$ (weakening) gives the required (4.13). ■

4.1.3 Relation with reduction semantics

Let us now check that the notion of internal movement engendered by actions-in-context coincides, more or less, with the reduction semantics of TYPED API; we need a typed version of Corollary 2.16. As in Section 2.3 we tackle this incrementally; indeed the arguments we use are only typed versions of those employed in that section. But first we need some more auxiliary results about the use of knowledge in actions-in-context.

Let us first show that actions-in-context are preserved by structural equivalence.

Proposition 4.14 In TYPED API *suppose $P \equiv Q$ and $\mathcal{I} \triangleright P \xrightarrow{\mu} P'$. Then there is some Q' such that $P' \equiv Q'$ and $\mathcal{I} \triangleright Q \xrightarrow{\mu} Q'$.*

Proof: This is a generalisation of Lemma 2.13 and the proof is an equally tedious argument by induction on the proof that $P \equiv Q$. The inductive cases are straightforward, as are most of the axioms; the only difficulty is the axiom (S-EXTR), when P, Q have the form $(\mathsf{new}\, n : \mathsf{D})(P_1 \mid P_2)$, $P_1 \mid (\mathsf{new}\, n : \mathsf{D})\, P_2$ respectively, or visa-versa, and n is not free in P_1. As an example let us outline how an action-in-context

$$\mathcal{I} \triangleright P_1 \mid (\mathsf{new}\, n : \mathsf{D})\, P_2 \xrightarrow{\mu} R$$

can be matched by a corresponding action from $(\mathsf{new}\, n : \mathsf{D})(P_1 \mid P_2)$.

One possibility is that P_1 is responsible for the move, that is it has the form

$$\mathcal{I} \triangleright P_1 \mid (\mathsf{new}\, n : \mathsf{D})\, P_2 \xrightarrow{\mu} \triangleright P_1' \mid (\mathsf{new}\, n : \mathsf{D})\, P_2$$

because $\mathcal{I} \triangleright P_1 \xrightarrow{\mu} P_1'$. In this case we know that n cannot appear in μ and therefore the required matching move is

$$\mathcal{I} \triangleright (\mathsf{new}\, n : \mathsf{D})(P_1 \mid P_2) \xrightarrow{\mu} (\mathsf{new}\, n : \mathsf{D})(P_1' \mid P_2)$$

which can be inferred from (L-CXT).

The second possibility is that $(\mathsf{new}\, n : \mathsf{D})\, P_2$ is responsible for the move. Here the argument is equally straightforward, although it depends on whether n appears in the label μ.

The final possibility is that μ is the internal label τ and the move is a communication between P_1 and $(\mathsf{new}\, n : \mathsf{D})\, P_2$. Here again there are two cases, when a value is sent by P_1 or received by P_1. Let us consider the latter, which is the more interesting. So the move is of the form

$$\mathcal{I} \triangleright P_1 \mid (\mathsf{new}\, n : \mathsf{D})\, P_2 \xrightarrow{\tau} (\mathsf{new}\, \tilde{c} : \tilde{\mathsf{D}})(P_1' \mid P_2')$$

because

$$\mathcal{I}_1 \triangleright P_1 \xrightarrow{\alpha_i} P_1'$$
$$\mathcal{I}_2 \triangleright (\mathsf{new}\, n : \mathsf{D})(P_2) \xrightarrow{\alpha_o} P_2'$$

for some environments $\mathcal{I}_1, \mathcal{I}_2$; moreover we can assume α_o is an output label, $(\tilde{c} : \tilde{\mathsf{D}})a!V$, and therefore α_i is some corresponding input label.

There are now two cases, depending on whether n is exported in α_o. If it is then let us suppose $(\tilde{c} : \tilde{\mathsf{D}})$ has the form $(n : \mathsf{D})(\tilde{d} : \tilde{\mathsf{D}}')$, α_o has the form $(n : \mathsf{D})\beta_o$ and the output move must have been inferred by (L-OPEN); the more general case is treated in a similar manner. So we must have

$$\mathcal{I}_2 \triangleright P_2 \xrightarrow{\beta_o} P_2' \tag{4.14}$$

The corresponding input label has the form $(n : \mathsf{D}')\beta_i$ and the input move must have been inferred by the rule (L-WEAK). So we have

$$\mathcal{I}_1, n : \mathsf{D}' \triangleright P_1 \xrightarrow{\beta_i} P_1'$$

The rule (L-COMM) can therefore be applied to give

$$\mathcal{I} \triangleright P_1 \mid P_2 \xrightarrow{\tau} (\mathsf{new}\,\tilde{d} : \tilde{\mathsf{D}}')(P_1' \mid P_2')$$

Then an application of (L-CTXT), gives the required matching move

$$\mathcal{I} \triangleright (\mathsf{new}\,n : \mathsf{D})(P_1 \mid P_2) \xrightarrow{\tau} (\mathsf{new}\,\tilde{c} : \tilde{\mathsf{D}})(P_1' \mid P_2')$$

The second case, when n is not exported in α_o is much more straightforward; P_2' must have the form $(\mathsf{new}\,n : \mathsf{D})\, P_2''$ and the output move must have been inferred using (L-CTXT) from

$$\mathcal{I}_2 \triangleright P_2 \xrightarrow{\alpha_o} P_2''$$

The required matching move may therefore be found by applying (L-COM) to this move and the corresponding input rule above, followed by an application of the second part of (L-CTXT). ■

From this it is straightforward to show that reductions can be captured, up to structural equivalence, by actions-in-context.

Corollary 4.15 Suppose $\mathcal{I} \triangleright P$ *is a configuration and* $P \longrightarrow Q$. *Then* $\mathcal{I} \triangleright P \xrightarrow{\tau} Q'$ *for some* $Q' \equiv Q$.

Proof: By induction on the inference of $P \longrightarrow Q$. The inductive case, when (R-STRUCT) is used, is catered for by the previous lemma and the only interesting axiom is (R-COMM):

$$c!\langle V\rangle \mid c?(X)\, R \longrightarrow R\{\!|{}^{V}\!/\!{}_{X}|\!\}$$

Since $\mathcal{I} \triangleright c!\langle V\rangle \mid c?(X)\, R$ is a configuration we know that there is some environment Γ_i compatible with $\mathcal{I}$ such that $\Gamma_i \vdash c!\langle V\rangle \mid c?(X)\, R$. This type judgement provides enough information to establish the premises to applications of the rules (L-OUT) and (L-IN) from Figure 4.1, to conclude ensure that

$$\Gamma_i \triangleright c!\langle V\rangle \xrightarrow{c!V} \mathsf{stop}$$
$$\Gamma_i \triangleright c?(X)\, R \xrightarrow{c?V} R\{\!|{}^{V}\!/\!{}_{X}|\!\}$$

respectively. An application of (L-COMM) from Figure 4.2 then gives the required

$$\mathcal{I} \triangleright c!\langle V\rangle \mid c?(X)\, R \xrightarrow{\tau} \mathsf{stop} \mid R\{\!|{}^{V}\!/\!{}_{X}|\!\}$$

■

The converse result requires, as in Proposition 2.15, an analysis of precise syntactic structure of actions-in-context.

Proposition 4.16 In TYPED API*:*

- *if* $\mathcal{I} \triangleright P \xrightarrow{(\tilde{c}:\tilde{\mathsf{D}})a!\langle V\rangle} Q$ *then P is structurally equivalent to* $(\mathsf{new}\,\tilde{c} : \tilde{\mathsf{D}})(a!\langle V\rangle \mid Q)$
- *if* $\mathcal{I} \triangleright P \xrightarrow{(\tilde{c}:\tilde{\mathsf{D}})a?V} Q$ *then P is structurally equivalent to a term of the form* $(\mathsf{new}\,\tilde{n} : \tilde{\mathsf{D}}')(P' \mid a?(X)\,R)$*, where no* n_i *appear in* V*, and* Q *is structurally equivalent to* $(\mathsf{new}\,\tilde{n} : \tilde{\mathsf{D}})(P' \mid R\{\!|^{V}/_{X}|\!\})$
- $\mathcal{I} \triangleright P \xrightarrow{\tau} \mathcal{I} \triangleright Q$ *implies* $P \longrightarrow Q$.

Proof: A straightforward proof by induction on the derivation of the actions-in-context; the details are very similar to the proof of the corresponding result in the untyped case, Proposition 2.15. ■

Putting these two results together we get the natural generalisation of Corollary 2.16 to the typed case.

Corollary 4.17 Suppose $\mathcal{I} \triangleright P$ *is a configuration. Then* $P \longrightarrow Q$ *if and only if* $\mathcal{I} \triangleright P \xrightarrow{\tau} Q'$ *for some* Q' *such that* $Q \equiv Q'$. ■

4.2 Typed bisimulation equivalence

We have now in place all the requirements to define an lts for TYPED API, and thereby induce a version of bisimulation equivalence. However there is a problem; the actions-in-context of the previous section induce an equivalence that is much too intensional to capture any reasonable adaptation of the touchstone equivalence $\cong$ to a typed setting.

Example 4.18 Let P, Q denote the processes

$$(\mathsf{new}\,n : \mathsf{rw})\,(\mathsf{new}\,m : \mathsf{rw})\,a!\langle m, n\rangle \qquad (\mathsf{new}\,m : \mathsf{w})\,(\mathsf{new}\,n : \mathsf{r})\,a!\langle m, n\rangle$$

respectively. Assuming some $\mathcal{I}_a$ that knows about the channel a at the type $\mathsf{rw}\langle(\mathsf{w}, \mathsf{r})\rangle$, the configurations $\mathcal{I}_a \triangleright P$ and $\mathcal{I}_a \triangleright Q$ can perform different output actions, labelled

$$(n : \mathsf{rw}, m : \mathsf{rw})a!(m, n) \qquad (m : \mathsf{w}, n : \mathsf{r})a!(m, n)$$

respectively. So a bisimulation equivalence based on these actions would distinguish them.

However one can argue that no reasonable observer, constrained by the type environment $\mathcal{I}$, would be able to distinguish between these two processes. Both deliver a new name on the channel a, and that is it. So although we have not yet reformulated $\cong$ to take types into account, any reasonable formulation would result in P and Q being considered indistinguishable. ■

Basically the output actions, labelled with the declaration types of new channels, are much too intensional.

4.2.1 The definition

First let us define a slightly more abstract version of the output actions-in-context.

Definition 4.19 (*untyped output actions-in-context*) For any *set* of names $\{\tilde{c}\}$ we write

$$\mathcal{I} \triangleright P \xrightarrow{(\tilde{c})a!V} \mathcal{I}' \triangleright Q$$

if there is some collection of types $(\tilde{\mathsf{D}})$ such that $\mathcal{I} \triangleright P \xrightarrow{(\tilde{c}:\tilde{\mathsf{D}})a!V} \mathcal{I}' \triangleright Q$. As with all action labels we make no distinction between the order in the bound names $(\tilde{c})$. ♦

Note that the various properties of actions-in-context developed in the previous section still apply to these less intensional actions. For example the definition of action residuals, Definition 4.6, still applies; if μ is an output action label then $(\mathcal{I}\ \mathsf{after}\ \mu)$ is independent of any types occurring in μ. Formally let $\mathsf{un}(\mu)$ denote the function that leaves the label μ untouched unless it is an output label, in which case it removes the type information. Furthermore we write $\mu \sim \mu'$ to mean $\mathsf{un}(\mu) = \mathsf{un}(\mu')$, that is μ and μ' are the same labels, except possibly for the types at which new names are exported. Then

$$\mu \sim \mu' \ \text{ implies } \ (\mathcal{I}\ \mathsf{after}\ \mu) = (\mathcal{I}\ \mathsf{after}\ \mu)$$
$$(\mathcal{I}\ \mathsf{allows}\ \ \mu) \ \text{ if and only if } \ (\mathcal{I}\ \mathsf{allows}\ \ \mu')$$

Similarly with the predicate $\mathcal{I}$ allows μ, Definition 4.9; so the determinacy of the change in the environment, Proposition 4.7, remains true when applied to these actions. However applications of subject reduction, Theorem 4.12, require knowledge of the types at which new names are exported. Indeed the main reason for recording these was to allow us to formulate correctly the actions-in-context; the rule (L-COMM) makes essential use of them.

Definition 4.20 (*lts for* TYPED API) This is defined as follows:

- the states consist of configurations $\mathcal{I} \triangleright P$
- the next state relations are the judgements of the form $\mathcal{I} \triangleright P \xrightarrow{\mu} \mathcal{I} \triangleright Q$, where μ can take the form
  - τ, for internal actions
  - $(\tilde{c} : \tilde{\mathsf{D}})a?V$, for input actions
  - $(\tilde{c})a!V$, for output actions.

We let $\approx_{bis}$ denote the standard bisimulation equivalence in the resulting lts; thus this is now a relation between *configurations*, rather than, as in Chapter 2, between processes. ♦

Example 4.21 Let us revisit Example 4.1 and the two processes

$$P_1 \Leftarrow (\text{new}\, c : \text{rw})(a!\langle c\rangle \mid c?P')$$

$$P_2 \Leftarrow (\text{new}\, c : \text{rw})(a!\langle c\rangle \mid \text{stop})$$

As in the previous example, let $\mathcal{I}_a$ denote some type environment in which $\mathcal{I}_a(a) = \text{rw}\langle \text{r}\rangle$, and let us assume that $\mathcal{I}_a \triangleright P_1$ and $\mathcal{I}_a \triangleright P_2$ are both configurations. To show

$$\mathcal{I}_a \triangleright P_1 \quad \approx_{bis} \mathcal{I}_a \triangleright P_2$$

we need to exhibit a bisimulation $\mathcal{R}$ containing the pair $\langle \mathcal{I}_a \triangleright P_1,\ \mathcal{I}_a \triangleright P_2\rangle$.

Let P_1', P_2' denote the processes $(\text{stop} \mid c?P')$, $(\text{stop} \mid \text{stop})$ respectively and $\mathcal{I}_{ac}$ denote the type environment $\mathcal{I}_a, c : \text{r}$. Then the required $\mathcal{R}$ consists of

$$\mathcal{I}_a \triangleright P_1 \leftrightarrow \mathcal{I}_a \triangleright P_2$$

$$\mathcal{I}_{ac} \triangleright P_1' \leftrightarrow \mathcal{I}_{ac} \triangleright P_2'$$

This is easy to check as the only actions-in-context that can be performed by these configurations are

$$\mathcal{I}_a \triangleright P_1 \xrightarrow{(c)a!c} \mathcal{I}_{ac} \triangleright P_1'$$

$$\mathcal{I}_a \triangleright P_2 \xrightarrow{(c)a!c} \mathcal{I}_{ac} \triangleright P_2'$$

■

Although in principle a bisimulation $\mathcal{R}$ may relate arbitrary configurations we will only ever use them to relate configurations with identical knowledge environments. A convenient way of specifying such restricted bisimulations is by defining a *family* of relations $\underline{\mathcal{R}}$ over processes, parameterised by type environments $\mathcal{I}$, with the property that whenever $\langle P, Q\rangle \in \mathcal{R}_{\mathcal{I}}$ then both $\mathcal{I} \triangleright P$ and $\mathcal{I} \triangleright Q$ are configurations. In this formulation we use the more suggestive notation

$$\mathcal{I} \models P \,\mathcal{R}\, Q \tag{4.15}$$

to denote the fact that $P\ \mathcal{R}_{\mathcal{I}}\ Q$, for a particular environment $\mathcal{I}$.

Because of Proposition 4.7, the transfer property for bisimulations then amounts to demanding that whenever (4.15) above holds then every action-in-context

$$\mathcal{I} \triangleright P \xrightarrow{\mu} P'$$

must be matched by an action

$$\mathcal{I} \triangleright Q \stackrel{\hat{\mu}'}{\Longrightarrow} Q' \tag{4.16}$$

for some Q' and μ', such that $\mu \sim \mu'$ and

$$(\mathcal{I} \text{ after } \mu) \models P' \mathcal{R} Q'$$

If we can show that each individual relation $\mathcal{R}_{\mathcal{I}}$ in the family, and its inverse, has this parameterised transfer property, then we know from (4.15) that $\mathcal{I} \triangleright P \approx_{bis} \mathcal{I} \triangleright Q$; continuing with our more suggestive notation we will write this as

$$\mathcal{I} \models P \approx_{bis} Q$$

It is worth emphasising that such a statement automatically means $\mathcal{I} \triangleright P$ and $\mathcal{I} \triangleright Q$ are both valid configurations.

This view of bisimulation relations also emphasises that many of the standard techniques can also be applied in this parameterised setting. For example, now viewing a bisimulation as a family of relations of the form (4.15) above, it is straightforward to check that each individual component is an equivalence relation over processes. Moreover, because of Proposition 4.14, in the transfer property it is sufficient to find a Q' as in (4.16) above, but satisfying the weaker condition that

$$(\mathcal{I} \text{ after } \mu) \models P' \mathcal{R} Q''$$

for some Q'' structurally equivalent to Q'. In other words the technique of *bisimulation equivalence up to structural equivalence*, given in Definition 2.18, generalises smoothly to the typed case. We refrain from spelling out the details; instead see Question 8 at the end of the chapter. But the technique will be used in some proofs, such as that of Proposition 4.24 below.

We finish this section with a brief look at the role of the knowledge environment $\mathcal{I}$, this time in the judgements

$$\mathcal{I} \models P \approx_{bis} Q \tag{4.17}$$

Our results will largely depend on the (sanity checks) in Lemma 4.11. One would not expect this relation to be preserved by *increasing* the environment's knowledge $\mathcal{I}$. That is if $\mathcal{I}_m <: \mathcal{I}$ then one would not expect (4.17) to imply $\mathcal{I}_m \models P \approx_{bis} Q$. Example 4.21 provides an instance. With $\mathcal{I}_a(a) = \mathsf{rw}\langle \mathsf{r} \rangle$ we have

$$\mathcal{I}_a \models (\mathsf{new}\, c : \mathsf{rw})(a!\langle c\rangle \mid c?P') \approx_{bis} (\mathsf{new}\, c : \mathsf{rw})(a!\langle c\rangle \mid \mathsf{stop})$$

but if the knowledge is increased to $\mathcal{I}_m <: \mathcal{I}_a$, with $\mathcal{I}_m(a) = \mathsf{rw}\langle \mathsf{rw} \rangle$, we have

$$\mathcal{I}_m \models (\mathsf{new}\, c : \mathsf{rw})(a!\langle c\rangle \mid c?P') \not\approx_{bis} (\mathsf{new}\, c : \mathsf{rw})(a!\langle c\rangle \mid \mathsf{stop})$$

It is more reasonable to expect that *restricting* the environments knowledge does not affect the equivalence of processes.

Proposition 4.22 (strengthening for bisimulation equivalence) Suppose $\mathcal{I} <: \mathcal{I}_l$. *Then* $\mathcal{I} \models P \approx_{bis} Q$ *implies* $\mathcal{I}_l \models P \approx_{bis} Q$.

Proof: Let the family $\underline{\mathcal{R}}$ be defined by letting

$$\mathcal{I} \models P \mathcal{R} Q$$

whenever $\mathcal{I}_m \models P \approx_{bis} Q$ for some $\mathcal{I}_m <: \mathcal{I}$. We show that this is a bisimulation; note that we are assured both $\mathcal{I} \triangleright P$ and $\mathcal{I} \triangleright Q$ are both configurations.

Suppose $\mathcal{I} \models P \mathcal{R} Q$ and $\mathcal{I} \triangleright P \xrightarrow{\mu} P'$. We must find a matching action-in-context, $\mathcal{I} \triangleright Q \stackrel{\hat{\mu}'}{\Longrightarrow} Q'$, where $\mu \sim \mu'$ such that $(\mathcal{I}\ \mathsf{after}\ \mu) \models P' \mathcal{R}\, Q'$.

Since $\mathcal{I} \models P \mathcal{R} Q$ we know $\mathcal{I}_m \models P \approx_{bis} Q$ for some $\mathcal{I}_m <: \mathcal{I}$. Moreover (weakening) from Lemma 4.11 gives the action-in-context $\mathcal{I}_m \triangleright P \xrightarrow{\mu} P'$. So there is a matching action-in-context

$$\mathcal{I}_m \triangleright Q \stackrel{\hat{\mu}'}{\Longrightarrow} Q' \qquad (4.18)$$

such that $\mathcal{I}_m\ \mathsf{after}\ \mu \models P' \approx_{bis} Q'$.

The existence of $(\mathcal{I}_m\ \mathsf{after}\ \mu)$ also ensures that $(\mathcal{I}\ \mathsf{after}\ \mu)$ is well-defined, and moreover $(\mathcal{I}_m\ \mathsf{after}\ \mu) <: (\mathcal{I}\ \mathsf{after}\ \mu)$; see Question 4 at the end of the chapter. In other words $\mathcal{I}\ \mathsf{after}\ \mu \models P' \mathcal{R}\, Q'$. Finally the existence of $\mathcal{I} \triangleright P \xrightarrow{\mu} P'$ means that $(\mathcal{I}\ \mathsf{allows}\ \mu')$ and therefore the second part of Proposition 4.10 can be applied to (4.18), to obtain the required matching move with the restricted environment $\mathcal{I} \triangleright Q \stackrel{\hat{\mu}'}{\Longrightarrow} Q'$. ■

An obvious consequence of this result is that rearranging the knowledge $\mathcal{I}$ to an equivalent environment $\mathcal{I}'$ has no effect on equivalences; that is $\mathcal{I} \models P \approx_{bis} Q$ and $\mathcal{I} \equiv \mathcal{I}'$ implies $\mathcal{I}' \models P \approx_{bis} Q$.

There is a partial converse to this (strengthening) result; the environment's knowledge can be increased by inventing new names, without affecting the equivalences.

Proposition 4.23 (fresh weakening for bisimulation equivalence) Let n be fresh to $\mathcal{I}$, P, Q. *Then* $\mathcal{I} \models P \approx_{bis} Q$ *implies* $\mathcal{I}, n : \mathsf{C} \models P \approx_{bis} Q$.

Proof: Let the family of relations $\underline{\mathcal{R}}$ be defined by letting

$$\mathcal{I} \models P \mathcal{R} Q$$

if $\mathcal{I} \equiv \mathcal{I}_1, n : \mathsf{C}$, for some n fresh to $\mathcal{I}_1, P$ and Q, where $\mathcal{I}_1 \models P \approx_{bis} Q$. We show that this family of relations generates a bisimulation.

Suppose $\mathcal{I} \models P \mathcal{R} Q$ and

$$\mathcal{I} \triangleright P \xrightarrow{\mu} P' \qquad (4.19)$$

We must find a corresponding action-in-context

$$\mathcal{I} \triangleright Q \overset{\hat{\mu}'}{\Longrightarrow} Q'$$

where $\mu \sim \mu'$, such that $(\mathcal{I} \text{ after } \mu) \models P' \mathcal{R} Q'$.

By the definition of $\mathcal{R}$ we know that $\mathcal{I} \equiv \mathcal{I}_1, n : \mathsf{C}$ and $\mathcal{I}_1 \models P \approx_{bis} Q$. Since n cannot appear in the label μ, (fresh strengthening) from Lemma 4.11 can be applied to (4.19) to give the action-in-context $\mathcal{I}_1 \triangleright P \xrightarrow{\mu} P'$, which we can therefore match with $\mathcal{I}_1 \triangleright Q \overset{\hat{\mu}'}{\Longrightarrow} Q'$ such that $(\mathcal{I}_1 \text{ after } \mu) \models P' \approx_{bis} Q'$.

(Weakening), again from Lemma 4.11, transforms this action into $\mathcal{I} \triangleright Q \overset{\hat{\mu}'}{\Longrightarrow} Q'$, which is the required corresponding move to (4.19) above. For

$$(\mathcal{I} \text{ after } \mu) \models P' \mathcal{R} Q' \tag{4.20}$$

follows because one can calculate that $(\mathcal{I} \text{after} \mu) \equiv (\mathcal{I}_1 \text{after} \mu), n : \mathsf{C}$. For example if μ is the output action $(\tilde{c} : \tilde{C})a!V$ then $(\mathcal{I} \text{ after } \mu) \equiv (\mathcal{I}_1, n : \mathsf{C}),\ \langle V{:}\mathcal{I}^r(a)\rangle$. But because of the freshness of n, $\mathcal{I}^r(a)$ coincides with $\mathcal{I}_1^r(a)$, and so this latter environment is equivalent to $(\mathcal{I}_1,\ \langle V{:}\mathcal{I}_1^r(a)\rangle),\ n : \mathsf{C}$, that is $(\mathcal{I}_1 \text{ after } \mu), n : \mathsf{C}$. ■

4.2.2 Compositionality

We wish to establish the compositionality principle (4.3) for bisimulation equivalence:

$$\text{from } \Gamma \vdash Q \text{ and } \Gamma \models P_1 \approx_{bis} P_2 \text{ it follows that } \Gamma \models P_1 \mid Q \approx_{bis} P_2 \mid Q \tag{4.21}$$

The idea is to mimic the proof of the corresponding result in the untyped setting, Proposition 2.21. There we needed the ability to decompose an internal action from the compound process $P \mid Q$ into the contributions from the individual processes P and Q, and conversely, the ability to compose appropriate contributions from P and Q back into an internal action from $P \mid Q$. For untyped actions this more or less follows by the inductive definition of $\xrightarrow{\tau}$ but here we have to deal with the more subtle actions-in-context; in particular with the presence of changing environments when internal actions are decomposed and subsequently recomposed.

Before embarking on the proof it is worthwhile considering in some detail the reason why the straightforward approach used in Proposition 2.21 does not work. Using this we would define the least family of relations $\underline{\mathcal{R}}$ satisfying

(i) $\mathcal{I} \models P_1 \approx_{bis} P_2$ implies $\mathcal{I} \models P_1 \mathcal{R} P_2$
(ii) $\mathcal{I} \models P_1 \mathcal{R} P_2$ implies $\mathcal{I} \models P_1 \mid Q \ \mathcal{R}\ P_2 \mid Q$ whenever $\mathcal{I} \vdash Q$
(iii) $\mathcal{I}, n : \mathsf{D} \models P_1 \mathcal{R} P_2$ implies $\mathcal{I} \models (\mathsf{new}\, n : \mathsf{D})\, P_1 \mathcal{R}\, (\mathsf{new}\, n : \mathsf{D})\, P_2$
(iv) $\mathcal{I} \models P_1 \mathcal{R} P_2$ and n fresh to $\mathcal{I}$ implies $\mathcal{I}, n : \mathsf{D} \models P_1 \mathcal{R} P_2$

and show that the result generates a bisimulation. There are at least two problems here.

The first is exemplified by Example 4.18. We will never be able to show that

$$\mathcal{I}_a \models (\mathsf{new}\, n : \mathsf{rw})\, a!\langle n\rangle \;\; \mathcal{R} \;\; (\mathsf{new}\, n : \mathsf{r})\, a!\langle n\rangle \tag{4.22}$$

The third clause in the definition of $\underline{\mathcal{R}}$ only allows the same binding to be applied to related processes. Although (4.22) is not a direct instance of the compositionality principle it will arise in an analysis of the case when Q, in (4.21) above, is $b?(x)\, a!\langle x\rangle$ and $P_1,\ P_2$ are $(\mathsf{new}\, n : \mathsf{rw})\, b!\langle n\rangle,\ (\mathsf{new}\, n : \mathsf{r})\, b!\langle n\rangle$ respectively.

An even worse inadequacy is seen by reconsidering Example 4.21. Referring to the definitions there we will never be able to establish

$$\mathcal{I}_a \models (\mathsf{new}\, c : \mathsf{rw})(a!\langle c\rangle \mid c?P') \;\; \mathcal{R} \;\; (\mathsf{new}\, c : \mathsf{rw})(a!\langle c\rangle \mid \mathsf{stop}) \tag{4.23}$$

This could only be inferred from

$$\mathcal{I}_a, c : \mathsf{rw} \models a!\langle c\rangle \mid c?P' \;\; \mathcal{R} \;\; a!\langle c\rangle \mid \mathsf{stop}$$

that would require

$$\mathcal{I}_a, c : \mathsf{rw} \models c?P' \;\; \mathcal{R} \;\; \mathsf{stop}$$

that will not follow from the proposed definition of $\mathcal{R}$. Again (4.23) above is not a direct instance of the compositionality principle, but it will arise, for example, when analysing the case when Q is $(\mathsf{new}\, c : \mathsf{rw})\, b!\langle c\rangle$ and $P_1,\ P_2$ are $b?(x)\,(a!\langle x\rangle \mid x?P'),\ \ b?(x)\,(a!\langle x\rangle \mid \mathsf{stop})$ respectively.

The definition of $\underline{\mathcal{R}}$ needs to be more sophisticated; in particular we need a more general form of the condition (iii) above, which will allow us to close related processes using scoped names with different declaration types.

Proposition 4.24 (compositionality) Suppose $\mathcal{I} \vdash Q$. *Then* $\mathcal{I} \models P_1 \approx_{bis} P_2$ *implies* $\mathcal{I} \models P_1 \mid Q \approx_{bis} P_2 \mid Q$.

Proof: In this proof, for convenience, we will not distinguish between sequences of bindings, $(\tilde{c}{:}\tilde{\mathsf{C}})$ and type environments, allowing meta-variables for the latter to appear in process terms.

Let $\underline{\mathcal{R}}$ be the family of relations defined by

$$\mathcal{I} \models (\mathsf{new}\, \Delta_0)(P_1 \mid Q) \;\; \mathcal{R} \;\; (\mathsf{new}\, \Delta_0')(P_2 \mid Q)$$

whenever there exist type associations $\mathcal{I}_0,\ \Delta,\ \Delta'$ such that

- $\mathcal{I}$ is compatible with both Δ and Δ'
- $\mathcal{I},\ \mathcal{I}_0$ is compatible with both Δ, Δ_0 and Δ', Δ_0'
- $\Delta, \Delta_0 \vdash P_1$ and $\Delta', \Delta_0' \vdash P_2$
- $\mathcal{I}, \mathcal{I}_0 \models P_1 \approx_{bis} P_2$ and $\mathcal{I}, \mathcal{I}_0 \vdash Q$.

We show that $\underline{\mathcal{R}}$ generates a bisimulation, up to structural equivalence, from which the result will follow.

Note that (4.22) and (4.23) are accommodated within this definition, at least up to structural equivalence. For example in the former case we can have

$$\mathcal{I}_a \models (\mathsf{new}\, n : \mathsf{rw})(a!\langle n\rangle \mid \mathsf{stop}) \quad \mathcal{R} \quad (\mathsf{new}\, n : \mathsf{r})(a!\langle n\rangle \mid \mathsf{stop})$$

because $\mathcal{I}_a, n : \mathsf{r} \models a!\langle n\rangle \approx_{bis} a!\langle n\rangle$.

Since each relation $\mathcal{R}_{\mathcal{I}}$ is symmetric it is sufficient to show how each action-in-context from the left-hand side

$$\mathcal{I} \triangleright (\mathsf{new}\,\Delta_0)(P_1 \mid Q) \xrightarrow{\mu} T \tag{4.24}$$

can be matched, up to structural induction, by one from the right-hand side. First consider the case when this is an external action, say an output $(\tilde{c} : \tilde{\mathsf{D}})a!V$; the case of input is similar but more straightforward. This action must be the responsibility of either P_1 or Q, and again we look at the more complicated case, the former. So (4.24) must take the form

$$\mathcal{I} \triangleright (\mathsf{new}\,\Delta_0)(P_1 \mid Q) \xrightarrow{\mu} (\mathsf{new}\,\Delta_l)(P_1' \mid Q)$$

In turn this must be derived using a sequence of applications of (L-OPEN) or the second part of (L-CTXT), from Figure 4.1, and one application of the first part of (L-CTXT), to

$$\mathcal{I} \triangleright P_1 \xrightarrow{\alpha} P_1' \tag{4.25}$$

Here the label α is obtained from μ by stripping off any binding $(n : \mathsf{D})$ used in an application of (L-OPEN). (In the input case, only (L-CTXT) is used and α coincides with μ.) We may apply (weakening) from Lemma 4.11 to this action, to obtain

$$\mathcal{I},\ \mathcal{I}_0 \triangleright P_1 \xrightarrow{\alpha} P_1' \tag{4.26}$$

Now using the hypothesis

$$\mathcal{I}, \mathcal{I}_0 \models P_1 \approx_{bis} P_2$$

we obtain a matching action-in-context

$$\mathcal{I}, \mathcal{I}_0 \triangleright P_2 \stackrel{\widehat{\alpha'}}{\Longrightarrow} P_2' \tag{4.27}$$

such that

$$(\mathcal{I}, \mathcal{I}_0)\ \mathsf{after}\ \alpha \models P_1' \approx_{bis} P_2'$$

Furthermore from (4.25) we know $\mathcal{I}$ allows α', and so Proposition 4.10 enables us to obtain

$$\mathcal{I} \triangleright P_2 \stackrel{\widehat{\alpha'}}{\Longrightarrow} P_2' \tag{4.28}$$

from which we can reconstruct

$$\mathcal{I} \triangleright (\mathsf{new}\,\Delta_0')(P_2 \mid Q) \stackrel{\widehat{\mu'}}{\Longrightarrow} (\mathsf{new}\,\Delta_r)(P_2' \mid Q)$$

This reconstruction uses the same sequence of applications of the rules (L-OPEN) and (L-CTXT) as used in the inference of the original move (4.24) from (4.25).

To prove that this is the required move to match (4.24), we have to establish

$$(\mathcal{I}\ \mathsf{after}\ \mu) \models (\mathsf{new}\,\Delta_l)(P_1' \mid Q)\ \ \mathcal{R}\ \ (\mathsf{new}\,\Delta_r)(P_2' \mid Q)$$

However this is easily achieved; $(\mathcal{I}\ \mathsf{after}\ \mu)$ unravels to $\mathcal{I}, \langle V{:}\mathcal{I}^r(a)\rangle$, which is equivalent to an environment of the form $(\mathcal{I}\ \mathsf{after}\ \mu), \mathcal{I}_0'$, where $\mathcal{I}_0'$ is an extension of $\mathcal{I}_0$. So the type associations required in the definition of $\mathcal{R}$ are $\mathcal{I}_0'$, and $(\Delta, \langle\tilde{c}{:}\tilde{\mathsf{D}}\rangle)$, $(\Delta', \langle\tilde{c}{:}\tilde{\mathsf{D}}'\rangle)$ where $(\tilde{\mathsf{D}}')$ are the declaration types of the exported names in the matching action μ'; subject reduction, Theorem 4.12, is useful when checking this.

Now consider the case when the action-in-context we are trying to match, (4.24) is internal. So it must take the form

$$\mathcal{I} \triangleright (\mathsf{new}\,\Delta_0)(P_1 \mid Q) \stackrel{\tau}{\longrightarrow} (\mathsf{new}\,\Delta_0, \Delta_1)(P_1' \mid Q') \tag{4.29}$$

If this derives from either Q or P_1 then we can proceed as before. So let us assume that it is the result of some communication between Q and P_1; in other words (4.29) is derived using an application of the rule (L-COMM) in Figure 4.2, followed of course by a sequence of applications of (L-CTXT). There are two possibilities.

Output from P_1 to Q: Here we have an output label $\alpha_o = (\tilde{c} : \tilde{\mathsf{D}})a!V$ and

(i) $\mathcal{I}_r \triangleright P_1 \stackrel{\alpha_o}{\longrightarrow} P_1'$
(ii) $\mathcal{I}_l \triangleright Q \stackrel{\overline{\alpha_o}}{\longrightarrow} Q'$
(iii) $\Delta_1 = \langle\tilde{c}{:}\tilde{\mathsf{D}}\rangle$

for some environments $\mathcal{I}_r$, $\mathcal{I}_l$. However since $(\mathcal{I}, \mathcal{I}_0)\ \mathsf{allows}\ \alpha_o$, Proposition 4.10 gives

(i') $\mathcal{I}, \mathcal{I}_0 \triangleright P_1 \stackrel{\alpha_o}{\longrightarrow} P_1'$.

We now use the hypothesis

$$\mathcal{I}, \mathcal{I}_0 \models P_1 \approx_{bis} P_2$$

to obtain a matching action-in-context

$$\mathcal{I}, \mathcal{I}_0 \triangleright P_2 \stackrel{(\tilde{c}:\tilde{\mathsf{D}}')a!V}{\Longrightarrow} P_2' \tag{4.30}$$

such that

$$(\mathcal{I},\ \mathcal{I}_0)\ \mathsf{after}\ (\tilde{c} : \tilde{\mathsf{D}}')a!V \models P_1' \approx_{bis} P_2'$$

Note that here the types of the exported names, $(\tilde{\mathsf{D}}')$, need not coincide with those in α_o. But this is irrelevant as a lookup of Definition 4.6 gives

$$(\mathcal{I},\ \mathcal{I}_0)\ \mathsf{after}\ (\tilde{c} : \tilde{\mathsf{D}}')a!V = (\mathcal{I},\ \mathcal{I}_0)\ \mathsf{after}\ \alpha$$

that is the form $\mathcal{I},\ \mathcal{I}_0,\ \mathcal{I}_1$.

An application of (L-COMM) to the moves (4.30) and (ii) above, followed by numerous applications of (L-CTXT) now gives, up to structural equivalence,

$$\mathcal{I} \triangleright (\mathsf{new}\ \Delta_0')(P_2 \mid Q) \stackrel{\tau}{\Longrightarrow} (\mathsf{new}\ \Delta_0', \Delta_1')(P_2' \mid Q')$$

where Δ_1' represents the environment $\langle\tilde{c}{:}\tilde{\mathsf{D}}'\rangle$.

One can then check that this is the required matching move since we have accumulated all the information necessary to establish

$$\mathcal{I} \models (\mathsf{new}\ \Delta_0, \Delta_1)(P_1' \mid Q')\ \ \mathcal{R}\ \ (\mathsf{new}\ \Delta_0', \Delta_1')(P_2' \mid Q')$$

To see this note that $(\mathcal{I}, \mathcal{I}_0)\ \mathsf{after}\ \alpha$ has the form $\mathcal{I},\ \mathcal{I}_0,\ \mathcal{I}_0'$ and so in this case we can take the typed associations required in the definition of $\mathcal{R}$ to be $(\mathcal{I}_0, \mathcal{I}_0')$ and the original Δ and Δ' respectively. Then by subject reduction, Theorem 4.12, we have

- $\Delta, \Delta_0, \Delta_1 \vdash P_1'$ and $\Delta, \Delta_0', \Delta_1' \vdash P_2'$
- $(\mathcal{I}, \mathcal{I}_0)\ \mathsf{after}\ \alpha \vdash Q'$, since we know $(\mathcal{I}, \mathcal{I}_0) \vdash Q$

and the required compatibilities between the various type environments are easily seen to be true.

Output from Q to P_1: This case is similar, consisting first of a decomposition of the move into the contributions from Q and P_1, finding a match to the latter from P_2 and a recomposition to obtain an internal move. The details are marginally simpler as the types of the imported names do not change. ■

This result gives a very powerful proof principle for reasoning about bisimulation equivalence $\approx_{bis}$ in a typed setting. Let us return to the discussion of Example 3.21 at the beginning of this chapter, and show that the results we have developed do indeed support the informal reasoning outlined there. First note that it is trivial to establish

$$\Gamma_{client} \models \mathsf{memSERV} \approx_{bis} \mathsf{stop}$$

as the relation

$$\Gamma_{client} \triangleright \mathsf{memSERV} \leftrightarrow \Gamma_{client} \triangleright \mathsf{stop}$$

is a bisimulation; neither configuration can perform any action in context. Also since $\Gamma_{client} \vdash \mathsf{Client}$ the compositionality principle immediately gives

$$\Gamma_{client} \models \mathsf{Client} \mid \mathsf{memSERV} \approx_{bis} \mathsf{Client} \mid \mathsf{stop}$$

It is also straightforward to show that

$$\Gamma_{client} \models \mathsf{Client} \mid \mathsf{stop} \approx_{bis} \mathsf{Client}$$

and therefore conclude

$$\Gamma_{client} \models \mathsf{Client} \mid \mathsf{memSERV} \approx_{bis} \mathsf{Client}$$

What we hope this chapter has demonstrated is that standard bisimulation theory can be adapted to our version of aPi with capability types. But of course the critique of bisimulation equivalence given in Section 2.5 applies equally well in the presence of types. To what extent is typed bisimulation equivalence an appropriate behavioural equivalence for typed aPi?

It is possible to develop a typed version of *reduction barbed congruence*, from Section 2.5, and the inadequacies of bisimulation equivalence with respect to this touchstone equivalence demonstrated there carry over to the typed case. However we can also develop a typed version of asynchronous bisimulations to overcome these inadequacies. But we postpone this discussion until Section 6.7, where it is examined in a distributed setting.

4.3 Questions

1. Suppose $\mathcal{I} \triangleright P \xrightarrow{\mu} \mathcal{I}' \triangleright P'$.
   (i) If μ is the input label $a?V$, prove
   - $\mathsf{fn}(P') \subseteq \mathsf{fn}(P) \cup \mathsf{n}(V)$.

   (ii) If μ is the output label $(\tilde{c} : \tilde{\mathsf{D}})a!V$, prove
   - $\mathsf{fn}(P') \subseteq \mathsf{fn}(P) \cup \mathsf{bn}(\tilde{c})$
   - $\mathsf{n}(V) \subseteq \mathsf{fn}(P) \cup \mathsf{bn}(\tilde{c})$.

   (iii) If μ is τ then $\mathsf{fn}(P') \subseteq \mathsf{fn}(P)$.
2. Suppose Γ_1, Γ_2 are two valid capability type environments, such that $\Gamma_1 <: \Gamma_2$, and suppose that $(\tilde{n})$ are fresh. Prove
   (i) $\Gamma_1, \langle\tilde{n}:\tilde{\mathsf{D}}\rangle \vdash V : \mathsf{T}$ implies $\Gamma_2, \langle V:\mathsf{T}\rangle \vdash \mathbf{env}$
   (ii) $\Gamma_1, \langle\tilde{n}:\tilde{\mathsf{D}}\rangle <: (\Gamma_2, \langle V:\mathsf{T}\rangle)$.
3. Use Question 2 to prove that if $\mathcal{I} \triangleright a!\langle V\rangle$ is a valid configuration and $\mathcal{I}^r(a)\downarrow_{\mathsf{def}}$, then $\mathcal{I}, \langle V{:}\mathcal{I}^r(a)\rangle$ is also a valid configuration.
   This means that when the rule (l-out) from Figure 4.1 is applied to a valid configuration, the conclusion is also a valid configuration.
4. Suppose $\mathcal{I}_m <: \mathcal{I}$, where $(\mathcal{I}_m\ \mathsf{after}\ \mu)$ is defined, and $\mathcal{I}$ allows μ. Prove that
   (i) $(\mathcal{I}\ \mathsf{after}\ \mu)$ is also defined
   (ii) $(\mathcal{I}_m\ \mathsf{after}\ \mu) <: (\mathcal{I}\ \mathsf{after}\ \mu)$.

5. Suppose $\mathcal{I}_m <: \mathcal{I}$. Which of the following statements are true:
   (i) $\mathcal{I}$ allows μ implies $\mathcal{I}_m$ allows μ
   (ii) $\mathcal{I}_m$ allows μ implies $\mathcal{I}$ allows μ?
6. Prove that bisimulation eqivalence is still an equivalence relation in the typed setting. Specifically, prove
   - $\mathcal{I} \models P \approx_{bis} P$ for all processes P
   - $\mathcal{I} \models P \approx_{bis} Q$ implies $\mathcal{I} \models Q \approx_{bis} P$
   - $\mathcal{I} \models P \approx_{bis} Q$ and $\mathcal{I} \models Q \approx_{bis} R$ implies $\mathcal{I} \models P \approx_{bis} R$.
7. Suppose $\mathcal{I} \triangleright P$ is a valid configuration. Prove $\mathcal{I} \models P \equiv Q$ implies $\mathcal{I} \models P \approx_{bis} Q$.
8. Let $\underline{\mathcal{R}}$ be a family of relations over TYPED APi processes such that every component $\mathcal{R}$ and its inverse satisfies the following transfer property: if $\mathcal{I} \models P \mathcal{R} Q$ then $\mathcal{I} \triangleright P \xrightarrow{\mu} P'$ implies $\mathcal{I} \triangleright Q \stackrel{\hat{\mu}'}{\Longrightarrow} Q'$ for some Q' and μ', such that $\mu \sim \mu'$ and

$$(\mathcal{I} \text{ after } \mu) \models P' \mathcal{R} Q''$$

   for some $Q'' \equiv Q'$. Prove $\mathcal{I} \models P \mathcal{R} Q$ implies $\mathcal{I} \models P \approx_{bis} Q$.
9. Suppose that $\mathcal{I} \triangleright (\text{new } c : \text{D})\, P$ and $\mathcal{I} \triangleright (\text{new } c : \text{D})\, Q$ are both configurations. Prove $\mathcal{I} \models (\text{new } c : \text{D})\, P \approx_{bis} (\text{new } c : \text{D})\, Q$ whenever $\mathcal{I} \models P \approx_{bis} Q$.
10. Give a definition of typed asynchonous bisimulation equivalence, $\mathcal{I} \models P \approx_a Q$, by adapting the rules in Figure 2.6 to give actions in context

$$\mathcal{I} \triangleright P \xrightarrow{\mu}_a \mathcal{I}' \triangleright P'$$

   With your definition prove
   (i) (Compositionality) $\mathcal{I} \models P_1 \approx_a P_2$ and $\mathcal{I} \vdash Q$ implies $\mathcal{I} \models P_1 \mid Q \approx_a P_2 \mid Q$
   (ii) $\mathcal{I} \models P_1 \approx_{bis} P_2$ implies $\mathcal{I} \models P_1 \approx_a P_2$.
11. Let API$_i$ be the language API augmented by the operator $!P$. The lts semantics for the operator is given by

$$\text{(L-ITER)}\quad \frac{P \xrightarrow{\mu} P'}{!P \xrightarrow{\mu} P' | !P}$$

   while the typing is handled by

$$\text{(TY-ITER)}\quad \frac{\Gamma \vdash P : \text{proc}}{\Gamma \vdash !P : \text{proc}}$$

   (i) Prove $\mathcal{I} \models !P \approx_{bis} \text{rec } x.\, (P \mid x)$, whenever $\mathcal{I} \triangleright P$ is a configuration.
   (ii) Suppose R contains no occurrence of the recursion operator rec, and $\mathcal{I} \triangleright \text{rec } x.\, R$ is a valid configuration. Then show that some process P in API$_i$ exists, containing no occurrence of recursion, such that $\mathcal{I} \models \text{rec } x.\, R \approx_{bis} P$.

5

A distributed asynchronous PI-CALCULUS

In this chapter we develop a language ADPI for describing *explicitly distributed* computations. The new concept is that of *location*, *site* or *domain*, an environment for computational activity. Intuitively a domain hosts *local resources* that *mobile agents* use to interact with each other. Thus a typical domain can be pictured as:

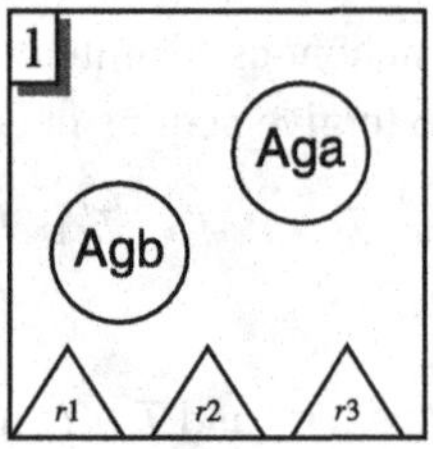

Here Aga and Agb represent two mobile agents currently residing at the domain l that contains the three local resources, $r1, r2$ and $r3$ that they may use to interact.

A distributed system may then be viewed as a collection of these independent domains. A typical example, consisting of three domains named s, k and l, is given in Figure 5.1. Here there are five agents distributed through the domains, Sa, Sb, A, R, S, and five local resources, a, b at domain s, e at k and c, d at l.

We use API to describe these mobile agents, although we require a new primitive to enable migration between domains. Thus we augment API with the construct

$$\mathsf{goto}\ l.P$$

If the agent $\mathsf{goto}\ l.P$ is currently residing at k it can migrate to the domain l and continue there with the execution of P.

To keep the language basic we have an extremely primitive notion of local resource, simply *locally declared channels*; thus throughout this chapter we will use *resource* and *channel* interchangeably. Then an agent currently residing at domain l may use the channels declared locally at l to communicate; referring to the diagram above, these would be channels named $r1$, $r2$ and $r3$. When an agent migrates to

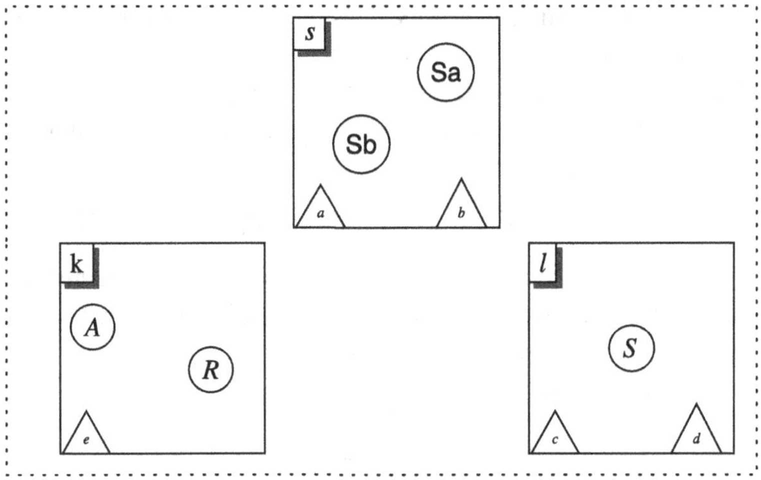

Figure 5.1 A distributed system

another domain k these resources at l are no longer available for it to use; of course it may subsequently migrate back from k to l and then they become available once more. More sophisticated notions of local resource need to be programmed in terms of these local channels. For example if the domain l wishes to offer a service for testing primality, as described in Example 2.10 then it would declare a local channel called in_p, start the agent primeS running locally, and distribute to its clients the *write* capability only on its local channel in_p. Retaining the *read* capability on the local in_p ensures the integrity of the service.

Also for simplicity we assume that the structure of domains is *flat*, that is there are no *subdomains*. However domains can be declared dynamically and knowledge of domains may be transmitted between agents along channels. Since the language is typed we need to introduce a new class of types for locations. These types describe the resources available at a location, together with the types at which the resources may be used. Thus the general form of a location type is

$$\mathsf{loc}[c_1 : \mathsf{C}_1, c_2 : \mathsf{C}_2, \ldots, c_n : \mathsf{C}_n],\ n \geq 0$$

If the name of a domain is received at this type then any one of the channels $c_1, \ldots, c_n$ located there may be exercised with the associated capabilities $\mathsf{C}_1, \ldots, \mathsf{C}_n$. For example a domain named m to be used to host a memory cell, along the lines of that described in Example 2.11, could be declared with the type

$$\mathsf{loc}[\mathsf{put} : \mathsf{rw}\langle \mathsf{C}_p \rangle, \mathsf{get} : \mathsf{rw}\langle \mathsf{C}_g \rangle, \mathsf{kill} : \mathsf{rw}\langle \mathsf{C}_k \rangle] \tag{5.1}$$

where C_p, C_g, C_k represent the capabilities allowed on the values transmitted by the located channels put, get, kill. The domain m could have in permanent residence an agent whose task would be to service calls on these resources; this agent would be defined as an elaboration on Example 2.11.

Knowledge of m may now be distributed via *supertypes* of the declaration type (5.1) above. The general rule determining the supertype relation over location types is given by

$$\mathsf{loc}[c_1 : \mathsf{C}_1, c_2 : \mathsf{C}_2, \ldots, c_k : \mathsf{C}_k, \ldots, c_n : \mathsf{C}_n] <: \mathsf{loc}[c_1 : \mathsf{C}'_1, c_2 : \mathsf{C}'_2, \ldots, c_k : \mathsf{C}'_k]$$

where $k \leq n$ and $\mathsf{C}_i <: \mathsf{C}'_i$ for each i between 1 and k. Thus an agent may know only a subset of the resources available at a domain, and may have limited capabilities at these resources. So, for example, the name m of the domain hosting the memory cell could be distributed at the type

$$\mathsf{loc}[\mathsf{put} : \mathsf{w}\langle \mathsf{C}_p \rangle, \mathsf{get} : \mathsf{w}\langle \mathsf{C}_g \rangle] \tag{5.2}$$

to the clients of the memory, and at the type

$$\mathsf{loc}[\mathsf{put} : \mathsf{r}\langle \mathsf{C}_p \rangle, \mathsf{get} : \mathsf{r}\langle \mathsf{C}_g \rangle, \mathsf{kill} : \mathsf{rw}\langle \mathsf{C}_k \rangle]$$

to the manager.

Individual resources or channels at a domain m may also be transmitted between agents. However in ADPI it is important to realise that all channels are *located*. Thus in general they are represented by *compound names* of the form

$$c@k$$

where k is the name of a domain and c is the name of a resource located there. So, for example, when a client sends a reply channel to a memory cell, the name of this reply channel is now a *compound name*, $r@k$, representing the channel named r located at the domain k. Of course the use of these compound values in turn leads to a new kind of type, that of *located channel types*.

The ability of channels to transmit compound names means that we have to extend the definition of *transmission types*, the types at which values may be sent and received, to include appropriate types for these structured values. Since domain names may also be transmitted, we must also include location types. For example a manager of a suite of memory cells, distributed throughout various domains, may maintain a *broadcasting agent* that informs clients of available cells. At a particular point in time this agent could contain the code

$$\ldots \mathsf{out}_{cl}!\langle m_i \rangle \ldots$$

where m_i is a domain hosting a cell. The declaration type of the channel out_{cl} would now be of the form $\mathsf{rw}\langle \mathsf{M} \rangle$, where M represents the type (5.2) above.

A priori sorting out the exact nature of what values may be transmitted, and how, looks complicated. However we show that an extension of the type system of Section 3.4 can be used in a natural manner to control the behaviour of agents. In effect these types enable system designers to specify *access control policies* for domains.

The elaboration of the language ADPI and its associated type system is the subject of this chapter. Later, in the following chapter, we will also see that a typed behavioural equivalence can be developed for the resulting typed language, and moreover this can be justified contextually.

5.1 The language ADPI

The explicitly typed language ADPI is obtained by adding one further syntactic category, called *Systems*, to those of API, or more accurately to the typed version of API of Chapter 3. However we postpone the discussion of the types until the next section.

A system is now essentially a set of *located* processes or agents, possibly sharing, as in API, private or local names. A typical system looks like

$$l[\![P_1]\!] \mid (\mathsf{new}\, e : \mathsf{D})(k[\![Q]\!] \mid l[\![P_2]\!])$$

Here we have three located processes, or agents, P_1 running at location l, Q running at location k and P_2 also running at location l. These latter two share a common resource e of type D.

The syntax of ADPI is given in Figure 5.2, with the new syntactic categories highlighted in bold. The simplest system, apart from the empty one **0**, takes the form $l[\![P]\!]$, consisting of essentially an API process P running at location l. These located agents may be combined using the parallel constructor $- \mid -$, and the new name constructor $(\mathsf{new}\, e : \mathsf{D})(-)$. It is important to note that there is not a direct connection between this formal syntax for systems and the informal pictorial representations, as in Figure 5.1. The latter emphasises the locality of the agents, while the former allows agents to be grouped together in an arbitrary manner. So, for example, if we ignore for a moment the declaration of the various local resources, the system in Figure 5.1 may be represented by any of the terms

$$s[\![\mathsf{Sa} \mid \mathsf{Sb}]\!] \mid \mathsf{k}[\![\mathsf{R} \mid \mathsf{A}]\!] \mid \mathsf{l}[\![\mathsf{S}]\!]$$
$$s[\![\mathsf{Sb}]\!] \mid \mathsf{k}[\![\mathsf{R}]\!] \mid \mathsf{k}[\![\mathsf{A}]\!] \mid \mathsf{l}[\![\mathsf{S}]\!] \mid \mathsf{s}[\![\mathsf{Sa}]\!]$$
$$s[\![\mathsf{Sa}]\!] \mid \mathsf{l}[\![\mathsf{S}]\!] \mid \mathsf{s}[\![\mathsf{Sb}]\!] \mid \mathsf{k}[\![\mathsf{R} \mid \mathsf{A}]\!]$$

However, as we will see, all of these will be *structurally equivalent*.

The syntax for processes or agents is inherited directly from API, with one major addition. There is the input and output of values as before, although now the values transmitted may be *compound*. The more general syntax for such values, and their

M, N ::=	***Systems***
$l[\![P]\!]$	**Located agents**
$M \mid N$	**Composition**
$(\text{new}\, e : \mathsf{D})\, M$	**Name Scoping**
$\mathbf{0}$	**Empty**

R, S, B ::=	*Process terms*
$u!\langle V\rangle$	Output
$u?(X)R$	Input
$\text{goto}\, v.R$	**Migration**
$(\text{newc}\, c : \mathsf{D}_c)\ R$	Channel Name creation
$(\text{newloc}\, k : \mathsf{D}_k)\ R$	**Location Name creation**
$\text{if}\ v_1 = v_2\ \text{then}\ R_1\ \text{else}\ R_2$	Matching
$R_1 \mid R_2$	Composition
$\text{rec}\ x.\ B$	Recursive definition
x	Recursion variable
stop	Termination

Figure 5.2 Syntax for ADPI

related patterns, is given in Figure 5.3, with the extra forms in bold. Recall that we tend to use the meta-variable u to denote *identifiers*, that is, either names or variables; in this chapter we will sometimes refer to these as *simple* identifiers and *simple* names. Also for the sake of clarity we tend to use $a, b, c, \ldots$ for (simple) names in Names that are used as channels, while (simple) names such as $k, l, \ldots$ will be used for locations. However this is an informal arrangement; formally the role of each name in a system will be determined by the type environment for that system.

The major addition to the syntax for processes is the construct for *migration*. Intuitively

$$\text{goto}\, k.P$$

running at any location l will migrate to location k where the code P is launched.

To make things clear, but perhaps at the price of verbosity, we have isolated the two kinds of names that can be declared by agents:

local channels: The agent $(\text{newc}\, c : \mathsf{D}_c)\ P$ creates a new local channel named c and then executes the code P. In a well-typed system D_c will be a *local channel type*.

locations: Similarly the agent $(\text{newloc}\, k : \mathsf{D}_k)\ P$ creates a new location k of type D_k and then launches the code P.

We will sometimes use the generic syntax $(\text{new}\, n : \mathsf{D})\, P$, when the exact nature of the name being declared is not important to the discussion at hand.

v, w ::=	*Simple values*
n	names
x	variables
bv	basic values
e ::=	*Compound values*
v	simple values
$u@w$	**located identifiers**
U, V, W ::=	*Values*
$(e_1, \ldots, e_n)$, $n \geq 0$	tupling
p ::=	*Compound variables*
x	variables
$x@y$	**located variables**
X, Y ::=	*Patterns*
$(p_1, \ldots, p_n)$, $n \geq 0$	tupling

Figure 5.3 Patterns and values in ADPI

The constructs for the testing of identifiers, parallel composition and recursion are as before, in API.

Example 5.1 [*A Distributed Compute Server*] Let us reconsider Example 2.10 in which a service of testing for primality is considered. In ADPI this service has to be located in some domain, say s, and therefore takes the form

$$s[\![\mathsf{DprimeS}]\!]$$

where DprimeS is the agent maintaining the service. This agent requires an *address* to which the result is to be returned and in ADPI this means both a location and a channel at that location. In other words the agent needs to be sent

- the value to be tested, an integer
- and a located resource name $c@h$, an *address*, where the result is to be sent.

Thus we may define the servicing agent as

$$\mathsf{DprimeS} \Leftarrow \mathsf{rec}\ z.\ \mathsf{in}_p?(x, y@w)\ (z \mid \mathsf{goto}\ w.y!\langle isprime(x)\rangle)$$

It receives a value, bound to x, and a compound name consisting of a reply channel, bound to y, located at a domain, bound to w. The required result is calculated, the computation of which we are ignoring by representing it by the predicate *isprime*, and then an agent is sent to the received location w to deliver it, at the reply channel y located there. To emphasise the fact that the computation is carried out at the server site this could be rendered as

$$\mathsf{DprimeS} \Leftarrow \mathsf{rec}\ z.\ \mathsf{in}_p?(x, y@w)\ (z \mid \mathsf{let}\ a = isprime(x)\ \mathsf{in}\ \mathsf{goto}\ w.y!\langle a\rangle)$$

if, as already suggested in Section 2.2, the language were augmented with a construct let $x = e_1$ in e_2 for explicitly sequencing computations.

A client generates a new reply channel at its current location, sends an agent to the service domain with the required information and awaits a reply. Thus this takes the form

$$h[\![\mathsf{Client}(v)]\!]$$

where the agent Client(v) is defined by

$$(\mathsf{newc}\ r : \mathsf{D}_r)\ (r?(x)\ \mathsf{print}!\langle x\rangle \quad | \quad \mathsf{goto}\ s.\mathsf{in}_p!\langle v, r@h\rangle) \qquad \blacksquare$$

The delivery of data at an address occurs so frequently in ADPI that it is worthwhile to introduce a shorthand notation.

Notation 5.2 We abbreviate the agent goto $l.c!\langle V\rangle$ to $l.c!\langle V\rangle$. We also inherit the various notations, introduced for API, such as abbreviating $c!\langle\rangle$ to $c!$, etc. Moreover types will sometimes be omitted from terms when they play no role in the discussion.

Example 5.3 [*Distributed Forwarders*] In a distributed setting a forwarder, based on that of Example 2.9, requires two addresses, located names $b@k_1$, $c@k_2$ between which it is to maintain the forwarding service. It can be defined by $h[\![\mathsf{DisF}(k_1, b, k_2, c)]\!]$, where the code is given by

$$\mathsf{DisF}(k_1, b, k_2, c) \Leftarrow \mathsf{goto}\ k_1.$$
$$\mathsf{rec}\ z.\ b?(x, y)\ \mathsf{goto}\ k_2.(\mathsf{new\ ack})(c!\langle x, \mathsf{ack}\rangle \mid \mathsf{ack}?\mathsf{goto}\ k_1.(y! \mid z))$$

The agent first goes to the source site k_1 and installs a recursive agent. From the local source channel b it inputs the value to be forwarded, bound to x, and an acknowledgement channel, bound to y. It then migrates to the second site k_2, generates a new acknowledgement channel ack that it transmits, together with the value x, to the target channel c at k_2. It waits at the delivery site, k_2, for the acknowledgement; when it arrives the agent returns to the source site k_1 where in turn it delivers its acknowledgement on y and awaits a new message on the source channel. ■

The language ADPI inherits from API all the standard notational conventions, the notions of free and bound variables and names, capture-avoiding substitutions and α-equivalence. However, as we have seen in the introduction to this chapter, channel names can appear in (location) types. This must be taken into account in the formal definitions of the function for calculating free and bound names, fn(−), bn(−) respectively, when applied to terms in ADPI. So for example in these definitions applied to processes we have clauses of the form

(R-COMM)
$$k[\![c!\langle V\rangle]\!] \mid k[\![c?(X)\,P]\!] \longrightarrow k[\![P\{^{V}\!/\!_{X}\}]\!]$$

(R-UNWIND)
$$k[\![\mathsf{rec}\ x.\ B]\!] \longrightarrow k[\![B\{^{\mathsf{rec}\ x.\ B}\!/\!_{x}\}]\!]$$

(R-EQ)
$$k[\![\mathsf{if}\ v = v\ \mathsf{then}\ P\ \mathsf{else}\ Q]\!] \longrightarrow k[\![P]\!]$$

(R-NEQ)
$$k[\![\mathsf{if}\ v_1 = v_2\ \mathsf{then}\ P\ \mathsf{else}\ Q]\!] \longrightarrow k[\![Q]\!], \quad v_1 \neq v_2$$

(R-STR)
$$\frac{M \equiv N,\ M \longrightarrow M',\ M' \equiv N'}{N \longrightarrow N'}$$

(R-SPLIT)
$$k[\![P \mid Q]\!] \longrightarrow k[\![P]\!] \mid k[\![Q]\!]$$

(R-MOVE)
$$k[\![\mathsf{goto}\ l.P]\!] \longrightarrow l[\![P]\!]$$

(R-L.CREATE)
$$k[\![(\mathsf{newloc}\ l : \mathsf{D}_l)\ P]\!] \longrightarrow (\mathsf{new}\ l : \mathsf{D}_l)(k[\![P]\!])$$

(R-C.CREATE)
$$k[\![(\mathsf{newc}\ c : \mathsf{D}_c)\ P]\!] \longrightarrow (\mathsf{new}\ c@k : \mathsf{D}_c)\, k[\![P]\!]$$

Figure 5.4 Reduction semantics for ADPI

$$\begin{aligned} \mathsf{bn}((\mathsf{new}\,n : \mathsf{D})\,R) &= \mathsf{bn}(R) \cup \{n\} \\ \mathsf{fn}((\mathsf{new}\,n : \mathsf{D})\,R) &= (\mathsf{fn}(R) \cup \mathsf{n}(\mathsf{D})) - \{n\} \end{aligned} \tag{5.3}$$

where $\mathsf{n}(\mathsf{D})$ denotes the names that occur in the type expression D; this will be empty unless D is a location type. A similar definition applies to system level terms, but there is a subtlety associated with the, as of yet unexplained, scoping mechanism $(\mathsf{new}\,e : \mathsf{D})\,M$ at the system level; this will be elaborated on below, in (5.4). We will use the word *system* to denote a *closed system term*, that is a system term that contains no free occurrences of variables. We will use the word *process* and *agent* for *closed process terms*.

The reduction semantics is similar in style to that of API, and uses a structural equivalence $\equiv$ to factor out inessential details in the syntax. The reduction relation is defined to be the least contextual relation between systems

$$M \longrightarrow N$$

that satisfies the rules in Figure 5.4. Note that the definition of contextual in Definition 2.5 can be applied to systems, as they have both a parallel constructor $- \mid -$ and a new name constructor $(\mathsf{new}\,e : \mathsf{D})(-)$. The axioms (R-EQ), (R-NEQ), (R-STR) and (R-UNWIND) are taken directly from the reduction semantics for API, but now apply to located processes; the structural equivalence used in (R-STR) is inherited from API, although there is a complication involving bound names; this will be explained presently.

The rule (R-COMM) is also inherited from API, although note that the communicating agents are obliged to be at the same location. Thus in ADPI communication is **local**; agents who wish to communicate must be co-located, and use a local channel for this communication.

The axiom (R-SPLIT) is novel. It allows the splitting of a concurrent agent located at k to evolve into two concurrent located agents, each of course still located at k. It is essentially a *housekeeping* move, as it allows systems to evolve into configurations from which *real* reductions, such as communication, migration, or value testing, can occur.

The new axiom (R-MOVE)

$$k[\![\mathsf{goto}\ l.P]\!] \longrightarrow l[\![P]\!]$$

accounts for migration. Note that migration is at the level of agent rather than domain. In fact the latter would not make any sense in view of the flat structure of domains.

Finally the creation rules allow us to export names declared by an individual agent to the system level. The rule for exporting domain declarations, (R-L.CREATE), is straightforward; $k[\![(\mathsf{newloc}\ l : \mathsf{D}_l)\ (R)]\!]$ evolves to $(\mathsf{new}\ l : \mathsf{D}_l)\ (k[\![R]\!])$. This may seem an innocuous move, but the code R may now send an agent to the new location, to install resources and run processes there. For example if R has the form $(P \mid \mathsf{goto}\ l.Q)$ then we will have the reductions

$$k[\![(\mathsf{newloc}\ l : \mathsf{D}_l)\ R]\!] \longrightarrow\longrightarrow\longrightarrow (\mathsf{new}\ l : \mathsf{D}_l)\ (k[\![P]\!] \mid l[\![Q]\!])$$

where now the residual P running at the original k can broadcast the existence of the new site l, and its resources; moreover the code Q has been installed at the new site to service these resources. This is such a natural manner for generating new locations that we introduce a specific notation for it.

Notation 5.4 We use $(\mathsf{newloc}\ l : \mathsf{D}_l)$ with Q in P to denote the process $(\mathsf{new}\ l : \mathsf{D}_l)\ (P \mid \mathsf{goto}\ l.Q)$ ■

The rules for creating local channels are similar. But note that in (R-C.CREATE), when the new channel c of type D_c, local to k, is exported to the system level, its location has to be noted; the name c created locally at site k is referred to globally as $c@k$. In other words at the system level we have simple names, k referring to locations, and *located names*, $c@k$, referring to actual *located channels* or *resources*. In future we use the meta-variable e to range over the corresponding *compound values*, which may be simple values v, or located identifiers $u@w$ where both u and w are simple identifiers, that is either names or variables; so when variables are not involved, these compound values are either simple names or located names.

There is a subtlety involved in the use of these located names. In the system $(\mathsf{new}\ c@k{:}\mathsf{D}_c)\ (M)$ only occurrences of c in M are bound; the location name k

(S-EXTR)	$(\mathsf{new}\, e : \mathsf{D})(M \mid N)$	=	$M \mid (\mathsf{new}\, e : \mathsf{D})\, N$	if $\mathsf{bn}(e) \notin \mathsf{fn}(M)$
(S-COM)	$M \mid N$	=	$N \mid M$	
(S-ASSOC)	$(M \mid N) \mid O$	=	$M \mid (N \mid O)$	
(S-ZERO)	$M \mid \mathbf{0}$	=	M	
	$k[\![\mathsf{stop}]\!]$	=	$\mathbf{0}$	
	$(\mathsf{new}\, e : \mathsf{D})\, \mathbf{0}$	=	$\mathbf{0}$	
(S-FLIP)	$(\mathsf{new}\, e_1 : \mathsf{D}_1)(\mathsf{new}\, e_2 : \mathsf{D}_2)\, M$	=	$(\mathsf{new}\, e_2 : \mathsf{D}_2)(\mathsf{new}\, e_1 : \mathsf{D}_1)\, M$	if $\mathsf{bn}(e_1) \notin (e_2 : \mathsf{D}_2),\ \mathsf{bn}(e_2) \notin (e_1 : \mathsf{D}_1)$

Figure 5.5 Structural equivalence for ADPI

is simply used as a tag, to denote where this private resource c exists. So when extending the notions of free and bound names to systems we must have the clauses

$$\begin{aligned} \mathsf{bn}(\,(\mathsf{new}\, c@k{:}\mathsf{D}_c)\, M) &= \{c\} \cup \mathsf{bn}(M) \\ \mathsf{fn}(\,(\mathsf{new}\, c@k{:}\mathsf{D}_c)\, M) &= (\{k\} \cup \mathsf{fn}(M) \cup \mathsf{n}(\mathsf{D}_c)) - \{c\} \end{aligned} \tag{5.4}$$

The corresponding clauses for the other kind of name declarations are as discussed above in (5.3).

These located names also have an effect on the definition of structural equivalence between systems. As with API this is defined to be the largest contextual equivalence that satisfies a set of axioms. These are given in Figure 5.5, and are modelled directly on those for API in Figure 2.3. But note that now in (S-EXTR) we have to be careful about the actual name being extruded; here $\mathsf{bn}(e)$ refers to c if e is the located name $c@k$ and otherwise is e itself. So for example, assuming there is no occurrence of c in P,

$$(\mathsf{new}\, c@l : \mathsf{D}_c)(l[\![P]\!] \mid k[\![Q]\!]) \equiv l[\![P]\!] \ \mid\ (\mathsf{new}\, c@l : \mathsf{D}_c)\, k[\![Q]\!]$$

Similarly in (S-FLIP) we have to make sure that the role of scoped names does not become confused. For example

$$(\mathsf{new}\, k : \mathsf{D}_k)\, (\mathsf{new}\, c@k : \mathsf{D}_c)\, M \not\equiv (\mathsf{new}\, c@k : \mathsf{D}_c)\, (\mathsf{new}\, k : \mathsf{D}_k) M$$

because k is contained in $c@k$. The side-conditions placed on (S-FLIP) are a slight generalisation of those used for TYPED API, discussed on page 61. Recall that types may now contain names, and therefore we need also to ensure that the bound names $\mathsf{bn}(e_1)$, $\mathsf{bn}(e_2)$ do not appear in the types D_2, D_1 respectively.

Let us now look at some examples of the use of this reduction semantics; as usual we will sometimes elide the actual types of bound names; indeed we continue to do so throughout the chapter unless they are relevant to the discussion at hand. The subject of the types required for bound names will be taken up in Section 5.2.

Example 5.5 Let us examine the possible reductions from the system

$$s[\![\mathsf{DprimeS}]\!] \ \mid\ h[\![\mathsf{Client}(11)]\!]$$

where the agents DprimeS and Client(11) are defined in Example 5.1.

These are two independent agents, each in evaluation contexts, and therefore are subject to any of the applicable rules in Figure 5.4. For example the rule (R-UNWIND) can be applied to $s[\![\mathsf{DprimeS}]\!]$ and we get the reduction

$$s[\![\mathsf{DprimeS}]\!] \mid h[\![\mathsf{Client}(11)]\!] \quad \longrightarrow \quad s[\![\mathsf{in}_p?(x, y@w)\,(\mathsf{DprimeS} \mid \mathsf{goto}\, w.y!\langle isprime(x)\rangle)]\!] \mid h[\![\mathsf{Client}(11)]\!] \tag{5.5}$$

The server is now in a stable state, waiting on input at the port in_p.

The client on the other hand needs first to extrude the new reply channel, using (R-C.CREATE):

$$h[\![\mathsf{Client}(11)]\!] \longrightarrow (\mathsf{new}\, r@h : \mathsf{D}_r)\, h[\![r?(x)\, \mathsf{print}!\langle x\rangle \mid \mathsf{goto}\, s.\mathsf{in}_p!\langle v, r@h\rangle]\!]$$

Putting this in context, that is applying the contextuality of reduction, we obtain

$$s[\![\mathsf{in}_p?(x, y@w)\ldots]\!] \mid h[\![\mathsf{Client}(11)]\!] \quad \longrightarrow \quad s[\![\mathsf{in}_p?(x, y@w)\ldots]\!] \mid (\mathsf{new}\, r@h : \mathsf{D}_r)\, h[\![r?(x)\, \mathsf{print}!\langle x\rangle \mid \mathsf{goto}\, s.\mathsf{in}_p!\langle 11, r@h\rangle]\!]$$

The client is now ready to send the requesting agent to the server. But in order to formally derive the reduction we need to use the structural equivalence to re-arrange the system so that the relevant axioms can be applied. We have already seen numerous instances of these re-arrangements in API, all using suitable applications of the extrusion axiom (S-EXTR); for one example see Example 2.9.

First note that

$$s[\![\ldots]\!] \mid (\mathsf{new}\, r@h : \mathsf{D}_r)\, h[\![\ldots]\!] \;\equiv\; (\mathsf{new}\, r@h : \mathsf{D}_r)(s[\![\ldots]\!] \mid h[\![\ldots]\!])$$

because of the rule (S-EXTR); r does not occur free in $h[\![\ldots]\!]$. Therefore applying the rule (R-STR) to the last reduction we obtain

$$s[\![\mathsf{in}_p?(x, y@w)\ldots]\!] \mid h[\![\mathsf{Client}(11)]\!] \quad \longrightarrow \quad (\mathsf{new}\, r : \mathsf{D}_r@h)(\, s[\![\mathsf{in}_p?(x, y@w)\ldots]\!] \mid h[\![r?(x)\, \mathsf{print}!\langle x\rangle \mid \mathsf{goto}\, s.\mathsf{in}_p!\langle 11, r@h\rangle]\!]) \tag{5.6}$$

This we may take to be the second reduction step of the system.

At this stage we may use the rule (R-SPLIT) to obtain

$$h[\![\mathsf{goto}\, s.\mathsf{in}_p!\langle 11, r@h\rangle \mid r?(x)\, \mathsf{print}!\langle x\rangle]\!] \longrightarrow h[\![r?(x)\, \mathsf{print}!\langle x\rangle]\!] \mid h[\![\mathsf{goto}\, s.\mathsf{in}_p!\langle 11, r@h\rangle]\!]$$

thereby isolating the agent, currently at h, which is about to move. Applying this reduction in context we obtain the third reduction step:

$$(\mathsf{new}\, r@h : \mathsf{D}_r)(\, s[\![\mathsf{in}_p?(x, y@w)\ldots]\!] \mid h[\![r?(x)\,\mathsf{print}!\langle x\rangle \mid \mathsf{goto}\, s.\mathsf{in}_p!\langle 11, r@h\rangle]\!]\,)$$
$$\longrightarrow (\mathsf{new}\, r@h : \mathsf{D}_r)(\, s[\![\mathsf{in}_p?(x, y@w)\ldots]\!] \mid$$
$$h[\![r?(x)\,\mathsf{print}!\langle x\rangle]\!] \mid h[\![\mathsf{goto}\, s.\mathsf{in}_p!\langle 11, r@h\rangle]\!]\,) \quad (5.7)$$

Here the migration of the agent may be derived using (R-MOVE):

$$h[\![\mathsf{goto}\, s.\mathsf{in}_p!\langle 11, r@h\rangle]\!] \longrightarrow s[\![\mathsf{in}_p!\langle 11, r@h\rangle]\!]$$

and applying this in context, together with an application of (R-STR), gives

$$(\mathsf{new}\, r : \mathsf{D}_r@h)(s[\![\mathsf{in}_p?(x, y@w)\ldots]\!] \mid h[\![r?(x)\,\mathsf{print}!\langle x\rangle]\!] \mid h[\![\mathsf{goto}\, s.\mathsf{in}_p!\langle 11, r@h\rangle]\!])$$
$$\longrightarrow \quad (5.8)$$
$$(\mathsf{new}\, r : \mathsf{D}_r@h)(s[\![\mathsf{in}_p?(x, y@w)\ldots]\!] \mid s[\![\mathsf{in}_p!\langle 11, r@h\rangle]\!] \mid h[\![r?(x)\,\mathsf{print}!\langle x\rangle]\!])$$

We now have at the server site s

- an agent who wishes to transmit a message along the local channel in_p
- and an agent who is willing to service this message.

The axiom (R-COMM) may be used to obtain

$$s[\![\mathsf{in}_p?(x, y@w)\ldots]\!] \mid s[\![\mathsf{in}_p!\langle 11, r@h\rangle]\!] \longrightarrow s[\![\mathsf{DprimeS} \mid \mathsf{goto}\, h.r!\langle isprime(11)\rangle]\!]$$

For variety let us use (R-SPLIT) on the resulting system, to obtain

$$s[\![\mathsf{in}_p?(x, y@w)\ldots]\!] \mid s[\![\mathsf{in}_p!\langle 11, r@h\rangle]\!] \longrightarrow\longrightarrow s[\![\mathsf{DprimeS}]\!]$$
$$\mid s[\![\mathsf{goto}\, h.r!\langle isprime(11)\rangle]\!]$$

Applying these two reductions in context we obtain the reductions

$$(\mathsf{new}\, r@h : \mathsf{D}_r)(s[\![\mathsf{in}_p?(x, y@w)\ldots]\!] \mid s[\![\mathsf{in}_p!\langle 11, r@h\rangle]\!] \mid h[\![r?(x)\,\mathsf{print}!\langle x\rangle]\!])$$
$$\longrightarrow\longrightarrow \quad (5.9)$$
$$(\mathsf{new}\, r@h : \mathsf{D}_r)(s[\![\mathsf{DprimeS}]\!] \mid s[\![\mathsf{goto}\, h.r!\langle isprime(11)\rangle]\!] \mid h[\![r?(x)\,\mathsf{print}!\langle x\rangle]\!])$$

Now there is the return agent, currently at s, which can migrate back to h. As explained in Example 2.10, let us elide the evaluation of $isprime(11)$, assuming it is some computation done at the server, and then (R-MOVE) can be used to give

$$s[\![\mathsf{goto}\, h.r!\langle isprime(11)\rangle]\!] \rightsquigarrow s[\![\mathsf{goto}\, h.r!\langle \mathbf{true}\rangle]\!] \longrightarrow h[\![r!\langle \mathbf{true}\rangle]\!]$$

where $\rightsquigarrow$ represents the elided evaluation of $isprime(11)$. In context this gives

$$(\mathsf{new}\, r@h : \mathsf{D}_r)(s[\![\mathsf{DprimeS}]\!] \mid s[\![\mathsf{goto}\, h.r!\langle isprime(11)\rangle]\!] \mid h[\![r?(x)\,\mathsf{print}!\langle x\rangle]\!])$$
$$\rightsquigarrow\longrightarrow \quad (5.10)$$
$$(\mathsf{new}\, r@h : \mathsf{D}_r)(s[\![\mathsf{DprimeS}]\!] \mid h[\![r!\langle \mathbf{true}\rangle]\!] \mid h[\![r?(x)\,\mathsf{print}!\langle x\rangle]\!])$$

Now there is a local communication possible at h, along the reply channel r. From (R-COMM) we obtain

$$h[\![r!\langle \mathbf{true}\rangle]\!] \mid h[\![r?(x)\, \mathsf{print!}\langle x\rangle]\!] \;\longrightarrow\; h[\![\mathsf{print!}\langle \mathbf{true}\rangle]\!]$$

that in context gives the reduction

$$\begin{aligned}&(\mathsf{new}\, r@h : \mathsf{D}_r)(s[\![\mathsf{DprimeS}]\!] \;\mid\; h[\![r!\langle \mathbf{true}\rangle]\!] \mid h[\![r?(x)\, \mathsf{print!}\langle x\rangle]\!])\\ &\longrightarrow\\ &(\mathsf{new}\, r@h : \mathsf{D}_r)(s[\![\mathsf{DprimeS}]\!] \;\mid\; h[\![\mathsf{print!}\langle \mathbf{true}\rangle]\!])\end{aligned}$$

However the channel name r does not appear free in the code DprimeS, or in the code at h and so using the derived structural equation

$$(\mathsf{new}\, e : \mathsf{D})\, N \;\equiv\; N \quad \text{if } \mathsf{bn}(e) \notin \mathsf{fn}(N)$$

similar to that discussed in Example 2.9, and an application of (R-STR) we obtain the final reduction

$$\begin{aligned}&(\mathsf{new}\, r@h : \mathsf{D}_r)(s[\![\mathsf{DprimeS}]\!] \;\mid\; h[\![r!\langle isprime(11)\rangle]\!] \mid h[\![r?(x)\, \mathsf{print!}\langle x\rangle]\!])\\ &\longrightarrow \qquad\qquad (5.11)\\ &s[\![\mathsf{DprimeS}]\!] \;\mid\; h[\![\mathsf{print!}\langle \mathbf{true}\rangle]\!]\end{aligned}$$

So in eight steps, ignoring the computation of *isprime*(11), we have seen the reduction of the system

$$s[\![\mathsf{DprimeS}]\!] \;\mid\; h[\![\mathsf{Client}(11)]\!]$$

with a server and a client, to one of the form

$$s[\![\mathsf{DprimeS}]\!] \;\mid\; h[\![\mathsf{print!}\langle \mathbf{true}\rangle]\!]$$

where the client has been serviced and the server is ready to accommodate further requests.

The first three reductions (5.5), (5.6), (5.7) are house-keeping in nature, preparing the system for the significant reductions, namely migration via the axiom (R-MOVE) and local communication via (R-COMM). The fourth reduction (5.8) sees the client send an agent to the server, while in (5.9) there is a communication at the server site; the server is informed of the client's request. After the evaluation of the call to *isprime*(−), the answer is given to an agent at the server site that, in the next move (5.10) migrates to the client site, and in (5.11) there is a local communication this time at the client site informing it of the result. ■

Example 5.6 [*A Located Memory*] Here we give a located version of the memory cell from Example 2.11. The cell takes the form

$$m[\![\mathsf{LMem}]\!]$$

where m is the location of the cell and LMem is the code running there. This is much the same as the code Mem from Example 2.11 except that now the *locations* of the methods must be catered for:

$$\mathsf{LMem} \Leftarrow (\mathsf{newc}\, s : \mathsf{S})\ (s!\langle 0\rangle \\ \mid \mathsf{rec}\ p.\ \mathsf{get}?(y@w)\ s?(z)\ (w.y!\langle z\rangle \mid s!\langle z\rangle \mid p) \\ \mid \mathsf{rec}\ g.\ \mathsf{put}?(x, y@w)\ s?(z)\ (w.y! \mid s!\langle x\rangle \mid g)$$

Here the access methods require *located* return channels, bound by the pattern $y@w$, at which to deliver the result of an access. Note that we are using the abbreviation introduced in Notation 5.2.

A client is in turn expected to be located, of the form

$$c[\![\mathsf{Client}]\!]$$

where Client, when calling the cell methods, must use c as the location of the return channels. It must also be aware of the location hosting the cell. The client corresponding to that in Example 2.11 is given by

$$\mathsf{Client} \Leftarrow (\mathsf{newc}\, a : \mathsf{D}_a)\ (m.\mathsf{put}!\langle 4, a@c\rangle \\ \mid a?\ (\mathsf{newc}\, r : \mathsf{D}_r)\ (\ m.\mathsf{get}!\langle r@c\rangle \mid r?(x)\ \mathsf{print}!\langle x\rangle\ )$$

The reduction semantics can be applied to the system

$$m[\![\mathsf{LMem}]\!] \ \mid\ c[\![\mathsf{Client}]\!]$$

and many different sequences of reductions are possible. But the variations are minor. All will involve four applications of the axiom (R-COMM), two at the memory site m and two at client site c. They will also require four applications of (R-MOVE), two in each direction, together with some house-keeping moves involving (R-C.CREATE), (R-SPLIT) and (R-UNWIND). There is some variation in the sequence of application of these rules but all sequences will eventually end in a system structurally equivalent to

$$m[\![\mathsf{LMem}]\!] \ \mid\ c[\![\mathsf{print}!\langle 4\rangle]\!]$$ ■

Although the mobility construct of ADPI, $\mathsf{goto}\, k.P$, is elementary it can be used to describe more complex frameworks, such as *code servers* that on request will initialise code at different locations. A typical generic example is given by:

$$\mathsf{server}[\![\mathsf{init}?(x, y)\ \mathsf{goto}\, y.\mathsf{code}(x)]\!]$$

Here $\mathsf{code}(x)$ represents some general useful code, with some initialisation paramater x. The *code server*, located at server receives requests at init, which expects to receive some initialisation data say n, to be bound to x, and a location k, to be bound to y. It spawns an agent that migrates to k and runs the intialised code $\mathsf{code}(n)$ there.

Of course to be useful this server must be able to respond to repeated requests. This is easily achieved, by transforming the body into a recursive agent. We pursue this idea in the following example.

Example 5.7 [*A Located Memory Server*] Let us now see how to describe a distributed version of the *memory service* described in Example 3.15. We will in fact see two versions.

The server takes the form

$$s[\![\mathsf{LmemS}]\!] \tag{5.12}$$

where LmemS is the code assuring the service. The server location s contains a request channel req where requests are received. A client sends a *reply address*, a located channel, the server generates a new located memory cell, using the code of the previous example LMem, and delivers the new location name at the reply address:

$$\mathsf{LmemS} \Leftarrow \mathsf{rec}\ z.\ \mathsf{req}?(y@w)\ (\mathsf{newloc}\ m : \mathsf{M})\ \ \mathsf{with}\ \mathsf{LMem}\ \mathsf{in}\ (z \mid w.y!\langle m\rangle)$$

A system containing the server and two clients takes the form

$$s[\![\mathsf{LmemS}]\!] \mid c_1[\![\mathsf{Client}_1]\!] \mid c_2[\![\mathsf{Client}_2]\!] \tag{5.13}$$

where now the client-side code is defined by

$$\mathsf{Client}_i \Leftarrow (\mathsf{newc}\ r : \mathsf{D}_r)\ (s.\mathsf{req}!\langle r@c_i\rangle \mid r?(x)\ C_i(x))$$

A client generates a new reply channel, sends a request to the server, for which it needs to know the *address* of the server, the location s and the appropriate method there req, and awaits for the server to deliver the location of the new memory cell.

The reduction semantics, including a judicious use of the structural equivalence, can be used to deduce a derivation from the system (5.13) to the system

$$\begin{aligned} s[\![\mathsf{LmemS}]\!] \mid &(\mathsf{new}\ m_1 : \mathsf{M})(m_1[\![\mathsf{LMem}]\!] \mid c_1[\![C_1(m_1)]\!]) \\ \mid &(\mathsf{new}\ m_2 : \mathsf{M})(m_2[\![\mathsf{LMem}]\!] \mid c_2[\![C_2(m_2)]\!]) \end{aligned} \tag{5.14}$$

There are a number of points worth making about this system. First the type system needs to ensure that friends of, say the first client, who have gained capabilities on the instances of put and get at m_1 cannot use these capabilities at m_2. Also the form of the resulting system (5.14) indicates that Client_i has control over knowledge of its respective memory m_i. By extending the capability based type system of Section 3.4 to ADPI we can ensure that these clients can selectively distribute restricted capabilities on their own memory cells.

Also the methods put and get now exist at two separate locations, m_1 and m_2. The type system will allow such use of method, or resource, names. Here the server ensures that they are declared with the same type but a priori our typechecking system will not impose any type consistency between the various instantiations of a resource name at different locations. This question will be addressed in Section 5.5.

The server we have defined, in (5.12) above, has the responsibility to generate the location of the memory cell. An alternative strategy would be for the clients themselves to generate the site, send the name to the server, who then installs the appropriate servicing code at the proffered site. Here the server code, running at the server site s, takes the form

$$\mathsf{LmemSV_{bis}} \Leftarrow \mathsf{rec}\ z.\ \mathsf{req}?(x, y@w)\ (z \mid \mathsf{goto}\, x.\mathsf{LMem} \mid w.y!)$$

whereas that of a client is given by

$$\begin{aligned}\mathsf{Client_{bis_i}} \Leftarrow\ & (\mathsf{newc}\, a : \mathsf{D}_a) \\ & (\mathsf{newloc}\, m : \mathsf{M})\ \ \mathsf{with}\ s.\mathsf{req}!\langle (m_i, a@c_i)\rangle\ \mathsf{in}\ a?\ C_i(m)\end{aligned}$$

A client, such as

$$c_1[\![\mathsf{Client_{bis_1}}]\!]$$

generates an acknowledgement channel a and a new location m with the installed code

$$s.\mathsf{req}!\langle (m_1, a@c_1)\rangle$$

This of course immediately leaves the newly created site to deliver a request to the server. Meanwhile at the client's site c_1 an acknowledgement is awaited from the server that the servicing code has been installed at m_1.

Once more the reduction semantics can be used to reduce the system

$$s[\![\mathsf{LmemSV_{bis}}]\!] \mid c_1[\![\mathsf{Client_{bis_1}}]\!] \mid c_2[\![\mathsf{Client_{bis_2}}]\!]$$

to one similar to (5.14) above; only the server is different. ■

5.2 Access control types for ADPI

In this section we explain the (capability) types for ADPI, and the typechecking system, a direct generalisation of the treatment of API in Section 3.4. This is best viewed as a mechanism for controlling the capabilities or permissions on declared names. Since these names now include domain or location names, and the names of resources local to these domains, controlling capabilities on them essentially amounts to controlling the access by agents to domain resources.

5.2.1 The types

The collection of types is described informally in Figure 5.6 and is an extension of those in Figure 3.6. Channel types remain the same, but now are considered to be the types appropriate to *local channels*. A value sent at a type such as $\mathsf{rw}\langle \mathsf{T}\rangle$ is considered to be a channel local to the domain in which the communication happens; recall that $\mathsf{rw}\langle \mathsf{T}\rangle$ is shorthand for the type $\mathsf{rw}\langle \mathsf{T}, \mathsf{T}\rangle$. Non-local channels must be transmitted at *global channel* types; a value at such a type is a located name $r@h$, where r is a channel located at the domain h. In Example 5.1 the service receives a value of this form, an address to which the result is to be returned. These global channel types take the form

$$\mathsf{C@loc}$$

with C representing the capabilities of the channel, and the tag loc the fact that the (unknown) location of the channel arrives with it.

We have already discussed, in the introduction to this chapter, the types of domain names, *location types*. These take the form

$$\mathsf{loc}[a_1 : \mathsf{C}_1, \ldots a_n : \mathsf{C}_n],\ n \geq 0$$

where all resource names a_i are distinct. We do not distinguish between location types that differ only in the ordering of the resource names; we also use loc as an abbreviation for the empty record type $\mathsf{loc}[]$.

The set of transmission types determines the values that can be legally sent and received along channels. As with API, these are tuples of *value types*. These in turn consist of the base types, local and global channel types, and location types. Note that in Figure 5.6 we have also introduced the meta-variable D for types that can be associated with name declarations in systems and agents. Unlike in the previous chapter, here, for the sake of clarity, we will tend to use the more specific meta-types, C for the declaration of a local channel and K for a location, when names are declared; but in the next chapter we will make heavy use of the more generic D.

Local channel types:	$\mathsf{C} ::= \mathsf{r}\langle \mathsf{T}\rangle \mid \mathsf{w}\langle \mathsf{T}\rangle \mid \mathsf{rw}\langle \mathsf{T}_r, \mathsf{T}_w\rangle$ provided $\mathsf{T}_w <: \mathsf{T}_r$
Location types:	$\mathsf{K} ::= \mathsf{loc}[a_1 : \mathsf{C}_1, \ldots, a_n : \mathsf{C}_n],\ n \geq 0$ provided $a_i = a_j$ implies $i = j$
Base types:	$\mathsf{base} ::= \mathsf{int} \mid \mathsf{bool} \mid \mathsf{unit} \mid \mathsf{str} \mid \ldots$
Declaration types	$\mathsf{D} ::= \mathsf{C} \mid \mathsf{K}$
Value types:	$\mathsf{A} ::= \mathsf{base} \mid \mathsf{C} \mid \mathsf{K} \mid \mathsf{C@loc}$
Transmission types:	$\mathsf{T} ::= (\mathsf{A}_1, \ldots, \mathsf{A}_n),\ n \geq 0$

Figure 5.6 Types for ADPI – informal

(SUB-LOC)

$$\frac{\mathsf{C}_i <: \mathsf{C}'_i, \quad 0 \le i \le k \le n}{\mathsf{loc}[a_1 : \mathsf{C}_1, \ldots, a_n : \mathsf{C}_n] <: \mathsf{loc}[a_1 : \mathsf{C}'_1, \ldots, a_k : \mathsf{C}'_k]}$$

(SUB-HOM)

$$\frac{\mathsf{C} <: \mathsf{C}'}{\mathsf{C}@\mathsf{loc} <: \mathsf{C}'@\mathsf{loc}}$$

(SUB-TUPLE) (SUB-BASE) (SUB-PROC) as in Figure 4.7
(SUB-CHAN.A) (SUB-CHAN.B)

Figure 5.7 Subtyping for ADPI

The subtyping relation between types is a direct generalisation of that used for API. The defining rules are given in Figure 5.7 and are a natural extension of those in Figure 3.7 for API types. As already mentioned in the introduction the main new rule pertains to location types. Whenever $k \le n$, and $\mathsf{C}_i <: \mathsf{C}'_i$ for each i between 0 and k, we can conclude

$$\mathsf{loc}[a_1 : \mathsf{C}_1, \ldots, a_n : \mathsf{C}_n] <: \mathsf{loc}[a_1 : \mathsf{C}'_1, \ldots, a_k : \mathsf{C}'_k]$$

Note that this implies $\mathsf{L} <: \mathsf{loc}$ for every location type L. The relation is extended to global channel types homomorphically with the rule (SUB-HOM).

Definition 5.8 (capability types for ADPI) We define the *capability types for* ADPI to be the set of all T such that

$$\mathsf{T} <: \mathsf{T}$$

can be derived using the subtyping rules, given in Figure 5.7. We reuse **Types** for this set of valid types, and will also use the notation $\vdash \mathsf{T} : \mathbf{ty}$ to denote the fact that T is a valid type. ♦

Proposition 5.9 The pre-order $\langle$**Types**, $<:\rangle$ *is partially complete.*

Proof: (outline) To show that $<:$ is actually a pre-order on **Types** the same technique as in Lemma 3.18 can be employed.

The definition of the partial meet and partial join operation given in Proposition 3.20 can be extended in a natural manner for the new types. On global channel types we simply use induction while on location types the (partial) meet operation is defined point-wise. If K, L are the types

$$\mathsf{loc}[a_1 : \mathsf{C}_1, \ldots a_n : \mathsf{C}_n] \text{ and } \mathsf{loc}[b_1 : \mathsf{C}'_1, \ldots b_{n'} : \mathsf{C}'_{n'}]$$

respectively, then $\mathsf{K} \sqcap \mathsf{L}$ is defined only when $a_i = b_j$ implies $\mathsf{C}_i \downarrow \mathsf{C}'_j$. In this case it is defined to be

$$\mathsf{loc}[c_1 : \mathsf{D}_1, \ldots, c_m : \mathsf{D}_k]$$

where $c_1, \ldots, c_k, \ldots, c_m$ consists of all the a_i and b_j, and D_k is given by:

- If $c_k = a_i = b_j$ then D_k is defined to be $\mathsf{C}_i \sqcap \mathsf{C}'_j$; because resource names are unique in location types there will be at most one such pair i, j.
- If $c_k = a_i$ and a_i does not appear in the L then D_k is defined to be C_i.
- Symmetrically if $c_k = b_j$ and b_j does not appear in K then D_k is defined to be C'_j.

The join operation, total on location types, is defined in a slightly different manner; $\mathsf{K} \sqcup \mathsf{L}$ is given by

$$\mathsf{loc}[c_1 : \mathsf{D}_1, \ldots, c_m : \mathsf{D}_k]$$

where this time $c_1, \ldots, c_k, \ldots, c_m$ is the set of names that appear in *both* $a_1 \ldots a_n$ and $b_1 \ldots b_{n'}$ and for which the corresponding type D_k exists; if $c_k = a_i = b_j$ then D_k is taken to be $\mathsf{C}_i \sqcup \mathsf{C}'_j$.

So for example if K, L are

$$\mathsf{loc}[a : \mathsf{w}\langle\mathsf{int}\rangle,\ b : \mathsf{w}\langle\mathsf{bool}\rangle] \qquad \mathsf{loc}[a : \mathsf{r}\langle\mathsf{int}\rangle,\ c : \mathsf{r}\langle\mathsf{bool}\rangle]$$

respectively, then $\mathsf{K} \sqcap \mathsf{L}$, $\mathsf{K} \sqcup \mathsf{L}$ are

$$\mathsf{loc}[a : \mathsf{rw}\langle\mathsf{int}\rangle,\ b : \mathsf{w}\langle\mathsf{bool}\rangle,\ c : \mathsf{r}\langle\mathsf{bool}\rangle] \qquad \text{and } \mathsf{loc}[]$$

respectively. If L had the additional resource $b : \mathsf{r}\langle\mathsf{int}\rangle$ then $\mathsf{K} \sqcap \mathsf{L}$ would no longer exist since $\mathsf{r}\langle\mathsf{bool}\rangle$ and $\mathsf{w}\langle\mathsf{int}\rangle$, the entries for b in K, L respectively, are not consistent. On the other hand $\mathsf{K} \sqcup \mathsf{L}$ would still be well-defined, as $\sqcup$ is a total operation on location types; it would still be equal to $\mathsf{loc}[]$. If the type of a in K were changed to $\mathsf{rw}\langle\mathsf{int}\rangle$ then $\mathsf{K} \sqcup \mathsf{L}$ would be the non-trivial type $\mathsf{loc}[a : \mathsf{r}\langle\mathsf{int}\rangle]$.

We leave the reader to check that the proof given in Proposition 3.20 can be extended, to these new definitions. ■

5.2.2 Type environments

Typechecking in ADPI is organised in a manner similar to that in API, but now with additional judgements of the form

$$\Gamma \vdash M$$

where M is a system term and Γ a type environment. Here type environments are more complicated, which is not surprising in view of the range of roles declared names may play. The main added complexity stems from the fact that some names only have local significance, those used for resources, while others, those used for locations, have global significance. Consequently we need to introduce some additional notation, which at first sight may seem unnecessarily tedious. However we will quickly develop some conventions that will tame the added complexity.

Again type environments are lists of associations between identifiers and types, and the following forms are allowed:

- $u : \mathsf{loc}$, indicating that u is the name of a domain
- $u@w : \mathsf{C}$, indicating that the identifier u, used at the domain w, represents a resource at type C there; these are *local channel type* associations
- $x@w : \mathsf{proc}$, indicating that the variable x is used in the definition of a recursive process, running at location w
- $x : \mathsf{base}$, indicating that the variable x is to be bound to a base value of type base.

It is important to note that in $u@w : \mathsf{C}$ both u and w may be identifiers; both may be either names or variables. These will be essential to type systems such as

$$k[\![a?(x@y)\ \mathsf{goto}\, y.x?(z)\, P]\!]$$

Here we will eventually end up typing the body $x?(z)\, P$ relative to an environment with the associations $x@y : \mathsf{C}$, and $y : \mathsf{loc}$.

As with API, it is convenient to have an extra meta-variable for the class of types that can appear in these new environments; we re-use that employed in Chapter 3:

$$\mathsf{E} ::= \mathsf{loc} \mid \mathsf{C} \mid \mathsf{base} \mid \mathsf{proc} \tag{5.15}$$

Thus environments will be restricted lists of the

$$e_1 : \mathsf{E}_1,\ e_2 : \mathsf{E}_2,\ \ldots, e_n : \mathsf{E}_n,\ n \geq 0$$

These restrictions are enforced by giving an inductive definition of valid environments, using an extension of the rules in Figure 3.8 for API, and, as in that case, the rules for the assignment of types to values are given simultaneously. But here there is a slight change. Certain resource names may exist in one domain and not in another, and therefore identifiers can only be assigned types, relative to a given domain. The judgements therefore take the form

$$\Gamma \vdash_w V : \mathsf{T} \tag{5.16}$$

and are designed so that they can only be inferred when w is known in Γ to be a domain name. But, as we shall see, in many cases the actual location w may be omitted from these judgements.

First let us consider the rules for valid environment formation. Recall that for TYPED API, because of our view of types as capabilities, we allowed multiple entries for a given identifier, provided all the entries were consistent. Here we carry over this idea, but now consistency will in general be relative to a specific location.

Definition 5.10 (*local consistency*) Let $\Gamma \downarrow_w u : \mathsf{E}$ denote the fact that for every type E', $\Gamma \vdash_w u : \mathsf{E}'$ implies $\mathsf{E}' \downarrow \mathsf{E}$.

(E-PROC)
$$\frac{\Gamma \vdash w : \mathsf{loc}}{\Gamma, x@w : \mathsf{proc} \vdash \mathbf{env}} \quad x \notin \Gamma$$

(E-BASE)
$$\frac{\Gamma \vdash \mathbf{env}}{\Gamma, x : \mathsf{base} \vdash \mathbf{env}} \quad \Gamma \downarrow_w x : \mathsf{base}$$

(E-LOC)
$$\frac{\Gamma \vdash \mathbf{env}}{\Gamma, u : \mathsf{loc} \vdash \mathbf{env}} \quad \Gamma \downarrow u : \mathsf{loc}$$

(E-CHAN)
$$\frac{\vdash \mathsf{C} : \mathbf{ty} \qquad \Gamma \vdash w : \mathsf{loc}}{\Gamma, u@w : \mathsf{C} \vdash \mathbf{env}} \quad \Gamma \downarrow_w u : \mathsf{C}$$

Figure 5.8 Type environments in ADPI

(TY-C.SUB)
$$\frac{\Gamma, u@w : \mathsf{C}, \Gamma' \vdash \mathbf{env}}{\Gamma, u@w : \mathsf{C}, \Gamma' \vdash_w u : \mathsf{C}'} \quad \mathsf{C} <: \mathsf{C}'$$

(TY-PROC.SUB)
$$\frac{\Gamma, x@w : \mathsf{proc}, \Gamma' \vdash \mathbf{env}}{\Gamma, x@w : \mathsf{proc}, \Gamma' \vdash_w x : \mathsf{proc}}$$

(TY-G.SUB)
$$\frac{\Gamma, u : \mathsf{E}, \Gamma' \vdash w : \mathsf{loc}}{\Gamma, u : \mathsf{E}, \Gamma' \vdash_w u : \mathsf{E}'} \quad \mathsf{E} <: \mathsf{E}'$$

(TY-LOC.SUB)
$$\frac{\Gamma, w : \mathsf{loc}, \Gamma' \vdash \mathbf{env}}{\Gamma, w : \mathsf{loc}, \Gamma' \vdash w : \mathsf{loc}}$$

(TY-LOC)
$$\frac{\Gamma \vdash_w v : \mathsf{loc} \qquad \Gamma \vdash_v a_i : \mathsf{C}_i,\ 0 \le i \le n}{\Gamma \vdash_w v : \mathsf{loc}[a_1 : \mathsf{C}_1, \ldots, a_n : \mathsf{C}_n]}$$

(TY-LOCATED.CHANNEL)
$$\frac{\Gamma \vdash_v u : \mathsf{C} \qquad \Gamma \vdash_w v : \mathsf{loc}}{\Gamma \vdash_w u@v : \mathsf{C}@\mathsf{loc}}$$

(STY-BASE)
$$\frac{\Gamma \vdash w : \mathsf{loc}}{\Gamma \vdash_w \mathsf{bv} : \mathsf{base}} \quad \mathsf{bv} \in \mathsf{base}$$

(TY-TUP), (TY-MEET)

adapted from Figure 4.9

Figure 5.9 Typing values in ADPI

As we shall see for many types, in particular location types, this predicate is actually independent of the particular location w, and therefore it will often be omitted. ♦

The rules for constructing new environments are given in Figure 5.8, although the base case, (E-EMPTY) from Figure 3.3 is omitted. It will be technically convenient to allow multiple entries of location name declarations, and variables of base type. This is allowed by the rules (E-LOC) and (E-BASE), where the side-conditions use the notation just introduced. Also note that the rule for introducing recursion variables, (E-PROC), ensures that these are declared at a specific location. The rule for adding local channel names is very natural. To add the entry $u@w : \mathsf{C}$ we have to ensure w is actually a location, and that the type C is consistent with all existing entries for u at the proposed location w, that is $\Gamma \downarrow_w u : \mathsf{C}$.

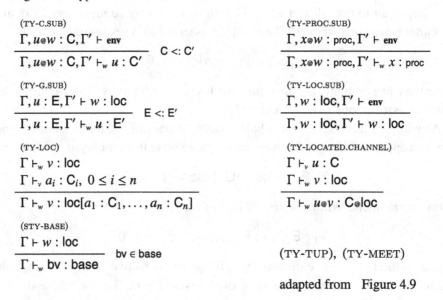

The rules for type assignment to values are given in Figure 5.9, and many are adapted directly from Figure 3.9, the corresponding rules for API, to take into account the fact that judgements are now local to a particular domain. The environment look-up rule from there, (TY-SUB), now has four different versions depending on the type of the identifier in question. The first two, (TY-C.SUB) for channels and (TY-PROC.SUB) for recursive definitions, are local. The slightly artificial rule (TY-LOC.SUB) for locations is required in order to be able to apply the global rule (TY-G.SUB); because of our constraints on environment formation this can only be used when E is either a base type, or the degenerate loc. The new rule (TY-LOC) is used to assign a location type $\mathsf{K} = \mathsf{loc}[a_1 : \mathsf{C}_1, \ldots a_n : \mathsf{C}_n]$ to an identifier, while (TY-LOCATED.CHANNEL) is the obvious rule to assign a global channel type to a located identifier. Notice that in both these new rules w, the location at which this typing is inferred, plays a limited role. This is true of many types in the judgements (5.16) above, and we will call such types global; specifically value types of the form base, K and $\mathsf{C@loc}$ are said to be *global*, while a transmission type T is *global* if all of its components are global. We leave the reader to check the following simple observation:

Lemma 5.11 If T *is a global type then* $\Gamma \vdash_w V : \mathsf{T}$ *implies* $\Gamma \vdash_{w'} V : \mathsf{T}$ *for every* w' *such that* $\Gamma \vdash w' : \mathsf{loc}$. ■

Consequently we will often omit these locations, for example writing $\Gamma \vdash w : \mathsf{K}$ for a location type K, if for any u, $\Gamma \vdash_u \mathsf{K}$.

As we have seen in Chapter 3 for API, typechecking requires the dynamic construction of environments, as the analysis of a term proceeds. For example the rule (TY-IN) in Figure 3.10, which is aimed at typing the API term $u?(X)\,R$ relative to the environment Γ, requires the analysis of R in the extended environment $\Gamma, \langle X{:}\mathsf{T}\rangle$, for some type T. This new environment is construed to be Γ to which has been added the association list $\langle X{:}\mathsf{T}\rangle$ obtained from the pattern X and the type T. In ADPI these patterns are more complicated as they involve compound values, and moreover typechecking will be relative to a specific location, as resources are location specific. We need a generalisation of Definition 3.2, for constructing environments from values and types.

(TY-CNEW)
$$\frac{\Gamma, c@k : \mathsf{C} \vdash M}{\Gamma \vdash (\mathsf{new}\, c@k : \mathsf{C})\, M}$$

(TY-LNEW)
$$\frac{\Gamma, \langle k{:}\mathsf{K}\rangle \vdash M}{\Gamma \vdash (\mathsf{new}\, k : \mathsf{K})\, M}$$

(TY-ZERO)
$$\frac{\Gamma \vdash \mathbf{env}}{\Gamma \vdash \mathbf{0}}$$

(TY-CON)
$$\frac{\Gamma \vdash M \qquad \Gamma \vdash N}{\Gamma \vdash M \mid N}$$

(TY-AGENT)
$$\frac{\Gamma \vdash_k P : \mathsf{proc}}{\Gamma \vdash k[\![P]\!]}$$

Figure 5.10 Typing systems

Definition 5.12 (*constructing environments*) We define an association list $\langle V{:}\mathsf{T}\rangle_{@w}$ from a value V, an identifier w and a transmission type T, by induction on the structure of the value.

- V is a base value bv. Then T must be the base type of bv and in this case the result is the empty list.
- V is a variable x and T is a base value base. Then $\langle V{:}\mathsf{T}\rangle_{@w}$ is the singleton list $x : \mathsf{base}$.
- V is an identifier u and T is a local channel type C. Then $\langle V{:}\mathsf{T}\rangle_{@w}$ is the singleton list $u_{@w} : \mathsf{C}$.
- V is an identifier u and T is a location type $\mathsf{loc}[a_1 : \mathsf{C}_1, \ldots, a_k : \mathsf{C}_k]$. Here $\langle V{:}\mathsf{T}\rangle_{@w}$ is the list $u : \mathsf{loc}, a_{1@u} : \mathsf{C}_1, \ldots, a_{k@u} : \mathsf{C}_k$. Note that in this case w plays no role in the construction of the list.
- V is the located identifier $u_{@v}$. Here T must have the form $\mathsf{C}_{@}\mathsf{loc}$ and again, the resulting list $\langle V{:}\mathsf{T}\rangle_{@w}$ will be independent of w. It is constructed in the natural manner, giving $v : \mathsf{loc},\ u_{@v} : \mathsf{C}$.
- V is the tuple $(V_1, \ldots, V_n)$. In this case we need T to be of the form $(\mathsf{A}_1, \ldots, \mathsf{A}_n)$, in which case the resulting list $\langle V{:}\mathsf{T}\rangle_{@w}$ is constructed by induction: $\langle V_1{:}\mathsf{A}_1\rangle_{@w}, \ldots, \langle V_n{:}\mathsf{A}_n\rangle_{@w}$.

♦

It is worthwhile comparing this definition with the corresponding one for API, Definition 3.2. Here we need the extra parameter, a location w, which is actually only used in the case of a (local) channel type C. In addition we need two new cases, for location types, and for located identifiers. But note that for global types, as we have defined above, w plays no role. For such types we will often abbreviate $\langle V{:}\mathsf{T}\rangle_{@w}$ to simply $\langle V{:}\mathsf{T}\rangle$. Indeed this *global* notation may be further extended by letting $\langle u_{@w}{:}\mathsf{C}\rangle$ be the singleton list, $u_{@w} : \mathsf{C}$. In this way we will have a way of constructing a type association list $\langle e{:}\mathsf{D}\rangle$ for every name creation $(\mathsf{new}\, e : \mathsf{D})(-)$ allowed in well-typed ADPI systems; this notation will be used extensively in the following chapter.

But again note that these lists, both located and unlocated, are only defined if the structure of the value V matches that of the type T, and in many cases the result is not a valid environment; for example in the case for tuples the different components may add conflicting information about an identifier to the list. However, there is a simple criterion for being able to extend well-defined type environments with these lists, at least in the case of simple values; this is a generalisation of the rule (E-CHAN) from Figure 5.8.

Lemma 5.13 (extension lemma) *Suppose* $\Gamma \vdash \mathbf{env}$. *Then* $\Gamma \downarrow_w u : \mathsf{D}$ *implies* $\Gamma, \langle u{:}\mathsf{D}\rangle_{@w} \vdash \mathbf{env}$.

Proof: If D is a local channel type this follows from (E-CHAN); so let us assume it is the location type $\mathsf{loc}[c_1 : \mathsf{C}_1, \ldots c_n : \mathsf{C}_n]$; we have to show $\Gamma, u : \mathsf{loc}, c_{1@u} : \mathsf{C}_1, \ldots, c_{n@w} : \mathsf{C}_n \vdash \mathbf{env}$.

First $\Gamma \downarrow_w u : \mathsf{D}$ implies $\Gamma \downarrow_w u : \mathsf{loc}$ and therefore an application of (E-LOC) gives $\Gamma, u : \mathsf{loc} \vdash \mathbf{env}$. Now, in order to apply (E-CHAN), suppose $\Gamma, u : \mathsf{loc} \vdash_u c_1 : \mathsf{C}$. This must mean that $\Gamma \vdash u : \mathsf{loc}$ and $\Gamma \vdash_u c_1 : \mathsf{C}$, and therefore $\Gamma \vdash u : \mathsf{loc}[c_1 : \mathsf{C}]$. From $\Gamma \downarrow_w u : \mathsf{D}$ it follows that $\mathsf{loc}[c_1 : \mathsf{C}] \downarrow \mathsf{D}$, which can only be the case if $\mathsf{C} \downarrow \mathsf{C}_1$. Therefore an application of (E-CHAN) gives $\Gamma, u : \mathsf{loc}, c_1@u : \mathsf{C}_1 \vdash \mathbf{env}$.

This argument can be repeated for each entry $c_i@u : \mathsf{C}_i$ because all c_j are distinct.

5.2.3 Typechecking

At last we are in a position to give the typechecking rules for aDpi systems. As we have already noted judgements are of the form

$$\Gamma \vdash M$$

where Γ is an association list and M a system; the inference rules are given in Figure 5.10. These are designed so that such a judgement can only be inferred when Γ is a valid type environment and, as usual, they can only be applied to systems M whose bound names do not appear in Γ. The rule (TY-ZERO) says that the empty system $\mathbf{0}$ is well-typed relative to any valid type environment Γ. To ensure the composite system $M \mid N$ is well-typed, the rule (TY-CON) dictates that it is sufficient to infer that the individual components M and N are well-typed. There are two different kinds of entities that can be declared globally for a system and for the sake of clarity each has its own inference rule. First let us consider the declaration of local resources, which is straightforward. According to (TY-CNEW) the system $(\mathsf{new}\, c@k : \mathsf{C})\, M$ is well-typed relative to Γ,

$$\Gamma \vdash (\mathsf{new}\, c@k : \mathsf{C})\, M \tag{5.17}$$

provided M is well-typed relative to the extended association list $\Gamma, c@k : \mathsf{C}$. In writing (5.17) we are assuming that the bound name c does not appear in Γ, but nevertheless we are not necessarily guaranteed that this extended association list is in fact a valid type environment; the location of the newly declared channel, k, needs to be known to Γ. Of course this is not stated explicitly as a requirement but at some point in the derivation of

$$\Gamma, c@k : \mathsf{C} \vdash M$$

it will be necessary to check that $\Gamma, c@k : \mathsf{C}$ is a valid environment, and to do so it will need to be the case that $\Gamma \vdash k : \mathsf{loc}$.

The declaration of new locations, in rule (TY-LNEW), is similar; the body M is typechecked relative to the association list $\Gamma, \langle k{:}\mathsf{K}\rangle$. Once more implicitly this will only be possible if the augmented list turns out to be a well-defined type environment. It is also worth noting that, using the notation introduced on page 146 after Definition 5.12, these two rules can be subsumed by the more generic:

$$\text{(TY-NEW)}\quad \frac{\Gamma, \langle e{:}\mathsf{D}\rangle \vdash M}{\Gamma \vdash (\mathsf{new}\, e : \mathsf{D})\, M}$$

However for the sake of clarity, we have preferred to spell out the individual cases.

Finally, to typecheck the located agent $k[\![P]\!]$ relative to Γ we use the rule (TY-AGENT); this ensures that the agent it well-typed to run at k. Agents need to be checked relative to locations because of the use of *local channels*. For example the agent

$$c?(x)\, R$$

will only be well-typed to run at a location k if there is a local channel named c declared at k. Thus for agents we require judgements of the form

$$\Gamma \vdash_w P : \mathsf{proc}$$

indicating that P is well-typed to run at location w. An instance of this is used in (TY-AGENT) to check that the located agent $k[\![P]\!]$ is well-typed.

So now let us turn to this typechecking of agent terms, relative to a location w. The inference rules are given in Figure 5.11 and, although relativised to the location w, have much in common with those for typechecking API, in Figure 3.10 and Figure 3.5. The rules (TY-STOP) and (TY-PAR) are inherited directly while the rules for input and output are minor variations. For example to infer

$$\Gamma \vdash_w u?(X)\, R : \mathsf{proc}$$

we must ensure that u is a channel declared *locally* at w, with an appropriate capability,

$$\Gamma \vdash_w u : \mathsf{r}\langle \mathsf{T}\rangle$$

and that the residual R can be typed, relative to w, in an extended environment. This is obtained by extending Γ with the type associations $\langle X{:}\mathsf{T}\rangle@w$. Again our assumption about bound identifiers ensures that the variables in X are new to Γ; so if Γ is a valid environment in which w is known to be a location, the extension will also be, provided that the structure of the pattern X matches that of the type T.

Similarly to ensure $u!\langle V\rangle$ is well-typed to run at w, relative to Γ, we must ensure

- u is declared at the location w and can be assigned some write capability appropriate to the transmission of V,

$$\Gamma \vdash_w u : \mathsf{w}\langle \mathsf{T}\rangle$$

- and *at* w the value to be transmitted, V, can be assigned the transmission type T,

$$\Gamma \vdash_w V : \mathsf{T}$$

(TY-OUT)

$$\frac{\Gamma \vdash_w V : \mathsf{T} \quad \Gamma \vdash_w u : \mathsf{w}\langle \mathsf{T} \rangle}{\Gamma \vdash_w u!\langle V \rangle : \mathsf{proc}}$$

(TY-IN)

$$\frac{\Gamma, \langle X{:}\mathsf{T} \rangle @ w \vdash_w R : \mathsf{proc} \quad \Gamma \vdash_w u : \mathsf{r}\langle \mathsf{T} \rangle}{\Gamma \vdash_w u?(X)\, R : \mathsf{proc}}$$

(TY-GO)

$$\frac{\Gamma \vdash u : \mathsf{loc} \quad \Gamma \vdash_u R : \mathsf{proc}}{\Gamma \vdash_w \mathsf{goto}\, u.R : \mathsf{proc}}$$

(TY-STOP)

$$\frac{\Gamma \vdash \mathbf{env}}{\Gamma \vdash_w \mathsf{stop} : \mathsf{proc}}$$

(TY-LP.NEW)

$$\frac{\Gamma, \langle k{:}\mathsf{K} \rangle \vdash_w R : \mathsf{proc}}{\Gamma \vdash_w (\mathsf{newloc}\, k : \mathsf{K})\ R : \mathsf{proc}}$$

(TY-CP.NEW)

$$\frac{\Gamma, c @ w : \mathsf{C} \vdash_w R : \mathsf{proc}}{\Gamma \vdash_w (\mathsf{newc}\, c : \mathsf{C})\ R : \mathsf{proc}}$$

(TY-MATCH)

$$\frac{\Gamma \vdash_w v_1 : \mathsf{A}_1, v_2 : \mathsf{A}_2 \quad \Gamma \vdash_w R_2 : \mathsf{proc} \quad \Gamma, \langle v_1{:}\mathsf{A}_2 \rangle @ w, \langle v_2{:}\mathsf{A}_1 \rangle @ w \vdash_w R_1 : \mathsf{proc}}{\Gamma \vdash_w \mathsf{if}\ v_1 = v_2\ \mathsf{then}\ R_1\ \mathsf{else}\ R_2 : \mathsf{proc}}$$

(TY-MIS.MATCH)

$$\frac{\Gamma \vdash_w v_1 : \mathsf{A}_1,\ v_2 : \mathsf{A}_2 \quad \Gamma \vdash_w R_2 : \mathsf{proc}}{\Gamma \vdash_w \mathsf{if}\ v_1 = v_2\ \mathsf{then}\ R_1\ \mathsf{else}\ R_2 : \mathsf{proc}}\ \mathsf{A}_1 \not\downarrow \mathsf{A}_2$$

(TY-REC)

$$\frac{\Gamma, x : \mathsf{proc} @ w \vdash_w B : \mathsf{proc}}{\Gamma \vdash_w \mathsf{rec}\ x.\ B : \mathsf{proc}}$$

(TY-PAR)

$$\frac{\Gamma \vdash_w R_1 : \mathsf{proc} \quad \Gamma \vdash_w R_2 : \mathsf{proc}}{\Gamma \vdash_w R_1 \mid R_2 : \mathsf{proc}}$$

Figure 5.11 Typing agents

Typing the migration construct, with (TY-GO), is straightforward. We can infer

$$\Gamma \vdash_w \mathsf{goto}\, u.R : \mathsf{proc}$$

provided u is known to Γ as a domain,

$$\Gamma \vdash u : \mathsf{loc}$$

and the agent R is well-typed to run at the target domain u,

$$\Gamma \vdash_u R : \mathsf{proc}$$

There are two rules for typing local declarations, (TY-CP.NEW), (TY-LP.NEW). We have already discussed at length the corresponding rules at the system level, and these are very similar. For example to typecheck

$$(\mathsf{newc}\, c : \mathsf{C})\ R$$

relative to Γ at the location w, we need to typecheck the process term R relative to the extended environment $\Gamma, c @ w : \mathsf{C}$. Because we are typechecking the process to run at w the locally declared channel c is added to the environment with the compound name $c @ w$.

Typechecking the match construct

$$\text{if } v_1 = v_2 \text{ then } R_1 \text{ else } R_2$$

is handled by the obvious localised versions of the corresponding rules for TYPED API. Finally note that the typechecking of a recursive process $\text{rec } x.\ B$, via (TY-REC), is always carried out relative to a specific domain w; in effect each recursive call to its body must be at the same location.

5.2.4 Examples

Throughout this section, and indeed for the remainder of the chapter we will abbreviate the agent judgements $\Gamma \vdash_w P : \text{proc}$ to simply $\Gamma \vdash_w P$.

As a first example let us consider how pattern matching, and the environment construction mechanism given in Definition 5.12, plays a central role in distinguishing between local and global channels.

Example 5.14 [*Pattern Matching*] First suppose that Γ_1 is a (valid) type environment that contains the type association $\text{in}@s : \text{rw}\langle\text{rw}\langle\text{int}\rangle\rangle$. Then one can check that

$$\Gamma_1 \vdash s[\![\text{in}?(x)\, x!\langle 7\rangle]\!]$$

This follows using (TY-AGENT) in Figure 5.10 from

$$\Gamma_1 \vdash_s \text{in}?(x)\, x!\langle 7\rangle$$

which in turn requires an application of (TY-IN) in Figure 5.11 to

$$\Gamma_1, \langle x{:}\text{rw}\langle\text{int}\rangle\rangle@s \vdash_s x!\langle 7\rangle \tag{5.18}$$

since, by (TY-C.SUB) of Figure 5.9, $\Gamma_1 \vdash_s \text{in} : \text{r}\langle\text{rw}\langle\text{int}\rangle\rangle$. The important point to note about this judgement, (5.18), is that the environment unravels, via Definition 5.12, to $\Gamma_1,\ x@s : \text{rw}\langle\text{int}\rangle$. In other words the incoming value on in, bound to x, is taken to be a channel name local to the site s; because of this the judgement (5.18) is easily established, via (TY-OUT).

For this reason a system such as

$$s[\![\text{in}?(x)\ \text{goto}\ k.x!\langle 7\rangle]\!]$$

cannot be typed relative to Γ_1, even if k is known in Γ_1 as a location. For this would require, via (TY-GO), the judgement

$$\Gamma_1,\ x@s : \text{rw}\langle\text{int}\rangle \vdash_k x!\langle 7\rangle$$

This in turn could only be inferred via (TY-OUT), which would require

$$\Gamma_1,\ x@s : \text{rw}\langle\text{int}\rangle \vdash_k x : \text{w}\langle\text{int}\rangle$$

This of course is impossible, as x has just been established as a channel name local to the original site at which it was received, s; as a bound variable in the system being typed, x cannot occur in Γ_1.

Channels that are not local to the domain s can only be received at s as part of a compound value. To see how these are typed let Γ_2 be an environment such that

$$\Gamma_2 \vdash_s \mathsf{in} : \mathsf{rw}\langle\ \mathsf{rw}\langle\mathsf{int}\rangle@\mathsf{loc}\ \rangle$$

Then we can infer the judgement

$$\Gamma_2 \vdash s[\![\mathsf{in}?(x@y)\ \mathsf{goto}\ y.x!\langle 7\rangle]\!] \tag{5.19}$$

Here a compound value is received at in, consisting of a location, bound to y, and a channel, bound to x, which is presumed to exist at the location y. Establishing (5.19) requires

$$\Gamma_2, \langle x@y{:}\mathsf{rw}\langle\mathsf{int}\rangle@\mathsf{loc}\rangle@s \vdash_s \mathsf{goto}\ y.x!\langle 7\rangle \tag{5.20}$$

Here the environment unravels, via Definition 5.12, to $\Gamma_2,\ y : \mathsf{loc},\ x@y : \mathsf{rw}\langle\mathsf{int}\rangle$ and consequently (5.20) is easily derived using (TY-GO) and (TY-OUT), as x has been recorded as a channel located at y.

However channels can sometimes be assumed to exist by virtue of their occurrence in a location type. To illustrate this consider a third environment Γ_3 such that

$$\Gamma_3 \vdash_s \mathsf{in} : \mathsf{rw}\langle\mathsf{L}\rangle \qquad \text{where } \mathsf{L} = \mathsf{loc}[r : \mathsf{w}\langle\mathsf{int}\rangle]$$

Then

$$\Gamma_3 \vdash s[\![\mathsf{in}?(y)\ \mathsf{goto}\ y.r!\langle 7\rangle]\!]$$

can be established. The crucial step is to derive

$$\Gamma_3,\ \langle y{:}\mathsf{L}\rangle@s \vdash_s \mathsf{goto}\ y.r!\langle 7\rangle$$

However this is straightforward as the augmented environment unravels to $\Gamma_3,\ y : \mathsf{loc},\ r@y : \mathsf{w}\langle\mathsf{int}\rangle$. Because of the type of the channel at which y is received, we know that it is a location at which there is a channel named r at type $\mathsf{w}\langle\mathsf{int}\rangle$. ■

In the next example we examine the declaration of channels and see how the typing system enforces the local nature of their use.

Example 5.15 (*Local Channel Declarations*) Consider the following system:

$$M_1 \Leftarrow l[\![(\mathsf{new}\ c : \mathsf{rw}\langle\mathsf{int}\rangle)\ \mathsf{goto}\ s.(c!\langle 1\rangle \mid c?(x)\ R)]\!]$$

An agent declares a channel c at the location l, migrates to s, and then tries to use c at the new location. Intuitively there is something amiss here; c is declared to be a resource available at l, but an attempt is made to use it at a different location.

Indeed one can check that for no Γ can the judgement

$$\Gamma \vdash M_1$$

be established. This would require an application of (TY-AGENT), preceded by an application of (TY-CP.NEW) to

$$\Gamma, c@l : \mathsf{rw}\langle\mathsf{int}\rangle \vdash_l \mathsf{goto}\, s.(c!\langle 1\rangle \mid c?(x)\, R)$$

that in turn would require establishing, among other things

$$\Gamma, c@l : \mathsf{rw}\langle\mathsf{int}\rangle \vdash_s c!\langle 1\rangle$$

But this is clearly impossible. We know c is fresh to Γ, and so (TY-OUT) can never be used here, since c only exists at the location l, and not s.

As a variation consider

$$M_2 \Leftarrow l[\![(\mathsf{new}\, c : \mathsf{rw}\langle\mathsf{int}\rangle)\, \mathsf{goto}\, s.\mathsf{in}!\langle c\rangle]\!]$$

and the type environment Γ_1 used in the previous example; it has the type association $\mathsf{in}@s : \mathsf{rw}\langle\mathsf{rw}\langle\mathsf{int}\rangle\rangle$. Then one can check that M_2 cannot be checked relative to Γ_1. Again the intuition should be clear. The channel in at location s can only transmit local resources, while an attempt is made to send the resource c, declared at l, on it. Formally the typing judgement $\Gamma_1 \vdash M_2$ cannot be established because it would require the judgement

$$\Gamma_1, c@l : \mathsf{rw}\langle\mathsf{int}\rangle \vdash_s c : \mathsf{rw}\langle\mathsf{int}\rangle$$

that is clearly not possible.

However if Γ_2 has the entry $\mathsf{in}@s : \mathsf{rw}\langle\, \mathsf{rw}\langle\mathsf{int}\rangle@\mathsf{loc}\,\rangle$, as in the previous example, then the reader should be able to establish $\Gamma \vdash M_3$ where

$$M_3 \Leftarrow l[\![(\mathsf{new}\, c : \mathsf{rw}\langle\mathsf{int}\rangle)\, \mathsf{goto}\, s.\mathsf{in}!\langle c@l\rangle]\!]$$

In other words non-local channels can be transmitted at s, provided their location is transmitted at the same time. ■

Now let us consider the typing of the distributed compute server in Example 5.1.

Example 5.16 (*Typing the Distributed Compute Server*) Let us first consider the service code DprimeS running at the site s. Here we also assume the rule

$$\text{(TY-OP)}\quad \frac{\Gamma \vdash u : \mathsf{int}}{\Gamma \vdash_w \mathit{isprime}(u) : \mathsf{bool}} \tag{5.21}$$

a distributed version of the rule (3.12) in Chapter 3, page 65; essentially this says that the *isprime* is available globally, as an operator from integers to booleans. Let Γ be any valid environment that contains the entry

$$\mathsf{in}_p@s : \mathsf{rw}\langle\, (\mathsf{int}, \mathsf{w}\langle\mathsf{bool}\rangle@\mathsf{loc})\,\rangle$$

So in_p is known to be a channel at the site s that can be used for both reading and writing of pairs, the first of which must be an integer. A value at the type $\mathsf{w}\langle\mathsf{bool}\rangle@\mathsf{loc}$ is a global channel along which may be sent a boolean; thus the value will be a located name, of the form $a@l$, where a is located at l. To see how we can derive the judgement

$$\Gamma \vdash s[\![\mathsf{DprimeS}]\!]$$

let us work backwards through a derivation. This will follow from

$$\Gamma \vdash_s \mathsf{DprimeS} \tag{5.22}$$

using (TY-AGENT). To get to (5.22) an application of (TY-REC) to

$$\Gamma, z@s : \mathsf{proc} \vdash_s \mathsf{in}_p?(x, y@w)\ (z \mid \mathsf{goto}\ w.y!\langle isprime(x)\rangle)$$

is required. Here we need an instance of (TY-IN). From our assumption we know that

$$\Gamma \vdash_s \mathsf{in}_p : \mathsf{r}\langle\mathsf{int}, \mathsf{w}\langle\mathsf{bool}\rangle@\mathsf{loc}\rangle$$

This judgement is an instance of (TY-C.SUB) from Figure 5.9 and uses the subtyping relation. Also Definition 5.12 can be applied to calculate the environment $\langle(x, y@w){:}(\mathsf{int}, \mathsf{w}\langle\mathsf{bool}\rangle@\mathsf{loc})\rangle@s$, giving

$$x : \mathsf{int}, w : \mathsf{loc}, y@w : \mathsf{w}\langle\mathsf{bool}\rangle$$

and therefore we need to establish

$$\Gamma, z@s : \mathsf{proc}, x : \mathsf{int}, w : \mathsf{loc}, y@w : \mathsf{w}\langle\mathsf{bool}\rangle\ \vdash_s z \mid \mathsf{goto}\ w.y!\langle isprime(x)\rangle \tag{5.23}$$

In this agent term the dominant operator is | and therefore to derive (5.23) an application of (TY-PAR) is required. One of the premises is a simple lookup of the located recursion variable $z@s$, using (TY-PROC.SUB), and therefore we are left with the premise

$$\Gamma, z@s : \mathsf{proc}, x : \mathsf{int}, w : \mathsf{loc}, y@w : \mathsf{w}\langle\mathsf{bool}\rangle\ \vdash_s \mathsf{goto}\ w.y!\langle isprime(x)\rangle$$

This will follow, by (TY-GO), from

$$\Gamma, z@s : \mathsf{proc}, x : \mathsf{int}, w : \mathsf{loc}, y@w : \mathsf{w}\langle\mathsf{bool}\rangle\ \vdash_w y!\langle isprime(x)\rangle \tag{5.24}$$

It is easy to derive

$$\Gamma, z@s : \mathsf{proc}, x : \mathsf{int}, w : \mathsf{loc}, y@w : \mathsf{w}\langle\mathsf{bool}\rangle\ \vdash_w y : \mathsf{w}\langle\mathsf{bool}\rangle$$

that is one of the premises for an application of (TY-OUT) with (5.24) as a conclusion. The other premise

$$\Gamma, z@w : \mathsf{proc}, x : \mathsf{int}, w : \mathsf{loc}, y@w : \mathsf{w}\langle\mathsf{bool}\rangle\ \vdash_w isprime(x) : \mathsf{bool}$$

follows, assuming an application of the rule (5.21) to the expression *isprime*(*x*), since we have

$$\Gamma, z@w : \mathsf{proc}, x : \mathsf{int}, w : \mathsf{loc}, y@w : \mathsf{w}\langle\mathsf{bool}\rangle \vdash x : \mathsf{int}$$

Let us now consider a typing for a client of this service:

$$h[\![(\mathsf{newc}\, r : \mathsf{D}_r)\ (r?(x)\, \mathsf{print}!\langle x\rangle \mid \mathsf{goto}\, s.\mathsf{in}_p!\langle 11, r@h\rangle)]\!]$$

A priori the client should also be typeable with the Γ used above, provided this also contains an appropriate type for the print channel:

$$\Gamma \vdash_h \mathsf{print} : \mathsf{w}\langle\mathsf{bool}\rangle$$

But we have to decide on the type D_r for the generated reply channel. We have seen that the server requires a *write* capability on any reply channel it receives while the client *reads* from it. So we let

$$\mathsf{D}_r = \mathsf{rw}\langle\mathsf{bool}\rangle$$

Then we can derive the judgement

$$\Gamma \vdash_h (\mathsf{newc}\, r : \mathsf{D}_r)\ (r?(x)\, \mathsf{print}!\langle x\rangle \mid \mathsf{goto}\, s.\mathsf{in}_p!\langle 11, r@h\rangle)$$

Note that this will only be typeable at the site *h* because the newly generated reply channel is exported as the global channel $r@h$.

The last step in this derivation is an application of (TY-CP.NEW) to

$$\Gamma, r@h : \mathsf{D}_r \vdash_h r?(x)\, \mathsf{print}!\langle x\rangle \mid \mathsf{goto}\, s.\mathsf{in}_p!\langle 11, r@h\rangle \tag{5.25}$$

Note that here the newly generated channel *r* has been added to the environment as existing at the site *h*. The derivation of (5.25) requires an application of (TY-PAR) to the two judgements

$$\Gamma, r@h : \mathsf{D}_r \vdash_h \mathsf{goto}\, s.\mathsf{in}_p!\langle 11, r@h\rangle \tag{5.26}$$

and

$$\Gamma, r@h : \mathsf{D}_r \vdash_h r?(x)\, \mathsf{print}!\langle x\rangle$$

We only consider the first of these, (5.26). As above we can deduce , via (TY-C.SUB),

$$\Gamma \vdash_s \mathsf{in}_p : \mathsf{w}\langle\ (\mathsf{int}, \mathsf{w}\langle\mathsf{bool}\rangle@\mathsf{loc})\ \rangle \tag{5.27}$$

and

$$\Gamma, r@h : \mathsf{D}_r \vdash_s \langle 11, r@h\rangle : \langle\mathsf{int}, \mathsf{w}\langle\mathsf{bool}\rangle@\mathsf{loc}\rangle \tag{5.28}$$

Note that this latter inference also involves the use of subtyping, and requires $\Gamma \vdash h : \mathsf{loc}$. Moreover these are global types, and so the actual location of the inference,

s, is unimportant. Now (5.27) and (5.28) can serve as premises to (TY-OUT) to deduce the judgement

$$\Gamma, r@h : \mathsf{D}_r \vdash_s \mathsf{in}_p!\langle 11, r@h\rangle$$

The rule (TY-GO) may then be applied, to obtain the required (5.26). ■

Example 5.17 (*Typing the Memory Cell*) Here we examine what is required to type the code for a memory cell

$$\begin{aligned}\mathsf{LMem} \Leftarrow\ & (\mathsf{new}\, s : \mathsf{S})(s!\langle 0\rangle \\ & \mid \mathsf{rec}\ g.\ \mathsf{get}?(y@w)\ s?(z)\ (w.y!\langle z\rangle \mid s!\langle z\rangle \mid g) \\ & \mid \mathsf{rec}\ p.\ \mathsf{put}?(x, y@w)\ s?(z)\ (w.y! \mid s!\langle x\rangle \mid p)\end{aligned}$$

as defined in Example 5.6. The internal resource s is both written to and read from, and so the declaration type S should be the type $\mathsf{rw}\langle\mathsf{int}\rangle$.

The method get expects to receive write permission on some located integer channel. That is, it expects values of type

$$\mathsf{T}_g = \mathsf{w}\langle\mathsf{int}\rangle@\mathsf{loc}$$

Similarly the method put expects an integer together with write permission on a located acknowledgement channel. So let

$$\mathsf{T}_p = (\mathsf{int}, \mathsf{w}@\mathsf{loc})$$

Then to type the code LMem at a site m we need

$$\begin{aligned}&\Gamma \vdash_m \mathsf{get} : \mathsf{r}\langle\mathsf{T}_g\rangle \\ &\Gamma \vdash_m \mathsf{put} : \mathsf{r}\langle\mathsf{T}_p\rangle\end{aligned}$$

Note that the functionality of the code LMem is independent of its location, provided that location hosts a declaration of put and get at these types.

In Example 5.6 we saw the behaviour of a typical client of a memory, residing at the site c:

$$\begin{aligned}\mathsf{Client} \Leftarrow\ & (\mathsf{newc}\, a : \mathsf{D}_a)\ (m.\mathsf{put}!\langle 4, a@c\rangle \\ & \qquad \mid a?\ (\mathsf{new}\, r : \mathsf{D}_r)(m.\mathsf{get}!\langle r@c\rangle \quad \mid r?(x)\ \mathsf{print}!\langle x\rangle\ )\end{aligned}$$

This generates two local channels, an acknowledgement channel a whose declaration type should be

$$\mathsf{D}_a = \mathsf{rw}$$

and an integer reply channel r whose declaration type is required to be

$$\mathsf{D}_r = \mathsf{rw}\langle\mathsf{int}\rangle$$

In each case the write permission is exported, to the memory, and the read permission is retained by the client. So, to type the client code we need

$$\Gamma \vdash_c \mathsf{get} : \mathsf{w}\langle \mathsf{T}_g \rangle$$
$$\Gamma \vdash_c \mathsf{put} : \mathsf{w}\langle \mathsf{T}_p \rangle$$
$$\Gamma \vdash_c \mathsf{print} : \mathsf{w}\langle \mathsf{int} \rangle$$

Then with such an environment Γ we can derive

$$\Gamma \vdash_c \mathsf{Client}$$

where c is the site of the client.

To sum up let us collect the requirements on a type environment necessary to type the overall system

$$m[\![\mathsf{LMem}]\!] \mid c[\![\mathsf{Client}]\!]$$

A review of the discussion will confirm that the system can be typed in any environment that has the entries

$$\mathsf{get}@m : \mathsf{rw}\langle \mathsf{T}_g \rangle,\ \mathsf{put}@m : \mathsf{rw}\langle \mathsf{T}_p \rangle,\ \mathsf{print}@c : \mathsf{w}\langle \mathsf{int} \rangle$$

provided that the locally declared names, a and r are declared at the types D_a and D_r respectively. Note that the client's code requires not only the knowledge of the server's location, m, but also its own location c. ■

Example 5.18 [*Typing the Located Memory Servers*] Let us consider the typing of the memory services discussed in Example 5.7. First let us consider the minimal requirements on Γ_{req} in order to be able to derive

$$\Gamma_{\mathsf{req}} \vdash s[\![\mathsf{LmemS}]\!] \mid c_1[\![\mathsf{Client}_1]\!] \mid c_2[\![\mathsf{Client}_2]\!] \tag{5.29}$$

where the code for LmemS and the clients may be found in Example 5.7. The server, in response to a request, generates a new location m at type M and installs the code LMem there. We have just discussed the typing of this code, and from this discussion it should be apparent that the declaration type M should be

$$\mathsf{loc}[\mathsf{put} : \mathsf{rw}\langle \mathsf{T}_p \rangle,\ \ \mathsf{get} : \mathsf{rw}\langle \mathsf{T}_g \rangle] \tag{5.30}$$

where T_p and T_g are $(\mathsf{int}, \mathsf{w}@\mathsf{loc})$ and $\mathsf{w}\langle \mathsf{int} \rangle @\mathsf{loc}$ respectively. Note that although the server only uses the read capability on put and get, clients require the write capability, and therefore both must be in the declaration type of m.

The clients generate return channels at type D_r on which the name of the newly generated channel is to be sent. Therefore we need to set this declaration type to be $\mathsf{rw}\langle \mathsf{M} \rangle$; again the clients only use the read capability but the sever uses the write.

The request channel req is a free name in the overall system, being read by the server, and written to by the clients; it must therefore be assigned a type by

Γ_{req}. The values being transmitted on req are the return channels generated by the clients. So one possibility would be for it to have the type $\text{rw}\langle \text{D}_r @ \text{loc}\rangle$; note that the transmission type is a *global channel*, as the return channel must be accompanied by its location. But this is unnecessarily liberal, as the return channels will only be written to by the server. So a sufficient type for req to have in Γ_{req} is the more restricted $\text{rw}\langle \text{w}\langle \text{M}\rangle @ \text{loc}\rangle$.

Summing up, we leave the reader to check that (5.29) can be derived whenever

- $\Gamma_{\text{req}} \vdash \text{req} : \text{rw}\langle \text{w}\langle \text{M}\rangle @ \text{loc}\rangle$
- the client code $r?(x)C_i(x)$ is properly typed, that is $\Gamma_{\text{req}}, \langle x{:}\text{M}\rangle \vdash_{c_i} C_i(x)$.

But there is a subtlety involved in establishing the judgement (5.29) above. The names put and get are used both by the server, in the declaration type M of the new locations, and the clients, in the declaration type D_r of the return channels. These are completely independent systems and a priori could independently assign conflicting types to these names. In Section 5.5 we outline an extension to our typing system that will enable the consistency of resource types to be maintained across different domains.

The treatment of the alternative server $s[\![\text{LmemSVbis}]\!]$ is very similar. Ignoring the residual client behaviour, in order to establish

$$\Gamma_{\text{req}} \vdash s[\![\text{LmemSVbis}]\!] \mid c_1[\![\text{Clientbis}_1(m_1)]\!] \mid c_2[\![\text{Clientbis}_2(m_2)]\!]$$

it is sufficient for Γ_{req} to have as an entry for the request channel req the type $\text{rw}\langle \text{M}, \text{w} @ \text{loc}\rangle$. ■

As a final example in this section let us re-emphasise the use of typed channels to implement the selective distribution of capabilities, already touched upon with API in Example 3.15.

Example 5.19 [*Distributing Capabilities*] We revisit the memory server of Example 5.7, used by two clients. Let us assume that the overlall system has reached the stage

$$\begin{aligned} \text{Sys} \Leftarrow\ & (\text{new}\, m_1 : \text{M})(m_1[\![\text{LMem}]\!] \mid c_1[\![C_1(m_1)]\!]) \mid \text{bob}[\![\text{codeB}]\!] \mid \\ & (\text{new}\, m_2 : \text{M})(m_2[\![\text{LMem}]\!] \mid c_2[\![C_2(m_2)]\!]) \mid \text{jane}[\![\text{codeJ}]\!] \end{aligned} \quad (5.31)$$

where for convenience we ignore the presence of the actual server, and assume the presence of friends bob and jane. Only c_1 knows about the memory m_1, which it uses in the code $C_1(m_2)$, while only c_2 knows about m_2, which it uses in $C_2(m_2)$. Let us see how bob and jane are informed aboout these new memories.

One possible instantiation of their respective codes is given by:

$$
\begin{aligned}
C_1(m) &\Leftarrow \mathsf{goto\,bob.xpt_1!}\langle m_1\rangle \\
C_2(m) &\Leftarrow \mathsf{goto\,jane.xpt_2!}\langle m_2\rangle \\
\mathsf{codeB} &\Leftarrow \mathsf{xpt_1?}(x)\,\mathsf{B}(x) \\
\mathsf{codeJ} &\Leftarrow \mathsf{xpt_2?}(x)\,\mathsf{J}(x)
\end{aligned}
$$

The channels xpt_i are used by the clients to inform bob and jane of these resources; the first client exports the name of its private cell m_1 to bob using xpt_1 while the second uses xpt_2 to inform jane of m_2. Using the reduction semantics one can show that Sys may evolve to

$$
\begin{aligned}
\mathsf{Sys}_1 \Leftarrow &(\mathsf{new}\, m_1 : \mathsf{M})(m_1[\![\mathsf{LMem}]\!] \mid \mathsf{bob}[\![\mathsf{B}(m_1)]\!]) \mid \\
&(\mathsf{new}\, m_2 : \mathsf{M})(m_2[\![\mathsf{LMem}]\!] \mid c_2[\![\mathsf{J}(m_2)]\!])
\end{aligned}
$$

The question now is what resources at m_i can bob and jane use in Sys_1; that is what resource access have they achieved at these sites?

This of course depends on the type environment used for (5.31). Here we assume that M is the type

$$\mathsf{loc}[\mathsf{put} : \mathsf{rw}\langle \mathsf{T}_p\rangle,\quad \mathsf{get} : \mathsf{rw}\langle \mathsf{T}_g\rangle]$$

as discussed in Example 5.18, and let Γ_{bj} contain the entries $\mathsf{xpt}_1@\mathsf{bob} : \mathsf{rw}\langle \mathsf{M}_p\rangle$ and $\mathsf{xpt}_2@\mathsf{jane} : \mathsf{M}_g$, where M_p, M_g denote $\mathsf{loc}[\mathsf{put} : \mathsf{w}\langle \mathsf{T}_p\rangle]$ and $\mathsf{loc}[\mathsf{get} : \mathsf{w}\langle \mathsf{T}_g\rangle]$ respecively, both of which are supertypes of M. By demanding that

$$\Gamma_{bj} \vdash \mathsf{Sys} \tag{5.32}$$

we are enforcing the access policy that bob has only write access on put at m_1 and that jane has only write access on get at m_2. For example establishing (5.32) requires, among other things,

$$\Gamma_{bj}, \langle x{:}\mathsf{M}_p\rangle \vdash_{\mathsf{bob}} \mathsf{B}(x)$$

that unravels to

$$\Gamma_{bj}, x : \mathsf{loc}, \mathsf{put}@x : \mathsf{w}\langle \mathsf{T}_p\rangle \vdash_{\mathsf{bob}} \mathsf{B}(x)$$

Since x is fresh to Γ_{bj}, in the code $\mathsf{B}(x)$ the only resource available at the location x is put, and this can only be used with the capability $\mathsf{w}\langle \mathsf{T}_p\rangle$. ■

5.3 Subject reduction for ADPI

The object of this section is to show that the approach to establishing subject reduction for API, in Section 3.4.3, which in turn is based on Section 3.3, can be adapted to ADPI. There are however some complications:

(1) In ADPI there are *three* different kinds of typing judgements, for values, agents and systems, in addition to the judgements for well-formed environments.

This is not a major issue; computations are essentially carried out by agents and therefore we concentrate on these judgements. In particular we need to develop *substitution* results, similar to those in Proposition 3.9 for agents; these of course will rely on similar results for values.

(2) Typing judgements for both agents and values are relative to locations, with judgements of the form $\Gamma \vdash_k P$ and $\Gamma \vdash_k V : \mathsf{T}$ respectively.

This means that our *substitution* results have to take into account both the location of the judgement being made and the location of the value being substituted, which may be different.

(3) (Interchange), as in Proposition 3.7, does not hold in ADPI.

As an example if both k and c are new to Γ we have

$$\Gamma, k : \mathsf{loc}, c@k : \mathsf{C} \vdash_k c : \mathsf{C}$$

but obviously we cannot derive

$$\Gamma, c@k : \mathsf{C}, k : \mathsf{loc} \vdash_k c : \mathsf{C}$$

for the simple reason that the result of switching the entries, $\Gamma, c@k : \mathsf{C}, k : \mathsf{loc}$, is not a valid environment.

Although this seems like a minor property to get worried about, it was used extensively in the proof of the *substitution* result for API, Proposition 3.9, at least for (processes). See for example the case (STY-IN) given there; but it is also required for the case (STY-NEW). What this means is that the statement of the corresponding *substitution* results for ADPI will have to be much more general; this has already been explored in the questions at the end of Chapter 3.

Let us first adapt the sanity checks given in Lemma 3.5 for API to ADPI.

Lemma 5.20 (sanity checks for ADPI)

(i) $\Gamma, \Gamma' \vdash \mathbf{env}$ *implies* $\Gamma \vdash \mathbf{env}$
(ii) $\Gamma \vdash_w u : \mathsf{E}$ *implies* $\Gamma \vdash \mathbf{env}$ *and* $\Gamma \vdash w : \mathsf{loc}$
(iii) $\Gamma \vdash_w R$ *implies* $\Gamma \vdash \mathbf{env}$
(iv) $\Gamma \vdash M$ *implies* $\Gamma \vdash \mathbf{env}$.

Proof: In each case a simple proof by rule induction suffices. ■

Recall that for ADPI valid type environments Γ can contain entries of the form $u : \mathsf{E}$ or $u@w : \mathsf{E}$, and consequently $\mathsf{dom}(\Gamma)$ will in general be a finite set of compound identifiers. Nevertheless modulo this slight complication, the interpretation of environments as functions from their domain to types given in Definition 3.25 carries over. Extending the notation used there, we let $\Gamma\{e\}$, for any e in $\mathsf{dom}(\Gamma)$, denote the non-empty set of types E such that $e : \mathsf{E}$ occurs in Γ.

Lemma 5.21 Suppose $\Gamma \vdash \mathbf{env}$. *Then*

- $e \in \mathsf{dom}(\Gamma)$ *implies* $\Gamma\{e\}\downarrow$
- $u \in \mathsf{dom}(\Gamma)$ *implies* $\Gamma \vdash u : \sqcap(\Gamma\{u\})$
- $u@w \in \mathsf{dom}(\Gamma)$ *implies* $\Gamma \vdash_w u : \sqcap(\Gamma\{u@w\})$.

Proof: Note that here, in the second clause, we are using the abbreviated form of typing judgements for global types, justified by Lemma 5.11, where the location subscript is omited from typing judgements. If a simple identifier u is in $\mathsf{dom}(\Gamma)$, then it will have associated with it a global type; specifically this can only be loc or a base type.

The proof is a straightforward adaptation of that of Lemma 3.24, to the notation for located judgements. ■

This allows us to generalise Definition 3.25 to ADPI environments:

Definition 5.22 (*environments as functions*) For every e in the domain of Γ, we use $\Gamma(e)$ to denote the type $\sqcap(\Gamma\{e\})$.

We also borrow the associated notation, such as $\Gamma^r(e)$ and $\Gamma^w(e)$, from Definition 3.25. ♦

The properties of value typing for API, given in Proposition 3.26, also generalise in the natural manner:

Proposition 5.23 In ADPI

(i) $\Gamma \vdash u : \mathsf{A}$ *implies* $\Gamma(u)$ *exists, and* $\Gamma(u) <: \mathsf{A}$
(ii) $\Gamma \vdash_w u : \mathsf{C}$ *implies* $\Gamma(u@w)$ *exists and* $\Gamma(u@w) <: \mathsf{C}$
(iii) $\Gamma \vdash_w u : \mathsf{r}\langle \mathsf{T}_1\rangle$ *and* $\Gamma \vdash_w u : \mathsf{w}\langle \mathsf{T}_2\rangle$ *implies* $\mathsf{T}_2 <: \mathsf{T}_1$
(iv) $\Gamma \vdash_w V : \mathsf{T}_1$ *and* $\Gamma \vdash_w V : \mathsf{T}_2$ *implies* $\mathsf{T}_1 \sqcap \mathsf{T}_2$ *exists and* $\Gamma \vdash_w V : (\mathsf{T}_1 \sqcap \mathsf{T}_2)$
(v) ***(subsumption)*** $\Gamma \vdash_w V : \mathsf{T}_1$ *and* $\mathsf{T}_1 <: \mathsf{T}_2$ *implies* $\Gamma \vdash V : \mathsf{T}_2$.

Proof: A simple adaptation of the corresponding results for TYPED API, in Proposition 5.23. Note that in (i) we could just have written $\Gamma(u) = \mathsf{A}$ because of the limited possibilities for the type A; it can either be a base type or loc. ■

Let us now check that apart from (interchange) most of the properties for capabilities typing given in Section 3.4.3 carry over. As usual we will leave the detailed proofs to the reader, and be content to lay down the sequence in which the various results can be established. We adapt the method used to compare type environments from the previous chapter, in Definition 3.27.

Definition 5.24 (*comparing environments*) For valid type environments let $\Gamma_1 <: \Gamma_2$ if for every identifier w, $\Gamma_2 \vdash_w u : \mathsf{E}$ implies $\Gamma_1 \vdash_w u : \mathsf{E}$. As in Section 3.4 we write $\Gamma_1 \equiv \Gamma_2$ whenever $\Gamma_1 <: \Gamma_2$ and $\Gamma_2 <: \Gamma_1$. ♦

To state uniformly results for both value and agent judgements, let us write $\Gamma \vdash_w J : \mathsf{G}$ to denote either of these kinds of judgements, $\Gamma \vdash_w V : \mathsf{T}$ or $\Gamma \vdash_w R : \mathsf{proc}$. Then

Proposition 5.25

- ***(Weakening)*** $\Gamma \vdash_w J : \mathsf{G}$ *and* $\Gamma' <: \Gamma$ *implies* $\Gamma' \vdash_w J : \mathsf{G}$.
- ***(Environment strengthening)*** *Suppose* $\Gamma, e : \mathsf{E}, \Delta \vdash \mathbf{env}$, *where* $\mathsf{bn}(e)$ *does not occur in* Δ. *Then* $\Gamma, \Delta \vdash \mathbf{env}$.
- ***(Strengthening)*** *Suppose* $\Gamma, e : \mathsf{E}, \Delta \vdash_w J : \mathsf{G}$, *where* $\mathsf{bn}(e)$ *does not occur in* Δ, w, J *or* G. *Then* $\Gamma, \Delta \vdash_w J : \mathsf{T}$.

Proof: The proof of (weakening) is by rule induction, with a (long) case analysis of the last rule used. That of (environment strengthening) is by induction on the size of Δ. The case when this is empty, the base case, is an instance of the first part of the (sanity checks), Proposition 5.20 above. Otherwise it has the form $\Delta', e' : \mathsf{E}'$ and again the (sanity checks) ensure that $\Gamma, e : \mathsf{E}, \Delta' \vdash \mathbf{env}$. So by induction $\Gamma, \Delta' \vdash \mathbf{env}$. We now have to argue that this can safely be extended by $e' : \mathsf{E}'$. There are four possible cases, and each in turn follows by virtue of the fact that $\Gamma, e : \mathsf{E}, \Delta'$ can be safely extended by $e' : \mathsf{E}'$. For example if $e' : \mathsf{E}'$ is $u@w : \mathsf{C}$ then we have to show that if $\Gamma, \Delta' \vdash_w u : \mathsf{C}'$ then $\mathsf{C} \downarrow \mathsf{C}'$. But by (weakening) $\Gamma, \Delta' \vdash_w u : \mathsf{C}'$ implies $\Gamma, e : \mathsf{E}, \Delta', u@w : \mathsf{C} \vdash_w u : \mathsf{C}'$ and therefore the required $\mathsf{C} \downarrow \mathsf{C}'$ follows from part (iv) of Proposition 5.23.

Finally (strengthening) is once more a long rule induction proof, with the various base cases, such as the application of (TY-C.SUB), (TY-ZERO), relying on the just established (environment strengthening). Let us examine one inductive case. Suppose

$$\Gamma, e : \mathsf{E}, \Delta \vdash_w (\mathsf{new}\, c : \mathsf{C})\, R$$

because

$$\Gamma, e : \mathsf{E}, \Delta, c@w : \mathsf{C} \vdash_w R$$

Then we are assured that $\mathsf{bn}(e)$ does not appear in $(\Delta, c@w : \mathsf{C})$, and therefore we can apply induction to obtain

$$\Gamma, \Delta, c@w : \mathsf{C} \vdash_w R$$

An application of (TY-CP.NEW) gives the required $\Gamma, \Delta \vdash_w (\mathsf{new}\, c : \mathsf{C})\, R$. ■

Note that this version of (strengthening) is somewhat more general than that stated in Proposition 3.30 for TYPED API; the generality means that it does not require any interchange property.

As we have already indicated, we do not have an interchange law for typing judgements. $\Gamma_1, e_1 : \mathsf{E}_1, e_2 : \mathsf{E}_2, \Gamma_2 \vdash_w J : \mathsf{G}$ does not necessarily imply $\Gamma_1, e_2 : \mathsf{E}_2, e_1 : \mathsf{E}_1, \Gamma_2 \vdash_w J : \mathsf{G}$ because $\Gamma_1, e_2 : \mathsf{E}_2, e_1 : \mathsf{E}_1, \Gamma_2$ may not be a valid type environment. However there are certain constraints on e_1, e_2, which ensure that they can be safely interchanged. One is given in the following lemma, although there are valid exchanges not covered by it; see Question 6 at the end of the chapter.

Proposition 5.26 (partial interchange) Suppose $\Gamma, e_1 : \mathsf{E}_1, e_2 : \mathsf{E}_2 \vdash \mathbf{env}$, *where* e_1 *does not occur in* e_2. *Then*

(i) $\Gamma, e_2 : \mathsf{E}_2, e_1 : \mathsf{E}_1 \vdash \mathbf{env}$
(ii) $\Gamma, e_1 : \mathsf{E}_1, e_2 : \mathsf{E}_2 \equiv \Gamma, e_2 : \mathsf{E}_2, e_1 : \mathsf{E}_1$.

Proof: The first result requires a tedious analysis of the possible forms of $e_1 : \mathsf{E}_1$ and $e_2 : \mathsf{E}_2$; in each case we have to first argue that $\Gamma, e_2 : \mathsf{E}_2 \vdash \mathbf{env}$, and then argue that it can safely be extended by the entry $e_1 : \mathsf{E}_1$. For example suppose $e_1 : \mathsf{E}$ is $w : \mathsf{loc}$ and $e_2 : \mathsf{E}_2$ is $u' @ w' : \mathsf{C}$. Then since w' must be different from w, the reason for being able to safely extend $\Gamma, e_1 : \mathsf{E}_1$ with $e_2 : \mathsf{E}_2$, an application of (E-CHAN), applies equally well to Γ, and so we have $\Gamma, e_2 : \mathsf{E}_2 \vdash \mathbf{env}$. The extension to $\Gamma, e_2 : \mathsf{E}_2, e_1 : \mathsf{E}_1$ is now justified by an application of (E-LOC).

The second result is a straightforward proof by rule induction, as typechecking essentially still uses environments as lookup tables, despite the presence of multiple entries for identifiers. ■

This exchange can be extended from single type association entries to the more general extensions given in Definition 5.12; we confine our attention to the global version of this notation.

Corollary 5.27 Suppose Γ, $\langle e_1{:}\mathsf{A}_1\rangle$, $\langle e_2{:}\mathsf{A}_2\rangle \vdash \mathbf{env}$. *Then* Γ, $\langle e_2{:}\mathsf{A}_2\rangle$, $\langle e_1{:}\mathsf{A}_1\rangle \vdash \mathbf{env}$, *provided* $\mathsf{bn}(e_1)$ *does not occur in* $e_2 : \mathsf{A}_2$.

Proof: A case by case analysis is required of the types A_i. The case when both are channel types is covered by the previous proposition (partial interchange), and when they are base types the proof is straightforward. The non-trivial case is when either are location types. The requirement that $\mathsf{bn}(e_1)$ occurs neither in e_2 nor in the type A_2, ensures that even in this case (partial interchange) can be applied; in general multiple applications will be required. ■

These permitted forms of interchange are not sufficiently general to allow the straightforward transfer of the *substitution* results from API to ADPI. But they do come into play when showing that structural equivalence is preserved by typing:

Proposition 5.28 *Suppose* $M \equiv N$. *Then* $\Gamma \vdash M$ *if and only if* $\Gamma \vdash N$.

Proof: The proof proceeds as in Proposition 3.11, by induction on why $M \equiv N$, and as with that proof, the only non-trivial part is dealing with the axioms, from Figure 5.5. The most important axiom is (S-EXTR) but the proof is virtually identical to the API case.

So instead let us consider briefly (S-FLIP). Suppose $\Gamma \vdash (\mathsf{new}\, e_1 : \mathsf{D}_1)$ $(\mathsf{new}\, e_2 : \mathsf{D}_2)\, M$, where $\mathsf{bn}(e_1)$ does not occur in $e_2 : \mathsf{D}_2$. The only way this judgement can be established is by applications of (TY-CNEW) or (TY-LNEW), depending on the form of the types, to the judgement $\Gamma, \langle e_1{:}\mathsf{D}_1\rangle, \langle e_2{:}\mathsf{D}_2\rangle \vdash M$. The side-condition means that we can apply the previous corollary to obtain $\Gamma, \langle e_2{:}\mathsf{D}_2\rangle, \langle e_1{:}\mathsf{D}_1\rangle \vdash M$, to which the rules (TY-LNEW) and (TY-CNEW) can again be applied, to obtain the required $\Gamma \vdash (\mathsf{new}\, e_2 : \mathsf{D}_2)\, (\mathsf{new}\, e_1 : \mathsf{D}_1)\, M$.

Finally consider the second rule in (S-ZERO). $\Gamma \vdash \mathbf{0}$ is true for any valid environment Γ. But so is $\Gamma \vdash k[\![\mathsf{stop}]\!]$, as this only requires that $\Gamma \vdash_k \mathsf{stop}$; note that this latter judgement does not actually require k to be known as a location in Γ. ■

Let us now turn our attention to the *substitution results*, which are a central component of subject reduction. As we have already explained these will be somewhat more complex than for API, because of the lack of (interchange). The complexity occurs because we have to consider not only substitutions into values and processes, but also environments. First let us look at value judgements.

Proposition 5.29 (*substitution for values*) *Suppose* $\Gamma \vdash_{w_1} v : \mathsf{A}$, *and that* $\Gamma, \langle x{:}\mathsf{A}\rangle @w_1, \Delta \vdash_{w_2} u : \mathsf{B}$, *where* x *is fresh to* Γ. *Then, assuming* $\Gamma, \Delta\{\!|^v/_x|\!\} \vdash \mathbf{env}$, *it follows that* $\Gamma, \Delta\{\!|^v/_x|\!\} \vdash_{w_2'} u\{\!|^v/_x|\!\} : \mathsf{B}$, *where* w_2' *denotes* $w_2\{\!|^v/_x|\!\}$.

Proof: Here Δ is a list of type associations, and $\Delta\{\!|^v/_x|\!\}$ is the result of substituting each occurrence of the variable x in Δ with v. But note that variables cannot occur in types, and therefore in effect the substitutions only take place in the compound identifiers in Δ. Also note that the locations w_1 and w_2 need not be the same, and that for the sake of clarity we use B to range over an arbitary value type.

The proof is by induction on the inference of $\Gamma, \langle x{:}\mathsf{A}\rangle @w_1, \Delta \vdash_{w_2} u : \mathsf{B}$, and an examination of the last rule used; throughout we use the notation J' as in Proposition 3.9, to denote the substitution $J\{\!|^v/_x|\!\}$, for any syntactic category J.

As an example suppose (TY-C.SUB) is the last rule used; this may be applied to an occurrence of $u@w_2 : \mathsf{B}_s$, for some subtype B_s of B, which may appear in Γ, in Δ, or in the list $\langle x{:}\mathsf{A}\rangle @w_1$. In the first case we know that $\Gamma \vdash_{w_2} u : \mathsf{B}$ and an application of (weakening), from Proposition 5.25, gives $\Gamma, \Delta' \vdash_{w_2} u : \mathsf{B}$ and the required result follows because we know both w_2 and u must be different from x.

If on the other hand $u@w_2 : \mathsf{B}_s$ occurs in Δ then $u'@w_2' : \mathsf{B}_s$ naturally occurs in Δ', which justifies the judgement $\Gamma, \Delta' \vdash_{w_2'} u' : \mathsf{B}$. Finally suppose it occurs somewhere in the list $\langle x{:}\mathsf{A}\rangle@w_1$. Here we do an analysis on the type A. Note that since v is a simple value the type A can only be either a base type base, a located channel type C or a location type K; we leave the case when it is a base type to the reader.

- A is a local channel type C. Then $\langle x{:}\mathsf{A}\rangle@w_1$ unravels to $x@w_1 : \mathsf{C}$, and the inference must be

$$\Gamma, x@w_1 : \mathsf{C}, \Delta \vdash_{w_1} x : \mathsf{B}$$

  where $\mathsf{C} <: \mathsf{B}$; note that here w_2 coincides with w_1, and is different from x. But one of our assumptions is that $\Gamma \vdash_{w_2} v : \mathsf{C}$, and therefore the required result, $\Gamma, \Delta' \vdash_{w_2} v : \mathsf{B}$, follows by (weakening) in Proposition 5.25 and (subsumption) in Proposition 5.23.
- A is the location type $\mathsf{K} = \mathsf{loc}[a_1 : \mathsf{C}_1, \ldots a_n : \mathsf{C}_n]$. Here $\langle x{:}\mathsf{A}\rangle@w_1$ unravels to $x : \mathsf{loc}, a_1@x : \mathsf{C}_1, \ldots, a_n@x : \mathsf{C}_n$ and there are two cases. The lookup may be a use of (TY-LOC.SUB) to infer the judgement $\Gamma, \langle x{:}\mathsf{A}\rangle@w_1, \Delta \vdash_{w_2} x : \mathsf{loc}$, which we leave to the reader. Otherwise it takes the form $\Gamma, \langle x{:}\mathsf{A}\rangle@w_1, \Delta \vdash_x a_i : \mathsf{C}_i'$ for some $\mathsf{C}_i <: \mathsf{C}_i'$; here w_2 coincides with x. Again we rely on the assumption $\Gamma \vdash_{w_1} v : \mathsf{K}$, from which we obtain $\Gamma \vdash_v a_i : \mathsf{C}_i$. So once more the required result follows from (weakening) and (subsumption).

This ends our analysis of the case when (TY-C.SUB) is the last rule used. There are seven other cases to consider, corresponding to each of the possible rules in Figure 5.9. But all are either a case analysis, much simpler than the one we have just done, or follow trivially by induction. ■

In this result the premise that $\Gamma, \Delta\{\!|^v\!/\!_x|\!\}$ is a valid environment is unfortunately required, as environment formation is not necessarily preserved by substitution.

Example 5.30 Let R_r, R_w denote the local channel types $\mathsf{r}\langle\mathsf{r}\rangle$, $\mathsf{r}\langle\mathsf{w}\rangle$ respectively; note that $\mathsf{R}_r \downarrow \mathsf{R}_w$. Also let T denote the type $\mathsf{rw}\langle\mathsf{r}\rangle$, and here note that $\mathsf{T} <: \mathsf{R}_r$ but $\mathsf{T} \not\downarrow \mathsf{R}_w$.

Now let the environment Γ be simply the two type associations $k : \mathsf{loc}$, $c@k : \mathsf{T}$, and Δ be the single type association $x@k : \mathsf{R}_w$. Then

$$\Gamma \vdash_k c : \mathsf{R}_r$$

$$\Gamma,\ x@k : \mathsf{R}_r,\ \Delta \vdash_k x : \mathsf{R}_r \sqcap \mathsf{R}_w$$

The first follows by an application of (TY-C.SUB), whereas the second uses two instances of this same rule followed by an application of (TY-MEET). But note that here it is essential that $\Gamma,\ x@k : \mathsf{R}_r,\ \Delta \vdash \mathbf{env}$. However we cannot conclude

$$\Gamma, \Delta\{\!|^c\!/\!_x|\!\} \vdash_k c : \mathsf{R}_r \sqcap \mathsf{R}_w$$

for the simple reason that the type association list $\Gamma, \Delta\{\!|^c\!/\!_x|\!\}$ is not a well-formed environment. This is a consequence of the fact that $\mathsf{T} \not\downarrow \mathsf{R}_w$. ■

We can now extend this generalised substitution result from value judgements, Proposition 5.29, to agent judgements:

Proposition 5.31 (simple substitution for agents) Suppose $\Gamma \vdash_{w_1} v : \mathsf{A}$ *and* x *is fresh to* Γ. *Then provided* $\Gamma, \Delta\{\!|^v/_x|\!\}$ *is a valid environment,* $\Gamma, \langle x{:}\mathsf{A}\rangle@w_1, \Delta \vdash_{w_2} R$ *implies* $\Gamma, \Delta\{\!|^v/_x|\!\} \vdash_{w_2'} R\{\!|^v/_x|\!\}$, *where* w_2' *denotes* $w_2\{\!|^v/_x|\!\}$.

Proof: This follows the lines of the proof of Proposition 3.9, using induction on the derivation of the judgement $\Gamma, \langle x{:}\mathsf{A}\rangle@w_1, \Delta \vdash_{w_2} R$, but the details are somewhat more subtle. We examine three cases; as usual we use the shorthand notation J' for $J\{\!|^v/_x|\!\}$.

Suppose $\Gamma, \langle x{:}\mathsf{A}\rangle@w_1, \Delta \vdash_{w_2} u?(Y)\, R$ because

(i) $\Gamma, \langle x{:}\mathsf{A}\rangle@w_1, \Delta \vdash_{w_2} u : \mathsf{r}\langle\mathsf{T}\rangle$
(ii) $\Gamma, \langle x{:}\mathsf{A}\rangle@w_1, \Delta, \langle Y{:}\mathsf{T}\rangle@w_2 \vdash_{w_2} R$

for some type T. In other words (TY-IN) was the last rule used in the inference. Now we are assuming $\Gamma, \Delta' \vdash \mathbf{env}$, and therefore we may apply Proposition 5.29 to (i) to obtain

(i') $\Gamma, \Delta' \vdash_{w_2'} u' : \mathsf{r}\langle\mathsf{T}\rangle$.

Since all the variables in the pattern Y can be assumed to be fresh we also have that $\Gamma, \Delta' \vdash \mathbf{env}$ implies $\Gamma, \Delta', \langle Y{:}\mathsf{T}\rangle@w_2' \vdash \mathbf{env}$. This latter environment is actually $\Gamma, (\Delta, \langle Y{:}\mathsf{T}\rangle@w_2)'$, which means that we can apply induction to (ii) to obtain

(ii') $\Gamma, \Delta', \langle Y{:}\mathsf{T}\rangle@w_2' \vdash_{w_2'} R'$.

So (TY-IN) can now be applied to (i') and (ii') to obtain the required $\Gamma, \Delta' \vdash_{w_2'} R'$. Note that this case, unlike in the proof of Proposition 3.9, we did not need to apply any (interchange).

The case when (TY-LP.NEW) is the last rule used is similar. Here we have

$$\Gamma, \langle x{:}\mathsf{A}\rangle@w_1, \Delta \vdash_{w_2} (\mathsf{newloc}\, k : \mathsf{K})\ R$$

because $\Gamma, \langle x{:}\mathsf{A}\rangle@w_1, \Delta, \langle k{:}\mathsf{K}\rangle \vdash_{w_2} R$. As before, we can assume k is fresh and therefore $\Gamma, \Delta', \langle k{:}\mathsf{K}\rangle$ is a well-formed environment; moreover it coincides with $\Gamma, (\Delta, \langle k{:}\mathsf{K}\rangle)'$. Therefore applying induction we get $\Gamma, \Delta', \langle k{:}\mathsf{K}\rangle \vdash_{w_2'} R'$. A final application of (TY-LP.NEW) gives the required result.

Let us now examine the most interesting case. Suppose (TY-MATCH) is the last rule used. So

$$\Gamma, \langle x{:}\mathsf{A}\rangle@w_1, \Delta \vdash_{w_2} \mathsf{if}\ v_1 = v_2\ \mathsf{then}\ R_1\ \mathsf{else}\ R_2$$

because for some types A_1, A_2

(i) $\Gamma, \langle x{:}\mathsf{A}\rangle@w_1, \Delta \vdash_{w_2} v_1 : \mathsf{A}_1$
(ii) $\Gamma, \langle x{:}\mathsf{A}\rangle@w_1, \Delta \vdash_{w_2} v_2 : \mathsf{A}_2$

(iii) $\Gamma, \langle x{:}\mathsf{A}\rangle @w_1, \Delta \vdash_{w_2} R_2$
(iv) $\Gamma, \langle x{:}\mathsf{A}\rangle @w_1, \Delta_e \vdash_{w_2} R_1$

where Δ_e is a notation for $\Delta, \langle v_1{:}\mathsf{A}_2\rangle @w_2, \langle v_2{:}\mathsf{A}_1\rangle @w_2$. Again since we are assuming $\Gamma, \Delta' \vdash \mathbf{env}$ we may apply Proposition 5.29 or induction to obtain

(i') $\Gamma, \Delta' \vdash_{w_2'} v_1' : \mathsf{A}_1$
(ii') $\Gamma, \Delta' \vdash_{w_2'} v_2' : \mathsf{A}_2$
(iii') $\Gamma, \Delta' \vdash_{w_2'} R_2'$.

If $\Gamma, (\Delta_e)' \vdash \mathbf{env}$ then we can also apply induction to (iv) to obtain

(iv') $\Gamma, \Delta', \langle v_1'{:}\mathsf{A}_2\rangle @w_2', \langle v_2'{:}\mathsf{A}_1\rangle @w_2' \vdash_{w_2'} R_1'$.

Then (TY-MATCH) can be applied to (i')–(iv') to obtain the required

$$\Gamma,\ \Delta' \vdash_{w_2'} \mathsf{if}\ v_1' = v_2'\ \mathsf{then}\ R_1'\ \mathsf{else}\ R_2' \tag{5.33}$$

So let us consider the possibility that $\Gamma, (\Delta_e)'$ is not a valid environment; note that here we can assume that v_1' and v_2' are different, as otherwise $\Gamma, (\Delta_e)' \equiv \Gamma, \Delta'$. We show that (TY-MIS.MATCH) can be applied to obtain (5.33), although not necessarily with the types A_1, A_2 used above in (i), (ii).

Now $\Gamma, (\Delta_e)'$ unravels to $\Gamma,\ \Delta',\ \langle v_1'{:}\mathsf{A}_2\rangle @w_2',\ \langle v_2'{:}\mathsf{A}_1\rangle @w_2'$ and there are only two reasons why it might not be a valid environment, although Γ, Δ' is.

- Suppose $\Gamma, \Delta', \langle v_1'{:}\mathsf{A}_2\rangle @w_2' \not\vdash \mathbf{env}$. Here A_2 cannot be a base type, and so we can apply the extension lemma, Lemma 5.13. This means that there must exist some type A such that $\mathsf{A} \not\downarrow \mathsf{A}_2$ and $\Gamma \vdash_{w_2'} v_1' : \mathsf{A}$. So we can use this, together with (ii') and (iii') above, as premises to (TY-MIS.MATCH) to obtain the required (5.33).
- So we can assume $\Gamma, \Delta', \langle v_1'{:}\mathsf{A}_2\rangle @w_2'$ is a valid type environment and therefore another application of the extension lemma gives a type B such that $\mathsf{B} \not\downarrow \mathsf{A}_1$ and $\Gamma,\ \Delta', \langle v_1'{:}\mathsf{A}_2\rangle @w_2' \vdash_{w_2'} v_2' : \mathsf{B}$. But since v_1' and v_2' are different this actually means that $\Gamma,\ \Delta' \vdash_{w_2'} v_2' : \mathsf{B}$, which again allows us to apply (TY-MIS.MATCH) to obtain the result. ■

Corollary 5.32 (substitution for agents) Suppose $\Gamma \vdash_{w_1} V : \mathsf{T}$ *and all variables in* X *are fresh to* Γ*. Then* $\Gamma, \langle X{:}\mathsf{T}\rangle @w_1 \vdash_{w_2} R$ *implies* $\Gamma \vdash_{w_2'} R\{\!|^V\!/\!_X|\!\}$*, where* w_2' *denotes* $w_2\{\!|^V\!/\!_X|\!\}$.

Proof: By induction on the structure of the pattern X. The base case, when it is a simple variable, is given in the previous proposition. So suppose it has the located form $x@y$, in which case the type T must be of the form $\mathsf{C}@\mathsf{loc}$, and the value V of the form $v@w$.

So we know, by unravelling the environment,

$$\Gamma, y : \mathsf{loc}, x_1@y : \mathsf{C} \vdash_{w_2} R$$

But $\Gamma \vdash_{w_1} V : \mathsf{T}$ means that $\Gamma \vdash w : \mathsf{loc}$, and the freshness of x ensures that $\Gamma, x@w : \mathsf{C}$ is a valid environment. So we may apply the previous result to obtain

$$\Gamma, x@w : \mathsf{C} \vdash_{w_2''} R\{\!|^{w}/_{y}|\!\}$$

where w_2'' denotes $w_2\{\!|^{w}/_{y}|\!\}$. But $\Gamma \vdash_{w_1} V : \mathsf{T}$ also means that $\Gamma \vdash_w v : \mathsf{C}$, and since this latter environment has the form $\Gamma, \langle x{:}\mathsf{C}\rangle @w$ the result can be applied again to obtain $\Gamma \vdash_{w_2'''} (R\{\!|^{w}/_{y}|\!\})\{\!|^{v}/_{x}|\!\}$, where w_2''' denotes $w_2''\{\!|^{v}/_{x}|\!\}$. But this is the required result since w_2''' is $w_2\{\!|^{V}/_{X}|\!\}$ and $(R\{\!|^{w}/_{y}|\!\})\{\!|^{v}/_{x}|\!\}$ is $R\{\!|^{V}/_{X}|\!\}$.

The final case, when X is the pattern $(X_1, \ldots, X_n)$ is handled in a similar manner, assuming by induction that the result already holds for the individual components X_i. ■

We need one more substitution result, to handle recursion.

Proposition 5.33 Suppose $\Gamma \vdash_w R_1$ *and* $\Gamma, x@w : \mathsf{proc}, \Delta \vdash_w R_2$. *Then* $R_2\{\!|^{R_1}/_{x}|\!\}$ *is well-defined and* $\Gamma, \Delta \vdash_w R_2\{\!|^{R_1}/_{x}|\!\}$.

Proof: This is a generalisation of Proposition 3.9 (recursion), but with the judgements now local to a site w. The proof proceeds by induction on the inference $\Gamma, x@w : \mathsf{proc}, \Delta \vdash_w R_2$.

The base case is when this uses the rule (TY-PROC.SUB) from Figure 5.9; the inference is therefore

$$\Gamma, x@w : \mathsf{proc}, \Delta \vdash_w x$$

and the result is given by (weakening) from the premise $\Gamma \vdash_w R_1$.

All other cases follow in a straightforward manner. Note however that the case when (TY-MATCH) is the last rule used requires the more general form of the result, involving Δ, rather than the simple form, as in Proposition 3.9 (recursion). ■

We have now accumulated all the auxiliary results required for subject reduction.

Theorem 5.34 (subject reduction for ADPI) Suppose $M \longrightarrow N$, *where* M, N *are systems in* ADPI. *Then* $\Gamma \vdash M$ *implies* $\Gamma \vdash N$.

Proof: The proof is by induction on the derivation of $M \longrightarrow N$. As in the proof of Theorem 3.12 we can concentrate on the defining rules, given in Figure 5.5. The rule (R-STR) has already been covered by Proposition 5.28 and so we look at some of the defining axioms.

Consider the axiom (R-COMM). By the hypothesis we know

$$\Gamma \vdash k[\![c!\langle V\rangle]\!] \mid k[\![c?(X)\, R]\!] \tag{5.34}$$

and we have to prove

$$\Gamma \vdash k[\![R\{\!|^{V}/_{X}|\!\}]\!]$$

that will follow if we can prove

$$\Gamma \vdash_k R\{\!\!\{^V/_X\}\!\!\} \tag{5.35}$$

Dissecting the premise (5.34) we know that

$$\Gamma \vdash_k V : \mathsf{T}_1$$
$$\Gamma \vdash_k u : \mathsf{w}\langle \mathsf{T}_1 \rangle$$
$$\Gamma \vdash_k u : \mathsf{r}\langle \mathsf{T}_2 \rangle$$
$$\Gamma, \langle X{:}\mathsf{T}_2\rangle@k \vdash_k R$$

for some types T_1 and T_2. Here we can apply part (iii) of Proposition 5.23 to deduce $\mathsf{T}_1 <: \mathsf{T}_2$. Then (subsumption), the final part of the same proposition, gives $\Gamma \vdash_k V : \mathsf{T}_2$ and we have the required hypothesis of Corollary 5.32, with Δ being the empty environment, to conclude (5.35) above.

The proofs for the two creation rules, (R-L.CREATE) and (R-C.CREATE) are very similar and rely on the relationship between the typing rules for systems, (TY-CNEW), (TY-LNEW) in Figure 5.10, and the corresponding rules for agents in Figure 5.11, (TY-CP.NEW) and (TY-LP.NEW). As an example consider the rule for location generation

$$\text{(R-L.CREATE)} \quad k[\![(\mathsf{newloc}\, l : \mathsf{L})\ P]\!] \longrightarrow (\mathsf{new}\, l : \mathsf{L})\, k[\![P]\!]$$

and suppose $\Gamma \vdash k[\![(\mathsf{newloc}\, l : \mathsf{L})\ P]\!]$. This means $\Gamma \vdash_k (\mathsf{newloc}\, l : \mathsf{L})\ P$, which can only be inferred using the rule (TY-LP.NEW) from $\Gamma, \langle l{:}\mathsf{L}\rangle \vdash_k P$. But this implies $\Gamma, \langle l{:}\mathsf{L}\rangle \vdash k[\![P]\!]$, which is the premise required for an application of (TY-LNEW) with the conclusion

$$\Gamma \vdash (\mathsf{new}\, l : \mathsf{L})\, k[\![P]\!]$$

Now consider the rule (R-EQ); from

$$\Gamma \vdash_k \mathsf{if}\ v = v\ \mathsf{then}\ P\ \mathsf{else}\ Q \tag{5.36}$$

we have to prove $\Gamma \vdash_k P$. This judgement cannot be derived from an application of (TY-MIS.MATCH); this would require two types A_i such that $\mathsf{A}_1 \not\downarrow \mathsf{A}_2$ and

$$\Gamma \vdash_k v : \mathsf{A}_i$$

which contradicts part (iv) of Proposition 5.23. So (5.36) can only be derived using the rule (TY-MATCH), in which case we have

$$\Gamma, \langle v{:}\mathsf{A}_1\rangle@k, \langle v{:}\mathsf{A}_2\rangle@k \vdash_k P$$

for some types A_i such that $\Gamma \vdash_k v : \mathsf{A}_i$. But here it is easy to show that

$$\Gamma, \langle v{:}\mathsf{A}_2\rangle@k, \langle v{:}\mathsf{A}_2\rangle@k \equiv \Gamma$$

from which the required $\Gamma \vdash_k P$ follows.

The remaining rules are straightforward. In (R-NEQ) we have to prove $\Gamma \vdash_k Q$ from

$$\Gamma \vdash_k \text{if } v_1 = v_2 \text{ then } P \text{ else } Q$$

But $\Gamma \vdash_k Q$ is a hypothesis to each of the possible rules, (TY-MATCH) or (TY-MIS.MATCH), which can be used to establish this. The case (R-MOVE) follows from (TY-AGENT) and (TY-GO), while the argument for (R-UNWIND) is similar to that used in Theorem 3.12, but using the appropriate substitution result, Proposition 5.33. ■

5.4 Type safety for ADPI

Here we review the purpose of the type system we have developed for ADPI and examine the extent to which it fulfils our expectations.

In Section 3.1 it was argued that one purpose of a type system is to eliminate *runtime errors* in programs, and one definition of such errors for API was given in Figure 3.1; essentially errors occur either when an attempt is made to use a value inappropriately; for example attempting to input or output on a value that does not represent a channel, or attempting to match a structured value against a differently structured pattern.

In extending this definition to ADPI a subtlety arises. Let us consider the rule (ERR-CHAN) from Figure 3.1; this states that, for example, $v!\langle V\rangle$ contains a runtime error if v is not a name. So $3!\langle V\rangle$ contains a runtime error but $n!\langle V\rangle$ does not, for any name n. This is because in API all names are assumed to be channel names; indeed there is no other syntactic construct to name. However, turning to ADPI, it is not so clear when

$$k[\![n!\langle V\rangle]\!] \tag{5.37}$$

contains a runtime error. Recall that n can come from the set of names Names, and a priori there is no indication whether it represents a channel or a location; although informally we have been using $a, b, c, \ldots$ as channel names and $l, k, \ldots$ as location names the set Names actually contains an undifferentiated set of names. In other words we can only tell if (5.37) contains a runtime error relative to some prescribed *intended use* of each of the names in Names.

Rather than get side-tracked in setting up appropriate definitions for this concept let us just use type environments for this purpose, although these prescribe the intended use of names in much more detail than we require here. In other words we define a relation

$$M \longrightarrow_{\Gamma}^{\text{err}}$$

indicating that M contains a runtime error, from the point of view of the intended use of names as described in Γ.

(ERR-READ)
$$k[\![v?(X)\,R]\!] \longrightarrow_{\Gamma}^{err} \quad \text{if } \Gamma \nvdash_k v : \mathsf{r}\langle\ldots\rangle$$

(ERR-WRITE)
$$k[\![v!\langle V\rangle]\!] \longrightarrow_{\Gamma}^{err} \quad \text{if } \Gamma \nvdash_k v : \mathsf{w}\langle\ldots\rangle$$

(ERR-LOC)
$$k[\![\mathsf{goto}\, v.R]\!] \longrightarrow_{\Gamma}^{err} \quad \text{if } \Gamma \nvdash v : \mathsf{loc}$$

(ERR-STR)
$$\frac{M \equiv M',\ M \longrightarrow_{\Gamma}^{err}}{M' \longrightarrow_{\Gamma}^{err}}$$

(ERR-REC)
$$k[\![\mathsf{rec}\ x.\ B]\!] \longrightarrow_{\Gamma}^{err}$$
if $B\{^{\mathsf{rec}\ x.\ B}/_x\}$ not defined

(ERR-COMM)
$$k[\![a?(X)\,T]\!] \mid k[\![a!\langle V\rangle]\!] \longrightarrow_{\Gamma}^{err}$$
if X, V do not match

(ERR-CXT)
$$\frac{M \longrightarrow_{\Gamma}^{err}}{\begin{array}{l} M \mid N \longrightarrow_{\Gamma}^{err} \\ N \mid M \longrightarrow_{\Gamma}^{err} \end{array}}$$

(ERR-CXT)
$$\frac{M \longrightarrow_{\Gamma,\langle e:\mathsf{D}\rangle}^{err}}{(\mathsf{new}\, e{:}\mathsf{D})\, M \longrightarrow_{\Gamma}^{err}}$$

Figure 5.12 Runtime errors in ADPI

The definition is given in Figure 5.12 and is modelled directly on that of Figure 3.1, although the presence of Γ allows us to be more specific in describing the cause of errors. The rule (ERR-LOC) states that $k[\![\mathsf{goto}\, v.R]\!]$ contains a runtime error, from the point of view of Γ, if v is not considered to be a location. The rules (ERR-READ) and (ERR-WRITE) are a generalisation of (ERR-NAME) from Figure 3.1; for example the latter states that $k[\![v!\langle V\rangle]\!]$ contains an error if v is not known by Γ to be a channel at k on which there is a write capability. The remaining rules are the obvious adjustments of the corresponding ones in Figure 3.1 to the syntax of ADPI. But it is worthwhile noting that the relation is not quite contextual; the second part of (ERR-CXT) requires an extension to Γ in its premise.

It is now a straightforward matter to show that our type system for ADPI eliminates the possibility of runtime errors, thus defined. This is the obvious extension of the corresponding result for API in Chapter 3 for API, Corollary 3.14.

Theorem 5.35 (simple type safety for ADPI) Suppose $\Gamma \vdash M$. *Then* $M \longrightarrow^* N$ *implies* $N \not\longrightarrow_{\Gamma}^{err}$.

Proof: By subject reduction, Theorem 5.34, we know that $\Gamma \vdash N$. Therefore we need only adapt the proof of Theorem 3.13 to show that this in turn implies that $N \not\longrightarrow_{\Gamma}^{err}$; in fact we prove the contra-positive, that $N \longrightarrow_{\Gamma}^{err}$ implies that $\Gamma \vdash N$ cannot be derived, by induction the derivation of $N \longrightarrow_{\Gamma}^{err}$.

As an example suppose $k[\![\mathsf{goto}\, v.R]\!] \longrightarrow_{\Gamma}^{err}$ because $\Gamma \nvdash v : \mathsf{loc}$. Now the only possible way to infer $\Gamma \vdash k[\![\mathsf{goto}\, v.R]\!]$ is via an application of (TY-AGENT) to $\Gamma \vdash_k \mathsf{goto}\, v.R$. But this in turn can only be derived via an application of (TY-GO), which requires the impossible $\Gamma \vdash v : \mathsf{loc}$.

As another example suppose $(\mathsf{new}\, e{:}\mathsf{D})\, M \longrightarrow^{\mathrm{err}}_{\Gamma}$ because $M \longrightarrow^{\mathrm{err}}_{\Gamma,\langle e:\mathsf{D}\rangle}$. By induction we have $\Gamma, \langle e{:}\mathsf{D}\rangle \nvdash M$. But the only way of inferring $\Gamma \vdash (\mathsf{new}\, e{:}\mathsf{D})\, M$ is by an application of one of the creation rules, (TY-CNEW) or (TY-LNEW) from Figure 5.10, all of which require the appropriate instance of $\Gamma, \langle e{:}\mathsf{D}\rangle \vdash M$. ■

However our typing system does much more than enforce the proper use of location and channel names. In the introduction to Section 5.2 we have proposed it as a mechanism for controlling *capabilities* on names, and therefore for implementing access control policies on domains. This idea was briefly alluded to at the end of Chapter 3, and now we explain it in detail. This is best approached via an example.

Example 5.36 Let us revisit Example 5.19 where clients have used the memory server to obtain their private instances of located memory cells; this in turn is based on Example 5.18 and the related Example 5.7. Here we consider the following variation:

$$\mathsf{Sys}^b \Leftarrow \mathsf{bob}[\![\mathsf{codeB}]\!] \mid (\mathsf{new}\, m : \mathsf{M})(m[\![\mathsf{LMem}]\!] \mid c[\![C(m)]\!]) \qquad (5.38)$$

where M is the type $\mathsf{loc}[\mathsf{put} : \mathsf{rw}\langle \mathsf{T}_p\rangle,\ \mathsf{get} : \mathsf{rw}\langle \mathsf{T}_g\rangle]$ and

$$\mathsf{codeB} \Leftarrow \mathsf{xpt}_p?(x)\, \mathsf{B}(x)$$

$$C(m) \Leftarrow \mathsf{goto}\ \mathsf{bob}.\mathsf{xpt}_p!\langle m\rangle$$

The client c makes available the existence of its private memory cell m to bob along the channel xpt_p. Moreover, as already explained in Example 5.19, it is made available with restricted access rights. Using the reduction semantics Sys^b evolves to

$$\mathsf{Sys}^b_1 \Leftarrow (\mathsf{new}\, m : \mathsf{M})(\ \mathsf{bob}[\![\mathsf{B}(m)]\!] \mid m[\![\mathsf{LMem}]\!]\ ) \qquad (5.39)$$

where, as we have seen, the resource capabilities at m accessible to bob are determined by the write capability on the export channel xpt_p.

Suppose Γ_b contains the entries

$$\ldots, \mathsf{xpt}_p @\mathsf{bob} : \mathsf{rw}\langle \mathsf{M}_p\rangle,\ \mathsf{print}\, @\mathsf{bob} : \mathsf{rw}\langle \mathsf{int}\rangle, \ldots$$

where M_p is $\mathsf{loc}[\mathsf{put} : \mathsf{w}\langle \mathsf{T}_p\rangle]$, a supertype of M. Thus, as explained in Example 5.19, intuitively Γ_b enforces the access policy in which bob has only write access on put at m. Yet, as we shall see, type safety, based on the runtime errors of Figure 5.12, is largely independent of the actual instantiations of $\mathsf{B}(x)$ in (5.38) above. For example with

$$\mathsf{B}(x) \Leftarrow (\mathsf{newc}\, r : \mathsf{R})\ (r?(y)\, \mathsf{print}!\langle y\rangle \mid \mathsf{goto}\, x.\mathsf{get}!\langle r @\mathsf{bob}\rangle)$$

the original system, Sys^b from (5.38), is type safe, assuming R is correctly instantiated; that is no runtime errors can occur, relative to Γ_b. Formally one can show that $S \not\longrightarrow^{\mathrm{err}}_{\Gamma_b}$ for every S such that $\mathsf{Sys}^b \longrightarrow^* S$.

An obvious S to worry about is

$$S \Leftarrow (\mathsf{new}\, m{:}\mathsf{M})((\mathsf{new}\, r{:}\mathsf{R})(\mathsf{bob}[\![r?(y)\, \mathsf{print}!\langle y\rangle]\!] \\ \mid m[\![\mathsf{get}!\langle r\rangle]\!]) \mid m[\![\mathsf{LMem}]\!]) \tag{5.40}$$

where bob has received the name m at the type M_p, but nevertheless has sent an agent there to collect the value in the memory via the method get. However one can check that there is no runtime error here; that is $S \not\longrightarrow^{\mathrm{err}}_{\Gamma_b}$. For $S \longrightarrow^{\mathrm{err}}_{\Gamma_b}$ could only be derived by applications of (ERR-CXT), which would require

$$m[\![\mathsf{get}!\langle r\rangle]\!] \longrightarrow^{\mathrm{err}}_{\Gamma_b, \langle m{:}\mathsf{M}\rangle,\, \langle r{:}\mathsf{R}\rangle}$$

However this is not possible since in the extended environment there is a write capability on get at m.

Thus the notion of runtime error is not sufficiently discriminating to pick up this misuse of capabilities by bob. Nevertheless the type system was designed to forbid such misuses, and one can show that

$$\Gamma_b \not\vdash \mathsf{Sys}^b$$

The problem arises when trying to establish $\Gamma_b \vdash_{\mathsf{bob}} \mathsf{xpt}_p?(x)\, \mathsf{B}(x)$. Because of the type of xpt_p at bob in Γ_b this requires deriving

$$\Gamma^e_b \vdash_x \mathsf{get} : \mathsf{w}\langle \mathsf{T}_g\rangle$$

where Γ^e_b is an extension of Γ_b in which the only entries involving x are $x : \mathsf{loc}$ and $\mathsf{put} : \mathsf{T}_p@x$. ∎

This example demonstrates that, although the type system does enforce some form of constraints on the capabilities available to agents, the current notion of runtime error is incapable of describing these constraints. In order to capture the power of the type system in an independent manner we need a version of the language in which the capabilities obtained by agents are explicitly described.

In the next section we describe such a language, TAGGED-ADPI. With this explicit representation of agent capabilities, it will be straightforward to define a version of runtime error that represents more clearly the misuse by agents of their acquired capabilities.

This is followed by a further section in which we explain how properly typed ADPI systems may be interpreted as tagged systems. Moreover these tagged systems will be guaranteed to be free from tag-based runtime errors. In other words the type system for ADPI alleviates the user from explicitly programming and reasoning about an agent's capabilities.

5.4.1 TAGGED-ADPI

It may seem rather daunting to embark on the definition of a new language, with its associated reduction semantics and typing system. But the only new construct we actually need is a representation of the capabilities, or *permissions* of agents. For this we employ the syntax

$$k[\![P]\!]_\Delta$$

where Δ is a list of type associations; this represents the agent P running at location k, with the permissions given in Δ. So the syntax of TAGGED-ADPI is given by simply replacing the syntax for systems, in Figure 5.2, with that given in Figure 5.13; we use M_t, N_t as meta-variables for tagged systems, in order to distinguish them from untagged systems of ADPI. Formally here Δ simply ranges over association lists between names and types. Although much of the technical development of this

Syntax:

M_t, N_t ::=	*Tagged systems*
$l[\![P]\!]_\Delta$	**Tagged agents**
$(\mathsf{new}\, e : \mathsf{D})\, M$	Name Scoping
...	Composition
...	Termination

Reductions:

(R$_\text{T}$-COMM)
$$k[\![c!\langle V\rangle]\!]_{\Delta_1} \mid k[\![c?(X)\,R]\!]_{\Delta_2} \longrightarrow_t k[\![R\{^V\!/\!_X\}]\!]_{\Delta_2,\langle V:\Delta_2^r(c@k)\rangle@k}$$

(R$_\text{T}$-MOVE)
$$k[\![\mathsf{goto}\, l.P]\!]_\Delta \longrightarrow_t l[\![P]\!]_\Delta$$

(R$_\text{T}$-C.CREATE)
$$k[\![(\mathsf{newc}\, c : \mathsf{C})\ P]\!]_\Delta \longrightarrow_t (\mathsf{new}\, c@k : \mathsf{C})(k[\![P]\!]_{\Delta,\langle c:\mathsf{C}\rangle@k})$$

(R$_\text{T}$-SPLIT)
$$k[\![P \mid Q]\!]_\Delta \longrightarrow_t k[\![P]\!]_\Delta \mid k[\![Q]\!]_\Delta$$

(R$_\text{T}$-L.CREATE)
$$k[\![(\mathsf{newloc}\, l : \mathsf{L})\ P]\!]_\Delta \longrightarrow_t (\mathsf{new}\, l : \mathsf{L})(k[\![P]\!]_{\Delta,\langle l:\mathsf{L}\rangle})$$

(R$_\text{T}$-UNWIND), (R$_\text{T}$-STR), (R$_\text{T}$-EQ), (R$_\text{T}$-NEQ)
as in Figure 5.6

Typing:

(TY$_\text{T}$-AGENT)
$$\frac{\Delta \vdash_k P : \mathsf{proc} \qquad \Gamma \vdash \mathbf{env}}{\Gamma \vdash k[\![P]\!]_\Delta}\ \Gamma <: \Delta$$

Figure 5.13 Tagged ADPI

section will only make sense when Δ is actually a valid type environment, in examples we will be less demanding. It is also worth noting that the definition allows the formation of tagged systems such as

$$(\mathsf{new}\, k{:}\mathsf{K})(l[\![P]\!]_{\Delta_1} \mid k[\![P]\!]_{\Delta_2})$$

where the bound name k may appear in either or both of the capability descriptions Δ_1, Δ_2.

This new language TAGGED-ADPI needs to be endowed with a new reduction semantics, describing the manner in which agents acquire new capabilities. As we have already indicated these are required as a result of a communication between two agents; after the communication of a value V along a location channel c at location k, the receiver obtains the capabilities on the values V ordained by its current read capabilities on c at k. To formalise this concept we use the notation developed in Definition 5.22 for interpreting environments as partial functions from compound identifiers, to types.

Let us consider the two agents

$$k[\![c!\langle v\rangle]\!]_{\Delta_1} \mid k[\![c?(x)\, P]\!]_{\Delta_2}$$

co-located at k. The first is willing to send a simple value v on c, while the second is waiting to receive a value on it. The latter's ability to use c is determined by its current capabilities, described in Δ_2. So for example if there is no read capability on c at k in Δ_2 then the communication is not possible. If there is, the communication can happen and moreover the capabilities received on v are determined by the read capability on c at the site k in Δ_2. After the communication the receiving agent, and its capabilities, are described by

$$k[\![P\{\!|^{v}\!/\!_{x}|\!\}]\!]_{\Delta_2, \langle v:\Delta_2^r(c@k)\rangle@k}$$

The value v may already be known in Δ_2, in which case extra capabilities on it have been acquired, or it may have been a completely unknown value, in which case it is now known by the receiver, and may be used in accordance with the capabilities described in $\langle v{:}\Delta_2^r(c@k)\rangle@k$; this represents the capabilities that the receiving agent can acquire using the channel c at k, according to its current permissions Δ_2.

Formally the reduction semantics is given as a binary relation between tagged systems

$$M_t \longrightarrow_t N_t$$

which is the least *contextual* relation satisfying the axioms and rules given in Figure 5.13. The main rule is (R_T-COMM), which we have just described in detail, at least for simple values. This axiom is interpreted to only hold when $\langle V{:}\Delta_2^r(c@k)\rangle@k$ is well-defined; that is, whenever it unravels according to Definition 5.12 to a list of type associations. So at the very least $\Delta_2^r(c@k)$ is required to exist, but it must also match the structure of the value V.

The remaining rules are inherited directly from the reduction semantics of ADPI, in Figure 5.5. Note that in (R_T-MOVE) agents retain their capabilities as they move between domains; also in the housekeeping move (R_T-SPLIT) capabilities are preserved as agents divide in preparation for communication or migration. The rules for newly created names, (R_T-C.CREATE) and (R_T-L.CREATE), need to update the agent's tag with the declared capabilities on the newly created name. The remaining rules are omitted, as the reader can reconstruct them directly from Figure 5.5. Of course (R_T-STR) requires a structural equivalence between tagged systems; its definition is in turn inherited from that for ADPI, in Figure 5.4; the only change required is to replace the untagged $k[\![\mathsf{stop}]\!]$ in the axiom (S-ZERO) with its tagged version $k[\![\mathsf{stop}]\!]_\Delta$.

Example 5.37 [*Tagged Systems*] Consider the following variation on the system described in Example 5.36:

$$\mathsf{Sys}_t^j \Leftarrow \mathsf{jane}[\![\mathsf{codeJ}]\!]_{\Delta_j} \mid (\mathsf{new}\, m : \mathsf{M})(m[\![\mathsf{LMem}]\!]_{\Delta_m} \mid c[\![C(m)]\!]_{\Delta_c}) \qquad (5.41)$$

where this time we have the code

$$C(m) \Leftarrow \mathsf{goto\,jane.xpt}_p!\langle m\rangle$$
$$\mathsf{codeJ} \Leftarrow \mathsf{xpt}_p?(x)\,(\mathsf{new}\, r : \mathsf{R})\,\mathsf{goto}\, x.\mathsf{put}!\langle 7, r@\mathsf{jane}\rangle$$

with R the type appropriate to a reply channel being sent on put, namely rw. Of course in a complete example jane would not only put the value $(7, r@\mathsf{jane})$ into the memory but would continue computing on receipt of an acknowledgement on r; but for simplicity we ignore this continuation. Suppose further that the current capabilities of jane and the client are

$$\Delta_c : \quad \mathsf{xpt}_p@\mathsf{jane} : \mathsf{w}\langle \mathsf{M}_p\rangle,\ m : \mathsf{loc},\ \mathsf{put}@m : \mathsf{T}_p,\ \mathsf{get}@m : \mathsf{T}_g$$
$$\Delta_j : \quad \mathsf{xpt}_p@\mathsf{jane} : \mathsf{r}\langle \mathsf{M}_p\rangle$$

Then a contextual application of (R_T-MOVE), followed by (R_T-STR), gives

$$\mathsf{Sys}_t^j \longrightarrow_t (\mathsf{new}\, m : \mathsf{M})(\,\mathsf{jane}[\![\mathsf{codeJ}]\!]_{\Delta_j} \mid \mathsf{jane}[\![\mathsf{xpt}!\langle m\rangle]\!]_{\Delta_c} \mid m[\![\mathsf{LMem}]\!]_{\Delta_m})$$

At this point note that the agent emanating from the client, $\mathsf{jane}[\![\mathsf{xpt}!\langle m\rangle]\!]_{\Delta_c}$ has both put and get capabilities at m, as evidenced in its set of permissions Δ_c. On the other hand jane still has no permissions at m, as evidenced in Δ_j, although it is within the scope of the declaration of m at type M.

But we can make a contextual application of (R_T-COMM) to obtain

$$(\mathsf{new}\, m : \mathsf{M})(\,\mathsf{jane}[\![(\mathsf{new}\, r : \mathsf{R})\,\mathsf{goto}\, m.\mathsf{put}!\langle 7, r@\mathsf{jane}\rangle]\!]_{\Delta_j^1} \mid m[\![\mathsf{LMem}]\!]_{\Delta_m})$$

where now the capabilities of jane are given by

$$\Delta_j^1 = \Delta_j,\ m{:}\mathsf{loc},\ \mathsf{put}@m{:}\mathsf{w}\langle \mathsf{T}_p\rangle$$

This is because $\langle m{:}\mathsf{M}_p\rangle@\mathsf{jane}$, the new capabilities acquired during the communication, unravels to $m : \mathsf{loc},\ \mathsf{put}@m : \mathsf{w}\langle \mathsf{T}_p\rangle$, by applying Definition 5.12. Then an application of (R_T-C.CREATE) followed by one of (R_T-MOVE) gives

$$(\mathsf{new}\, m : \mathsf{M})\ (\mathsf{new}\, r@\mathsf{jane} : \mathsf{R})(\ m[\![\mathsf{put}!\langle 7, r@\mathsf{jane}\rangle]\!]_{\Delta_j^2}\ \mid\ m[\![\mathsf{LMem}]\!]_{\Delta_m})$$

Here the migrating agent has acquired the declared permissions on the newly generated reply channel r; Δ_j^2 represents

$$\Delta_j^1,\ \mathsf{jane}{:}\mathsf{loc},\ r@\mathsf{jane}{:}\mathsf{rw}$$

Now, assuming m has a read capability on put in its current capabilities Δ_m, a communication can happen along put, as a consequence of which m will acquire some capability on r at jane. If, as expected, Δ_m contains the entry $\mathsf{put}{:}\mathsf{rw}\langle \mathsf{T}_p\rangle$, then it will acquire the new capability $\langle (7, r@\mathsf{jane}){:}\mathsf{T}_p\rangle@m$. Since T_p is $(\mathsf{int}, \mathsf{w}@\mathsf{loc})$ this unravels to $\mathsf{jane}{:}\mathsf{loc}, r@\mathsf{jane}{:}\mathsf{w}$; the memory has acquired the permission to write an acknowledgement along r at jane. ■

Typechecking TAGGED-ADPI: Our reduction semantics for TAGGED-ADPI appears to correctly implement the informal idea of the selective distribution of capabilities via typed channels. However there are problems; the agent on the receiving end of a communication obtains the capabilities dictated by the communication channel, even if these are not owned by the sender.

Example 5.38 Consider the system

$$\mathsf{Sys} \Leftarrow l[\![\mathsf{goto}\, k.\mathsf{in}!\langle s\rangle]\!]_{\Delta_l}\ \mid\ k[\![\mathsf{in}?(x)\ \mathsf{goto}\, x.\mathsf{info}!\langle news\rangle]\!]_{\Delta_k}$$

Here l informs k of an information gathering service at s; k goes there and sends some *news* along a channel info, which it knows should be available at s.

Suppose Δ_l and Δ_k both contain the permission $\mathsf{in}@k : \mathsf{rw}\langle \mathsf{loc}[\mathsf{info} : \mathsf{w}\langle \mathsf{str}\rangle]\rangle$. So both sites have permission to use in at location k for transmitting locations of type $\mathsf{loc}[\mathsf{info} : \mathsf{w}\langle \mathsf{str}\rangle]$. Suppose further, for the sake of argument, that these are the *only* permissions in Δ_l and Δ_k; note that this implies that l has *no* permissions for the site s.

According to our semantics we obtain the reductions

$$\mathsf{Sys} \longrightarrow_t k[\![\mathsf{goto}\, s.\mathsf{info}!\langle news\rangle]\!]_{\Delta_k^n}$$

where Δ_k^n is the updated set of permissions $\Delta,\ s{:}\mathsf{loc},\ \mathsf{info}@s{:}\mathsf{w}\langle \mathsf{str}\rangle$; the agent k has gained permission to use info at s, despite the fact that l did not have this permission to pass on; indeed this permission did not exist anywhere in the system. ■

So we must restrict attention to tagged systems that are in some sense *consistent*; there must be some coherency between an agent's code and its permissions. There are further issues, concerning consistency between the views of different agents.

Example 5.39 Suppose in the previous example that Δ_l, Δ_k are

$$s{:}\mathsf{loc},\ \mathsf{req}@s{:}\mathsf{r}\langle\mathsf{str}\rangle,\ \mathsf{in}@k{:}\mathsf{rw}\langle\mathsf{L}_s\rangle$$
$$\mathsf{in}@k{:}\mathsf{rw}\langle\mathsf{K}_s\rangle$$

respectively, where L_s, K_s are $\mathsf{loc}[\mathsf{req} : \mathsf{r}\langle\mathsf{int}\rangle]$, $\mathsf{loc}[\mathsf{info} : \mathsf{w}\langle\mathsf{str}\rangle]$, respectively. Here there is a fundamental misunderstanding between l and k about the type of the channel $\mathsf{in}@k$; the agent l has permission to use it for locations of type L_s, and it uses it correctly with respect to this permission. On the other hand k believes it is for locations of type K_s, and also uses it in accordance with this belief.

In the end, after the communication on in, k obtains a permission on s that bears no relation to those of l; it obtains permission to use a resource info there, although l only has permission related to a resource called req there. ■

To rule out these abuses of explicit permissions, and to adjudicate between conflicting permissions of different agents we need a typing system.

The judgements of the type system for TAGGED-ADPI are inherited directly from those for ADPI, and take the form

$$\Gamma \vdash M_t$$

Here, as with ADPI, Γ dictates the roles of the names used in M_t, and their types; in this way inconsistencies between different agents' permissions are eliminated. The typechecking rules are a minor adaptation from those in Figure 5.10, the only change being the replacement of (TY-AGENT) with

$$\text{(TY}_\text{T}\text{-AGENT)}\quad \frac{\Delta \vdash_k P : \mathsf{proc} \qquad \Gamma \vdash \mathbf{env}}{\Gamma \vdash k[\![P]\!]_\Delta}\quad \Gamma <: \Delta$$

So in order for the tagged agent $k[\![P]\!]_\Delta$ to be well-typed with respect to Γ we require the following:

(i) Γ has to be a valid type environment; this is simply a sanity check on judgements.
(ii) The agent's code P must be well-typed with respect to its permissions, $\Delta \vdash_k P : \mathsf{proc}$. This is checked using the rules for ADPI agents in Figure 5.11. Note that this will imply that Δ has to be a well-typed environment.
(iii) Δ can only use permissions from Γ, $\Gamma <: \Delta$; agents are not allowed to invent permissions that do not exist.

Referring to Example 5.38 one can check that there is no possible Γ for which $\Gamma \vdash \mathsf{Sys}$ can be derived. The problem occurs when trying to establish

$$\Delta_l \vdash l[\![\mathsf{goto}\, k.\mathsf{in}!\langle s\rangle]\!]_{\Delta_l}$$

This is ruled out by (ii) above, as we would need to establish

$$\Delta_l \vdash_l \mathsf{goto}\, k.\mathsf{in}!\langle s\rangle$$

and Δ_l has no information of any kind about s.

Typing Example 5.39 is ruled out by condition (iii). It is possible to find a Γ_1 and a Γ_2 such that

$$\Gamma_1 \vdash l[\![\mathsf{goto}\, k.\mathsf{in}!\langle \mathsf{info}@s\rangle]\!]_{\Delta_l}$$
$$\Gamma_2 \vdash k[\![\mathsf{in}?(x)\, \mathsf{goto}\, s.\mathsf{info}!\langle news\rangle]\!]_{\Delta_k}$$

But there is no Γ such that $\Gamma \vdash \mathsf{Sys}$, as this would imply

$$\Gamma <: \Delta_l$$
$$\Gamma <: \Delta_k$$

But this is clearly impossible because Δ_1 and Δ_k contain conflicting type information on $\mathsf{in}@k$.

Theorem 5.40 (subject reduction for TAGGED-ADPI*) In* TAGGED-ADPI, *suppose* $\Gamma \vdash M_t$ *and* $M_t \longrightarrow_t N_t$. *Then* $\Gamma \vdash N_t$.

Proof: The proof is by induction on the inference of $M_t \longrightarrow_t N_t$, and most cases are treated as in Theorem 5.34. We examine two, both instances of the axioms in Figure 5.13.

Consider the rule (R$_\mathrm{T}$-MOVE). So let us assume $\Gamma \vdash k[\![\mathsf{goto}\, l.P]\!]_\Delta$, from which we have to show $\Gamma \vdash l[\![P]\!]_\Delta$. Since the hypothesis can only be derived from an application of (TY$_\mathrm{T}$-AGENT) we have

(i) $\Gamma \vdash \mathbf{env}$
(ii) $\Delta \vdash_k \mathsf{goto}\, l.P$
(iii) $\Gamma <: \Delta$.

However from (ii) we know

(ii') $\Delta \vdash_l P$

and therefore an application of the same rule to (i), (ii') and (iii) gives the required $\Gamma \vdash l[\![P]\!]_\Delta$.

As a second example consider (R$_\mathrm{T}$-COMM); so we know $\Gamma \vdash k[\![c!\langle V\rangle]\!]_{\Delta_1} \mid k[\![c?(X)\, R]\!]_{\Delta_2}$ and we have to prove

$$\Gamma \vdash k[\![R\{\!|^{V}\!/\!_{X}|\!\}]\!]_{\Delta_2^n}, \tag{5.42}$$

where, for convenience, we have abbreviated $\Delta_2, \langle V{:}\Delta_2^r(c@k)\rangle@k$ to Δ_2^n. From the fact that the outputting agent is typeable relative to Γ, we know $\Delta_1 \vdash_k V : \Delta_1^w(c@k)$, and therefore that $\Gamma \vdash_k V : \Delta_1^w(c@k)$, since $\Gamma <: \Delta_1$.

This last fact also implies $\Gamma \vdash_k c : \mathsf{w}\langle\Delta_1^w(c@k)\rangle$, and in turn $\Gamma <: \Delta_2$ implies $\Gamma \vdash_k c{:}\mathsf{r}\langle\Delta_2^r(c@k)\rangle$. So by part (iii) of Proposition 5.23 we know $\Delta_1^w(c@k) <: \Delta_2^r(c@k)$. By (subsumption) in the same proposition we therefore have $\Gamma \vdash_k V{:}\Delta_2^r(c@k)$, which is sufficient to establish that $\Delta_2^n \vdash \mathbf{env}$ and

(i) $\Gamma <: \Delta_2^n$.

This follows from Question 5 at the end of the chapter. Moreover since Δ_2^n is a well-defined environment

(ii) $\Delta_2^n \vdash_k V{:}\Delta_2^r(c@k)$.

The typing of the input agent implies $\Delta_2 \vdash_k c?(X)\,R$ that, by virtue of (TY-IN), means $\Delta_2, \langle X{:}\Delta_2^r(c@k)\rangle@k \vdash_k R$. Therefore in view of (ii) the substitution result, Corollary 5.32, gives

(iii) $\Delta_2^n \vdash_k R\{\!|^V\!/\!_X|\!\}$.

An application of the new rule (TY$_\mathrm{T}$-AGENT) to (i) and (iii) now gives the required (5.42). ■

Runtime errors in TAGGED-ADPI: Since the capabilities or permissions of agents are explicitly represented in TAGGED-ADPI, it is straightforward to define a version of runtime error that represents the misuse of capabilities. Intuitively such a runtime error occurs in

$$k[\![P]\!]_\Delta$$

if P is about to use a capability that is not in its permission set Δ. Because we have concentrated on two specific capabilities there are principally two ways in which this might occur. The first is when P attempts to output on some channel c and there is no permission to write on c at k in Δ. This is covered by the rule (ERR$_\mathrm{T}$-OUT) in Figure 5.14. The rule (ERR$_\mathrm{T}$-IN) takes care of the misuse of input capabilities; $k[\![c?(X)\,R]\!]_\Delta$ contains a runtime error if there is no mention of a read capability on c at k in the agent's permissions Δ. Formally the relation

$$M \longrightarrow^{\mathrm{err}}$$

is defined to be the least *contextual* relation over tagged systems that satisfies the two axioms (ERR$_\mathrm{T}$-IN), (ERR$_\mathrm{T}$-OUT).

Example 5.41 Let us consider a tagged version of the system in Example 5.36:

$$\mathsf{Sys}_t \Leftarrow \mathsf{bob}[\![\mathsf{codeB}]\!]_{\Delta_b} \mid (\mathsf{new}\, m : \mathsf{M})(m[\![\mathsf{LMem}]\!]_{\Delta_m} \mid c[\![C(m)]\!]_{\Delta_c})$$

where Δ_b, Δ_c are given by

$$\mathsf{xpt}_p@\mathsf{bob}:\mathsf{rw}\langle \mathsf{M}_p\rangle,\ \mathsf{print}@\mathsf{bob}:\mathsf{rw}\langle \mathsf{int}\rangle \qquad \text{and} \qquad \mathsf{xpt}_p@\mathsf{bob}:\mathsf{rw}\langle \mathsf{M}_p\rangle$$

respectively. Then $\mathsf{Sys}_t \longrightarrow_t^* \mathsf{Sys}_t^n$, where

$$\begin{aligned}\mathsf{Sys}_t^n \Leftarrow (\mathsf{new}\, m{:}\mathsf{M})\ (\mathsf{new}\, r{:}\mathsf{R})(\ \mathsf{bob}[\![r?(y)\, \mathsf{print}!\langle y\rangle]\!]_{\Delta_b^n} \\ \mid\ m[\![\mathsf{get}!\langle r\rangle]\!]_{\Delta_b^n}\ \mid\ m[\![\mathsf{LMem}]\!]_{\Delta^c})\end{aligned}$$

and Δ_b^n is the augmented set of permissions Δ_b, $\mathsf{put}@m{:}\mathsf{T}_p$. But here there is a runtime error, in the agent $m[\![\mathsf{get}!\langle r\rangle]\!]_{\Delta_b^n}$, picked up by the rule (ERR$_\mathrm{T}$-OUT); the agent is about to write on the channel get at m, although this resource does not appear in its permission set Δ_b^n. ■

Proposition 5.42 (type safety in TAGGED-ADPI) Suppose $\Gamma \vdash M_t$. *Then* $M_t \longrightarrow_t^* N_t$ *implies* $N_t \not\longrightarrow^{err}$.

Proof: Because of subject reduction, Theorem 5.40, it is sufficient to show $N_t \longrightarrow^{\mathrm{err}}$ implies $\Gamma \not\vdash N_t$ for every Γ. The proof is by induction on the derivation of $N_t \longrightarrow^{\mathrm{err}}$.

The two axioms, given in Figure 5.14, are straightforward. For example to derive $\Gamma \vdash k[\![c?(X)\, R]\!]_\Delta$ it is necessary, among other things, to establish $\Delta \vdash_k c?(X)\, R$. But this is not possible, as the side-condition on (ERR$_\mathrm{T}$-IN) says that $c@k$ contains no read capabilities in Δ.

The two (implicit) rules, generated by the contextuality of $\longrightarrow^{\mathrm{err}}$, are handled by induction. For example suppose $(\mathsf{new}\, e : \mathsf{D})\, N_t \longrightarrow^{\mathrm{err}}$ because $N_t \longrightarrow^{\mathrm{err}}$. Then $\Gamma' \vdash N_t$ for no possible Γ'. In particular $\Gamma, \langle e{:}\mathsf{D}\rangle \not\vdash N_t$, and therefore $\Gamma \vdash (\mathsf{new}\, e : \mathsf{D})\, N_t$ cannot be derived. ■

5.4.2 Types versus tags

We have just seen that TAGGED-ADPI is a language in which capabilities/permissions are explicitly represented in the syntax and are explicitly managed by the runtime semantics; moreover in well-typed systems of TAGGED-ADPI we are assured that permissions are never violated by agents. However it is quite onerous on programmers or designers to develop system descriptions in which all capabilities are required to be explicit. Also, as we have seen, even with this explicitness a type system is required.

(ERR$_\mathrm{T}$-IN)

$$k[\![c?(X)\, R]\!]_\Delta \longrightarrow^{\mathrm{err}} \quad \text{if } c@k{:}\mathsf{r}\langle\ldots\rangle \notin \Delta$$

(ERR$_\mathrm{T}$-OUT)

$$k[\![c!\langle V\rangle]\!]_\Delta \longrightarrow^{\mathrm{err}} \quad \text{if } c@k{:}\mathsf{w}\langle\ldots\rangle \notin \Delta$$

Figure 5.14 Runtime errors in TAGGED-ADPI

Here we show that ADPI alleviates the burden of runtime management of these explicit tags. We explain how systems written in ADPI may be viewed as representations for explicitly annotated systems in TAGGED-ADPI, and how the type system in ADPI may be viewed as a systematic mechanism for implicitly handling the capabilities of these annotated systems correctly.

Definition 5.43 (*tagging systems*) For any list of type associations Γ and any ADPI system M let $\mathsf{tag}_\Gamma(M)$ be the TAGGED-ADPI system defined as follows:

- $\mathsf{tag}_\Gamma(\mathbf{0}) = \mathbf{0}$
- $\mathsf{tag}_\Gamma(k[\![P]\!]) = k[\![P]\!]_\Gamma$
- $\mathsf{tag}_\Gamma(M \mid N) = \mathsf{tag}_\Gamma(M) \mid \mathsf{tag}_\Gamma(N)$
- $\mathsf{tag}_\Gamma((\mathsf{new}\, e : \mathsf{D})\, M) = (\mathsf{new}\, e : \mathsf{D})(\mathsf{tag}_{\Gamma, \langle e:\mathsf{D}\rangle}(M))$. ♦

So $\mathsf{tag}_\Gamma(M)$ systematically distributes the permissions in Γ to every agent in the system M.

Theorem 5.44 (*tagging preserves well-typing*) *$\Gamma \vdash M$ if and only if $\Gamma \vdash \mathsf{tag}_\Gamma(M)$.*

Proof: By structural induction on M. For example suppose M is $k[\![P]\!]$. Then $\Gamma \vdash \mathsf{tag}_\Gamma(M)$ is equivalent to $\Gamma \vdash_k P$, which in turn is equivalent to $\Gamma \vdash k[\![P]\!]$. ■

This result has an interesting corollary, which says that if the unannotated ADPI system M is well-typed with respect to Γ, then no runtime errors will occur in the annotated version of M, where all agents are initialised with the permissions described in Γ:

Corollary 5.45 Suppose $\Gamma \vdash M$. Then $N_t \not\longrightarrow^{err}$ for every N_t such that $\mathsf{tag}_\Gamma(M) \longrightarrow_t^* N_t$.

Proof: From the previous theorem we know $\Gamma \vdash \mathsf{tag}_\Gamma(M)$ and the result therefore follows immediately from type safety for TAGGED-ADPI, Proposition 5.42. ■

It is worth emphasising the import of this corollary. It means that there is no reason to get involved in the complexities of TAGGED-ADPI, in which capabilities need to be explicitly represented and managed at runtime. Instead of considering the tagged system $\mathsf{tag}_\Gamma(M)$ and its behaviour relative to the tagged reduction semantics, it is sufficient to consider the untagged system M and its behaviour relative to the simpler untagged reduction semantics. So long as $\Gamma \vdash M$ we are assured that $\mathsf{tag}_\Gamma(M)$, running relative to the tagged reduction semantics, will never give rise to a runtime error.

Example 5.46 Let us reconsider the ADPI system

$$\mathsf{Sys}^j \Leftarrow \mathsf{jane}[\![\mathsf{codeJ}]\!] \mid (\mathsf{new}\, m : \mathsf{M})(m[\![\mathsf{LMem}]\!] \mid c[\![C(m)]\!])$$

where the code for $C(m)$ and codeJ is given in Example 5.37. And suppose Δ_j is such that $\Delta_j \vdash_{\mathsf{jane}} \mathsf{xpt}_p : \mathsf{rw}\langle \mathsf{M}_p \rangle$, and it has sufficient capabilities to type the memory correctly.

Then one can check that $\Delta_j \vdash \mathsf{Sys}^j$ and consequently the explicitly annotated system $\mathsf{tag}_{\Delta_j}(\mathsf{Sys}^j)$ will never raise a runtime error relative to the tagged reduction semantics; agents will only ever use resources for which they have explicit permission.

However this is not the case for the system involving bob, Sys^b in Example 5.36. A corresponding type environment is some Δ_b, with respect to which the only type that can be inferred for xpt_p at bob is $\mathsf{rw}\langle \mathsf{M}_p \rangle$. Here we have $\Delta_b \not\vdash \mathsf{Sys}^b$ and therefore the explicitly annotated system $\mathsf{tag}_{\Delta_b}(\mathsf{Sys}^b)$ is not type-safe; consequently there is a possibility of runtime errors. Indeed a runtime error does occur, as detailed in Example 5.41. There the explicit permissions are slightly different, but the same runtime error occurs in $\mathsf{tag}_{\Delta_b}(\mathsf{Sys}^b)$; an agent emanating from bob that tries to use the get method at m without permission. ■

Corollary 5.45 justifies the type system for ADPI in terms of the reduction semantics of TAGGED-ADPI. But we can go even further by showing that this reduction semantics of TAGGED-ADPI is essentially the same as that of ADPI. The relationship is not completely straightforward, as reductions are not preserved under the function $\mathsf{tag}_\Delta(\,)$. That is $M \longrightarrow N$ does not necessarily imply $\mathsf{tag}_\Delta(M) \longrightarrow_t \mathsf{tag}_\Delta(N)$, as the following very simple example shows.

Example 5.47 Let Γ be a type environment such that $\Gamma \vdash_k c : \mathsf{rw}\langle \mathsf{w} \rangle$ and let M denote the system

$$k[\![c?(x)\, x!]\!] \mid (\mathsf{new}\, a@k{:}\mathsf{rw})\, k[\![c!\langle a \rangle]\!]$$

Note that $\Gamma \vdash M$. Then $M \longrightarrow N$, where N is $(\mathsf{new}\, a@k : \mathsf{rw})(k[\![a!]\!])$ but $\mathsf{tag}_\Gamma(M) \not\longrightarrow_t \mathsf{tag}_\Gamma(N)$. For $\mathsf{tag}_\Gamma(M)$ decodes to the tagged system

$$k[\![c?(x)\, x!]\!]_\Gamma \mid (\mathsf{new}\, a@k : \mathsf{rw})(k[\![c!\langle a \rangle]\!]_{\Gamma^{\mathsf{rw}}})$$

where Γ^{rw} represents $\Gamma, a@k{:}\mathsf{rw}$. Note that the channel c can only transmit write capabilities, and therefore the only tagged reduction from this, according to the rules in Figure 5.13, is to a system structurally equivalent to $(\mathsf{new}\, a@k : \mathsf{rw})\, k[\![a!]\!]_{\Gamma^{\mathsf{w}}}$ where Γ^{w} represents $\Gamma, a@k{:}\mathsf{w}$.

But $\mathsf{tag}_\Gamma(N)$, which decodes to $(\mathsf{new}\, a@k : \mathsf{rw})\, k[\![a!]\!]_{\Gamma^{\mathsf{rw}}}$, cannot be structurally equivalent to this system. ■

Of course this is not surprising as the tagged reduction semantics keeps a detailed account of the distributions of permissions, which is not even represented in the untagged systems. So to relate reductions in the two languages we need a more subtle analysis.

Definition 5.48 (tagging systems loosely) For each ADPI system M let $\mathsf{Tag}_\Gamma(M)$ be the least (finite) set of TAGGED-ADPI systems that satisfies

- $\mathbf{0} \in \mathsf{Tag}_\Gamma(\mathbf{0})$ whenever $\Gamma \vdash \mathbf{env}$
- $k[\![P]\!]_\Delta \in \mathsf{Tag}_\Gamma(k[\![P]\!])$ if $\Gamma <: \Delta$ and $\Delta \vdash_k P$
- $M_t \mid N_t \in \mathsf{Tag}_\Gamma(M \mid N)$ if $M_t \in \mathsf{Tag}_\Gamma(M)$ and $N_t \in \mathsf{Tag}_\Gamma(N)$
- $(\mathsf{new}\, e : \mathsf{D})\, M_t \in \mathsf{Tag}_\Gamma((\mathsf{new}\, e : \mathsf{D})\, M)$ if $M_t \in \mathsf{Tag}_{\Gamma,\langle e:\mathsf{D}\rangle}(M)$. ♦

Intuitively $\mathsf{Tag}_\Gamma(M)$ returns the set of tagged systems structurally similar to M, whose components have *at most* the permissions defined in Γ. For example, using the notation of Example 5.47 we have $(\mathsf{new}\, a@k : \mathsf{rw})$ $k[\![a!]\!]_{\Gamma^w} \in \mathsf{Tag}_\Gamma(N)$; recall that $k[\![a!]\!]_{\Gamma^w}$ is the tagged system to which $\mathsf{tag}_\Gamma(M)$ reduces.

The definition of $\mathsf{Tag}_\Gamma(M)$ is really only designed with the case when $\Gamma \vdash M$ in mind, in which case we are guaranteed that it is non-empty; the first part of the next result shows that it will always contain $\mathsf{tag}_\Gamma(M)$.

Lemma 5.49

(i) $\Gamma \vdash M$ *if and only if* $\mathsf{tag}_\Gamma(M) \in \mathsf{Tag}_\Gamma(M)$.
(ii) $M_t \in \mathsf{Tag}_\Gamma(M)$ *implies* $\Gamma \vdash M_t$.

Proof: The first statement is proved by induction on the structure of M. The two base cases, when M is $\mathbf{0}$ or $k[\![P]\!]$ follow by definition, and the remaining two cases follow trivially by induction.

The second statement also follows by a simple inductive argument on the structure of M, the interesting case being when it has the form $k[\![P]\!]$. By definition M_t must, in this case, take the form $k[\![P]\!]_\Delta$ for some Δ such that $\Gamma <: \Delta$ and $\Delta \vdash_k P$. But (weakening) immediately gives $\Gamma \vdash M_t$. ■

Theorem 5.50 Suppose $M_t \in \mathsf{Tag}_\Gamma(M)$. Then

(i) $M \longrightarrow N$ *implies* $M_t \longrightarrow_t N_t$ *for some* $N_t \in \mathsf{Tag}_\Gamma(N)$
(ii) $M_t \longrightarrow_t N_t$ *implies* $M \longrightarrow N$ *for some* N *such that* $N_t \in \mathsf{Tag}_\Gamma(N)$.

Proof: The first statement is proved by induction on why $M \longrightarrow N$. We look at some cases.

- Suppose it is an instance of the rule (R-COMM),

$$k[\![c!\langle V\rangle]\!] \mid k[\![c?(X)\, R]\!] \longrightarrow k[\![R\{\!|^V\!/\!_X|\!\}]\!]$$

Here M_t must have the form

$$k[\![c!\langle V\rangle]\!]_{\Delta_1} \mid k[\![c?(X)\, R]\!]_{\Delta_2}$$

where $\Delta_1 \vdash_k c!\langle V\rangle$, $\Delta_2 \vdash_k c?(X)\, R$, and $\Gamma <: \Delta_1$, $\Gamma <: \Delta_2$. The typing of the input agent ensures that $\Delta_2^r(c@k)$ exists. The typing of the output agent, and (weakening), means $\Gamma \vdash_k V : \Delta_1^w(c@k)$, and the third part of Proposition 5.23 can be employed to derive $\Delta_1^w(c@k) <: \Delta_2^r(c@k)$. This is enough to ensure that V and $\Delta_2^r(c@k)$ match, and therefore that $\langle V{:}\Delta_2^r(c@k)\rangle@k$ is well-defined.

So we can apply the rule (R_T-COMM) of the reduction semantics for TAGGED-ADPI to get

$$M_t \longrightarrow_t k[\![R\{\!|{}^V\!/\!x|\!\}]\!]_{\Delta_2'}$$

where Δ_2' is $\Delta_2, \langle V{:}\Delta_2^r(c@k)\rangle@k$.

We know by the previous lemma that $\Gamma \vdash M_t$, and therefore using subject reduction for TAGGED-ADPI, Theorem 5.40, we have

$$\Gamma \vdash k[\![R\{\!|{}^V\!/\!x|\!\}]\!]_{\Delta_2'}$$

However this typing judgement is enough to ensure that $k[\![R\{\!|{}^V\!/\!x|\!\}]\!]_{\Delta_2'} \in \mathsf{Tag}_\Gamma(k[\![R\{\!|{}^V\!/\!x|\!\}]\!])$.

- Suppose the reduction is an instance of (R-C.CREATE):

$$k[\![(\mathsf{newc}\, c : \mathsf{C})\ P]\!] \longrightarrow (\mathsf{new}\, c@k : \mathsf{C})\, k[\![P]\!]$$

Here M_t must take the form

$$k[\![(\mathsf{newc}\, c : \mathsf{C})\ P]\!]_\Delta$$

where $\Gamma <: \Delta$ and $\Delta \vdash_k (\mathsf{newc}\, c : \mathsf{C})\ P$.

The reduction semantics for TAGGED-ADPI gives

$$M_t \longrightarrow_t (\mathsf{new}\, c@k{:}\mathsf{C})\, k[\![P]\!]_{\Delta'}$$

where Δ' denotes $\Delta, c@k{:}\mathsf{C}$. Again the typing judgement is sufficient to ensure the inclusion of $(\mathsf{new}\, c@k{:}\mathsf{C})\, k[\![P]\!]_{\Delta'}$ in $\mathsf{Tag}_\Gamma((\mathsf{new}\, c@k : \mathsf{C})\, k[\![P]\!])$.

The remaining axioms are similar, and all of the rules, apart from (R-STR), follow by induction. For (R-STR) we need to establish the relationship between structural equivalence and $\mathsf{Tag}_\Gamma(\,)$. See Question 11 at the end of this chapter.

The second statement is proved in a similar manner, by induction on the inference of $M_t \longrightarrow_t N_t$, and an analysis of why M_t is in $\mathsf{Tag}_\Gamma(M)$. The details are left to the reader. The only non-trivial case is when the tagged reduction is an instance of (R_T-COMM), where subject reduction for TAGGED-ADPI is used. ■

The next, and final, result emphasises the import of this theorem. It shows that the computations in the untagged language from system M, well-typed with respect to Γ, are essentially the same as the tagged computations from $\mathsf{tag}_\Gamma(M)$.

Corollary 5.51 Suppose $\Gamma \vdash M$. *Then* $M \longrightarrow^* N$ *if and only if* $\mathsf{tag}_\Gamma(M) \longrightarrow_t^* N_t$ *for some* $N_t \in \mathsf{Tag}_\Gamma(N)$.

Proof: Since $\Gamma \vdash M$ we know $\mathsf{tag}_\Gamma(M) \in \mathsf{Tag}_\Gamma(M)$. Therefore the result follows by repeated application of the previous theorem. ■

To summarise this section, we have shown that the resource access types for ADPI developed in Section 5.2.1 enforce an implicit regime of access permissions to resources. Specifically an ADPI system M, well-typed with respect to Γ, may be taken to represent the explicitly annotated system $\mathsf{Tag}_\Gamma(M)$. Because it is well-typed we are assured that $\mathsf{Tag}_\Gamma(M)$, when run relative to the reduction semantics in which permissions are explicitly manipulated and managed, will never misuse these permissions. Moreover this runtime behaviour, with explicit management of permissions, is adequately modelled in the reduction semantics of ADPI, when restricted to well-typed systems.

5.5 Distributed consistency of local channels

In ADPI channel or resource names have only local significance, in that such a name is only useful if the owner also knows its location; thus the importance of located names, such as $c@l$ and $c@k$. In this framework the same name can be used at different locations, for what are essentially independent resources. For example consider the system $s[\![P]\!]$ where P is the code

$$\begin{aligned}&(\mathsf{newloc}\, s_1 : \mathsf{S}_1)\ \mathsf{with}\ P_1\ \mathsf{in}\\ &\quad(\mathsf{newloc}\, s_2 : \mathsf{S}_2)\ \mathsf{with}\ P_2\ \mathsf{in}\quad \mathsf{xpt}_1!\langle \mathsf{print}\,@s_1\rangle \mid \mathsf{xpt}_2!\langle \mathsf{print}\,@s_2\rangle\end{aligned} \tag{5.43}$$

where the location types S_i contain the local resource name print. This sets up two new sites s_1, s_2, which are locally serviced by the code P_1, P_2 respectively, and the print, created at each site, is exported along the distribution channels xpt_i; the actual values exported are *located*, consisting of the name print together with where it is defined. A user or client, with access to both export channels, xpt_1 and xpt_2 will gain knowledge of the existence of the resource print at these two distinct locations, via the located names $\mathsf{print}\,@s_1$ and $\mathsf{print}\,@s_2$ respectively.

However despite sharing the same name, a priori, there is no reason for these two local resources to have anything in common. In this instance their types are determined by the type associated with the newly created locations. These, for example, could be given by

$$\begin{aligned}\mathsf{S}_1 &= \mathsf{loc}[\mathsf{print} : \mathsf{rw}\langle \mathsf{str}\rangle, \ldots]\\ \mathsf{S}_2 &= \mathsf{loc}[\mathsf{print} : (\mathsf{int}, \mathsf{r}\langle \mathsf{w}\langle \mathsf{bool}\rangle\rangle), \ldots]\end{aligned}$$

Then at location s_1, print is a resource for handling strings, while at s_2 print expects pairs, the first of which should be an integer, and the second a local channel, with some specific capabilities. Although our type system will correctly manage the disparity between the two instances of the resource name print, it puts considerable strain on any user of these resources, since they have to continually remember which occurrence of print is being used.

But the type system can be modified so as to ensure consistency between multiple instances of the same local resource name. There are various approaches, depending on the level of consistency one wishes to enforce, and in the remainder of this chapter we outline one possibility. The general idea is to introduce a new form of global declaration, for *registered resource names*, and to insist that when new locations are generated they can only use resource names that have already been registered; moreover the types at which the locations use these names must be *consistent* with the types at which they have been registered. There are various possibilities for what is meant by *consistent* here. We outline a simple example, demanding that the type of a resource at each location must be a supertype of the type at which it has been registered. With such an approach there will be no type environment Γ for which

$$\Gamma \vdash s[\![P]\!]$$

where P is given by (5.43) above. For the resource name print must be registered in Γ at some type, say T_p; this we will denote as an entry $\mathsf{print} : \mathsf{rc}\langle \mathsf{T}_p \rangle$ in Γ, and well-typing will impose the two constraints

$$\mathsf{T}_p <: \mathsf{rw}\langle \mathsf{str} \rangle \qquad \mathsf{T}_p <: (\mathsf{int}, \mathsf{r}\langle \mathsf{w}\langle \mathsf{bool} \rangle \rangle)$$

which are unsatisfiable; these two types have no lower bound.

We now outline the changes necessary to implement this scheme as part of the typing system; for clarity let us use $\vdash^{rc}$ in place of $\vdash$ when discussing the extra requirements. First we must adapt the formation rules for well-formed environments to allow the new kind of entries, of the form $n : \mathsf{rc}\langle \mathsf{C} \rangle$, indicating that n is a globally defined registered resource name. The details are outlined in Figure 5.15. The new rule (E-RC) allows new registered names to be added to environments at a so-called *registration* type $\mathsf{rc}\langle \mathsf{C} \rangle$; note that for simplicity we will only allow names, and not variables, to be registered.

The effect of the presence of registered names is felt in the new rules for adding information about a local channel u, which replace the general rule (E-CHAN) in Figure 5.9. The first, (E-CHAN.RC), applies when u already appears in Γ as a globally defined registered name; in this case the newly added capability, at any site w, must be supported by the registration type. The second rule, (E-CHAN.NRC), is essentially the same as the old rule; when u is not registered the added capability must be consistent with all existing capabilities on u at the site in question; the notation $\Gamma \nvdash^{rc} u : \mathsf{rc}$ just means that there is no entry of the form $u : \mathsf{rc}\langle \mathsf{C} \rangle$ in Γ. Note that these rules rely on value typing judgements; these remain unchanged, inheriting the judgements from Figure 5.9.

However the most significant modification is to the subtyping rules in Figure 5.7, which also implicitly dictate the rules for constructing well-formed types. Now the

Type environments: replace (E-CHAN) in Figure 5.8 with

(E-RC)

$$\frac{\Gamma \vdash^{rc} \mathbf{env} \qquad \Gamma \vdash^{rc} \mathsf{C} : \mathbf{ty}}{\Gamma, n : \mathsf{rc}\langle \mathsf{C} \rangle \vdash^{rc} \mathbf{env}} \quad n \notin \Gamma$$

(E-CHAN.RC)

$$\frac{\Gamma \vdash^{rc} n : \mathsf{rc}\langle \mathsf{C} \rangle \qquad \Gamma \vdash^{rc} w : \mathsf{loc}}{\Gamma, n@w : \mathsf{C} \vdash^{rc} \mathbf{env}}$$

(E-NRC.CHAN)

$$\frac{\Gamma \nvdash^{rc} u : \mathsf{rc} \qquad \Gamma \vdash^{rc} \mathsf{C} : \mathbf{ty} \qquad \Gamma \vdash^{rc} w : \mathsf{loc}}{\Gamma, u@w : \mathsf{C} \vdash^{rc} \mathbf{env}} \quad \Gamma \downarrow_w (u : \mathsf{C})$$

Subtyping: replace Figure 5.7 with

(SUB-LOC)

$$\frac{\Gamma \vdash^{rc} \mathsf{C}_i <: \mathsf{C}'_i, \;\; 0 \leq i \leq k \leq n \qquad \Gamma \vdash^{rc} a_i : \mathsf{rc}\langle \mathsf{C}_i \rangle, \;\; 0 \leq i \leq n}{\Gamma \vdash^{rc} \mathsf{loc}[a_1 : \mathsf{C}_1, \ldots, a_n : \mathsf{C}_n] <: \mathsf{loc}[a_1 : \mathsf{C}'_1, \ldots, a_k : \mathsf{C}'_k]}$$

(SUB-HOM)

$$\frac{\Gamma \vdash^{rc} \mathsf{C} <: \mathsf{C}'}{\begin{array}{l}\Gamma \vdash^{rc} \mathsf{C}@\mathsf{loc} <: \mathsf{C}'@\mathsf{loc} \\ \Gamma \vdash^{rc} \mathsf{rc}\langle \mathsf{C} \rangle <: \mathsf{rc}\langle \mathsf{C}' \rangle\end{array}}$$

(SUB-TUPLE) (SUB-BASE)
(SUB-CHAN.A) (TY-CHAN.B)

adapted from Figure 3.7

Figure 5.15 Types for registered resource names

judgements must take the form

$$\Gamma \vdash^{rc} \mathsf{T}_1 <: \mathsf{T}_2$$

in which subtyping, and therefore type construction, is relative to a well-formed type environment. The only place in which the presence of Γ has an effect is in constructing location types, (SUB-LOC). To deduce

$$\Gamma \vdash^{rc} \mathsf{loc}[a_1 : \mathsf{C}_1, \ldots, a_n : \mathsf{C}_n] <: \mathsf{loc}[a_1 : \mathsf{C}_1, \ldots, a_n : \mathsf{C}_n]$$

that is to construct the type $\mathsf{loc}[a_1 : \mathsf{C}_1, \ldots, a_n : \mathsf{C}_n]$, each a_i has to be registered in Γ as a resource name; moreover the proposed type of a_i must be consistent with its registered type.

As in Definition 5.8, these subtyping rules determine when types are well-formed; we write $\Gamma \vdash^{rc} \mathsf{T} : \mathbf{ty}$ to mean that we can derive the judgement $\Gamma \vdash^{rc} \mathsf{T} <: \mathsf{T}$. Here the only real role for Γ is to ensure that if T is a location type, or uses a location type, then all resource names in that type are registered in Γ. Adapting Definition 5.8, we let $\mathbf{Types}_\Gamma$ denote the set of all types T for which we can derive $\Gamma \vdash^{rc} \mathsf{T} : \mathbf{ty}$.

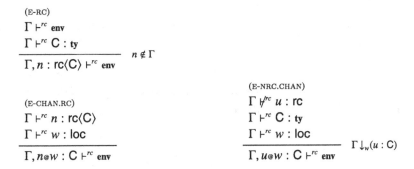

Proposition 5.52 For every valid type environment Γ*, the pre-order* $\langle \mathbf{Types}_\Gamma, <: \rangle$ *is partially complete.*

Proof: The proof is virtually identical to that of Proposition 5.9, despite the presence of the extra parameter Γ. ■

The requirement to establish the validity of a type expression relative to a type environment really only has an impact for location types. The rule (SUB-LOC) from Figure 5.15 can be specialised to

$$\text{(TY-L.TYPE)}\quad \frac{\Gamma \vdash^{rc} a_i : \mathsf{rc}\langle \mathsf{C}_i \rangle,\ \ 0 \le i \le n}{\Gamma \vdash^{rc} \mathsf{loc}[a_1 : \mathsf{C}_1, \ldots, a_n : \mathsf{C}_n] : \mathbf{ty}} \tag{5.44}$$

Indeed it is easy to see that if $\Gamma \vdash^{rc} \mathsf{loc}[a_1 : \mathsf{C}_1, \ldots, a_n : \mathsf{C}_n] : \mathbf{ty}$ then it can be established by an instance of this rule.

Note that in this modified typing framework the rules for environment construction, subtyping, and value typing are all mutually dependent. This may seem somewhat complex, but nevertheless rule induction can still be used to establish the various required properties of all these judgements. One significant new property emphasises the role of registered names:

Proposition 5.53 Suppose $\Gamma \vdash^{rc} n : \mathsf{rc}$*. Then* $\Gamma \vdash^{rc}_{w} n : \mathsf{C}$ *implies* $\Gamma \vdash^{rc} n : \mathsf{rc}\langle \mathsf{C} \rangle$*.*

Proof: By induction on the proof of $\Gamma \vdash^{rc}_{w} n : \mathsf{C}$. The only non-trivial case is the base case, when this is inferred from (TY-C.SUB) in Figure 5.9. Here Γ has the form $\Gamma_1,\ n@w : \mathsf{C}',\ \Gamma_2$ where $\mathsf{C}' <: \mathsf{C}$. The (sanity checks) on environment formation give that

$$\Gamma_1,\ n@w : \mathsf{C}' \vdash^{rc} \mathbf{env} \tag{5.45}$$

and moreover since registered name declarations are unique we must have that $\Gamma_1 \vdash^{rc} n : \mathsf{rc}$. So (5.45) can only be inferred using the rule (E-CHAN.RC) from Figure 5.8, which means that $\Gamma_1 \vdash^{rc} u : \mathsf{rc}\langle \mathsf{C}' \rangle$. The required $\Gamma \vdash^{rc} n : \mathsf{rc}\langle \mathsf{C} \rangle$ follows by (subsumption) and (weakening), which can be established for the extended typechecking system. ■

This new notion of type environment can now be used in typing judgements for systems and processes. The rules in Figures 5.10 and 5.11 can remain virtually unchanged. But we need to modify the manner in which new location declarations are handled; see Figure 5.16. For example to ensure that $(\mathsf{new}\, k : \mathsf{K})\, M$ typechecks relative to Γ we need to check that M typechecks relative to the augmented environment $\Gamma, \langle k{:}\mathsf{K} \rangle$ as before, but also that K is a well-formed location type, that is $\Gamma \vdash^{rc} \mathsf{K} : \mathbf{ty}$; this ensures that all the resource names used in K have already been registered.

Process typing:

- change (TY-LP.NEW) to

$$\frac{\begin{array}{l}\text{(TY-LP.NEW)}\\ \Gamma \vdash^{rc} \mathsf{K} : \mathbf{ty} \\ \Gamma, \langle k{:}\mathsf{K}\rangle \vdash^{rc}_{w} R : \mathsf{proc}\end{array}}{\Gamma \vdash^{rc}_{w} (\mathsf{newloc}\, k : \mathsf{K})\ R : \mathsf{proc}}$$

- replace (TY-MIS.MATCH) with

$$\frac{\begin{array}{l}\text{(TY-MIS.MATCH.GEN)}\\ \Gamma \vdash^{rc}_{w} v_1 : \mathsf{A}_1,\ v_2 : \mathsf{A}_2 \\ \Gamma \vdash^{rc}_{w} R_2 : \mathsf{proc} \\ \Gamma, \langle v_1{:}\mathsf{A}_2\rangle@w, \langle v_2{:}\mathsf{A}_1\rangle@w \not\vdash^{rc} \mathbf{env}\end{array}}{\Gamma \vdash^{rc}_{w} \mathsf{if}\ v_1 = v_2\ \mathsf{then}\ R_1\ \mathsf{else}\ R_2 : \mathsf{proc}}$$

System typing:

- change (TY-LNEW) to

$$\frac{\begin{array}{l}\text{(TY-LNEW)}\\ \Gamma \vdash^{rc} \mathsf{K} : \mathbf{ty} \\ \Gamma, \langle k{:}\mathsf{K}\rangle \vdash^{rc} M\end{array}}{\Gamma \vdash^{rc} (\mathsf{new}\, k : \mathsf{K})\, M}$$

Figure 5.16 Typing with registered resource names

However we also need to revise our rules for typing the match construct $\mathsf{if}\ v_1 = v_2\ \mathsf{then}\ R_1\ \mathsf{else}\ R_2$. Recall that for ADPI the rule (TY-MIS.MATCH) in Figure 5.11 is necessary in order to cover the possibility that the augmented environment used in the premise of (TY-MATCH), $\Gamma, \langle v_1{:}\mathsf{A}_2\rangle@w, \langle v_2{:}\mathsf{A}_1\rangle@w \vdash_w R_1$, is not well-defined. In ADPI if Γ is a well-defined environment, then so is $\Gamma, \langle v_1{:}\mathsf{A}_2\rangle@w, \langle v_2{:}\mathsf{A}_1\rangle@w$, unless $\mathsf{A}_1 \not\downarrow \mathsf{A}_2$. However in the presence of *registered names* it turns out that there are more reasons for this augmented environment to be ill-defined, not covered by the rule (TY-MIS.MATCH). To cover all possibilities we therefore use the rule (TY-MIS.MATCH.GEN), which simply says that when the augmented environment is not well-defined it is sufficient to type R_2 in the original environment. We are guaranteed that if $\Gamma, \langle v_1{:}\mathsf{A}_2\rangle@w, \langle v_2{:}\mathsf{A}_1\rangle@w$, is not a well-defined environment, then v_1 and v_2 must be different and therefore only the else branch will ever actually be executed. See Question 17 at the end of this chapter for an alternative approach to typing the match construct.

This new typechecking framework enforces a primitive form of consistency between independent systems that use the same name for independent local resources. A typical example occurs in the typing of the memory servers from Example 5.7, discussed in Example 5.18.

Example 5.54 (*Located Memory Servers, Again*) Let us reconsider the system

$$s[\![\mathsf{LmemS}]\!] \mid c_1[\![\mathsf{Client}_1]\!] \mid c_2[\![\mathsf{Client}_2]\!]$$

from Example 5.7, where the server at s generates memory cells at type M and clients generate reply channels at type R to be sent to the server. *A priori* these clients are completely independent from the server, but there is an implicit dependency between them, in the requirements on these types. Both use the resource names put, get and there is an agreement in principle that they are each declared locally at the same types, T_p and T_g respectively.

First let us see that the type judgement for this example system, given in Example 5.18, no longer works in the presence of resource registration types. Let us assume Γ_{req} has as an entry $\mathsf{req} : \mathsf{rw}\langle \mathsf{w}\langle \mathsf{M}\rangle @\mathsf{loc}\rangle$, in addition to whatever is required to type the clients; moreover since Γ_{req} is inherited from the previous section we also assume it contains no registered resources names. Typechecking now breaks down when we try to establish

$$\Gamma_{\mathsf{req}} \vdash^{rc} s[\![\mathsf{LmemS}]\!]$$

that requires the judgement

$$\Gamma_{\mathsf{req}} \vdash^{rc}_{s} (\mathsf{new}\, m : \mathsf{M})(\mathsf{LmemS} \mid \ldots)$$

The only possible rule to apply here is the revised (TY-LP.NEW), which now requires the premise

$$\Gamma_{\mathsf{req}} \vdash^{rc} \mathsf{M} : \mathbf{ty} \tag{5.46}$$

Recall from (5.30) on page 156 that M is the type $\mathsf{loc}[\mathsf{put} : \mathsf{rw}\langle \mathsf{T}_p\rangle,\ \mathsf{get} : \mathsf{rw}\langle \mathsf{T}_g\rangle]$, and so establishing (5.46) via the derived rule (TY-L.TYPE) in (5.44) above would require $\Gamma \vdash^{rc} \mathsf{put} : \mathsf{rc}\langle \mathsf{T}_p\rangle$. But this is not possible, as neither of the resources put and get are registered in Γ_{req}.

However let Γ_{pg} be a type environment with the entries

$$\mathsf{put} : \mathsf{rc}\langle \mathsf{T}_p\rangle,\ \mathsf{get} : \mathsf{rc}\langle \mathsf{T}_g\rangle,\ \mathsf{req} : \mathsf{req} : \mathsf{rw}\langle \mathsf{w}\langle \mathsf{M}\rangle @\mathsf{loc}\rangle$$

Then any system defined relative to this type environment is working under clear assumptions about the purpose of the two names put and get; they must be used at all locations in a manner consistent with their registered types. This refers to clients generating reply channels at types that use these names, but more importantly to the server when it wishes to generate new domains that offer resources with these names.

Indeed it is now easy to see that the derivation of the original type judgement can easily be adapted to obtain

$$\Gamma_{pg} \vdash^{rc} s[\![\mathsf{LmemS}]\!] \mid c_1[\![\mathsf{Client}_1]\!] \mid c_2[\![\mathsf{Client}_2]\!]$$

Here we can derive the required judgement $\Gamma_{pg} \vdash^{rc} \mathsf{M} : \mathbf{ty}$ using (TY-L.TYPE) because put and get have been declared as registered resources in Γ_{pg}. But equally important is the fact that any other client, who wishes to use the resource names put and get, for example in new location declarations, is obliged to use them at a type consistent with their registration type in Γ_{pg}. ■

The standard properties of typechecking systems developed in Section 5.3 can also be shown to hold for this framework with registered resources. However we need to be careful about the manner in which envionments are compared, generalising Definition 5.24 to: WW

Definition 5.55 (*comparing environments with registered resources*) For valid type environments, we write $\Gamma_1 <: \Gamma_2$ if for every identifier w,

(i) $\Gamma_2 \vdash^{rc}_w u : \mathsf{A}$ implies $\Gamma_1 \vdash_w u : \mathsf{A}$
(ii) $\Gamma_1 \vdash^{rc}_w u : \mathsf{rc}\langle \mathsf{C} \rangle$ if and only if $\Gamma_1 \vdash^{rc}_w u : \mathsf{rc}\langle \mathsf{C} \rangle$. ♦

In other words we do not allow any subtyping with respect to the types at which resources are declared; $\Gamma_1 <: \Gamma_2$ only if both environments have exactly the same registered resources, with exactly the same declaration types.

With this generalisation the properties such as (weakening), (strengthening), etc., from Section 5.3 still hold. We leave their proofs to the reader, and simply state the most important one:

Theorem 5.56 (*subject reduction with registered resources*) *Suppose* $\Gamma \vdash^{rc} M$ *and* $M \longrightarrow N$. *Then* $\Gamma \vdash^{rc} N$. ■

5.6 Questions

1. Prove that $(\mathsf{new}\, e : \mathsf{D})\, M \equiv M$ whenever the bound names in e does not occur free in M.
2. • Show that the subtyping relation over the set **Types**, as given in Definition 5.8, is a partial order.
   • Prove that $\langle \mathbf{Types}, <: \rangle$ is partially complete; that is fill in the details to the proof of Proposition 5.9.
3. Consider the following server for generating *distributed forwarders*, based on Example 5.3: $s[\![\mathsf{DisFServ}]\!]$ where the code DisFServ is given by

$$\mathsf{DisFServ} \Leftarrow \mathsf{rec}\; z.\; \mathsf{req?}(x_1@y_1, x_2@y_2, x@y)\; (z \mid y.x! \mid \mathsf{DisF}(y_1, x_1, y_2, x_2))$$

   where $\mathsf{DisF}(y_1, x_1, y_2, x_2)$ is obtained from $\mathsf{DisF}(k_1, b, k_2, c)$ in the obvious manner. Give a type environment, containing only an entry for $\mathsf{req}@s$, with respect to which the server is well-typed.

4. Consider the searching process defined by:

$$\mathsf{Search} \Leftarrow \mathsf{rec}\ z.\ \mathsf{test}?(x)\ \mathsf{if}\ \mathsf{good}(x)\ \mathsf{then}\ \mathsf{goto}\ \mathsf{h.report!}\langle x\rangle\ \mathsf{else}$$
$$\mathsf{neigh}?(y)\ \mathsf{goto}\ y.z$$

When run at a specific domain, it reads some data from the channel test, and runs a check on it, with the predicate good. If the check passes it reports to some home base h. Otherwise it uses the channel neigh to find a neighbour of the current location, and starts the searching process all over again from there.
Show that it is not possible to type the system $k[\![\mathsf{Search}]\!]$, for any location k.
How could the typing system be extended so that $k[\![\mathsf{Search}]\!]$ could be properly typed?
5. This is a generalisation of Question 2 from Chapter 4 to ADPI. Suppose $\Gamma_1,\ \Gamma_2$ are two valid type environments with $\Gamma_1 <: \Gamma_2$. Prove

   (i) $\Gamma_1, \langle \tilde{e}:\tilde{\mathsf{D}}\rangle \vdash \mathbf{env}$ implies $\Gamma_2, \langle \tilde{e}:\tilde{\mathsf{D}}\rangle \vdash \mathbf{env}$.
   Note that here there is no assumption about identifiers in $(\tilde{e})$ being fresh.
   (ii) If $\mathsf{bn}(\tilde{e})$ are fresh to Γ_1 then $\Gamma_2, \langle \tilde{e}:\tilde{\mathsf{D}}\rangle \vdash \mathbf{env}$ implies $\Gamma_1, \langle \tilde{e}:\tilde{\mathsf{D}}\rangle \vdash \mathbf{env}$.
   (iii) $\Gamma_1 \vdash_w V : \mathsf{T}$ implies $\Gamma_2,\ \langle V{:}\mathsf{T}\rangle@w \vdash \mathbf{env}$.
   (iv) $\Gamma_1 <: \Gamma_2, \langle V{:}\mathsf{T}\rangle@w$.

   Show that these four results also hold for type environments with registered resources, from Section 5.5.
6. Let us say that e_1, e_2 *interchange*, if one of the following conditions hold:

   - both $e_1,\ e_2$ are located identifiers
   - both are simple names
   - e_1 is a simple name that does not occur in e_2.

   Suppose $\Gamma_1, e_1 : \mathsf{A}_1, e_2 : \mathsf{A}_2 \vdash \mathbf{env}$, where e_1 and e_2 *interchange*. Prove that $\Gamma_1, e_2 : \mathsf{A}_2, e_1 : \mathsf{A}_1$ is also a valid type environment.
7. Suppose Γ is a closed environment, that is contains no variables, such that $\Gamma \vdash k : \mathsf{loc}$. Show that there is an environment Γ' not containing k and a location type K such that $\Gamma \equiv \Gamma', \langle k{:}\mathsf{K}\rangle$.

   Is this true when $\Gamma \vdash^{rc} k : \mathsf{loc}$?; that is when the type environment can contain registered resources?
8. Again suppose $\Gamma \vdash \mathbf{env}$ is a closed environment. Prove that there exists a sequence of names $k_1, \ldots, k_n$, and location types $\mathsf{K}_1, \ldots, \mathsf{K}_n$, for some $n \geq 0$, such that $\Gamma \equiv \langle k_1{:}\mathsf{K}_1\rangle, \ldots, \langle k_n{:}\mathsf{K}_n\rangle$.
9. An environment Γ is in *standard form* if there is at most one entry for every compound value e in Γ.

   (i) Prove that for every well-defined environment, $\Gamma \vdash^{rc} \mathbf{ty}$, there is one in standard form Γ' such that $\Gamma \equiv \Gamma'$.
   (ii) Suppose Γ is in standard form and $\Gamma \vdash_w V : \mathsf{T}$. Show that there is a derivation of this judgement that does not use the rule (TY-MEET).

10. Here we generalise Question 11 of Chapter 3 Let σ be a mapping over $\mathsf{Names} \cup \mathsf{Vars}$ that maps names to names and variables to variables. Let $\Gamma\sigma$ be the type association list obtained from Γ by
    - replacing every occurrence of $u : \mathsf{E}$ with $\sigma(u) : (\mathsf{E}\sigma)$
    - replacing every occurrence of $u@w : \mathsf{C}$ with $\sigma(u)@\sigma(w) : (\mathsf{C}\sigma)$.

    Note that channel types and registered name types can contain names; thus $(\mathsf{E})\sigma$ is the result of substituting every occurrence of n by $\sigma(n)$ in E. Assuming σ is injective on the set of (simple) identifiers that occur in Γ, prove:

    (i) $\Gamma \vdash M$ implies $\Gamma\sigma \vdash M\sigma$
    (ii) $\Gamma \vdash^{rc} M$ implies $\Gamma\sigma \vdash^{rc} M\sigma$.
11. Suppose $M \equiv N$. Prove that $M_t \in \mathsf{Tag}_\Gamma(M)$ implies there exists some $N_t \in \mathsf{Tag}_\Gamma(N)$ such that $M_t \equiv N_t$.
12. Show that subject reduction still holds in the typing system of Figure 5.10, if (TY-MIS.MATCH) in Figure 5.11 is replaced by (TY-MIS.MATCH.GEN) from Figure 5.16.
13. Consider the type system with registered names from Section 5.5. A type environment is called *reduced* if $\Gamma \vdash^{rc}_{w_1} n : \mathsf{C}_1$ and $\Gamma \vdash^{rc}_{w_2} n : \mathsf{C}_2$ implies $w_1 = w_2$, whenever $\Gamma \not\vdash^{rc} n : \mathsf{rc}$. In other words local channel names exist at a unique site unless they have been declared as a registered resource.

    Suppose $\Gamma \vdash^{rc} M$, where Γ is reduced. Then show that $\Gamma \vdash^{rc} M$ can be inferred using judgements that *only* contain reduced environments.
14. Prove Theorem 5.56, subject reduction for the typing system with registered resource names.
15. Show that the substitution result Proposition 5.31 no longer holds in the presence of registered resources if (TY-MIS.MATCH.GEN) is replaced by (TY-MIS.MATCH).
16. Use the previous question to show that subject reduction also does *not* hold in the presence of registered resources, if (TY-MIS.MATCH.GEN) is replaced by (TY-MIS.MATCH).
17. Prove that subject reduction will hold for the system with registered resource names if (TY-MIS.MATCH.GEN) is replaced by (TY-MIS.MATCH) together with the following two rules:

(TY-MIS.MATCH.R1)
$$\frac{\Gamma \vdash_w v_1 : \mathsf{A}_1 \quad \Gamma \vdash^{dec} v_2 : \mathsf{rc}\langle \mathsf{A}_2 \rangle \quad \Gamma \vdash_w R_2 : \mathsf{proc}}{\Gamma \vdash_w \mathsf{if}\ v_1 = v_2\ \mathsf{then}\ R_1\ \mathsf{else}\ R_2 : \mathsf{proc}} \quad \mathsf{A}_2 \not<: \mathsf{A}_1$$

(TY-MIS.MATCH.R2)
$$\frac{\Gamma \vdash_w v_2 : \mathsf{A}_2 \quad \Gamma \vdash^{dec} v_1 : \mathsf{rc}\langle \mathsf{A}_1 \rangle \quad \Gamma \vdash_w R_2 : \mathsf{proc}}{\Gamma \vdash_w \mathsf{if}\ v_1 = v_2\ \mathsf{then}\ R_1\ \mathsf{else}\ R_2 : \mathsf{proc}} \quad \mathsf{A}_1 \not<: \mathsf{A}_2$$

Here the notation $\Gamma \vdash^{dec} v : \mathsf{rc}\langle \mathsf{A} \rangle$ means that the type association $v : \mathsf{rc}\langle \mathsf{A} \rangle$ occurs in Γ.

6

Behavioural equivalences for ADPI

In this chapter we apply the theory developed for API in Chapter 4 to ADPI. For technical reasons it is best to work relative to the extended typing system developed in Section 5.5, although to avoid unnecessary clutter we will abbreviate $\vdash^{rc}$ to simply $\vdash$.

The motivation for this theory, the relativisation of behavioural equivalences to the partial knowledge of observers as explained in Chapter 4, applies equally well, if not more so, in a distributed setting. Consequently it is not repeated here. Moreover the technical framework, developed in detail in Chapter 4, is easily adapted to ADPI. So we simply apply it, modifying the various concepts as necessary to the distributed setting, in what we hope is a natural manner.

In the first section we discuss *distributed* actions-in-context and the associated typed bisimulation equivalence, $\approx_{bis}$, for ADPI systems. Most proofs of the expected properties of this equivalence are left to the reader as they can be easily constructed from the corresponding ones in Sections 4.1 and 4.2.

This is followed by a section on examples, which demonstrates that at least in principle standard bisimulation-based proof methodologies can be adapted to our setting. Necessarily there are more syntactic details to contend with; but in time appropriate software tools, based for example on theorem provers, could be developed to partially alleviate the tedium.

In the final section we revisit the subject first broached in the untyped setting of API, in Section 2.5, namely the justification of our typed bisimulation equivalence for ADPI. This involves developing a typed version of the touchstone equivalence $\eqsim$ and applying it to the distributed setting of ADPI. We show that bisimulation equivalence $\approx_{bis}$ is sound with respect to $\eqsim$, thus establishing that bisimulations provide an adequate technique for establishing behavioural identities. Of course readers still familiar with the contents of Section 2.5 will realise that the converse is not true; Example 2.29 is readily adapted to ADPI. So there are distributed systems that cannot be reasonably distinguished, but that can never be related using a bisimulation. The attentive reader will also know the remedy. We develop an asynchronous version of bisimulation for ADPI, and adapt the technique of Section 2.7 to show that this asynchronous version of bisimulation equivalence is complete relative to $\approxeq$; if two ADPI configurations are related via $\approxeq$ then there exists some (typed) asynchronous bisimulation that relates them.

6.1 Actions-in-context for ADPI

As in Chapter 4 we consider *configurations*, this time consisting of ADPI systems, coupled with partial knowledge of their resources encapsulated in a type environment.

Definition 6.1 (*configurations in* ADPI) A configuration is a pair

$$\mathcal{I} \triangleright M$$

where M is a system from ADPI such that $\Gamma \vdash M$ for some type environment Γ compatible with $\mathcal{I}$, that is $\Gamma <: \mathcal{I}$. It is assumed that both $\mathcal{I}$ and Γ are valid environments; moreover since M is a closed term, that is it contains no free variables, we may assume that the domain of $\mathcal{I}$, and also that of the implicit Γ, only contains names, and located names. ♦

We define (distributed) *actions-in-context*

$$\mathcal{I} \triangleright M \xrightarrow{\mu} \mathcal{I}' \triangleright M' \tag{6.1}$$

representing the ability of M to interact with its environment, together with the ability of the environment, with knowledge $\mathcal{I}$, to participate in the interaction. As in API the only forms of possible interaction are input or output along a communication channel; but now these channels, or resources, are *located*. Consequently the possible typed action labels μ are as follows:

- $\alpha_i = (\tilde{e} : \tilde{\mathsf{D}})k.a?V$: the input of value V along the channel a, *located at the site* k; the *bound* names in the set $(\tilde{e})$ are freshly generated by the environment.
- $\alpha_o = (\tilde{e} : \tilde{\mathsf{D}})k.a!V$: the output of value V along the channel a, *located at the site* k; here the *bound* names in $(\tilde{e})$ are freshly generated by the system.
- τ: this represents, as usual, some internal activity.

We extend the complementary notation for action labels, $\overline{\mu}$, used for API, in the obvious manner; $\overline{\tau}$ is τ itself; if α_o is $(\tilde{e} : \tilde{\mathsf{D}})k.a!V$ then $\overline{\alpha_o}$ is the corresponding input label $(\tilde{e} : \tilde{\mathsf{D}})k.a?V$, while $\overline{\alpha_i}$ is the output label $(\tilde{e} : \tilde{\mathsf{D}})k.a!V$, if α_i is the output $(\tilde{e} : \tilde{\mathsf{D}})k.a!V$.

As usual the standard assumptions on bound variables in these actions (6.1) are in force. Thus all bound names are assumed to be *fresh*, relative to the environment $\mathcal{I}$ and system M, although for emphasis this requirement is sometimes explicitly mentioned. We also employ the same consistency requirements on these μ as in

Section 4.1, adapted to take into account possible compound names. So for example for $(e : \mathsf{D})\alpha$ to be well-formed we require α to be well-formed, and the bound name in e to

- be different from the location and channel used in α
- be different from the bound names in α
- appear somewhere in α.

The occurrence of these actions-in-context depends on the environment having appropriate capabilities on *located* channels. To describe these we use the notation referred to after Definition 3.25, on page 87, to describe the read/write capabilities associated with a given channel in a type environment, *relative* to a given location; for example $\mathcal{I}^r(a@k)$ gives the read capability, known to $\mathcal{I}$, on the channel a at the location k.

The actions-in-context (6.1) are defined to be the least relations over configurations satisfying the axioms and rules in Figures 6.1 and 6.2. These are simply a *localised* adaptation of the corresponding axioms and rules for TYPED API in Figures 4.1 and 4.2; each possible action may occur at a specific location, say k, and the various requirements for the action-in-context to be defined are checked locally, at this k. Input is governed by two rules, (L-IN) for values that are already known to the environment, and therefore the system being observed, and (L-WEAK) for names newly invented by the observer; in the latter we use the general notation $\langle e{:}\mathsf{D}\rangle$ developed after Definition 5.12, for extracting type association lists from system level name creations. The (implicit) requirement in this rule that $\mathcal{I}, \langle e{:}\mathsf{D}\rangle$ is a well-defined environment, is crucial to the proper management of new names. For example consider the judgement

$$\mathcal{I} \triangleright k[\![a?(X)\, R]\!] \xrightarrow{\alpha_i} \mathcal{I}' \triangleright N$$

Let us look at three instances of the input action label α_i.

- α_i is $(b@l : \mathsf{C})k.a?b@l$: here, in order for $\mathcal{I}, \langle e{:}\mathsf{D}\rangle$, that is $\mathcal{I}, b@l : \mathsf{C}$, to be well-defined, it is necessary for l to be already known as a location in $\mathcal{I}$, that is $\mathcal{I} \vdash l : \mathsf{loc}$. So the label represents the transmission at location k, from the observer to the observed system, of the name of a new resource b, with type C, at a location already known to both observer and observed, namely l.
- If α_i is $(l : \mathsf{loc},\ b@l : \mathsf{C})k.a?b@l$ then the label represents the transmission, again at k, of a new resource b at the newly created location l.
- If it is $(l : \mathsf{loc}[\mathsf{in} : \mathsf{I}])k.a?l$ then it represents the transmission of a new location l, which has been created at type $\mathsf{loc}[\mathsf{in} : \mathsf{I}]$; here the receiving agent, in addition to being able to use the newly acquired location name l, may also use the located name $\mathsf{in}@l$, of a non-local resource at type I. Because we are using ADPI with distributed consistency of resource names this channel in must be a registered resource.

(L-IN)

$$\frac{\mathcal{I}^w(a@k)\downarrow_{\mathsf{def}} \qquad \mathcal{I} \vdash_k V : \mathcal{I}^w(a@k)}{\mathcal{I} \triangleright k[\![a?(X)\,R]\!] \xrightarrow{k.a?V} \mathcal{I} \triangleright k[\![R\{^V\!/\!_X\}]\!]}$$

(L-WEAK)

$$\frac{\mathcal{I}, \langle e{:}\mathsf{D}\rangle \triangleright M \xrightarrow{\alpha_i} \mathcal{I}' \triangleright M'}{\mathcal{I} \triangleright M \xrightarrow{(e:\mathsf{D})\alpha_i} \mathcal{I}' \triangleright M'} \quad \mathsf{bn}(e) \text{ fresh}$$

(L-OUT)

$$\frac{\mathcal{I}^r(a@k)\downarrow_{\mathsf{def}}}{\mathcal{I} \triangleright k[\![a!\langle V\rangle]\!] \xrightarrow{k.a!V} \mathcal{I},\ \langle V{:}\mathcal{I}^r(a@k)\rangle@k \triangleright k[\![\mathsf{stop}]\!]}$$

(L-OPEN)

$$\frac{\mathcal{I} \triangleright M \xrightarrow{\alpha_o} \mathcal{I}' \triangleright M'}{\mathcal{I} \triangleright (\mathsf{new}\, e : \mathsf{D})\, M \xrightarrow{(e:\mathsf{D})\alpha_o} \mathcal{I}' \triangleright M'}$$

(L-CTXT)

$$\frac{\mathcal{I} \triangleright M \xrightarrow{\mu} \mathcal{I}' \triangleright M'}{\begin{array}{l}\mathcal{I} \triangleright M \mid N \xrightarrow{\mu} \mathcal{I}' \triangleright M' \mid N \\ \mathcal{I} \triangleright N \mid M \xrightarrow{\mu} \mathcal{I}' \triangleright N \mid M'\end{array}} \quad \mathsf{bn}(\mu) \cap \mathsf{fn}(N) = \emptyset$$

$$\frac{\mathcal{I} \triangleright M \xrightarrow{\mu} \mathcal{I}' \triangleright M'}{\mathcal{I} \triangleright (\mathsf{new}\, e : \mathsf{D})\, M \xrightarrow{\mu} \mathcal{I}' \triangleright (\mathsf{new}\, e : \mathsf{D})\, M'} \quad \mathsf{bn}(e) \notin \mu$$

Figure 6.1 External actions-in-context for ADPI

Finally note that although the moves are decorated only with new global information, $(\tilde{e} : \tilde{\mathsf{D}})$, new *local* information can also be generated. For example when α_i is $(b@k : \mathsf{C})k.a?b$ the label represents the transmission of a newly created local channel b, created at the site local to the action, namely k.

Output is also governed by two rules, (L-OUT) for the transmission of values that intuitively are assumed to be known to the observer, and (L-OPEN) for the transmission of newly created names, this time newly created by the system being observed. Note that, as with TYPED API, there is an important implicit side-condition here, namely that the resulting label is well-defined. Thus to apply this rule the bound name in e must appear somewhere in the label α_o, although it is also required to be different from all the existing bound names there. Also as in TYPED API the observer receives values at the *transmission type* of channel a at k, rather than at the declaration type; the example discussed on page 102 is easily

(L-COMM)
$$\frac{\mathcal{I}_1 \triangleright M \xrightarrow{(\tilde{e}:\tilde{\mathsf{D}}')k.a?V} \mathcal{I}_1' \triangleright M' \quad \mathcal{I}_2 \triangleright N \xrightarrow{(\tilde{e}:\tilde{\mathsf{D}})k.a!V} \mathcal{I}_2' \triangleright N'}{\mathcal{I} \triangleright M \mid N \xrightarrow{\tau} \mathcal{I} \triangleright (\mathsf{new}\,\tilde{e}:\tilde{\mathsf{D}})(M' \mid N')}$$

(L-COMM)
$$\frac{\mathcal{I}_1 \triangleright M \xrightarrow{(\tilde{e}:\tilde{\mathsf{D}})k.a!V} \mathcal{I}_1' \triangleright M' \quad \mathcal{I}_2 \triangleright N \xrightarrow{(\tilde{e}:\tilde{\mathsf{D}}')k.a?V} \mathcal{I}_2' \triangleright N'}{\mathcal{I} \triangleright M \mid N \xrightarrow{\tau} \mathcal{I} \triangleright (\mathsf{new}\,\tilde{e}:\tilde{\mathsf{D}})(M' \mid N')}$$

(L-EQ)
$$\mathcal{I} \triangleright k[\![\mathsf{if}\ v = v\ \mathsf{then}\ P\ \mathsf{else}\ Q]\!] \xrightarrow{\tau} \mathcal{I} \triangleright k[\![P]\!]$$

(L-NEQ)
$$\mathcal{I} \triangleright k[\![\mathsf{if}\ v_1 = v_2\ \mathsf{then}\ P\ \mathsf{else}\ Q]\!] \xrightarrow{\tau} \mathcal{I} \triangleright k[\![Q]\!] \quad v_1 \neq v_2$$

(L-SPLIT)
$$\mathcal{I} \triangleright k[\![P \mid Q]\!] \xrightarrow{\tau} \mathcal{I} \triangleright k[\![P]\!] \mid k[\![Q]\!]$$

(L-MOVE)
$$\mathcal{I} \triangleright k[\![\mathsf{goto}\ l.P]\!] \xrightarrow{\tau} \mathcal{I} \triangleright l[\![P]\!]$$

(L-C.CREATE)
$$\mathcal{I} \triangleright k[\![(\mathsf{newc}\ c:\mathsf{C})\ P]\!] \xrightarrow{\tau} \mathcal{I} \triangleright (\mathsf{new}\ c@k:\mathsf{C})\ k[\![P]\!]$$

$\mathcal{I}\triangleright$(L-L.CREATE)
$$k[\![(\mathsf{newloc}\ l:\mathsf{L})\ P]\!] \xrightarrow{\tau} \mathcal{I} \triangleright (\mathsf{new}\ l:\mathsf{L})(k[\![P]\!])$$

(L-REC)
$$\mathcal{I} \triangleright k[\![\mathsf{rec}\ x.\ B]\!] \xrightarrow{\tau} \mathcal{I} \triangleright k[\![B\{^{\mathsf{rec}\ x.\ B}/_{x}\}]\!]$$

Figure 6.2 Internal actions-in-context for ADPI

generalised to the distributed case. Again as in TYPED API, in (L-OUT) the fact that $\mathcal{I} \triangleright k[\![a!\langle V\rangle]\!]$ is a configuration ensures that the augmented association list, namely $\mathcal{I}, \langle V{:}\mathcal{I}^r(a@k)\rangle@k$, is always a well-defined type environment; see Question 3 at the end of the chapter. The final rule in Figure 4.1 (L-CTXT) is a standard contextual rule; but note that the side-condition in the second clause, $\mathsf{bn}(e) \notin \mu$ has extra significance here as $\mathsf{bn}(e)$ may in principle occur in the types used in μ.

Most of the rules governing internal actions-in-context are taken directly from the reduction semantics; the only exception, (L-COMM), is adapted from TYPED API. The internal communication does not change the external knowledge $\mathcal{I}$, and is independent of the actual environments $\mathcal{I}_1$ and $\mathcal{I}_2$ necessary to provoke the constituent actions.

In Chapter 4 we went into considerable detail developing the properties of actions-in-context for API. Here we spare the reader many of the detailed proofs; instead we will simply state their properties, leaving it to the reader to check that the proofs given there can be adapted to ADPI. But we do need to develop the notation required to state these properties.

Notation 6.2 We first define the effect of actions on environments, generalising Definition 4.6. Let the partial function after be defined by

- $(\mathcal{I}\ \mathsf{after}\ \tau)$ is $\mathcal{I}$.
- If μ is the input label $(\tilde{e}:\tilde{\mathsf{D}})k.a?V$ then $(\mathcal{I}\ \mathsf{after}\ \mu)$ is defined to be $\mathcal{I}, \langle\tilde{e}{:}\tilde{\mathsf{D}}\rangle$; recall that here we know that all the bound names in $(\tilde{e})$ are fresh to $\mathcal{I}$.
- If μ is the output label $(\tilde{e}:\tilde{\mathsf{D}})k.a!V$ then $(\mathcal{I}\ \mathsf{after}\ \mu)$ is defined to be $\mathcal{I}, \langle V{:}\mathcal{I}^r(a@k)\rangle@k$.

Of course in each case the result is only defined if it is a valid environment.

Next let us define another partial predicate allows, which determines when an action is possible in an environment.

- $\mathcal{I}$ allows τ is always true.
- $\mathcal{I}$ allows $(\tilde{e} : \tilde{\mathsf{D}})k.a?V$ is true whenever $\mathcal{I}^w(a@k)$ is defined and $\mathcal{I}, \langle \tilde{e}:\tilde{\mathsf{D}}\rangle \vdash_k V : \mathcal{I}^w(a@k)$.
- $\mathcal{I}$ allows $(\tilde{e} : \tilde{\mathsf{D}})k.a!V$ is true whenever $\mathcal{I}^r(a@k)$ is defined.

Finally we write, mimicking Notation 4.8, $M \xrightarrow{\mu} N$ to mean that there exist *some* environments $\mathcal{I}$, $\mathcal{I}'$, such that $\mathcal{I} \triangleright M \xrightarrow{\mu} \mathcal{I}' \triangleright N$; this means that M can in principle perform the action μ. ■

Note that as with TYPED API, the definitions of ($\mathcal{I}$ after μ) and ($\mathcal{I}$ allows μ) are independent of the types in μ, whenever it is an output label. Specifically let $\mu \sim \mu'$ mean that $\mathsf{un}(\mu) = \mathsf{un}(\mu')$, where $\mathsf{un}(\,)$ is the obvious generalisation of the function given in Section 4.2.1, which eliminates the types from output labels, and leaves others untouched. Then

- ($\mathcal{I}$ after μ) = ($\mathcal{I}$ after μ')
- ($\mathcal{I}$ allows μ) if and only if ($\mathcal{I}$ allows μ').

Let us now simply enumerate the important properties of actions-in-context for ADPI, expected in the light of Section 4.1.

1. (Determinacy on environments) If $\mathcal{I} \triangleright M \xrightarrow{\mu} \mathcal{I}' \triangleright N$ then ($\mathcal{I}$ after μ) is well-defined and coincides with $\mathcal{I}'$. (See Proposition 4.7.)
   In view of this result we abbreviate actions-in-context to the form $\mathcal{I} \triangleright M \xrightarrow{\mu} N$. ■
2. (Allowing actions) If $\mathcal{I}$ allows μ and $M \xrightarrow{\mu} N$ then $\mathcal{I} \triangleright M \xrightarrow{\mu} N$, for any configuration $\mathcal{I} \triangleright M$. (Again see Proposition 4.10.)
   Intuitively this means that if M is capable of performing an action, and $\mathcal{I}$ allows it, then the action can be performed by the configuration $\mathcal{I} \triangleright M$. ■
3. (Subject reduction) If $\mathcal{I} \triangleright M \xrightarrow{\mu} N$ and $\Gamma \vdash M$ then

   - if μ is τ then $\Gamma \vdash N$
   - if μ is the output action $(\tilde{e} : \tilde{\mathsf{D}})k.a!V$ then $\Gamma^w(a@k)\downarrow_{\mathsf{def}}$, ($\Gamma$ after $\overline{\mu}$) $\vdash_k V : \Gamma^w(a@k)$ and (Γ after $\overline{\mu}$) $\vdash N$
   - if μ is the input action $(\tilde{e} : \tilde{\mathsf{D}})k.a?V$ then $\Gamma^r(a@k)\downarrow_{\mathsf{def}}$, and ($\Gamma$ after $\overline{\mu}$) $\vdash$ **env** implies (Γ after $\overline{\mu}$) $\vdash N$.

   (See Theorem 4.12.)
   As in the previous chapter the proof here depends on the fact that $\mathcal{I} \triangleright M$ is a configuration. ■
4. (Configurations) If $\mathcal{I} \triangleright M$ is a configuration and $\mathcal{I} \triangleright M \xrightarrow{\mu} N$ then ($\mathcal{I}$ after μ) $\triangleright N$ is also a configuration. (See Corollary 4.13.)
   The proof, as with TYPED API, relies on subject reduction. ■

5. (Structural equivalence) Suppose $M \equiv N$. Then $\mathcal{I} \triangleright M \xrightarrow{\mu} M'$ implies $\mathcal{I} \triangleright N \xrightarrow{\mu} N'$ for some N' such that $M' \equiv N'$. (See Proposition 4.14.) ■
6. (Reduction semantics) Suppose $\mathcal{I} \triangleright M$ is a configuration. Then $M \longrightarrow M'$ if and only if $\mathcal{I} \triangleright M \xrightarrow{\tau} M''$ for some M'' such that $M' \equiv M''$. (See Corollary 4.17.)
   The proof involves describing the precise structure of external actions, as in Proposition 4.16. ■

6.2 Typed bisimulation equivalence for ADPI

We now have in place the necessary machinery to define a bisimulation equivalence for ADPI, mimicking Definition 4.20. We have the following lts:

- The states consist of all ADPI configurations $(\mathcal{I} \triangleright M)$.
- The action labels consist of:
  - input: $(\tilde{e} : \tilde{\mathsf{D}})k.a?V$
  - output: $(\tilde{e})k.a!V$
  - internal: τ

  where the standard consistency requirements on the bound names are enforced.
- The next state relations are given by:
  - the judgements
    $$(\mathcal{I} \triangleright M) \xrightarrow{\mu} (\mathcal{I}\ \mathsf{after}\ \mu \triangleright N)$$
    that are derivable from the rules in Figures 6.1 and 6.2, when μ is an input action or the internal action τ;
  - the judgements
    $$(\mathcal{I} \triangleright M) \xrightarrow{(\tilde{e}:\tilde{E})k.a!V} (\mathcal{I}\ \mathsf{after}\ \mu \triangleright N)$$
    for *some* collection of types $(\tilde{E})$, when μ is the output action $(\tilde{e})k.a!V$.

The reason for abstracting away from the types in output moves is explained in detail in Example 4.18 for API but it applies equally well to ADPI. Essentially observers are oblivious to the declaration types of newly acquired resource names, and simply receive them at the capabilities determined by the output type of the channel through which they are transmitted. We also extend the equivalence between action labels for API, given on page 113, in the obvious manner. If μ and μ' are output labels then $\mu \sim \mu'$ means that their untyped versions are the same; otherwise μ and μ' must be identical.

Consequently we can apply the standard definition, to obtain a bisimulation equivalence between ADPI configurations. As usual we are principally interested in comparing systems under the same external assumptions and consequently we use the same notation as in Chapter 4:

$$\mathcal{I} \models M \approx_{bis} N$$

means that the configurations $(\mathcal{I} \triangleright M)$ and $(\mathcal{I} \triangleright N)$ are bisimilar. Indeed we can also adapt the terminology developed there and specify bisimulations for ADPI by defining a parameterised family of relations $\underline{\mathcal{R}}$, with the property that $\langle M, N\rangle \in \mathcal{R}_I$ implies that both $\mathcal{I} \triangleright M$ and $\mathcal{I} \triangleright N$ are configurations; moreover this will often be written as $\mathcal{I} \models M \; \mathcal{R} \; N$. The required transfer property then amounts to demanding that every action-in-context

$$(\mathcal{I} \triangleright M) \xrightarrow{\mu} M'$$

has a matching one

$$(\mathcal{I} \triangleright N) \xRightarrow{\widehat{\mu'}} N'$$

such that

$$(\mathcal{I} \text{ after } \mu) \models M' \, \mathcal{R} \, N'$$

and $\mu \sim \mu'$; recall from page 113 that this relation between action labels simply abstracts away from the types of extruded names in output actions. If the relations $\mathcal{R}_{\mathcal{I}}$ are not symmetric we will also require the corresponding transfer property for actions-in-context from $(\mathcal{I} \triangleright N)$.

In Section 4.2 we expended considerable effort in developing non-trivial properties of this relation for API. Here we simply enumerate the more interesting ones: we omit the proofs as these follow the same lines as those elaborated for API.

(A) (Strengthening) Let $\mathcal{I} <: \mathcal{I}_l$. Then $\mathcal{I} \models M \approx_{bis} N$ implies $\mathcal{I}_l \models M \approx_{bis} N$. (See Proposition 4.22.) Note however that the proof requires some properties of actions-in-context for ADPI, which we have not enumerated in the previous section. See Questions 4 and 5 at the end of the chapter. ■

(B) (Fresh weakening) Suppose $\mathcal{I}, \langle e{:}E\rangle$ is a valid environment, where $\mathsf{bn}(e)$ do not appear in $\mathcal{I}$. Then $\mathcal{I} \models M \approx_{bis} N$ implies $\mathcal{I}, \langle e{:}E\rangle \models M \approx_{bis} N$. (See Proposition 4.23.) ■

(C) (Compositionality) Let $\mathcal{I} \vdash O$. Then $\mathcal{I} \models M \approx_{bis} N$ implies $\mathcal{I} \models O \mid M \approx_{bis} O \mid N$. (See Proposition 4.24.) As we have seen the proof of this result for API requires the definition of a rather complicated typed relation between configurations. However exactly the same proof will apply to ADPI, although establishing that the adapted relation is indeed a bisimulation is somewhat more tedious, because the formation of valid type environments for ADPI is more subtle. ■

However rather than spend more effort on repeating these proofs let us consider how we may adapt standard techniques to demonstrate the parameterised equivalence between systems.

6.3 Describing bisimulations

To show that two systems M and N are equivalent relative to a configuration $\mathcal{I}$ it is sufficient to exhibit a relation $\mathcal{R}$ that contains the pair $\langle \mathcal{I} \triangleright M, \mathcal{I} \triangleright N \rangle$ and that satisfies the requirements of being a bisimulation. In fact as we have already stated, witness bisimulations are often more conveniently presented as a family of relations $\underline{\mathcal{R}}$ parameterised on type environments. However even for very simple systems describing bisimulations in any form can be quite onerous, as the required relations can be difficult to describe precisely.

There are numerous ways of alleviating this burden, some of which we examine here. One method is to develop *algebraic laws* that are satisfied by semantically equivalent systems. Structural equivalence gives one simple set of such laws.

Corollary 6.3 Suppose $M \equiv N$. *Then* $\mathcal{I} \models M \approx_{bis} N$.

Proof: An immediate consequence of Proposition 4.14, which has been generalised to ADPI in (5) on page 200. ■

What this means is that axioms for structural equivalence in Figure 5.4 can be used as equational laws for manipulating system descriptions. So for example we now know

$$(\mathsf{new}\, e : \mathsf{D})(M \mid N) \approx_{bis} M \mid (\mathsf{new}\, e : \mathsf{D})\, N \qquad \text{whenever } \mathsf{bn}(e) \notin \mathsf{fn}(M)$$

We will later see more such laws.

Another approach to alleviating the burden of exhibiting witness bisimulations is to extract structure common from the system descriptions. (Compositionality), item (C) above, justifies one such instance, where the common structure involves a concurrent system. Another instance is justified by the following result.

Proposition 6.4 (scoping) Suppose that both $\mathcal{I} \triangleright (\mathsf{new}\, e : \mathsf{D})\, M$ *and* $\mathcal{I} \triangleright (\mathsf{new}\, e : \mathsf{D})\, N$ *are configurations. Then* $\mathcal{I} \models M \approx_{bis} N$ *implies* $\mathcal{I} \models (\mathsf{new}\, e : \mathsf{D})\, M \approx_{bis} (\mathsf{new}\, e : \mathsf{D})\, N$.

Proof: Note that our ongoing implicit assumptions about the freshness of bound names, ensures that in this statement we know that the bound name in e does not appear in $\mathcal{I}$.

Let $\underline{\mathcal{R}}$ be the family of relations defined as follows: $\mathcal{I} \models M\, \mathcal{R}\, N$ if

(i) $\mathcal{I} \models M \approx_{bis} N$
(ii) or M, N have the form $(\mathsf{new}\, e : \mathsf{D})\, M_1$, $(\mathsf{new}\, e : \mathsf{D})\, N_1$ respectively, where $\mathcal{I} \models M_1 \approx_{bis} N_1$.

The result will follow if we show that $\underline{\mathcal{R}}$ is a bisimulation. So suppose $\mathcal{I} \models M\, \mathcal{R} N$ and $\mathcal{I} \triangleright M \xrightarrow{\mu} M'$. We have to find a matching action-in-context $\mathcal{I} \triangleright N \stackrel{\widehat{\mu'}}{\Longrightarrow} N'$ such that $(\mathcal{I}\ \mathsf{after}\ \mu) \models M\, \mathcal{R}\, M'$ and $\mu \sim \mu'$.

The non-trivial case is (ii), when M, N have the form $(\mathsf{new}\, e : \mathsf{D})\, M_1$, $(\mathsf{new}\, e : \mathsf{D})\, N_1$ respectively, where we have to examine the inference of the action-in-context; in particular the last rule used in the inference. There are only two possibilities; we examine one, when it is (L-OPEN). So μ has the form $(e : \mathsf{D})\alpha_o$ for some output label α_o, and $\mathcal{I} \triangleright M_1 \xrightarrow{\alpha_o} M_1'$.

Since $\mathcal{I} \models M_1 \approx_{bis} N_1$, this move can be matched by an action-in-context $\mathcal{I} \triangleright N_1 \stackrel{\widehat{\alpha_o'}}{\Longrightarrow} N_1'$ such that $\alpha_o \sim \alpha_o'$ and $\mathcal{I}\, \mathsf{after}\, \alpha_o \models M_1' \approx_{bis} N_1'$. Now (L-OPEN) can also be applied to this move, to obtain $\mathcal{I} \triangleright (\mathsf{new}\, e : \mathsf{D})\, N_1 \stackrel{\widehat{\mu'}}{\Longrightarrow} N_1'$ where μ' is $(e : \mathsf{D})\alpha_o'$. This is the required matching move, since $\mathcal{I}\, \mathsf{after}\, \alpha_o$ coincides with $\mathcal{I}\, \mathsf{after}\, \mu$. ■

Another convenient technique allows us to use witness bisimulations in which moves need only be matched approximately. For example in the untyped setting Proposition 2.19 means that the matching need only be carried out relative to structural equivalence; in effect in a bisimulation up to structural equivalence each occurrence of a process actually represents all processes structurally equivalent to it. This result can easily be generalised to ADPI, under the convention, which we will apply in this section, that structural equivalence applies to configurations. However here we will generalise the result further, allowing us to abstract away from many of the *housekeeping* moves in the operational semantics of ADPI.

Consider the rules for internal actions-in-context given in Figure 6.2. It turns out that all of these, except (L-COMM), give rise to moves whose occurrence does not really affect the subsequent behaviour of systems. To see this let us revise the operational semantics by labelling all internal moves, other than communications, with τ_β replacing the label τ used on the internal moves inferred from all the axioms with the annotated label τ_β. In other words the axioms (L-EQ), (L-NEQ), ..., (L-L.CREATE) and (L-C.CREATE) in Figure 6.2 now all give rise to instances of

$$\mathcal{I} \triangleright M \xrightarrow{\tau_\beta} N$$

so-called β-moves. So for example we have

$$\begin{aligned}
&\mathcal{I} \triangleright (\mathsf{new}\, r@k : \mathsf{R})(k[\![r?(x)\, Q]\!] \mid k[\![\mathsf{goto}\, l.\mathsf{in}!\langle r\rangle]\!]) \\
&\quad \xrightarrow{\tau_\beta} (\mathsf{new}\, r@k : \mathsf{R})(k[\![r?(x)\, Q]\!] \mid l[\![\mathsf{in}!\langle r\rangle]\!]) \\
&\mathcal{I} \triangleright k[\![\mathsf{if}\; a = b\; \mathsf{then}\; P\; \mathsf{else}\; (\mathsf{newc}\, c : \mathsf{C})\; (Q_1 \mid Q_2)]\!] \\
&\quad \xrightarrow{\tau_\beta}{}^{*} (\mathsf{new}\, c@k : \mathsf{C})(k[\![Q_1]\!] \mid k[\![Q_2]\!])
\end{aligned}$$

In the sequel we will continue to use $(\mathcal{I} \triangleright M) \xrightarrow{\tau} N$ to refer to *any* internal move, annotated or not. We will also use the notation $M \xrightarrow{\tau_\beta} N$ for the fact that $(\mathcal{I} \triangleright M) \xrightarrow{\tau_\beta} N$, for some $\mathcal{I}$. Thus, as with $\xrightarrow{\tau}$, we will use $\xrightarrow{\tau_\beta}$ interchangeably as a relation over systems, or over configurations; it will also be convenient to consider structural equivalence as a relation over configurations, by letting $(\mathcal{I} \rhd M) \equiv (\mathcal{I}' \rhd N)$ if $\mathcal{I}$ coincides with $\mathcal{I}'$ and $M \equiv N$. We leave the reader to check that the following two properties, which we have already established for τ, specialise to the annotated version:

Lemma 6.5

- $M \xrightarrow{\tau_\beta} N$ implies $\mathcal{I} \rhd M \xrightarrow{\tau_\beta} N$ for every configuration $\mathcal{I} \rhd M$.
- $M \equiv N$ and $\mathcal{I} \rhd M \xrightarrow{\tau_\beta} M'$ implies $\mathcal{I} \rhd N \xrightarrow{\tau_\beta} N'$ for some N' such that $M' \equiv N'$. ∎

The main technical property of β-moves is given in the following lemma. Here, and often in the sequel, for the sake of clarity we revert to the original notation for describing actions-in-context, as relations over configurations.

Lemma 6.6 (β-commutativity) Suppose $\mathcal{I} \rhd M \xrightarrow{\tau_\beta} \mathcal{I} \rhd M'$. Then for every other move $\mathcal{I} \rhd M \xrightarrow{\mu} (\mathcal{I} \text{ after } \mu) \rhd N$ either

(i) *μ is τ and N is M',*
(ii) *or there is a system N' and moves $(\mathcal{I} \text{ after } \mu) \rhd N \xrightarrow{\tau_\beta} (\mathcal{I} \text{ after } \mu) \rhd N'$ and $\mathcal{I} \rhd M' \xrightarrow{\mu} (\mathcal{I} \text{ after } \mu) \rhd N'$.*

Diagrammatically we can say that given

$$
\begin{array}{ccc}
\mathcal{I} \rhd M & \xrightarrow{\ \tau_\beta\ } & \mathcal{I} \rhd M' \\
\Big\downarrow{\scriptstyle \mu} & & \\
(\mathcal{I} \text{ after } \mu) \rhd N & &
\end{array}
$$

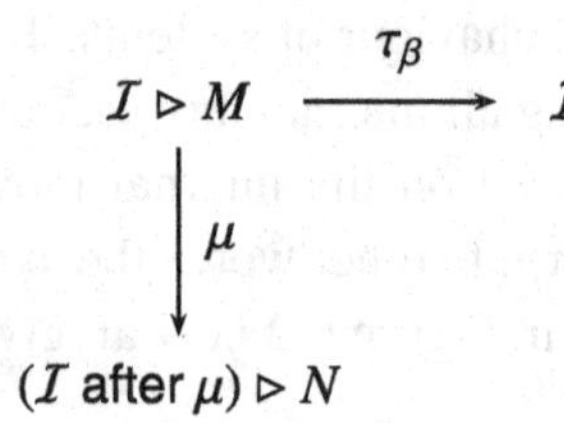

then either μ is τ and N is M', or there exists commuting moves:

$$
\begin{array}{ccc}
\mathcal{I} \rhd M & \xrightarrow{\ \tau_\beta\ } & \mathcal{I} \rhd M' \\
\Big\downarrow{\scriptstyle \mu} & & \Big\vdots{\scriptstyle \mu} \\
(\mathcal{I} \text{ after } \mu) \rhd M & \overset{\tau_\beta}{\cdots\cdots\!\!\rightarrow} & (\mathcal{I} \text{ after } \mu) \rhd N'
\end{array}
$$

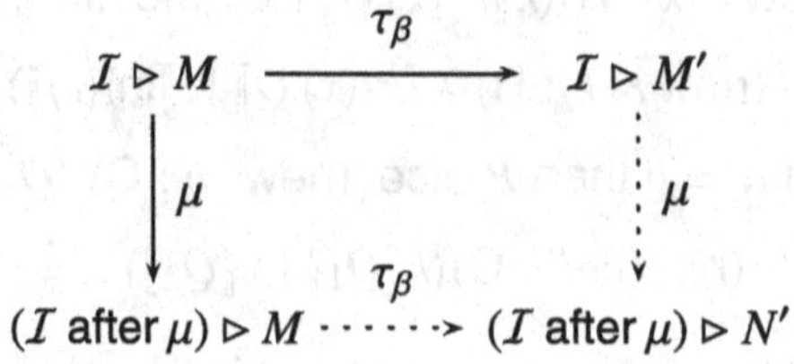

In such diagrams we use the solid lines to indicate the moves that are given, and the dotted lines those that are required.

Proof: Intuitively the reason why this is true is that if $\mathcal{I} \triangleright M \xrightarrow{\tau_\beta} \mathcal{I} \triangleright M'$ and $\mathcal{I} \triangleright M$ does any different move then both moves must have occurred in different *independent* components of M. Formally the proof proceeds by induction on the inference of $\mathcal{I} \triangleright M \xrightarrow{\tau_\beta} \mathcal{I} \triangleright M'$, with a sub-induction when appropriate on the derivation of $\mathcal{I} \triangleright M \xrightarrow{\mu} N$. We proceed by examining the last rule used in the former derivation.

All the axioms are trivial; these are the annotated versions of the axioms in Figure 6.2, and in each case the required clause (i) holds.

Note that the rule (L-COMM) from the same figure does not occur in any derivation of a β-move. So for the inductive case this leaves one of the three instances of the contextual rule, (L-CTXT). As an example suppose $\mathcal{I} \triangleright M_1 \mid M_2 \xrightarrow{\tau_\beta} \mathcal{I} \triangleright M_1' \mid M_2$ because $\mathcal{I} \triangleright M_1 \xrightarrow{\tau_\beta} \mathcal{I} \triangleright M_1'$. We now examine the proof of the second move, which must be of the form $\mathcal{I} \triangleright M_1 \mid M_2 \xrightarrow{\mu} (\mathcal{I}\ \mathsf{after}\ \mu) \triangleright N$. There are three possibilities for this move:

- N is $M_1 \mid M_2'$ and $\mathcal{I} \triangleright M_2 \xrightarrow{\mu} (\mathcal{I}\ \mathsf{after}\ \mu) \triangleright M_2'$.
  Diagrammatically we have

$$
\begin{array}{ccc}
\mathcal{I} \triangleright M_1 \mid M_2 & \xrightarrow{\quad\tau_\beta\quad} & \mathcal{I} \triangleright M_1' \mid M_2 \\
\Big\downarrow{\scriptstyle \mu} & & \\
(\mathcal{I}\ \mathsf{after}\ \mu) \triangleright M_1 \mid M_2' & &
\end{array}
$$

  Here the second clause (ii) is automatically fulfilled, with the required N' being $M_1' \mid M_2'$. To see this note that the first part of the previous lemma can be applied to $\mathcal{I} \triangleright M_1 \xrightarrow{\tau_\beta} \mathcal{I} \triangleright M_1'$ to obtain $(\mathcal{I}\ \mathsf{after}\ \mu) \triangleright M_1 \xrightarrow{\tau_\beta} (\mathcal{I}\ \mathsf{after}\ \mu) \triangleright M_1'$ and an application of (L-CTXT) gives the move $(\mathcal{I}\ \mathsf{after}\ \mu) \triangleright M_1 \mid M_2' \xrightarrow{\tau_\beta} (\mathcal{I}\ \mathsf{after}\ \mu) \triangleright M_1' \mid M_2'$.
  Since the free names of M_1' are contained in those of M_1, the contextual rule (L-CTXT) can be applied to $\mathcal{I} \triangleright M_2 \xrightarrow{\mu} (\mathcal{I}\ \mathsf{after}\ \mu) \triangleright M_2'$, to obtain the move $\mathcal{I} \triangleright M_1' \mid M_2 \xrightarrow{\mu} \mathcal{I} \triangleright M_1' \mid M_2'$. In other words we have the required commuting diagram

$$
\begin{array}{ccc}
\mathcal{I} \triangleright M_1 \mid M_2 & \xrightarrow{\quad\tau_\beta\quad} & \mathcal{I} \triangleright M_1' \mid M_2 \\
\Big\downarrow{\scriptstyle \mu} & & \Big\downarrow{\scriptstyle \mu} \\
(\mathcal{I}\ \mathsf{after}\ \mu) \triangleright M_1 \mid M_2' & \xrightarrow{\quad\tau_\beta\quad} & (\mathcal{I}\ \mathsf{after}\ \mu) \triangleright M_1' \mid M_2'
\end{array}
$$

- The label μ is τ, N is $(\mathsf{new}\,\tilde{e}:\tilde{\mathsf{D}})(M_1'' \mid M_2'')$ and $\mathcal{I}_1 \triangleright M_1 \xrightarrow{\alpha_1} \mathcal{I}_1' \triangleright M_1''$, $\mathcal{I}_2 \triangleright M_2 \xrightarrow{\alpha_2} \mathcal{I}_2' \triangleright M_2''$, for some suitable labels $\alpha_1,\ \alpha_2$. In other words we have to complete the diagram:

$$\begin{array}{ccc} \mathcal{I} \triangleright M_1 \mid M_2 & \xrightarrow{\tau_\beta} & \mathcal{I} \triangleright M_1' \mid M_2 \\ \big\downarrow \tau & & \\ \mathcal{I} \triangleright (\mathsf{new}\,\tilde{e}:\tilde{\mathsf{D}})(M_1'' \mid M_2'') & & \end{array} \tag{6.2}$$

First note that we also have the diagram

$$\begin{array}{ccc} \mathcal{I} \triangleright M_1 & \xrightarrow{\tau_\beta} & \mathcal{I} \triangleright M_1' \\ \big\downarrow \alpha_1 & & \\ \mathcal{I}\ \mathsf{after}\ \alpha_1 \triangleright M_1'' & & \end{array}$$

that can be completed, by induction, as

$$\begin{array}{ccc} \mathcal{I} \triangleright M_1 & \xrightarrow{\tau_\beta} & \mathcal{I} \triangleright M_1' \\ \big\downarrow \alpha_1 & & \big\downarrow \alpha_1 \\ \mathcal{I}\ \mathsf{after}\ \alpha_1 \triangleright M_1'' & \xrightarrow{\tau_\beta} & \mathcal{I}\ \mathsf{after}\ \alpha_1 \triangleright M_1''' \end{array}$$

We use these commuting moves to construct the moves required to complete the diagram (6.2) above:

$$\begin{array}{ccc} \mathcal{I} \triangleright M_1 \mid M_2 & \xrightarrow{\tau_\beta} & \mathcal{I} \triangleright M_1' \mid M_2 \\ \big\downarrow \tau & & \vdots\ \tau \\ \mathcal{I} \triangleright (\mathsf{new}\,\tilde{e}:\tilde{\mathsf{D}})(M_1'' \mid M_2'') & \overset{\tau_\beta}{\cdots\cdots\rightarrow} & \mathcal{I} \triangleright (\mathsf{new}\,\tilde{e}:\tilde{\mathsf{D}})(M_1''' \mid M_2'') \end{array}$$

An application of (L-COMM) to $\mathcal{I} \triangleright M_1' \xrightarrow{\alpha_1} \mathcal{I}\ \mathsf{after}\ \alpha_1 \triangleright M_1'''$ and $\mathcal{I}_2 \triangleright M_2 \xrightarrow{\alpha_2} \mathcal{I}_2' \triangleright M_2''$, gives the first required move:

$$\mathcal{I} \triangleright M_1' \mid M_2 \xrightarrow{\tau} \mathcal{I} \triangleright (\mathsf{new}\,\tilde{e}:\tilde{\mathsf{D}})(M_1''' \mid M_2'')$$

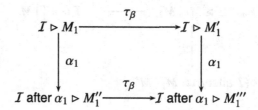

The second is obtained from $\mathcal{I}$ after $\alpha_1 \triangleright M_1'' \xrightarrow{\tau_\beta} \mathcal{I}$ after $\alpha_1 \triangleright M_1'''$; note that by the first part of the previous lemma the environment used here, $\mathcal{I}$ after α_1, can be replaced by any environment $\mathcal{I}'$ for which $\mathcal{I}' \triangleright M_1''$ is a configuration. An argument using subject reduction, (3) on page 199, can be made to show that this includes $\mathcal{I}, \langle\tilde{e}{:}\tilde{\mathsf{D}}\rangle$; the reasoning depends on whether α is an input or output action. Then two applications of (L-CTXT) gives the required

$$\mathcal{I} \triangleright (\mathsf{new}\,\tilde{e} : \tilde{\mathsf{D}})(M_1'' \mid M_2'') \xrightarrow{\tau_\beta} \mathcal{I} \triangleright (\mathsf{new}\,\tilde{e} : \tilde{\mathsf{D}})(M_1''' \mid M_2'')$$

- The final possibility is that N is $M_1' \mid M_2$ and $\mathcal{I} \triangleright M_1 \xrightarrow{\mu} \mathcal{I} \triangleright M_1'$. Here the argument is a simpler form of the one we have just made, and is left to the reader. ■

This result is lifted to sequences of β-moves, by the use of some more convenient notation. Extending the ^ notation introduced in Chapter 1, let $\mathcal{I} \triangleright M \xrightarrow{\hat{\mu}} \mathcal{I}' \triangleright N$ if

- $\mathcal{I} \triangleright M \xrightarrow{\mu} \mathcal{I}' \triangleright N$, whenever μ is an external action
- $\mathcal{I} \triangleright M \xrightarrow{\tau} \mathcal{I} \triangleright N$, or $\mathcal{I} = \mathcal{I}'$ and $N = M$, whenever μ is an internal action, that is τ annotated or not; so $\hat{\tau}$ represents 0 or 1 internal moves.

Corollary 6.7 Suppose $\mathcal{I} \triangleright M \xrightarrow{\tau_\beta}{}^{*} \mathcal{I} \triangleright M'$. *Then for every move* $\mathcal{I} \triangleright M \xrightarrow{\mu} (\mathcal{I}$ after $\mu) \triangleright N$ *there is a system* N' *and moves* $(\mathcal{I}$ after $\mu) \triangleright N \xrightarrow{\tau_\beta}{}^{*} (\mathcal{I}$ after $\mu) \triangleright N'$ *and* $\mathcal{I} \triangleright M' \xrightarrow{\hat{\mu}} (\mathcal{I}$ after $\mu) \triangleright N'$. *Diagrammatically given*

$$\begin{array}{ccc}
\mathcal{I} \triangleright M & \xmapsto{\ \tau_\beta\ }{}^{*} & \mathcal{I} \triangleright M' \\
\Big\downarrow \mu & & \\
(\mathcal{I} \text{ after } \mu) \triangleright N & &
\end{array}$$

there exist commuting *moves such that*

$$\begin{array}{ccc}
\mathcal{I} \triangleright M & \xrightarrow{\ \tau_\beta\ }{}^{*} & \mathcal{I} \triangleright M' \\
\Big\downarrow \mu & & \vdots\ \hat{\mu} \\
(\mathcal{I} \text{ after } \mu) \triangleright N & \overset{\tau_\beta}{\cdots\cdots\rightarrow}{}^{*} & (\mathcal{I} \text{ after } \mu) \triangleright N'
\end{array}$$

Proof: By repeated application of the previous lemma. ■

Thus in some sense sequences of β-moves do not affect the possible occurrence of other moves. For this reason they preserve bisimulation equivalence.

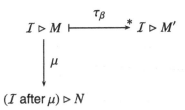

Proposition 6.8 Suppose $\mathcal{I} \triangleright M \xrightarrow{\tau_\beta}{}^* M'$. *Then* $\mathcal{I} \models M \approx_{bis} M'$.

Proof: It is sufficient to prove this result in the case when $\mathcal{I} \triangleright M \xrightarrow{\tau_\beta} M'$. Let $\underline{\mathcal{R}}$ be the parameterised family of relations defined by letting $\mathcal{I} \models M \;\; \mathcal{R} \;\; M'$ whenever

- $\mathcal{I} \triangleright M$ is a configuration
- either $M = M'$ or $M \xrightarrow{\tau_\beta} M'$.

We show $\underline{\mathcal{R}}$ is a bisimulation; note that the individual relations $\mathcal{R}_{\mathcal{I}}$ are not necessarily symmetric.

Let $\mathcal{I} \models M \, \mathcal{R} M'$ and first suppose that $\mathcal{I} \triangleright M \xrightarrow{\mu} N$. If M and M' are the same then the matching move is trivial. Otherwise we know $\mathcal{I} \triangleright M \xrightarrow{\tau_\beta} M'$ and we can apply Lemma 6.6, which gives two cases; both result in the required matching move. In the first case μ is τ and the matching move is the empty one $\mathcal{I} \triangleright M' \xrightarrow{\tau}{}^* M'$, since N and M' coincide. In the second it is the move furnished by the lemma, $\mathcal{I} \triangleright M' \xrightarrow{\mu} N'$, since $(\mathcal{I}\ \mathsf{after}\ \mu) \models N \;\; \mathcal{R} \;\; N'$.

Suppose on the other hand that $\mathcal{I} \triangleright M' \xrightarrow{\mu} N'$. If $M \xrightarrow{\tau_\beta} M'$ then the required matching move from $\mathcal{I} \triangleright M$ is simply $\mathcal{I} \triangleright M \xrightarrow{\tau_\beta} M' \xrightarrow{\mu} N'$. ■

This result gives us many useful instances of bisimulation equivalence, all albeit expected. Examples include

$$
\begin{aligned}
&\mathcal{I} \models k[\![P \mid Q]\!] \approx_{bis} k[\![P]\!] \mid k[\![Q]\!] \\
&\mathcal{I} \models k[\![\mathsf{rec}\ z.\ B]\!] \approx_{bis} k[\![P\{\!|^{\mathsf{rec}\ z.\ B}/_{z}|\!\}]\!] \\
&\mathcal{I} \models k[\![(\mathsf{newc}\, c : \mathsf{C})\ P]\!] \approx_{bis} (\mathsf{new}\, c@k : \mathsf{C})(k[\![P]\!] \\
&\mathcal{I} \models k[\![\mathsf{goto}\ l.P]\!] \approx_{bis} l[\![P]\!]
\end{aligned}
\tag{6.3}
$$

assuming of course that $\mathcal{I}$ is such that all of these are configurations.

More importantly β-moves enable us to develop a notion of bisimulation-up-to-β-reduction, which can cut down considerably on the complexity of exhibiting bisimulations. The general idea is to define a modified bisimulation relation $\mathcal{R}$ in which the condition for matching residuals is relaxed; instead of demanding that they be again related by $\mathcal{R}$ we allow an *approximate matching*. We have already seen one instance of this, where the approximation is implemented with structural equivalence. Here we use β-moves; our formulation takes advantage of the fact that both $\xrightarrow{\tau_\beta}{}^*$ and structural equivalence, $\equiv$, can be viewed as relations over both systems and configurations. Most of the abstract reasoning we are about to perform is independent of the precise syntax for configurations, and holds in an arbitrary lts. Consequently we will often use general meta-variables such as $\mathcal{C}$, $\mathcal{D}$ to range over configurations; indeed the previous two results, Corollary 6.7 and Proposition 6.8 could also have been treated at this level of abstraction.

Definition 6.9 (β-transfer properties) A relation $\mathcal{S}$ over ADPI configurations is said to satisfy the *strong β-transfer property* if

$$\begin{array}{ccc} \mathcal{C} & \mathcal{S} & \mathcal{D} \\ \downarrow \mu & & \\ \mathcal{C}' & & \end{array} \quad \text{implies} \quad \begin{array}{ccc} \mathcal{C} & \mathcal{S} & \mathcal{D} \\ \downarrow \mu & & \Downarrow \widehat{\mu'} \\ \mathcal{C}' & \mathcal{A}_l \circ \mathcal{S} \circ \mathcal{A}_r & \mathcal{D}'' \end{array}$$

for some label μ' such that $\mu \sim \mu'$, where $\mathcal{A}_l,\ \mathcal{A}_r$ are the approximation relations

$$(\xrightarrow{\tau_\beta}{}^*) \circ \equiv \quad \text{and} \quad \approx_{bis}$$

respectively. In other words the move $\mathcal{C} \xrightarrow{\mu} \mathcal{C}'$ need only be matched by a move $\mathcal{D} \overset{\widehat{\mu'}}{\Longrightarrow} \mathcal{D}'$ where some β-residual of $\mathcal{C}'$ is approximately related to $\mathcal{D}'$. This means the existence of $\mathcal{C}' \xrightarrow{\tau_\beta}{}^* \mathcal{C}''$ such that

$$\mathcal{C}'' \quad \equiv \circ \mathcal{S} \circ \approx_{bis} \quad \mathcal{D}'$$

On the other hand we say $\mathcal{S}$ satisfies the *weak β-transfer property* if

$$\begin{array}{ccc} \mathcal{C} & \mathcal{S} & \mathcal{D} \\ \Downarrow \mu & & \\ \mathcal{C}' & & \end{array} \quad \text{implies} \quad \begin{array}{ccc} \mathcal{C} & \mathcal{S} & \mathcal{D} \\ \Downarrow \mu & & \Downarrow \widehat{\mu'} \\ \mathcal{C}' & \mathcal{A}_l \circ \mathcal{S} \circ \mathcal{A}_r & \mathcal{D}'' \end{array}$$

for some label μ' such that $\mu \sim \mu'$. ♦

These relations allow considerable flexibility in how actions are matched, with the result that they are in general much smaller than real bisimulations. Intuitively in such an $\mathcal{S}$ the single pair $\langle \mathcal{C}, \mathcal{D} \rangle$ represents any pair $\langle \mathcal{C}', \mathcal{D}' \rangle$, where $\mathcal{D} \approx_{bis} \mathcal{D}'$, and $\mathcal{C}$ β-reduces to some configuration structurally equivalent to $\mathcal{C}'$.

Definition 6.10 (bisimulation up-to-β) We say that a relation $\mathcal{R}$ over configurations is a *bisimulation-up-to-β* if it and its inverse $\mathcal{R}^{-1}$ satisfy the strong β-transfer property. ♦

As with standard bisimulations, we tend to present these relations over configurations in terms of *families* of relations over systems, parameterised by type environments, as explained on page 201. This presentation is used in the following example.

Example 6.11 Let DelP and DelS denote the following systems

$$k[\![\, \mathsf{goto}\, l.\ (\mathsf{del}!\langle v_1\rangle \mid \mathsf{del}!\langle v_2\rangle \mid \mathsf{del}!\langle v_3\rangle)\ ]\!]$$

$$k[\![\, \mathsf{goto}\, l.\mathsf{del}!\langle v_1\rangle \ \mid\ (\mathsf{goto}\, l.\mathsf{del}!\langle v_2\rangle \ \mid\ \mathsf{goto}\, l.\mathsf{del}!\langle v_3\rangle)\,]\!]$$

respectively. DelS is a system that delivers, from k to l, three values v_1, v_2, v_3 in a sequential manner; each value is transported individually, by migrating an individual process for it. On the other hand DelP transports all three simultaneously, in one migration.

Suppose $\mathcal{I}_d$ is a type environment that can type both systems. This means

$$\mathcal{I}_d \vdash k : \mathsf{loc}$$

$$\mathcal{I}_d \vdash l : \mathsf{loc}[\mathsf{del} : \mathsf{w}\langle \mathsf{T}_v\rangle]$$

$$\mathcal{I}_d \vdash_l v_i : \mathsf{T}_v$$

for some appropriate type T_v. Then the relation

$$\mathcal{R}_{\mathcal{I}} = \{\, (M, M) \mid \mathcal{I} \triangleright M \ \text{ is a configuration}\,\}$$
$$\cup \{\, \langle \mathsf{DelP}, \mathsf{DelS}\rangle \mid \text{if } \mathcal{I} \equiv \mathcal{I}_d \,\}$$

is a bisimulation-up-to-β.

To see this let Dvl denote the system

$$l[\![\mathsf{del}!\langle v_1\rangle]\!] \ \mid\ l[\![\mathsf{del}!\langle v_2\rangle]\!] \ \mid\ l[\![\mathsf{del}!\langle v_3\rangle]\!]$$

Then it is easy to check that

- DelS and DelP both reduce via β-moves to Dvl
- every β-residual of DelS and DelP can be reduced, via β-moves, to Dvl.

Formally to show that $\mathcal{R}$ is a bisimulation-up-to-β-moves it is sufficient to show that all initial derivatives of $(\mathcal{I}_d \triangleright \mathsf{DelS})$ and $(\mathcal{I}_d \triangleright \mathsf{DelP})$ are correctly matched. For example the only possibility from DelS is

$$\mathcal{I}_d \triangleright \mathsf{DelS} \xrightarrow{\tau} \mathcal{I}_d \triangleright N_1$$

where N_1 is $k[\![\, \mathsf{goto}\, l.\mathsf{del}!\langle v_1\rangle]\!] \ \mid\ k[\![\mathsf{goto}\, l.\mathsf{del}!\langle v_2\rangle \mid \mathsf{goto}\, l.\mathsf{del}!\langle v_3\rangle]\!]$; in fact this is a β-move. This can be matched by the move

$$(\mathcal{I}_d \triangleright \mathsf{DelP}) \xrightarrow{\tau}{}^{*} (\mathcal{I}_d \triangleright \mathsf{Dvl})$$

(again a sequence of β-moves) since $(\mathcal{I}_d \triangleright N_1)\ \ \mathcal{A}_l \circ \mathcal{R} \circ \mathcal{A}_r\ \ (\mathcal{I}_d \triangleright \mathsf{Dvl})$.

It is possible to construct a standard bisimulation containing the pair $\langle \mathsf{DelP}, \mathsf{DelS}\rangle$, but it is much more difficult, since explicit relationships must be enumerated for all of the β-residuals. ■

The relevant properties of the left-hand approximation relation are given by:

Lemma 6.12

- $\mathcal{A}_l \subseteq \approx_{bis}$
- $\mathcal{A}_l \circ \mathcal{A}_l = \mathcal{A}_l$, *that is* $\mathcal{A}_l$ *is idempotent.*

Proof: Note that $\mathcal{A}_l$ is a relation both over configurations and over systems; here we view it as being over configurations.

The proof of the first property is straightforward, in view of Proposition 6.8. To prove the second, let Id denote the identity relation on configurations. Since $\mathsf{Id} \subseteq (\xrightarrow{\tau_b}{}^*)$ and $\mathsf{Id} \subseteq \equiv$ it follows trivially that $\mathsf{Id} \subseteq \mathcal{A}_l$. Therefore $\mathcal{A}_l \subseteq \mathcal{A}_l \circ \mathcal{A}_l$, because if $\mathcal{C}\ \mathcal{A}_l\ \mathcal{D}$ then we have $\mathcal{C}\ \mathcal{A}_l\ \mathcal{C}\ \mathcal{A}_l\ \mathcal{D}$.

So we prove the converse, and for the sake of variety let us reason directly on the relations. First note that expanding out $\mathcal{A}_l \circ \mathcal{A}_l$ we get

$$\xrightarrow{\tau_b}{}^* \circ \equiv \circ \xrightarrow{\tau_b}{}^* \circ \equiv \tag{6.4}$$

However the second part of Lemma 6.5 implies

$$\equiv \circ \xrightarrow{\tau_b}{}^* \quad \subseteq \quad \xrightarrow{\tau_b}{}^* \circ \equiv$$

For if $\mathcal{D} \equiv \circ \xrightarrow{\tau_b}{}^* \mathcal{C}'$ then we know that there is some $\mathcal{C}$ such that $\mathcal{D} \equiv \mathcal{C}$ and $\mathcal{C} \xrightarrow{\tau_b}{}^* \mathcal{C}'$. Repeated application of the lemma to $\mathcal{C} \xrightarrow{\tau_b}{}^* \mathcal{C}'$ gives some $\mathcal{D}'$ such that $\mathcal{D} \xrightarrow{\tau_b}{}^* \mathcal{D}'$ and $\mathcal{D}' \equiv \mathcal{C}'$. The existence of this $\mathcal{D}'$ ensures that $\mathcal{D} \xrightarrow{\tau_b}{}^* \circ \equiv \mathcal{C}'$.

So (6.4) above can be rewritten to

$$\xrightarrow{\tau_b}{}^* \circ \xrightarrow{\tau_b}{}^* \equiv \circ \equiv$$

that coincides with $\mathcal{A}_l$, since both component relations are transitive. ■

Lemma 6.13 $\mathcal{A}_l$ *satisfies the following transfer property:*

$$\begin{array}{ccc} \mathcal{C} & \mathcal{A}_l & \mathcal{D} \\ \big\downarrow \mu & & \\ \mathcal{C}' & & \end{array} \qquad \textit{implies} \qquad \begin{array}{ccc} \mathcal{C} & \mathcal{A}_l & \mathcal{D} \\ \big\downarrow \mu & & \vdots\ \hat{\mu} \\ \mathcal{C}' & \mathcal{A}_l & \mathcal{D}' \end{array}$$

Proof: Here let us argue diagrammatically. Suppose

$$\begin{array}{ccc} \mathcal{C} & \mathcal{A}_l & \mathcal{D} \\ \big\downarrow \mu & & \\ \mathcal{C}' & & \end{array}$$

This actually means that there exists some $\mathcal{C}_1$ such that

$$\begin{array}{ccccc}
\mathcal{C} & \xrightarrow{\tau_\beta}{}^{*} & \mathcal{C}_1 & \equiv & \mathcal{D} \\
\big\downarrow \mu & & & & \\
\mathcal{C}' & & & &
\end{array}$$

By Corollary 6.7 we can find a $\mathcal{C}_1'$ such that

$$\begin{array}{ccccc}
\mathcal{C} & \xrightarrow{\tau_\beta}{}^{*} & \mathcal{C}_1 & \equiv & \mathcal{D} \\
\big\downarrow \mu & & \big\downarrow \hat{\mu} & & \\
\mathcal{C}' & \xrightarrow{\tau_\beta}{}^{*} & \mathcal{C}_1' & &
\end{array}$$

Then the second part of Lemma 6.5 allows us to find $\mathcal{D}'$ such that

$$\begin{array}{ccccc}
\mathcal{C} & \xrightarrow{\tau_\beta}{}^{*} & \mathcal{C}_1 & \equiv & \mathcal{D} \\
\big\downarrow \mu & & \big\downarrow \hat{\mu} & & \big\downarrow \hat{\mu} \\
\mathcal{C}' & \xrightarrow{\tau_\beta}{}^{*} & \mathcal{C}_1' & \equiv & \mathcal{D}'
\end{array}$$

The result now follows, since this means $\mathcal{C}' \ \mathcal{A}_l \ \mathcal{D}'$. ■

Proposition 6.14 Suppose $\mathcal{S}$ is a relation over configurations that satisfies the strong β-transfer property. Then it also satisfies the weak β-transfer property.

Proof: Suppose

$$\begin{array}{ccc}
\mathcal{C} & \mathcal{S} & \mathcal{D} \\
\Big\Downarrow \mu & & \\
\mathcal{C}' & &
\end{array}$$

We use induction on the *size* of the action-in-context $\mathcal{C} \overset{\mu}{\Longrightarrow} \mathcal{C}'$ to show the existence of some $\mathcal{D}'$ such that

$$\begin{array}{ccc}
\mathcal{C} & \mathcal{S} & \mathcal{D} \\
\Big\Downarrow \mu & & \Big\Downarrow \widehat{\mu'} \\
\mathcal{C}' & \mathcal{A}_l \circ \mathcal{S} \circ \mathcal{A}_r & \mathcal{D}'
\end{array} \qquad (*)$$

and $\mu \sim \mu'$. Here *size* means the number of actual strong moves $\xrightarrow{\tau}$ and $\xrightarrow{\mu}$ used in the derivation of $\mathcal{C} \xRightarrow{\mu} \mathcal{C}'$. There are three cases.

- Suppose $\mathcal{C} \xrightarrow{\mu} \mathcal{C}'$. Then the result follows from the strong β-transfer property.
- Suppose $\mathcal{C} \xrightarrow{\tau} \mathcal{C}_1 \xRightarrow{\mu} \mathcal{C}'$. Applying the strong transfer property to

$$\begin{array}{ccc} \mathcal{C} & \mathcal{S} & \mathcal{D} \\ \big\downarrow \tau & & \\ \mathcal{C}_1 & & \end{array}$$

gives

$$\begin{array}{ccc} \mathcal{C} & \mathcal{S} & \mathcal{D} \\ \big\downarrow \tau & & \Big\Downarrow \hat{\tau} \\ \mathcal{C}_1 & \mathcal{A}_l \circ \mathcal{S} \circ \mathcal{A}_r & \mathcal{D}_1 \end{array}$$

This means we have $\mathcal{C}_1 \;\; \mathcal{A}_l \;\; \mathcal{C}_2 \;\; \mathcal{S} \;\; \mathcal{D}_2 \;\; \mathcal{A}_r \;\; \mathcal{D}_1$. Repeated application of Lemma 6.13 to

$$\begin{array}{ccc} \mathcal{C}_1 & \mathcal{A}_l & \mathcal{C}_2 \\ \Big\Downarrow \mu & & \\ \mathcal{C}' & & \end{array}$$

gives

$$\begin{array}{ccc} \mathcal{C}_1 & \mathcal{A}_l & \mathcal{C}_2 \\ \Big\Downarrow \mu & & \Big\Downarrow \hat{\mu} \\ \mathcal{C}' & \mathcal{A}_l & \mathcal{C}_2' \end{array}$$

Here the essential point is that the size of the derivation $\mathcal{C}_2 \xRightarrow{\hat{\mu}} \mathcal{C}_2'$ is at most that of $\mathcal{C}_1 \xRightarrow{\mu} \mathcal{C}'$. So we may apply induction to

$$\begin{array}{ccc} \mathcal{C}_2 & \mathcal{S} & \mathcal{D}_2 \\ \Big\Downarrow \hat{\mu} & & \\ \mathcal{C}_2' & & \end{array}$$

to obtain

$$\begin{array}{ccc} \mathcal{C}_2 & \mathcal{S} & \mathcal{D}_2 \\ \Big\Downarrow \hat{\mu} & & \Big\Downarrow \widehat{\mu''} \\ \mathcal{C}'_2 & \mathcal{S} & \mathcal{D}'_2 \end{array}$$

for some $\mu'' \simeq \mu$. Now we can use the fact that $\mathcal{D}_2 \;\; \mathcal{A}_r \;\; \mathcal{D}_1$, that is $\mathcal{D}_2 \approx_{bis} \mathcal{D}_1$, to obtain a move $\mathcal{D}_1 \stackrel{\widehat{\mu'}}{\Longrightarrow} \mathcal{D}'$ such that $\mathcal{D}'_2 \;\; \mathcal{A}_r \;\; \mathcal{D}'$. The matching move required in $(*)$ above is $\mathcal{D} \stackrel{\hat{\tau}}{\Longrightarrow} \mathcal{D}_1 \stackrel{\widehat{\mu'}}{\Longrightarrow} \mathcal{D}'$, since by the second part of Lemma 6.12 $\mathcal{C}' \;\; \mathcal{A}_l \circ \mathcal{S} \circ \mathcal{A}_r \;\; \mathcal{D}'$.

- The final possibility, which we leave to the reader, is that $\mathcal{C} \xrightarrow{\mu} \mathcal{C}_1 \stackrel{\tau}{\Longrightarrow} \mathcal{C}'$; the proof is similar to the case we have just completed. ■

This result is the essential ingredient in the proof that bisimulations-up-to-β yield bisimulation equivalence.

Theorem 6.15 If $\mathcal{I} \models M \;\; \mathcal{R} \;\; N$, *where* $\mathcal{R}$ *is a bisimulation-up-to-*β, *then* $\mathcal{I} \models M \approx_{bis} N$.

Proof: Let $\mathcal{S}$ denote the relation $\approx_{bis} \circ \mathcal{R} \circ \approx_{bis}$ over configurations. We show that this is a bisimulation, from which the result follows. The proof relies on the fact that $\mathcal{R}$ and its inverse satisfy the weak β-transfer property, which we know to be true from the previous proposition.

First suppose

$$\begin{array}{ccc} \mathcal{C} & \mathcal{S} & \mathcal{D} \\ \Big\downarrow \mu & & \\ \mathcal{C}' & & \end{array}$$

We have to find a matching move

$$\begin{array}{ccc} \mathcal{C} & \mathcal{S} & \mathcal{D} \\ \Big\downarrow \mu & & \Big\Downarrow \widehat{\mu'} \\ \mathcal{C}' & \mathcal{S} & \mathcal{D}' \end{array} \qquad (**)$$

Now $\mathcal{C} \;\mathcal{S}\; \mathcal{D}$ actually means

$$\mathcal{C} \approx_{bis} \mathcal{C}_1 \;\; \mathcal{R} \;\; \mathcal{D}_1 \approx_{bis} \mathcal{D}$$

So we can find a move $\mathcal{C}_1 \stackrel{\widehat{\mu''}}{\Longrightarrow} \mathcal{C}'_1$ such that $\mathcal{C}' \approx_{bis} \mathcal{C}'_1$. Since $\mathcal{R}$ satisfies the weak β-transfer property we can find a move $\mathcal{D}_1 \stackrel{\widehat{\mu'''}}{\Longrightarrow} \mathcal{D}'_1$ such that

$$\mathcal{C}'_1 \;\; \mathcal{A}_l \circ \mathcal{S} \circ \mathcal{A}_r \;\; \mathcal{D}'_1$$

But Lemma 6.12 ensures that $\mathcal{A}_l \subseteq \approx_{bis}$ and therefore we actually have $\mathcal{C}' \; \widehat{\mathcal{S}} \; \mathcal{D}_1'$; recall that $\mathcal{A}_r$ is actually $\approx_{bis}$. Now since $\mathcal{D}_1 \approx_{bis} \mathcal{D}$ we can find a move $\mathcal{D} \stackrel{\hat{\mu}'}{\Longrightarrow} \mathcal{D}'$ such that $\mathcal{D}_1' \approx_{bis} \mathcal{D}'$. This is the matching move required in (**) above, since $\mathcal{C}' \; \mathcal{S} \; \mathcal{D}'$.

Note that the relation $\mathcal{S}$ is not necessarily symmetric, since $\mathcal{R}$ may not be. So we have to also prove that every move from $\mathcal{D}$, $\mathcal{D} \xrightarrow{\mu} \mathcal{D}'$, must be properly matched by an appropriate one from $\mathcal{C}$. However the argument is essentially the same, but this time relying on the fact that $\mathcal{R}^{-1}$ satisfies the weak β-transfer property. ■

Referring back to Example 6.11, the exhibited bisimulation-up-to-β, is therefore a straightforward demonstration that

$$\mathsf{DelS} \;\approx_{bis}\; \mathsf{DelP}$$

6.4 Servers and clients

Let us now revisit another example, the server that checks whether integers are prime, from Example 5.1, $s[\![\mathsf{DprimeS}]\!]$, where $\mathsf{DprimeS}$ is the following code installed at a site s:

$$\mathsf{DprimeS} \Leftarrow \mathsf{rec}\; z.\; (z \mid \mathsf{in}_p?(x, y@w)\; \mathsf{goto}\; w.y!\langle isprime(x)\rangle)$$

We would like to prove that in some sense this does indeed act like a *prime-checking server*. Of course this server requires clients using it to conform to the required protocol; namely a client must send, in addition to the integer to be checked, a return address of the appropriate type on which the answer is to be returned. The format for such clients has already been given, also in Example 5.1. These must take the form $h[\![\mathsf{Client}(v)]\!]$, where

$$\mathsf{Client}(v) \Leftarrow (\mathsf{newc}\; r : \mathsf{R})\; (\mathsf{goto}\; s.\mathsf{in}_p!\langle v, r@h\rangle \mid r?(x)\; \mathsf{print}!\langle x\rangle)$$

and R is the type $\mathsf{rw}\langle \mathsf{bool}\rangle$.

As explained in Example 5.16, the clients use the channel in_p, located at s, at type $\mathsf{w}\langle \mathsf{T}_{in}\rangle$, and the server uses it at type $\mathsf{r}\langle \mathsf{T}_{in}\rangle$, where T_{in} is the type $(\mathsf{int}, \mathsf{w}\langle \mathsf{bool}\rangle@\mathsf{loc})$. So assuming Γ assigns the type $\mathsf{rw}\langle \mathsf{T}_{in}\rangle$ to in_p at site s and $\mathsf{w}\langle \mathsf{bool}\rangle$ to print at the sites h_1, h_2, one might expect

$$\begin{aligned} \Gamma \;\models\; & s[\![\mathsf{DprimeS}]\!] \mid h_1[\![\mathsf{Client}(27)]\!] \mid h_2[\![\mathsf{Client}(11)]\!] \\ & \approx_{bis} \\ & s[\![\mathsf{DprimeS}]\!] \mid h_1[\![\mathsf{print}!\langle \mathbf{false}\rangle]\!] \mid h_1[\![\mathsf{print}!\langle \mathbf{true}\rangle]\!] \end{aligned} \tag{6.5}$$

to be true. This would show, for example, that different clients can use the service simultaneously, with each client getting its correct response.

But unfortunately this statement is not true. The basic reason is that this framework allows a context in which there is another server, providing a different, perhaps unexpected, response to requests on the resource in_p at site s; we have already come across this argument, in a slightly different setting, in Example 3.15. Consider the system

$$s[\![\mathsf{badServer}]\!]$$

where badServer is the code

$$\mathsf{in}_p?(x, y@w)\ \mathsf{goto}\ w.y!\langle\mathbf{true}\rangle$$

This server, which also uses in_p at s with the type $\mathsf{r}\langle\mathsf{T}_{in}\rangle$, simply decrees that all integers are prime. Now if the statement (6.5) above were true, then since $\Gamma \vdash s[\![\mathsf{badServer}]\!]$, the compositionality principle would dictate that

$$\begin{aligned}\Gamma \ \models\ & s[\![\mathsf{DprimeS}]\!] \mid h_1[\![\mathsf{Client}(27)]\!] \mid h_2[\![\mathsf{Client}(11)]\!] \mid s[\![\mathsf{badServer}]\!] \\ \approx_{bis}\ & \\ & s[\![\mathsf{DprimeS}]\!] \mid h_1[\![\mathsf{print}!\langle\mathbf{false}\rangle]\!] \mid h_1[\![\mathsf{print}!\langle\mathbf{true}\rangle]\!] \mid s[\![\mathsf{badServer}]\!]\end{aligned}$$

would also be true. But this is obviously not the case. In the first system, the client at h_1 could communicate with badServer, and get back the answer **true** and print it. This behaviour is not possible in the second system. Formally the first configuration can perform the weak move

$$\xRightarrow{h_1.\mathsf{print}!(\mathbf{true})}$$

and this cannot be matched by the second.

Nevertheless we would still like to prove that the server/client interaction works correctly, *provided* $s[\![\mathsf{DprimeS}]\!]$ is the only server in the environment. By restricting the type environment Γ we can prove a slightly stronger result; in any environment in which the read capability on in_p is not available, the statement (6.5) above is true.

As a first step towards this proof we consider a slightly simpler situation.

Example 6.16 Let $\mathcal{I}_s$ be any environment that satisfies

$$\begin{aligned}&\mathcal{I}_s \vdash_{h_i} \mathsf{print} : \mathsf{w}\langle\mathsf{bool}\rangle \\ &\mathcal{I}_s \vdash_s \mathsf{in}_p : \mathsf{w}\langle\mathsf{T}_{in}\rangle \text{ where } \mathsf{T}_{in} \text{ is } (\mathsf{int}, \mathsf{w}\langle\mathsf{bool}\rangle@\mathsf{loc}) \\ &\mathcal{I}_s \vdash_s \mathsf{in}_p : \mathsf{T} \text{ implies } \mathsf{w}\langle\mathsf{T}_{in}\rangle <: \mathsf{T}\end{aligned}$$

So we confine our contexts to those in which $\mathsf{in}_p@s$ can only be used to send values, of the appropriate type.

Let $\mathsf{DprimeS}_1$ be the code

$$\mathsf{in}_p?(x, y@w)\ \mathsf{goto}\ w.y!\langle isprime(x)\rangle$$

This code, placed at the server site s, responds correctly to one client request. We show this formally by proving

$$\mathcal{I}_s \models s[\![\mathsf{DprimeS}_1]\!] \mid h_1[\![\mathsf{Client}(27)]\!] \approx_{bis} h_1[\![\mathsf{print}!\langle \mathbf{false}\rangle]\!] \qquad (6.6)$$

Let $\mathcal{R}$ be the relation over configurations consisting of all pairs of the form

$$\langle \mathcal{I}_s \triangleright M_l,\ \mathcal{I}_s \triangleright M_r\rangle$$

where $\langle M_l, M_r\rangle$ ranges over the following pairs:

$$\begin{array}{rcl}
s[\![\mathsf{DprimeS}_1]\!] \mid h_1[\![\mathsf{Client}(27)]\!] & \leftrightarrow & h_1[\![\mathsf{print}!\langle \mathbf{false}\rangle]\!] \\
(\mathsf{new}\ r@h_1 : \mathsf{R})(s[\![\mathsf{DprimeS}_1]\!] \mid & & \\
s[\![\mathsf{in}_p!\langle 27, r\rangle]\!] \mid h_1[\![\mathsf{wait}]\!]) & \leftrightarrow & h_1[\![\mathsf{print}!\langle \mathbf{false}\rangle]\!] \\
(\mathsf{new}\ r@h_1 : \mathsf{R})(h_1[\![r!\langle \mathbf{false}\rangle]\!] \mid h_1[\![\mathsf{wait}]\!]) & \leftrightarrow & h_1[\![\mathsf{print}!\langle \mathbf{false}\rangle]\!] \\
h_1[\![\mathsf{print}!\langle \mathbf{false}\rangle]\!] & \leftrightarrow & h_1[\![\mathsf{print}!\langle \mathbf{false}\rangle]\!] \\
\mathbf{0} & \leftrightarrow & \mathbf{0}
\end{array}$$

Here wait is the code $r?(x)\ \mathsf{print}!\langle x\rangle$.

Then it is easy to check that $\mathcal{R}$ is a bisimulation-up-to-β. For example the only possible move from an instance of $\mathcal{I}_s \triangleright M_r$ is

$$\mathcal{I}_s \triangleright M_r \xrightarrow{s.\mathsf{print}!(\mathbf{false})} h[\![\mathsf{stop}]\!]$$

This can be matched by a move from any corresponding $\mathcal{I} \triangleright M_l$. For example if M_l is

$$(\mathsf{new}\ r@h_1 : \mathsf{R})(h_1[\![r!\langle \mathbf{false}\rangle]\!] \mid h_1[\![\mathsf{wait}]\!])$$

then the required move is

$$\mathcal{I}_s \triangleright M_l \xrightarrow{\tau} \xrightarrow{s.\mathsf{print}!(\mathbf{false})} (\mathsf{new}\ r@h_1 : \mathsf{R})(h[\![\mathsf{stop}]\!])$$

This follows since one can show

$$(\mathsf{new}\ e : \mathsf{D})\ M \equiv M$$

whenever $\mathsf{bn}(e)$ does not occur free in M; and of course from (S-ZERO) in Figure 5.4 we have $h[\![\mathsf{stop}]\!] \equiv \mathbf{0}$; see Question 1 at the end of Chapter 5.

Similarly all the moves from $\mathcal{I}_s \triangleright M_l$ can be matched by the corresponding $\mathcal{I}_s \triangleright M_r$; in fact other than the actual print move, the matching is by the empty move. For example suppose M_l is

$$(\mathsf{new}\ r@h_1 : \mathsf{R})(s[\![\mathsf{DprimeS}_1]\!] \mid s[\![\mathsf{in}_p!\langle 27, r\rangle]\!] \mid h_1[\![\mathsf{wait}]\!])$$

Then the only possible move is the communication of the value 27 to the server:

$$\mathcal{I}_s \triangleright M_l \xrightarrow{\tau} M_l'$$

where M_l' denotes $(\mathsf{new}\, r@h_1 : \mathsf{R})(s[\![\mathsf{goto}\, h_1.r!\langle \mathbf{false}\rangle]\!] \mid s[\![\mathsf{stop}]\!] \mid h_1[\![\mathsf{wait}]\!])$. The required matching move is

$$\mathcal{I}_s \triangleright M_r \xrightarrow{\tau}{}^0 M_r$$

This is because

$$M_l' \xrightarrow{\tau_\beta} (\mathsf{new}\, r@h_1 : \mathsf{R})(h_1[\![r!\langle \mathbf{false}\rangle]\!] \mid s[\![\mathsf{stop}]\!] \mid h_1[\![\mathsf{wait}]\!])$$

and this latter system is structurally equivalent to $(\mathsf{new}\, r@h_1 : \mathsf{R})(h_1[\![r!\langle \mathbf{false}\rangle]\!] \mid h_1[\![\mathsf{wait}]\!])$, which in turn is related to M_r at $\mathcal{I}_s$ by $\mathcal{R}$.

This ends our proof of the statement (6.6) above. ■

It would be tempting to use this result, (6.6), to establish the more general

$$\mathcal{I}_s \models s[\![\mathsf{DprimeS}]\!] \mid h_1[\![\mathsf{Client(27)}]\!] \;\approx_{bis}\; s[\![\mathsf{DprimeS}]\!] \mid h_1[\![\mathsf{print}!\langle \mathbf{false}\rangle]\!] \quad (6.7)$$

By exhibiting a specific bisimulation-up-to-β, it is possible to show

$$\mathcal{I}_s \models s[\![\mathsf{DprimeS}]\!] \;\approx_{bis}\; s[\![\mathsf{DprimeS}]\!] \mid s[\![\mathsf{DprimeS}_1]\!]$$

An application of (compositionality) then gives

$$\mathcal{I}_s \models s[\![\mathsf{DprimeS}]\!] \mid h_1[\![\mathsf{Client(27)}]\!] \approx_{bis} s[\![\mathsf{DprimeS}]\!] \mid s[\![\mathsf{DprimeS}_1]\!] \mid h_1[\![\mathsf{Client(27)}]\!]$$

since $\mathcal{I}_s \vdash h_1[\![\mathsf{Client(27)}]\!]$. From this we could then conclude (6.7), again by (compositionality), under the hypothesis

$$\mathcal{I}_s \vdash s[\![\mathsf{DprimeS}]\!]$$

But unfortunately this hypothesis is not true; indeed the knowledge environment was designed to explicitly rule out systems that can read from the request service in_p at s.

However we can establish (6.7) directly by giving a witness bisimulation-up-to-β slightly more complicated than that in Example 6.16.

Example 6.17 Let S denote the system

$$s[\![\mathsf{in}_p?(x, y@w)\, \mathsf{goto}\, w.y!\langle isprime(x)\rangle \mid \mathsf{DprimeS}]\!]$$

Note that $s[\![\mathsf{DprimeS}]\!] \xrightarrow{\tau_\beta} S$ and therefore by Proposition 6.8

$$\mathcal{I}_s \models s[\![\mathsf{DprimeS}]\!] \approx_{bis} S.$$

In this example we will show

$$\mathcal{I}_s \models S \mid h_1[\![\mathsf{Client(27)}]\!] \;\approx_{bis}\; S \mid h_1[\![\mathsf{print}!\langle \mathbf{false}\rangle]\!] \quad (6.8)$$

Note that $\mathcal{I}_s \vdash h_1[\![\mathsf{Client}(27)]\!]$ and $\mathcal{I}_s \vdash h_1[\![\mathsf{print}!\langle\mathbf{false}\rangle]\!]$. Therefore our second goal (6.7) will follow by (compositionality).

Let $\mathcal{R}$ be the relation containing all pairs of configurations

$$\langle \mathcal{I} \triangleright M_l, \ \ \mathcal{I} \triangleright M_r \rangle$$

that satisfy the following requirements:

(i) M_r is of the form

$$h_1[\![\mathsf{print}!\langle\mathbf{false}\rangle]\!] \mid B \mid S$$

where B is a system

$$\Pi_{j\in J} h_j[\![r_j!\langle b_j\rangle]\!]$$

for some index set J, and collection of names h_j, r_j and boolean values b_j. Here $\Pi_{j\in J} M_j$ represents a series of systems M_j running in parallel, one for each index in J.

(ii) M_l takes one of the forms

(a) $h_1[\![\mathsf{Client}(27)]\!] \mid B \mid S$
(b) $(\mathsf{new}\, r@h_1 : \mathsf{R})\, s[\![\mathsf{in}_p!\langle 27, r@h_1\rangle]\!] \mid h_1[\![\mathsf{wait}]\!] \mid B \mid S$
(c) $(\mathsf{new}\, r@h_1 : \mathsf{R})\, h_1[\![r!\langle\mathbf{false}\rangle]\!] \mid h_1[\![\mathsf{wait}]\!] \mid B \mid S$.

(iii) $\mathcal{I}$ satisfies the requirements on $\mathcal{I}_s$ given in Example 6.16, together with

$$\mathcal{I} \vdash h_j : \mathsf{loc}$$
$$\mathcal{I} \vdash_{h_j} r_j : \mathsf{w}\langle\mathsf{bool}\rangle$$

Note that the pair

$$\langle \mathcal{I}_s \triangleright h_1[\![\mathsf{Client}(27)]\!] \mid S, \ \ \mathcal{I}_s \triangleright h_1[\![\mathsf{print}!\langle\mathbf{false}\rangle]\!] \mid S\rangle$$

is in $\mathcal{R}$, simply by taking the index set in the system B to be empty. So (6.8) follows if we can show that $\mathcal{R}$ is contained in a bisimulation-up-to-β. In fact if Id denotes the identity relation over configurations then $(\mathcal{R} \cup \mathsf{Id})$ turns out to be a bisimulation-up-to-β. This requires a considerable amount of checking, but all of it is mundane.

For example consider a move from $\mathcal{I} \triangleright M_r$. There are three possibilities:

- It is the print action at h_1;

$$\mathcal{I} \triangleright h_1[\![\mathsf{print}!\langle\mathbf{false}\rangle]\!] \mid B \mid S \xrightarrow{h_1.\mathsf{print}!\mathbf{false}} h_1[\![\mathsf{stop}]\!] \mid B \mid S$$

  But this can be matched precisely by every possible M_l, as

$$\mathcal{I} \triangleright M_l \xrightarrow{\tau}{}^{*} \xrightarrow{h_1.\mathsf{print}!\mathbf{false}} M'$$

  for some M' structurally equivalent to $h_1[\![\mathsf{stop}]\!] \mid B \mid S$; the presence of the relation Id is necessary to take care of this possibility.

- It is a move from S. Here there are a number of possibilities, depending on whether the location and/or the channel received on in_p at s is fresh. When both are fresh we get moves of the form

$$\mathcal{I}\triangleright h_1[\![\mathsf{print!}\langle\mathbf{false}\rangle]\!] \mid B \mid S \xrightarrow{\alpha_i} h_1[\![\mathsf{print!}\langle\mathbf{false}\rangle]\!] \mid B \mid s[\![\mathsf{goto}\, h.r\langle isprime(v_j)\rangle \mid \mathsf{DprimeS}]\!] \qquad (6.9)$$

where α_i is the action $(h : \mathsf{H}, r@h : \mathsf{T}_r)s.\mathsf{in}_p?(v, r@h)$. Note that this action can be continued, via τ_β moves, to a system that is once more of the form M_r, up to structural induction:

$$h_1[\![\mathsf{print!}\langle\mathbf{false}\rangle]\!] \mid B \mid s[\![\mathsf{goto}\, h.r\langle isprime(v)\rangle \mid \mathsf{DprimeS}]\!] \xrightarrow{\tau_\beta}{}^{*} h_1[\![\mathsf{print!}\langle\mathbf{false}\rangle]\!] \;\mid\; (B \mid h[\![r!\langle isprime(v)\rangle]\!]) \;\mid\; S$$

Each possible M_l can allow the S component to execute the same input action, followed by a τ move to obtain

$$\mathcal{I} \triangleright M_l \quad \stackrel{\alpha_i}{\Longrightarrow} M'$$

for some M' that is once more of the required form M_l. Here matching the residuals is with respect to the augmented environment $\mathcal{I}$ after α_i, which unravels to $\mathcal{I}, \langle h{:}\mathsf{H}\rangle,\ r@h : \mathsf{T}_r$. Note that requirements (iii) above are satisfied by this environment, because the action-in-context (6.9) can only be inferred provided

$$\mathcal{I}, \langle h{:}\mathsf{H}\rangle,\ r@h : \mathsf{T}_r \vdash_s r@h : \mathsf{w}\langle\mathsf{bool}\rangle@\mathsf{loc}$$

There are a number of mild variations to the exact form of α_i in the move (6.9) above; for example it could be $(r@h_j : \mathsf{T}_r)s.\mathsf{in}_p?(r@h_j)$, for some h_j already known to $\mathcal{I}$. But in each case the reasoning is more or less the same.
- Finally it might be a move from B. Here we can argue as in the previous case that it can be matched by a similar move from $\mathcal{I} \triangleright M_l$; indeed in this case reasoning up-to-β is not necessary.

We also have to consider all possible moves from each of the forms of M_l. If B or S is responsible arguments similar to those already employed can be repeated. As an example of the remaining cases let us consider when M_l has the form (*a*) and the move is

$$\mathcal{I}\triangleright h_1[\![\mathsf{Client(27)}]\!] \mid B \mid S \xrightarrow{\tau_\beta} (\mathsf{new}\, r_1@h_1 : \mathsf{R})\; h_1[\![\mathsf{goto}\, s.\mathsf{in}_p!\langle 27, r@h\rangle \;\mid\; \mathsf{wait}]\!] \mid B \mid S$$

Now this move can also be continued via τ_β steps, to reach a system that is once more of a form required on the left-hand side M_l :

$$(\mathsf{new}\, r_1@h_1 : \mathsf{R})\; h_1[\![\mathsf{goto}\, s.\mathsf{in}_p!\langle 27, r_1@h\rangle \;\mid\; \mathsf{wait}]\!] \mid B \mid S \xrightarrow{\tau_\beta}{}^{*} (\mathsf{new}\, r_1@h_1 : \mathsf{R})\; s[\![\mathsf{in}_p!\langle 27, r\rangle]\!] \;\mid h_1[\![\mathsf{wait}]\!] \;\mid\; B \mid S$$

This can now be matched by the empty move from the right-hand side:

$$\mathcal{I} \triangleright M_r \stackrel{\hat{\tau}}{\Longrightarrow} M_r$$

The remaining possibilities of moves from the left-hand side are treated similarly; in each case the corresponding move from the right-hand side is the empty move.■

So we have established that one client can interact successfully with the server, (6.7) above:

$$\mathcal{I}_s \models s[\![\mathsf{DprimeS}]\!] \mid h_1[\![\mathsf{Client}(27)]\!] \quad \approx_{bis} \quad s[\![\mathsf{DprimeS}]\!] \mid h_1[\![\mathsf{print}!\langle \mathbf{false} \rangle]\!]$$

But simple compositional reasoning can now be used to generalise this to an arbitrary number of clients. As an example let us consider a second client $h_2[\![\mathsf{Client}(11)]\!]$, and let us assume that $\mathcal{I}_s$ also types this correctly; that is, it knows that h_2 is a location. Then, since $\mathcal{I}_s \vdash h_2[\![\mathsf{Client}(11)]\!]$, (compositionality) applied to (6.7) gives

$$\begin{aligned} \mathcal{I}_s \models\ & s[\![\mathsf{DprimeS}]\!] \mid h_1[\![\mathsf{Client}(27)]\!] \mid h_2[\![\mathsf{Client}(11)]\!] \\ \approx_{bis}\ & s[\![\mathsf{DprimeS}]\!] \mid h_1[\![\mathsf{print}!\langle \mathbf{false} \rangle]\!] \mid h_2[\![\mathsf{Client}(11)]\!] \end{aligned} \tag{6.10}$$

A repeat of the argument in Example 6.17 establishes

$$\begin{aligned} \mathcal{I}_s \models\ & s[\![\mathsf{DprimeS}]\!] \mid h_2[\![\mathsf{Client}(11)]\!] \\ \approx_{bis}\ & s[\![\mathsf{DprimeS}]\!] \mid h_2[\![\mathsf{print}!\langle \mathbf{true} \rangle]\!] \end{aligned}$$

A further application of (compositionality) to this, gives

$$\begin{aligned} \mathcal{I}_s \models\ & s[\![\mathsf{DprimeS}]\!] \mid h_2[\![\mathsf{Client}(11)]\!] \mid h_1[\![\mathsf{print}!\langle \mathbf{false} \rangle]\!] \\ \approx_{bis}\ & s[\![\mathsf{DprimeS}]\!] \mid h_2[\![\mathsf{print}!\langle \mathbf{true} \rangle]\!] \mid h_1[\![\mathsf{print}!\langle \mathbf{false} \rangle]\!] \end{aligned}$$

Then, by the transitivity of $\approx_{bis}$, and the commutativity of $\mid$, (6.10) gives

$$\begin{aligned} \mathcal{I}_s \models\ & s[\![\mathsf{DprimeS}]\!] \mid h_1[\![\mathsf{Client}(27)]\!] \mid h_2[\![\mathsf{Client}(11)]\!] \\ \approx_{bis}\ & s[\![\mathsf{DprimeS}]\!] \mid h_1[\![\mathsf{print}!\langle \mathbf{false} \rangle]\!] \mid h_2[\![\mathsf{print}!\langle \mathbf{true} \rangle]\!] \end{aligned}$$

This argument can be extended to demonstrate that the server can properly handle an arbitrary number of clients.

6.5 Modelling a firewall

Intuitively a firewall is an administrative domain to which access is restricted; only agents that are *permitted*, in some sense, by the firewall are allowed in. A simple example of such a firewall is given by

$$F \Leftarrow (\mathsf{new\,f} : \mathsf{F})\, \mathsf{f}[\![\mathsf{Inform} \ \mid \ P]\!]$$

where Inform is the code

$$\mathsf{rec}\ z.\ (z \mid \mathsf{goto}\, a.\mathsf{tell!}\langle \mathsf{f} \rangle)$$

Here f is the name of the firewall, which is created with the capabilities described in the location type F, and P is some code that maintains the internal business of the firewall. A typical example of the capabilities of a firewall could be given by

$$\mathsf{F} = \mathsf{loc}[\mathsf{info} : \mathsf{rw}\langle \mathsf{I} \rangle,\ \mathsf{req} : \mathsf{rw}\langle \mathsf{R} \rangle]$$

that allows access to two resources info and req in f. Then P could, for example, maintain appropriate services at these resources; of course P would also be able to use non-local resources it knows about in its current environment.

In this very simplified scenario the existence of the firewall is made known to only one (trusted) agent, a, which is strictly speaking another domain, via the information channel tell located at a; a more realistic scenario would have some method for generating such trusted agents. A typical example of the code for this trusted agent is given by

$$A \Leftarrow a[\![\mathsf{tell?}(x)\ \mathsf{goto}\, x.Q \mid R]\!]$$

where a is informed of f by inputting on the local channel tell: we have the execution

$$F \mid A \longrightarrow^* (\mathsf{new}\, \mathsf{f} : \mathsf{F})(\mathsf{f}[\![P \mid \mathsf{Inform}]\!] \mid \mathsf{f}[\![Q]\!]) \mid a[\![R]\!] \qquad (6.11)$$

and the code Q is allowed to execute locally within the firewall.

Moreover the resources to which Q has access within the firewall are controlled by the capability type associated with the information channel tell. For example suppose the type associated with this channel is $\mathsf{rw}\langle \mathsf{F}_r \rangle$ where

$$\mathsf{F}_r = \mathsf{loc}[\mathsf{info} : \mathsf{w}\langle \mathsf{I} \rangle,\ \mathsf{req} : \mathsf{r}\langle \mathsf{R} \rangle]$$

a supertype of the declaration type F. Then in (6.11) Q, having gained entry into the firewall, can only write to resource info and read from req.

Let us now consider the correctness of this simple protocol for allowing access to one agent, a to the firewall. Let Γ be any type environment such that

$$\Gamma \vdash F \mid A \qquad (6.12)$$

Then one might expect to be able to derive

$$\Gamma \models F \mid A \approx_{bis} (\mathsf{new}\, \mathsf{f} : \mathsf{F})\, \mathsf{f}[\![\mathsf{Inform} \mid P \mid Q]\!] \mid a[\![R]\!] \qquad (6.13)$$

But this happens not to be true, because of an implicit assumption; namely that the information channel tell can only be accessed by partners in the entry protocol, f and a; we have already seen this phenomenon when considering servers and clients.

In order for (6.12) to be true we must have $\Gamma \vdash_a \mathsf{tell} : \mathsf{rw}\langle \mathsf{F}_s \rangle$, and this allows other agents in the environment access to tell. For example consider

$$\mathsf{Rogue} \Leftarrow b[\![\mathsf{goto}\, a.\mathsf{tell}!\langle b \rangle]\!]$$

and suppose that $\Gamma \vdash \mathsf{Rogue}$. Then (compositionality) applied to (6.13) would give

$$\Gamma \models F \mid A \mid \mathsf{Rogue} \approx_{bis} (\mathsf{new}\, \mathsf{f} : \mathsf{F})(\mathsf{f}[\![\mathsf{Inform} \mid P \mid Q]\!]) \mid a[\![R]\!] \mid \mathsf{Rogue}$$

But this is obviously not the case. The left hand system can reduce via a series of τ steps (representing the interaction between A and Rogue) to the state

$$F \mid a[\![R]\!] \mid b[\![Q]\!]$$

Under reasonable assumptions about the code Q, the right-hand system has no corresponding reduction to a similar state. On the left-hand side the code Q is running at the site b while on right-hand side it is executing at f. Thus (6.13) cannot be true.

However, as with the previous example on the server and its clients, our framework allows us to amend the correctness statement (6.13) above, to take into account the implicit assumption about the information channel tell. The essential point is that the protocol works provided that *only the firewall can write on* tell. This can be formalised by proving the equivalence between the two systems relative to a restricted environment, one that does not allow write access to tell.

Suppose $\mathcal{I}$ is a type environment that satisfies

(i) $\mathcal{I} \vdash_a \mathsf{tell} : \mathsf{T}$ implies $\mathsf{r}\langle \mathsf{F}_r \rangle <: \mathsf{T}$
(ii) $\mathcal{I} \vdash a[\![R]\!]$
(iii) $\mathcal{I} \vdash (\mathsf{new}\, \mathsf{f} : \mathsf{F})\, \mathsf{f}[\![P]\!]$.

The import of the first requirement, which is the most important, is that systems in the computational context cannot write on tell. The other requirements, which are mainly for convenience, ensure that the residual behaviour at a and f is well-behaved, although a side-effect is that they also cannot write on tell. Note that in (iii), because we are using ADPI, the capabilities in the firewall type F are expected to be registered resources. Under these assumptions we prove

$$\mathcal{I} \models F \mid A \approx_{bis} (\mathsf{new}\, \mathsf{f} : \mathsf{F})(\mathsf{f}[\![\mathsf{Inform} \mid P \mid Q]\!]) \mid a[\![R]\!] \qquad (6.14)$$

First note that (up to structural equivalence)

$$F \mid A \xrightarrow{\tau_\beta} F \mid A_t \mid a[\![R]\!]$$

via (L-SPLIT), where we use A_t as a shorthand for $a[\![\mathsf{tell}?(x)\, \mathsf{goto}\, x.Q]\!]$. So by Proposition 6.8 it is sufficient to prove

$$\mathcal{I} \models F \mid A_t \mid a[\![R]\!] \approx_{bis} (\mathsf{new}\, \mathsf{f} : \mathsf{F})(\mathsf{f}[\![\mathsf{Inform} \mid P \mid Q]\!]) \mid a[\![R]\!]$$

Here assumption (ii) comes in useful, as by (compositionality) it is now sufficient to prove

$$\mathcal{I} \models F \mid A_t \approx_{bis} (\mathsf{new\,f : F})(\mathsf{f}[\![\mathsf{Inform} \mid P \mid Q]\!])$$

Here the left-hand side can be manipulated using the structural equivalence rules, in particular (S-EXT), thereby reducing the proof burden to

$$\mathcal{I} \models (\mathsf{new\,f : F})(\mathsf{f}[\![P \mid \mathsf{Inform}]\!] \mid A_t) \approx_{bis} (\mathsf{new\,f : F})(\mathsf{f}[\![\mathsf{Inform} \mid P \mid Q]\!])$$

An application of (scoping), Proposition 6.4, reduces this further to

$$\mathcal{I} \models \mathsf{f}[\![P \mid \mathsf{Inform}]\!] \mid A_t \approx_{bis} \mathsf{f}[\![\mathsf{Inform} \mid P \mid Q]\!]$$

Expanding further using β-moves, we get

- $\mathsf{f}[\![P \mid \mathsf{Inform}]\!] \mid A_t \xrightarrow{\tau_\beta} \mathsf{f}[\![P]\!] \mid \mathsf{f}[\![\mathsf{Inform}]\!] \mid A_t$
- $\mathsf{f}[\![\mathsf{Inform} \mid P \mid Q]\!] \xrightarrow{\tau_\beta} \mathsf{f}[\![\mathsf{Inform}]\!] \mid \mathsf{f}[\![P]\!] \mid \mathsf{f}[\![Q]\!]$.

So further applications of Proposition 6.8, and (compositionality), give the requirement

$$\mathcal{I} \models \mathsf{f}[\![\mathsf{Inform}]\!] \mid A_t \approx_{bis} \mathsf{f}[\![\mathsf{Inform}]\!] \mid \mathsf{f}[\![Q]\!] \tag{6.15}$$

This we establish directly by exhibiting a particular bisimulation.

We define the parameterised relation $\mathcal{R}$ by letting

$$\mathcal{J} \models M \,\mathcal{R}\, N$$

whenever

(a) $\mathcal{J} \triangleright M$ is a configuration and N is the same as M
(b) or $\mathcal{J} \equiv \mathcal{I}$ and
- M has the form $\mathsf{f}[\![\mathsf{Inform}]\!] \mid A_t \mid \Pi_{(j+1)}(a[\![\mathsf{tell!}\langle \mathsf{f}\rangle]\!])$
- N has the form $\mathsf{f}[\![\mathsf{Inform}]\!] \mid \mathsf{f}[\![Q]\!] \mid \Pi_j(a[\![\mathsf{tell!}\langle \mathsf{f}\rangle]\!])$

for some $j \geq 0$.

Proposition 6.18 The parameterised relation $\mathcal{R}$ *defined above is a bisimulation up-to-*β.

Proof: Suppose $\mathcal{J} \models M \mathcal{R} N$. First let us see that actions-in-context from $\mathcal{J} \triangleright M$ can be matched by corresponding actions-in-context from $\mathcal{J} \triangleright N$. In fact it is sufficient to consider case (b) above, when $\mathcal{J} \equiv \mathcal{I}$ and M and N are of the prescribed form. The actions fall into one of three categories:

- Here $\mathsf{f}[\![\mathsf{Inform}]\!]$ is responsible, so it takes the form

$$\mathcal{I} \triangleright M \xrightarrow{\tau} \mathcal{I} \triangleright \mathsf{f}[\![\mathsf{Inform} \mid \mathsf{goto}\, a.\mathsf{tell!}\langle \mathsf{f}\rangle]\!] \mid A_t \mid \Pi_{(j+1)}(\ldots)$$

But

$$\mathcal{I} \triangleright \mathsf{f}[\![\mathsf{Inform} \mid \mathsf{goto}\, a.\mathsf{tell!}\langle \mathsf{f}\rangle]\!] \mid A_t \mid \Pi_{(j+1)}(\ldots) \xrightarrow{\tau_\beta}{}^{*} \mathsf{f}[\![\mathsf{Inform}]\!] \mid a[\![\mathsf{tell!}\langle \mathsf{f}\rangle]\!] \mid A_t \mid \Pi_{(j+1)}(\ldots)$$

and this can be matched, up to structural equivalence, by essentially the same moves:

$$\mathcal{I} \triangleright N \xrightarrow{\tau}{}^{*} \mathcal{I} \triangleright \mathsf{f}[\![\mathsf{Inform}]\!] \mid \mathsf{f}[\![Q]\!] \mid \Pi_{(j+1)}(\ldots)$$

- The second possibility is that the third component, $\Pi_{(j+1)}(a[\![\mathsf{tell!}\langle \mathsf{f}\rangle]\!])$ is responsible for the action, which therefore must be $a.\mathsf{tell!}f$. It is easy to see that $\mathcal{I} \triangleright N$ can perform exactly the same action, to a related configuration.
- Finally the middle component A_t might be involved in the action. Note that the action cannot be external, as $a.\mathsf{tell?}V$ cannot be performed by the environment. So it must be a communication, of the form

$$\mathcal{I} \triangleright M \xrightarrow{\tau} \mathcal{I}_f \triangleright \mathsf{f}[\![\mathsf{Inform}]\!] \mid a[\![\mathsf{goto}\, \mathsf{f}.Q]\!] \mid \Pi_j(\ldots)$$

But once more this can be matched, up-to-β, since

$$\mathcal{I} \triangleright \mathsf{f}[\![\mathsf{Inform}]\!] \mid a[\![\mathsf{goto}\, \mathsf{f}.Q]\!] \mid \Pi_j(\ldots) \xrightarrow{\tau}{}^{*}_{\beta} \mathcal{I} \triangleright \mathsf{f}[\![\mathsf{Inform}]\!] \mid \mathsf{f}[\![Q]\!] \mid \Pi_j(\ldots)$$

and this can be matched by the empty sequence of internal actions from $\mathcal{I} \triangleright N$.

We leave the reader to check the converse; namely that every action-in-context from $\mathcal{J} \triangleright N$ can also be matched by actions from $\mathcal{J} \triangleright M$. The details are similar, but somewhat simpler. ■

This completes our proof of (6.14) above. Note that the firewall F allows in principle multiple entries of agents from a. So, for example suppose R, in (6.14) above, has the form

$$S \mid \mathsf{tell?}(x)\, \mathsf{goto}\, x.Q_1$$

Let us show how the second agent, executing Q_1, can also gain access through the firewall.

Let F_1 denote the firewall containing the first agent Q:

$$F_1 \Leftarrow (\mathsf{new}\, \mathsf{f} : \mathsf{F})\, \mathsf{f}[\![P \mid Q \mid \mathsf{Inform}]\!]$$

Then the reasoning we have just completed could be repeated, to prove

$$\mathcal{I} \models F_1 \mid a[\![R]\!] \approx_{bis} (\mathsf{new}\, \mathsf{f} : \mathsf{F})(\mathsf{f}[\![\mathsf{Inform} \mid P \mid Q \mid Q_1]\!]) \mid a[\![S]\!]$$

This, combined with (6.14), gives

$$\mathcal{I} \models F \mid A \approx_{bis} (\mathsf{new}\, \mathsf{f} : \mathsf{F})(\mathsf{f}[\![\mathsf{Inform} \mid P \mid Q \mid Q_1]\!]) \mid a[\![S]\!]$$

Here the domain a has managed to send two separate agents into the firewall.

6.6 Typed contextual equivalences

In Chapter 2 we put forward the idea that bisimulation equivalence should be looked upon as a mechanism for providing a proof technique for relating systems, rather than giving a definitive notion of when systems should be considered behaviourally equivalent. Here we pursue this idea, applying it to ADPI; we define a touchstone behavioural equivalence for ADPI, and examine its relationship with bisimulation equivalence. There are two complications to the scenario discussed in Section 2.5, namely types and locations. We need to generalise the definition of reduction barbed congruence, Definition 2.25 so as to take these into account.

As argued in Chapter 4, the presence of types means that behavioural equivalences have to move from relating processes, or their corresponding syntactic category in ADPI systems, to relating configurations. So we need to revisit the justification for reduction barbed congruence, and recast it in terms of configurations.

Recall that this relation was defined to be the largest relation that satisfies three intuitive properties; thus API processes are deemed equivalent unless they can be shown to be distinguished by one of these properties. So we have to generalise these properties, from relations over processes in API, to relations over configurations in ADPI. However we will only wish to relate two configurations if their external knowledge coincides. Therefore we revert to the technique we have already been using informally for presenting bisimulations, representing relations over configurations by parameterised families of relations over systems, which we recall in the following definition:

Definition 6.19 (typed relations) A *typed relation* in ADPI, is any family of relations $\mathcal{R}$, parameterised over type environments $\mathcal{I}$, which satisfies: $M\ \mathcal{R}_{\mathcal{I}}\ N$ implies $(\mathcal{I} \triangleright M)$ and $(\mathcal{I} \triangleright N)$ are both configurations.
We continue using the suggestive notation

$$\mathcal{I} \models M\ \mathcal{R}\ N$$

to indicate that M and N are related by the component $\mathcal{R}_{\mathcal{I}}$. ♦

We now generalise reduction barbed congruence, Definition 2.25, to a typed relation, by in turn generalising its three defining properties to typed relations.

Definition 6.20 (typed observations in ADPI*)* Let $M \Downarrow_{\mathcal{I}}^{\mathsf{barb}} k.a$ if

- $\mathcal{I}^r(a@k)\downarrow_{\mathsf{def}}$ and $\mathcal{I}^w(a@k)\downarrow_{\mathsf{def}}$
- $M \xrightarrow{(\tilde{e}:\tilde{\mathsf{D}})k.a!V} M'$, for some M', $(\tilde{e} : \tilde{\mathsf{D}})$ and V.
  When $\mathcal{I} \triangleright M$ is a configuration this amounts to demanding $\mathcal{I} \triangleright M \xrightarrow{(\tilde{e}:\tilde{\mathsf{D}})k.a!V} \mathcal{I}' \triangleright M'$, for some configuration $\mathcal{I}' \triangleright M'$.

So observations are *localised* to specific locations, and note that the observer requires both the read and write capability on the channel being observed.

We say a typed relation $\mathcal{R}$ *preserves observations* if
$\mathcal{I} \models M \mathcal{R} N$ implies $P \Downarrow^{\mathsf{barb}}_{\mathcal{I}} k.a$ if and only if $Q \Downarrow^{\mathsf{barb}}_{\mathcal{I}} k.a$
for all names k and a. ♦

The definition of *reduction-closure* is borrowed directly from Definition 2.24:

Definition 6.21 (*reduction-closure*) A typed relation $\mathcal{R}$ is reduction-closed, if each of its individual components is in turn reduction-closed. That is $\mathcal{I} \models M \mathcal{R} N$ and $\mathcal{I} \triangleright M \longrightarrow \mathcal{I} \triangleright M'$ implies $\mathcal{I} \triangleright N \longrightarrow^* \mathcal{I} \triangleright N'$ for some N' such that $\mathcal{I} \models M' \mathcal{R} N'$. ♦

The generalisation of *contextuality*, Definition 2.5, needs to take the presence of the observer's knowledge into account.

Definition 6.22 (*typed contextual relations*) A typed relation $\mathcal{R}$ is called *contextual* if it satisfies:

- (Compositional) $\mathcal{I} \models M \mathcal{R} N$ and $\mathcal{I} \vdash O$ implies $\mathcal{I} \models M \,|\, O \;\mathcal{R}\; N \,|\, O$ and $\mathcal{I} \models O|M \;\mathcal{R}\; O|N$.
- (Fresh weakening) $\mathcal{I} \models M \mathcal{R} N$ implies $\mathcal{I}, \langle e{:}\mathsf{D}\rangle \models M \mathcal{R} N$, whenever $\mathsf{bn}(e)$ is fresh (to M, N and $\mathcal{I}$).
- $\mathcal{I}, \langle e{:}\mathsf{D}\rangle \models M \mathcal{R} N$ implies $\mathcal{I} \models (\mathsf{new}\, e : \mathsf{D})\, M \;\mathcal{R}\; (\mathsf{new}\, e : \mathsf{D})\, N$, whenever both $\mathcal{I} \triangleright (\mathsf{new}\, e : \mathsf{D})\, M$ and $\mathcal{I} \triangleright (\mathsf{new}\, e : \mathsf{D})\, N$ are valid configurations. ♦

The major change from the untyped case, Definition 2.5, is that we only expect related systems to remain related when run in parallel with a restricted set of other systems, namely those that can be typed by the current knowledge of the observers. However knowledge of names is carefully managed by type environments and so we also need to add a form of weakening. We expect *contextual* relations to be preserved by inventing completely new names; with ADPI these could be new locations, new resources at existing locations, or even new registered resources.

Definition 6.23 (*reduction barbed congruence for* ADPI) We use $\cong$ to denote the largest typed relation in ADPI that

- preserves typed observations
- is typed contextual
- is reduction-closed. ♦

Note that although typed relations are formally families of relations over ADPI systems, the standard set theoretic operations, such as $\subseteq$, $\cup$, $\cap$ can be defined point-wise on them, and consequently it makes sense to talk of the *largest typed relation* satisfying a collection of properties. ♦

This is the natural generalisation of Definition 2.23 to typed relations. Indeed we use the same notation, $\cong$, for the two concepts; it should be apparent from the context whether it refers to a relation over untyped processes from API or a typed relation over systems in ADPI, that is a relation over ADPI configurations.

This behavioural equivalence inherits all the advantages and disadvantages discussed in Section 2.5. The advantages include:

- It is intuitively reasonable, as systems are only distinguished on the basis of three intuitively appealing behavioural properties.
- It takes into account the observer's current knowledge of the capabilities of systems, in a manner consistent with the ideas elaborated in the introduction to Chapter 4.
- By definition it satisfies the compositionality principle, given in (4.3).

The major disadvantage is that in general it is difficult to prove that two systems are equivalent relative to a given $\mathcal{I}$. To emphasise this let us attempt such a proof.

Example 6.24 Let us revisit the *located memory* $m[\![\mathsf{LMem}]\!]$ discussed in Examples 5.17 and 5.6. In order for a client to use the memory it needs to know the access methods at the appropriate types $\mathsf{get}@m : \mathsf{w}\langle \mathsf{T}_g \rangle$, $\mathsf{put}@m : \mathsf{w}\langle \mathsf{T}_p \rangle$. Suppose on the contrary that $\mathcal{I}_r$ is some type environment that has no entries for $\mathsf{get}@m$ and $\mathsf{put}@m$. Then one would expect

$$\mathcal{I}_r \models m[\![\mathsf{LMem}]\!] \cong \mathbf{0} \tag{6.16}$$

to be true; this formalises the intuitive idea that knowledge of the memory's access methods, and their location, is necessary in order to use it.

To prove (6.16) we need to construct a typed relation $\mathcal{R}$, which satisfies the three defining properties of $\cong$, such that

$$\mathcal{I}_r \models m[\![\mathsf{LMem}]\!] \;\; \mathcal{R} \;\; \mathbf{0}$$

The obvious approach is to define the family of relations $\mathcal{R}$ inductively as the least ones such that

- $m[\![\mathsf{LMem}]\!] \; \mathcal{R}_{\mathcal{I}_r} \; \mathbf{0}$
- for every $\mathcal{I}$, $M \;\; \mathcal{R}_{\mathcal{I}} \;\; N$ implies $M \mid O \;\; \mathcal{R}_{\mathcal{I}} \;\; N \mid O$ and $O \mid M \;\; \mathcal{R}_{\mathcal{I}} \;\; O \mid N$ for every O such that $\mathcal{I} \vdash O$
- $M \;\; \mathcal{R}_{\mathcal{I},\langle e:\mathsf{D}\rangle} \;\; N$ implies $(\mathsf{new}\, e : \mathsf{D})\, M \;\; \mathcal{R}_{\mathcal{I}} \;\; (\mathsf{new}\, e : \mathsf{D})\, N$
- $M \;\; \mathcal{R}_{\mathcal{I}} \;\; N$ implies $M \;\; \mathcal{R}_{\mathcal{I},\langle e:\mathsf{D}\rangle} \;\; N$, whenever the bound name of e is fresh to $\mathcal{I}, M, N$.

Note that for many $\mathcal{I}$, the relation $\mathcal{R}_{\mathcal{I}}$ is actually empty.

This gives a typed relation that by definition is contextual. But the difficulty is to show that it is reduction-closed; if $\mathcal{I} \models M \,\mathcal{R}\, N$ and $M \longrightarrow M'$ then we need to find a corresponding N' such that $N \longrightarrow^* N'$ and $\mathcal{I} \models M' \mathcal{R} N'$. We could try to proceed by induction on the derivation of the move $M \longrightarrow M'$. The base case is vacuous but how to proceed for the inductive cases is far from obvious. For example consider the case when M, N have the forms $M_1 \mid O$, $N_1 \mid O$ for some $\mathcal{I} \vdash O$ respectively, and $M_1 \mathcal{R} N_1$. Here we need to match every move $\mathcal{I} \triangleright M_1 \mid O \longrightarrow S$ with a matching one from $\mathcal{I} \triangleright N_1 \mid O$. Unfortunately this move may arise through communication between M_1 and O, and there is no obvious way to proceed to find the matching move. ■

However, as with API, bisimulations provide a conceptually convenient method for establishing behavioural equivalences:

Proposition 6.25 $\mathcal{I} \models M \approx_{bis} N$ *implies* $\mathcal{I} \models M \underset{\approx}{=} N$.

Proof: A priori bisimulation equivalence can relate configurations with different environments, and is therefore not a typed relation, as defined in Definition 6.19. However our method of presenting witness bisimulations, as families of parameterised relations over systems, allows us to transform $\approx_{bis}$ into a typed relation.

Let $\underline{\mathcal{B}}$ be the typed relation defined by letting $\mathcal{I} \models M \;\mathcal{B}\; N$ whenever $(\mathcal{I} \triangleright M) \approx_{bis} (\mathcal{I} \triangleright N)$. Then it is simply a matter of checking that $\mathcal{B}$ satisfies all the defining properties of $\underset{\approx}{=}$. It is reduction-closed by definition, and it preserves observations since bisimilar configurations must perform the same actions-in-context. Finally the first two requirements for contextuality are covered by (B) and (C) on page 201; the third follows from (scoping), Proposition 6.4, and strengthening for $\approx_{bis}$, given in (A) on the same page, page 201.

Since $\underset{\approx}{=}$ is the largest typed relation satisfying the defining properties the result follows. ■

It is a trivial matter to show that $\mathcal{I}_r \models m[\![\mathsf{LMem}]\!] \approx_{bis} \mathbf{0}$; the family of relations $\underline{\mathcal{R}}$ containing only one non-empty relation

$$\mathcal{I}_r \models m[\![\mathsf{LMem}]\!] \;\;\mathcal{R}\;\; \mathbf{0}$$

is trivially a bisimulation, as neither configuration can make any action-in-context. Consequently we can finish Example 6.24 and conclude

$$\mathcal{I}_r \models m[\![\mathsf{LMem}]\!] \underset{\approx}{=} \mathbf{0}$$

However the reader still familiar with the contents of Chapter 2 should easily be able to establish that this proof method for $\underset{\approx}{=}$ is not complete:

- $\mathcal{I} \models M \underset{\approx}{=} N$ does **not** necessarily imply $\mathcal{I} \models M \approx_{bis} N$.

It is simply a matter of adapting Example 2.29 to the distributed language:

Example 6.26 Let $\mathcal{I}_a$ be a type environment in which k is a location and $\mathcal{I}_a \vdash_k a$: rw. Then obviously

$$\mathcal{I}_a \models k[\![a?a!]\!] \not\approx_{bis} k[\![\mathsf{stop}]\!]$$

because one of these systems can perform an action-in-context, namely an input on a at k, while the other can perform no action-in-context. On the other hand by adapting the proof given in Example 2.29 we can show

$$\mathcal{I}_a \models k[\![a?a!]\!] \approx k[\![\mathsf{stop}]\!]$$

■

6.7 Justifying bisimulation equivalence contextually in ADPI

The object of this section is to define a version of bisimulation equivalence that does indeed coincide with the touchstone equivalence. The approach is straightforward; we adapt the development in Section 2.7 and define an *asynchronous* bisimulation equivalence for ADPI; this needs to take into account both the distributed nature of computation, and the presence of types.

As argued in Section 2.6 the inadequacy of bisimulation equivalence lies in the definition of the input actions-in-context. Consequently we define new actions

$$\mathcal{I} \triangleright M \xrightarrow{\alpha}_a \mathcal{I}' \triangleright N$$

where α is an input label, of the form $(\tilde{e} : \tilde{\mathsf{D}})k.a?V$. These are the least relations satisfying the rules in Figure 6.3 and are based directly on those in Figure 2.6, which define the untyped asynchronous actions for API. The rule (A-CON) coincides with the standard rule for inputing values, (L-IN) from Figure 6.1, while (A-DELV) is the typed version of (A-DELV) from Figure 2.6. The latter represents the delivery of the value V to the channel a located at k, while the former represents its consumption. Note that both require the environment to have the ability to send the value along a at k. The two final rules (A-WEAK) and (A-CTXT) simply allow these asynchronous actions to happen within evaluation contexts.

We leave the reader to check that the properties (1)–(5) on page 199 also apply to these asynchronous actions-in-context, and we use the associated notation without comment. The main extra property of these new actions is summarised in the following result:

Proposition 6.27 (asynchronous actions) Let α_i denote the input label $(\tilde{e} : \tilde{\mathsf{D}})k.a?V$ and suppose $\mathcal{I}$ allows α_i. Then

(i) $\mathcal{I} \triangleright M \xrightarrow{\alpha_i}_a N$ implies $\mathcal{I}, \langle \tilde{e}{:}\tilde{\mathsf{D}}\rangle \triangleright M \mid k[\![a!\langle V\rangle]\!] \xrightarrow{\tau}{}^{*} N'$, for some $N' \equiv N$.
(ii) Conversely, assuming $(\tilde{e})$ are fresh to M, $\mathcal{I}, \langle \tilde{e}{:}\tilde{\mathsf{D}}\rangle \triangleright M \mid k[\![a!\langle V\rangle]\!] \xrightarrow{\tau}{}^{*} N$ implies $\mathcal{I} \triangleright M \xRightarrow{\alpha_i}_a N'$ for some $N' \equiv N$.

Proof: Part (i) is proved by induction on the derivation of the asynchronous action-in-context $\mathcal{I} \triangleright M \xrightarrow{\alpha_i}_a N$, and there are four cases, depending on the last rule applied; in the first two α_i is guaranteed to be of the simple form $k.a?V$.

(A-CON)
$$\frac{\mathcal{I}^w(a@k)\downarrow_{\mathsf{def}} \qquad \mathcal{I} \vdash_k V : \mathcal{I}^w(a@k)}{\mathcal{I} \triangleright k[\![a?(X)\,R]\!] \xrightarrow{k.a?V}_a \mathcal{I} \triangleright k[\![R\{\!\!|^V/x|\!\!\}]\!]}$$

(A-DELV)
$$\frac{\mathcal{I}^w(a@k)\downarrow_{\mathsf{def}} \qquad \mathcal{I} \vdash_k V : \mathcal{I}^w(a@k)}{\mathcal{I} \triangleright M \xrightarrow{k.a?V}_a \mathcal{I} \triangleright M \mid k[\![a!V]\!]}$$

(A-WEAK), (A-CTXT) adapted from Figure 7.1

Figure 6.3 Asynchronous actions-in-context for ADPI

(A-CON): Here we have $\mathcal{I} \triangleright k[\![a?(X)\,R]\!] \xrightarrow{k.a?V}_a k[\![R\{\!\!|^V/X|\!\!\}]\!]$ because $\mathcal{I}^w(a@k)\downarrow_{\mathsf{def}}$ and $\mathcal{I} \vdash_k V : \mathcal{I}^w(a@k)$. But this information is sufficient to allow an application of (L-IN) to obtain the action-in-context

$$\mathcal{I} \triangleright k[\![a?(X)\,R]\!] \xrightarrow{k.a?V} k[\![R\{\!\!|^V/X|\!\!\}]\!]$$

Now (L-COMM), after an obvious application of (L-OUT), can be applied to obtain

$$\mathcal{I} \triangleright k[\![a?(X)\,R]\!] \mid k[\![a!\langle V\rangle]\!] \xrightarrow{\tau} k[\![R\{\!\!|^V/X|\!\!\}]\!] \mid k[\![\mathsf{stop}]\!]$$

(A-DELV): Here we have $\mathcal{I} \triangleright M \xrightarrow{k.a?V}_a M \mid k[\![a!\langle V\rangle]\!]$, and the result is trivial; $\mathcal{I} \triangleright M \mid k[\![a!\langle V\rangle]\!] \xrightarrow{\tau}{}^* M \mid k[\![a!\langle V\rangle]\!]$ in zero steps.

(A-WEAK): Here α_i takes the form $(e : \mathsf{D})\beta_i$, where β_i is $(\tilde{d} : \tilde{\mathsf{D}}')k.a?V$ and

$$\mathcal{I}, \langle e{:}\mathsf{D}\rangle \triangleright M \xrightarrow{\beta_i}_a N$$

We can apply induction to this action-in-context, which will actually give us the required sequence of τ moves:

$$\mathcal{I}, \langle e{:}\mathsf{D}\rangle, \langle \tilde{d}{:}\tilde{\mathsf{D}}'\rangle \triangleright M \mid k[\![a!\langle V\rangle]\!] \xrightarrow{\tau}{}^* N'$$

(A-CTXT): We leave this case, which is similar, to the reader.

Let us now prove the converse, part (ii); we use induction on the number of steps in the computation

$$\mathcal{I}, \langle \tilde{e}{:}\tilde{\mathsf{D}}\rangle \triangleright M \mid k[\![a!\langle V\rangle]\!] \xrightarrow{\tau}{}^* N$$

zero: From the relation ($\mathcal{I}$ allows α_i), and the fact that $(\tilde{e})$ are fresh, we have enough information to enable an application of (A-DELV) to obtain

$$\mathcal{I}, \langle \tilde{e}{:}\tilde{\mathsf{D}}\rangle \triangleright M \xrightarrow{k.a?V}_a M \mid k[\![a!\langle V\rangle]\!]$$

Then the required move, $\mathcal{I} \triangleright M \xrightarrow{\alpha_i}_a M \mid k[\![a!\langle V\rangle]\!]$ follows by a series of applications of (A-WEAK).

non-zero: If the derivation is of the form

$$\mathcal{I}, \langle\tilde{e}:\tilde{\mathsf{D}}\rangle \triangleright M \mid k[\![a!\langle V\rangle]\!] \xrightarrow{\tau} \mathcal{I}, \langle\tilde{e}:\tilde{\mathsf{D}}\rangle \triangleright M' \mid k[\![a!\langle V\rangle]\!] \xrightarrow{\tau}{}^{*} \mathcal{I}, \langle\tilde{e}:\tilde{\mathsf{D}}\rangle \triangleright N$$

we can apply induction. Otherwise the first step must involve an application of (L-COMM), and so the derivation takes the form

$$\mathcal{I}, \langle\tilde{e}:\tilde{\mathsf{D}}\rangle \triangleright M \mid k[\![a!\langle V\rangle]\!] \xrightarrow{\tau} \mathcal{I}, \langle\tilde{e}:\tilde{\mathsf{D}}\rangle \triangleright M' \mid k[\![\mathsf{stop}]\!]) \xrightarrow{\tau}{}^{*} \mathcal{I}, \langle\tilde{e}:\tilde{\mathsf{D}}\rangle \triangleright N$$

for some M' such that $\mathcal{I}_M \triangleright M \xrightarrow{\beta_i} M'$, for some $\mathcal{I}_M$, where β_i denotes the label $k.a?V$. But $\mathcal{I}$ **allows** α_i implies $\mathcal{I}, \langle\tilde{e}:\tilde{\mathsf{D}}\rangle$ **allows** β_i, and so we can apply (2) on page 199 to obtain $\mathcal{I}, \langle\tilde{e}:\tilde{\mathsf{D}}\rangle \triangleright M \xrightarrow{\beta_i} M'$. Also synchronous actions-in-context are also asynchronous, and so we have $\mathcal{I}, \langle\tilde{e}:\tilde{\mathsf{D}}\rangle \triangleright M \xrightarrow{\beta_i}_a M'$. Now a series of applications of (A-WEAK) will give $\mathcal{I} \triangleright M \xrightarrow{\alpha_i}_a M'$.

Moreover in this case N must be of the form $M'' \mid k[\![\mathsf{stop}]\!]$, where $M' \xrightarrow{\tau}{}^{*} M''$. Therefore the required asynchronous action-in-context is $\mathcal{I} \triangleright M \stackrel{\alpha_i}{\Longrightarrow}_a M''$. ■

Following the development in Section 2.6, these revised input actions give rise to an *observational lts* for ADPI. Here the configurations are of the form $\mathcal{I} \triangleright M$, as before, and the actions over configurations are given by

input: $\mathcal{I} \triangleright M \xrightarrow{(\tilde{e}:\tilde{\mathsf{D}})k.c?V}_a \mathcal{I}' \triangleright N$
output: $\mathcal{I} \triangleright M \xrightarrow{(\tilde{e})k.c!V} \mathcal{I}' \triangleright N$
internal: $\mathcal{I} \triangleright M \xrightarrow{\tau} \mathcal{I} \triangleright N$

This is called the *asynchronous lts* for ADPI, and for notational convenience, as in Chapter 2, we will denote an arbitrary action in this lts by $\mathcal{I} \triangleright M \xrightarrow{\mu}_a \mathcal{I}' \triangleright N$, although in two cases this coincides with the standard action $\mathcal{I} \triangleright M \xrightarrow{\mu} \mathcal{I}' \triangleright N$.

Definition 6.28 (*asynchronous bisimulations for* ADPI) A relation over ADPI systems is called an *asynchronous* bisimulation if it satisfies the standard transfer properties in the asynchronous lts.

We let $\mathcal{I} \models M \approx_a N$ denote the fact that there is some asynchronous bisimulation $\mathcal{R}$ such that $\mathcal{I} \triangleright M \;\; \mathcal{R} \;\; \mathcal{I} \triangleright N$. ♦

We leave the reader to check that this new equivalence corrects the mismatch in Example 6.26 between bisimulation equivalence and reduction barbed congruence; see Question 7 at the end of the chapter. Indeed the aim of this section is to show that these asynchronous bisimulations capture exactly reduction barbed congruence.

Theorem 6.29 $\mathcal{I} \models M \approx_a N$ *implies* $\mathcal{I} \models M \cong N$.

Proof: It is simply a matter of checking that $\approx_a$, viewed as a typed relation, satisfies the defining properties of $\cong$, in Definition 6.23 applied to ADPI. By definition it is reduction-closed, and it is simple to prove that it preserves typed observations. The proof that it is contextual is, of course, non-trivial. However the proof of Proposition 4.24 can be adapted to ADPI with asynchronous actions, as can that of Proposition 4.23. The final requirement, that $\mathcal{I}, \langle n{:}\mathsf{D}\rangle \models M \approx_a N$ implies $\mathcal{I} \models (\mathsf{new}\, e : \mathsf{D})\, M \approx_a (\mathsf{new}\, e : \mathsf{D})\, N$, whenever both $\mathcal{I} \triangleright (\mathsf{new}\, e : \mathsf{D})\, M$ and $\mathcal{I} \triangleright (\mathsf{new}\, e : \mathsf{D})\, M$ are configurations, requires a typed version of Proposition 2.20; see Question 6 at the end of the chapter. ■

What this means is that in order to show $\mathcal{I} \models M \cong N$ it is sufficient to exhibit an asynchronous bisimulation containing the configurations $(\mathcal{I} \triangleright M,\ \mathcal{I} \triangleright N)$. As we have seen, in the untyped case of API, asynchronous bisimulations are not quite as convenient to exhibit as synchronous ones. But synchronous bisimulations also provide a sound proof method:

Proposition 6.30 $\mathcal{I} \models M \approx_{bis} N$ *implies* $\mathcal{I} \models M \approx_a N$.

Proof: It is sufficient to show that $\approx_{bis}$ satisfies the requirements for being an asynchronous bisimulation, as given in Definition 6.28. To this end suppose $M \approx_{bis} N$ and $\mathcal{I} \triangleright M \xrightarrow{\mu}_a M'$; we must find a matching asynchronous move from N. The only non-trivial case is where μ is an input label, say $\alpha_i = (\tilde{e} : \tilde{\mathsf{D}})k.a?V$, where we need a move $\mathcal{I} \triangleright N \overset{\alpha_i}{\Longrightarrow} N'$ such that $(\mathcal{I}\ \mathsf{after}\ \alpha_i) \models M' \approx_{bis} N'$.

From part (i) of Proposition 6.27 we have $\mathcal{I}, \langle \tilde{e}{:}\tilde{\mathsf{D}}\rangle \triangleright M \mid k[\![a!\langle V\rangle]\!] \xrightarrow{\tau}{}^{*} M''$, for some $M'' \equiv M'$. Now $\approx_{bis}$ is compositional, and is preserved by fresh weakening; see (B), (C) on page 201. This means that

$$\mathcal{I}, \langle \tilde{e}{:}\tilde{\mathsf{D}}\rangle \models M \mid k[\![a!\langle V\rangle]\!] \approx_{bis} N \mid k[\![a!\langle V\rangle]\!]$$

and so the above sequence of τ actions can be matched; we have

$$\mathcal{I}, \langle \tilde{e}{:}\tilde{\mathsf{D}}\rangle \triangleright N \mid k[\![a!\langle V\rangle]\!] \xrightarrow{\tau}{}^{*} N'' \tag{6.17}$$

for some N'' such that $\mathcal{I}, \langle \tilde{e}{:}\tilde{\mathsf{D}}\rangle \models M'' \approx_{bis} N''$. In fact this can be rendered as $(\mathcal{I}\ \mathsf{after}\ \alpha_i) \models M'' \approx_{bis} N''$. But part (ii) of Proposition 6.27 can now be applied to (6.17), to obtain

$$\mathcal{I} \triangleright N \xrightarrow{\alpha_i}_a N'$$

for some $N' \equiv N''$; this is the required matching move. ■

Thus the various examples treated in Section 6.3, and the general proof methods developed there, can now be considered to pertain to our touchstone equivalence, $\cong$.

Our aim is to show that asynchronous bisimulations actually provide a *complete* proof method; that is whenever $\mathcal{I} \models M \cong N$ we can exhibit an asynchronous bisimulation $\mathcal{R}$ containing the pair $(\mathcal{I} \triangleright M,\ \mathcal{I} \triangleright N)$. However this is only true in a restricted setting.

Example 6.31 Let Γ be any environment that types both the systems

$$k[\![b!\langle a\rangle]\!] \qquad (\mathsf{new}\, c@k : \mathsf{rw})\, k[\![b!\langle c\rangle]\!]$$

Let $\mathcal{I}$ be obtained from Γ by omitting the typing for a at k.

Then one can check (how?) that

$$\mathcal{I} \models k[\![b!\langle a\rangle]\!] \approx (\mathsf{new}\, c@k : \mathsf{rw})\, k[\![b!\langle c\rangle]\!] \tag{6.18}$$

The problem is that any observer typeable by $\mathcal{I}$ does not know of the existence of a and therefore cannot distinguish it from the completely new name c. ■

To avoid this kind of anomaly we restrict our attention to *strict* configurations.

Definition 6.32 (*strict configurations*) A configuration $\mathcal{I} \triangleright M$ is *strict* if there is a type environment Γ such that

- $\Gamma <: \mathcal{I}$
- $\Gamma \vdash M$
- $\mathsf{dom}(\Gamma) \subseteq \mathsf{dom}(\mathcal{I})$

Note that it is only the last clause that is different from Definition 6.1; it requires that all names necessary to type M must be at least known to $\mathcal{I}$. ♦

Proposition 6.33 Suppose $\mathcal{I} \triangleright M$ is a strict configuration. Then $\mathcal{I} \triangleright M \xrightarrow{\mu} \mathcal{I}' \triangleright M'$ implies $\mathcal{I}' \triangleright M'$ is also a strict configuration.

Proof: From result (4) on page 199 we know that $\mathcal{I}' \triangleright M'$ is a configuration; that is $\Gamma \vdash M$ for some Γ such that $\Gamma <: \mathcal{I}$. To establish the current proposition we re-do the proof of this result, mimicking that of the corresponding result for API, Corollary 4.13, checking the extra requirement, that a Γ' can be found whose domain is contained within that of $\mathcal{I}'$.

First suppose μ is the output action $(\tilde{e}{:}\tilde{\mathsf{D}})k.a!V$, in which case $\mathcal{I}'$ is $\mathcal{I}, \langle V{:}\mathcal{I}^r(a@k)\rangle@k$, and subject reduction, (3) on page 199, gives $\Gamma, \langle\tilde{e}{:}\tilde{\mathsf{D}}\rangle \vdash M'$. A careful analysis of the rules for generating actions-in-context will reveal that each e_i will actually appear in the domain of $\langle V{:}\mathcal{I}^r(a@k)\rangle@k$, from which it follows that the required Γ' is $\Gamma, \langle\tilde{e}{:}\tilde{\mathsf{D}}\rangle$; such an analysis is given in Question 1 at the end of the chapter.

Now suppose μ is the input label $(\tilde{e} : \tilde{\mathsf{D}})k.a?V$. Here we know that $\mathcal{I}'$ is $\mathcal{I}, \langle\tilde{e}{:}\tilde{\mathsf{E}}\rangle$, where $(\tilde{e})$ are fresh to $\mathcal{I}$. They can also be assumed to be fresh to Γ and therefore Question 5 of the previous chapter assures us that $\Gamma, \langle\tilde{e}{:}\tilde{\mathsf{E}}\rangle$ is a valid environment. We can now mimic the input case in the proof of Corollary 4.13 to obtain $\Gamma, \langle\tilde{e}{:}\tilde{\mathsf{E}}\rangle \vdash M'$, which establishes the required result. ■

So for the remainder of this section let us consider the restricted *asynchronous lts* consisting only of strict configurations. The previous proposition means that bisimulation equivalence is also well-defined in this restricted setting. Moreover within this restricted setting we are able to repeat the general completeness argument of the untyped setting of Section 2.7. But this time round it is considerably more complicated due to the presence of types, and the parameterisation of the equivalences with respect to knowledge environments.

A typical example is the *definability of actions-in-context*, generalising Theorem 2.37, in which contexts are defined for mimicking actions. These actions are located, and the values that are sent and received may only make sense at the location of the action. But we will need to manipulate these values, perhaps at varying locations. Consequently we need to transform them into *global values*, with *global types*.

Moreover, as in Theorem 2.37, we need to make available at some standardised place the new names generated by the action we are defining. But here, in addition, we need to also make available their capabilities, and even new capabilities on names that are already known. So first let us develop some notation.

Definition 6.34 (*standard environment extensions*) The type environment $\Gamma, \langle V\!:\!\mathsf{T}\rangle$ is said to be a *standard* extension of Γ if

- T is a global type
- for every component v_i of V of the form $u@w$, if $u@w$ is new to Γ, that is, is not in $\mathsf{dom}(\Gamma)$, then $\Gamma \nvdash u : \mathsf{rc}$.

What this means is that new located channels in the extension cannot be registered resources. ♦

Lemma 6.35 If $\mathcal{I} \triangleright M \xrightarrow{\mu}_a M'$ *then* $(\mathcal{I}\ \mathsf{after}\ \mu)$ *is a standard extension of* $\mathcal{I}$.

Proof: If μ is the internal label τ then this is immediate, since $\mathcal{I}\ \mathsf{after}\ \tau$ coincides with $\mathcal{I}$. If it is the input action $(\tilde{e} : \tilde{\mathsf{D}})k.a?U$ then $\mathcal{I}\ \mathsf{after}\ \mu$ is $\mathcal{I}, \langle\tilde{e}\!:\!\tilde{\mathsf{D}}\rangle$. There may be a non-global entry in $\tilde{\mathsf{D}}$, a local channel type C. But this can be replaced by the global entry $\mathsf{C@loc}$.

Also if $c@l$ is new to $\mathcal{I}$ it must appear in $(\tilde{e})$. Therefore we know, because of the well-definedness of the label μ, that c must be new to $\mathcal{I}$, and therefore is certainly not a registered resource known to $\mathcal{I}$.

When μ is the output action label $(\tilde{e} : \tilde{\mathsf{D}})k.a!U$, the reason is the same. First if $c@l$ is new to $\mathcal{I}$ in $\mathcal{I}\ \mathsf{after}\ \mu$, which in this case unravels to $\mathcal{I}, \langle U\!:\!\mathcal{I}^r(a@k)\rangle$, then $c@l$ must again appear in $(\tilde{e})$. This follows from subject reduction, (3) on page 199, from which we can deduce that $\Gamma, \langle\tilde{e}\!:\!\tilde{\mathsf{D}}\rangle \vdash_k U : \Gamma^w(a@k)$, for some Γ whose domain coincides with that of $\mathcal{I}$. Secondly the types used in the extended environment, $\mathcal{I}^r(a@k)$, can easily be globalised, by replacing each occurrence of C with $\mathsf{C@loc}$. ■

So $(\mathcal{I}\ \mathsf{after}\ \alpha)$ always has the form $\mathcal{I}, \langle V\!:\!\mathsf{T}\rangle$, where $\langle V\!:\!\mathsf{T}\rangle$ represents the new information learnt by performing the action. Let us use $\mathsf{v}_{\mathcal{I}}(\alpha)$ to denote this value V and $\mathsf{ty}_{\mathcal{I}}(\alpha)$ the corresponding type T. Then the context we design for mimicking the performance of the action labelled α in the environment $\mathcal{I}$ will make available the new information $\mathsf{v}_{\mathcal{I}}(\alpha)$ at the type $\mathsf{ty}_{\mathcal{I}}(\alpha)$ at some fresh location. To this end, when discussing an action labelled α we use $\mathcal{I}_h$ to denote the extended environment

$$\mathcal{I}, \mathsf{succ} : \mathsf{rc}\langle \mathsf{rw}\langle \mathsf{ty}_{\mathcal{I}}(\alpha)\rangle\rangle, \mathsf{fail} : \mathsf{rc}\langle \mathsf{rw}\langle\rangle\rangle,$$
$$\mathsf{h} : \mathsf{loc}, \mathsf{succ}@\mathsf{h} : \mathsf{rw}\langle \mathsf{ty}_{\mathcal{I}}(\alpha)\rangle, \mathsf{fail}@\mathsf{h} : \mathsf{rw}\langle\rangle$$

where succ, $\mathsf{fail}, \mathsf{h}$ are all assumed to be fresh to $\mathcal{I}$. Here the location h may be viewed as a *home base* at which information may be collected. But its actual identity is not important. For if $\mathcal{I}_{\mathsf{h}} \models M \approx N$ for a particular h, then we can assume $\mathcal{I}_{\mathsf{h}'} \models M \approx N$ for *any* fresh h', where $\mathcal{I}_{\mathsf{h}'}$ is obtained from $\mathcal{I}_{\mathsf{h}}$ in the obvious manner, by renaming the entries at h, to h'. This follows because $\approx$ is preserved by injective renamings; see Question 10 at the end of the chapter.

Theorem 6.36 (definability in ADPI) *Let α denote an external action, $(\tilde{e} : \tilde{\mathsf{D}})k.a!V$ or $(\tilde{e} : \tilde{\mathsf{D}})k.a?V$, and suppose $\mathcal{I}$ allows α. Then there is a system $T(\alpha)$ with the following properties:*

1. $\mathcal{I}_{\mathsf{h}} \vdash T(\alpha)$.
2. *If $\mathcal{I} \triangleright M$ is a strict configuration then*
   (a) *$\mathcal{I} \triangleright M \xrightarrow{\alpha}_a M'$ implies $T(\alpha) \mid M \longrightarrow^* (\mathsf{new}\, \tilde{e} : \tilde{\mathsf{D}})(\mathsf{h}[\![\mathsf{succ}!\langle \mathsf{v}_{\mathcal{I}}(\alpha)\rangle]\!] \mid M')$*
   (b) *$T(\alpha) \mid M \longrightarrow^* R$, where $R \Downarrow^{\mathsf{barb}} \mathsf{h.succ}$ and $R \not\Downarrow^{\mathsf{barb}} \mathsf{h.fail}$ implies that R is structurally equivalent to $(\mathsf{new}\, \tilde{e} : \tilde{\mathsf{D}}')(\mathsf{h}[\![\mathsf{succ}!\langle \mathsf{v}_{\mathcal{I}}(\alpha)\rangle]\!] \mid M')$ for some M' such that $\mathcal{I} \triangleright M \stackrel{\alpha'}{\Longrightarrow}_a M'$, where $\alpha \sim \alpha'$.*

Proof: First consider the output case. We give the proof for a specific instance $\alpha_o = (c@k : \mathsf{C})k.a!\langle c, l\rangle$; the general case should be apparent from this example. Let $T(\alpha_o)$ denote

$$\begin{aligned}\mathsf{h}[\![\mathsf{fail}!]\!] \mid k[\![a?(x, y)\ \mathsf{if}\ P(x, y, l, \mathcal{I})\\ &\mathsf{then\ goto\ h.fail?succ!}\langle x@k, y\rangle\\ &\mathsf{else\ stop}]\!]\end{aligned}$$

Here $P(x, y, l, \mathcal{I})$ is shorthand for code that checks the incoming values at k, bound to x and y, are what is expected; the second must be equal to l while the first must be completely new. This means being completely new at k in the implicit underlying type environment with respect to which we are working. But since we are restricting attention to *strict* configurations this can be checked by ensuring that the first value is not declared at k in the domain of $\mathcal{I}$. So the testing code can be expressed as

$$\mathsf{if}\ y = l\ \mathsf{then\ (if}\ x \notin \mathcal{I}\ \mathsf{then\ goto\ h.fail?succ!}\langle x@k, y\rangle\ \mathsf{else\ stop)\ else\ stop}$$

where in turn $x \notin \mathcal{I}$ can be coded up as a sequence of tests of x against the names b such that $b@k$ is in the domain of $\mathcal{I}$. The use of fail in $T(\alpha_o)$ is to be able to guarantee, by the absence of a barb on fail, that the output action and subsequent tests have indeed occurred.

1. It is straightforward to show that the test is well-typed, $\mathcal{I}_{\mathsf{h}} \vdash T(\alpha_o)$.
2. (a) Suppose $\mathcal{I} \triangleright M \xrightarrow{\alpha_o}_a N$; recall that synchronous and asynchronous outputs coincide. Then an application of (L-COMM) from Figure 6.2, followed by applications of the (L-EQ), and then (L-MOVE) followed by another (L-COMM) to affect the synchronisation on fail, gives

$$\mathcal{I} \triangleright T(\alpha_o) \mid M \xrightarrow{\tau}{}^{*} (\mathsf{new}\, \tilde{e} : \tilde{\mathsf{D}})(\mathsf{h}[\![\mathsf{succ}!\langle c@k, l\rangle]\!] \mid N)$$

Now (6) on page 200 can be used to turn these τ moves into reductions.

   (b) Finally suppose $T(\alpha_o) \mid M \longrightarrow^{*} R$, where $R \Downarrow^{\mathsf{barb}} \mathsf{h.succ}$ and $R \not\Downarrow^{\mathsf{barb}} \mathsf{h.fail}$. Then by the same point we also know $\mathcal{I} \triangleright T(\alpha_o) \mid M \xrightarrow{\tau}{}^{*} R_\tau$, where $R_\tau \Downarrow^{\mathsf{barb}} \mathsf{h.succ}$ and $R_\tau \not\Downarrow^{\mathsf{barb}} \mathsf{h.fail}$, since barbs are preserved by structural equivalence. Here the inability to do a barb on fail is crucial; by examining the possible execution tree we see that R_τ must be of the form $(\mathsf{new}\, \tilde{e} : \tilde{\mathsf{D}}')(\mathsf{h}[\![\mathsf{succ}!\langle c@k, l\rangle]\!] \mid M')$ for some M' for which we can derive $\mathcal{I} \triangleright M \overset{\alpha'}{\Longrightarrow}_a M'$, where $\alpha' \sim \alpha$.

Now let us consider the input case, and again we only consider a typical example, when α_i is $(c@k : \mathsf{C}, d@l_1 : \mathsf{C}')k.a?(c, d@l_1, l_2)$. Here the test has to generate the new names, c at k and d at l_1 and then send them, together with the existing l_2, along a at location k; at the same time it exports the new names, suitably globalised at h. Let $T(\alpha_i)$ denote the system

$$\begin{aligned}
&\mathsf{h}[\![\mathsf{fail}! \mid \\
&\quad \mathsf{goto}\, l_1.(\mathsf{new}\, d : \mathsf{C}')\, \mathsf{goto}\, k.(\mathsf{new}\, c : \mathsf{C})\, a!\langle c, d@l_1, l_2\rangle \mid \\
&\qquad\qquad \mathsf{goto}\, \mathsf{h.fail?succ}!\langle c@k, d@l_1, l_2\rangle]\!]
\end{aligned}$$

Here we leave the reader to check that $T(\alpha_i)$ has the required properties; the reasoning is similar to that in the proof of Proposition 6.27. Here the role of fail is less important; it merely ensures that the various new names, declared locally, have been exported to the systems level. However the use of the asynchronous actions-in-context instead of synchronous ones is crucial, as the test $T(\alpha_i)$ cannot guarantee that the actual communication along a at k has happened. ■

As in the untyped case for API, these tests do not provoke exactly the same reaction in systems as the actions-in-context they are mimicking. When the test is applied the bound names of the action still scope the residual of the system. We need an *extrusion* lemma, generalising Lemma 2.38, which will allow us to strip off these from the residuals. It helps to simplify the situation a little if we use a slightly weaker version of $\approxeq$, which we call $\approxeq_p$.

Definition 6.37 (*pcontextuality*) A typed relation $\mathcal{R}$ is *pcontextual* if it is preserved by parallel contexts and a restricted form of weakening. Referring to Definition 6.22, we only require that the first clause and special instances of the third clause be satisfied. Specifically we say $\mathcal{R}$ is *pcontextual* if it satisfies:

- (Parallel) $\mathcal{I} \models M \;\; \mathcal{R} \;\; N$ and $\mathcal{I} \vdash k[\![P]\!]$ implies $\mathcal{I} \models M \mid k[\![P]\!] \;\; \mathcal{R} \;\; Q \mid k[\![P]\!]$ and $\mathcal{I} \models k[\![P]\!] \mid M \;\; \mathcal{R} \;\; k[\![P]\!] \mid N$.
- (Fresh location weakening) $\mathcal{I} \models M \,\mathcal{R}\, N$ implies that for every location type L there is some l fresh to $\mathcal{I}$ such that $\mathcal{I}, \langle l{:}\mathsf{L}\rangle \models M \,\mathcal{R}\, N$. ♦

Let $\eqsim_p$ be the largest typed relation over processes that is reduction-closed, preserves typed observations, and is *pcontextual.* Note that we only require weakening with respect to *some* fresh location l. But it turns out that Weakening follows for *arbitrary* fresh locations; see Question 10 at the end of the chapter. The purpose of this restricted form of contextual equivalence is to facilitate the proof of the following result.

Lemma 6.38 (extrusion for ADPI*) Suppose $\mathcal{I}, \langle V{:}\mathsf{T}\rangle$ is a standard extension of $\mathcal{I}$, and that in the extended environment $\mathcal{I}_{\mathsf{h}}$ the type of* succ *at* h *is* $\mathsf{rw}\langle\mathsf{T}\rangle$. *If*

$$\mathcal{I}_{\mathsf{h}} \models (\mathsf{new}\,\tilde{e} : \tilde{\mathsf{D}})\, M \mid \mathsf{h}[\![\mathsf{succ!}\langle V\rangle]\!] \eqsim_p (\mathsf{new}\,\tilde{e} : \tilde{\mathsf{D}}')\, N \mid \mathsf{h}[\![\mathsf{succ!}\langle V\rangle]\!],$$

where each e_i occurs in V then $\mathcal{I}, \langle V{:}\mathsf{T}\rangle \models M \eqsim_p N$.

Proof: We define the typed relation $\underline{\mathcal{R}}$ by letting $\mathcal{J} \models M \,\mathcal{R}\, N$ whenever

(i) $\mathcal{J} \equiv \mathcal{I}, \langle V{:}\mathsf{T}\rangle$, for some standard extension of $\mathcal{I}$
(ii) $\mathcal{I}_{\mathsf{h}} \models (\mathsf{new}\,\tilde{e} : \tilde{\mathsf{D}})(M \mid \mathsf{h}[\![\mathsf{succ!}\langle V\rangle]\!]) \eqsim_p (\mathsf{new}\,\tilde{e} : \tilde{\mathsf{D}}')(N \mid \mathsf{h}[\![\mathsf{succ!}\langle V\rangle]\!])$, for some fresh h, where we assume each e_i occurs in V.

Note that in the decomposition of $\mathcal{J}$ we do not require the values in V to be fresh to $\mathcal{I}$. We show that $\underline{\mathcal{R}}$ satisfies the defining properties of $\eqsim_p$, from which the result will follow.

Reduction closure is straightforward, but let us look at the preservation of barbs. Suppose $\mathcal{J} \models M \,\mathcal{R}\, N$, that is

$$\mathcal{I}_{\mathsf{h}} \models (\mathsf{new}\,\tilde{e} : \tilde{\mathsf{D}})(M \mid \mathsf{h}[\![\mathsf{succ!}\langle V\rangle]\!]) \eqsim_p (\mathsf{new}\,\tilde{e} : \tilde{\mathsf{D}}')(N \mid \mathsf{h}[\![\mathsf{succ!}\langle V\rangle]\!] \quad (6.19)$$

and $M \Downarrow^{\mathsf{barb}}_{\mathcal{J}} k.a$. We have to show that $N \Downarrow^{\mathsf{barb}}_{\mathcal{J}} k.a$. We know $\mathcal{J} \equiv \mathcal{I}, \langle V{:}\mathsf{T}\rangle$, and if $M \Downarrow^{\mathsf{barb}}_{\mathcal{I}} k.a$, then this is straightforward. But it may be that a at k is not known in $\mathcal{I}$; if not we can still check that N can perform an output on a at k, by examining the data produced at succ@h.

Let h′ be a fresh name, and let $\mathcal{I}_{\mathsf{h},\mathsf{h}'}$ be the extension of $\mathcal{I}_{\mathsf{h}}$ by the declaration $\mathsf{h}' : \mathsf{loc}[\mathsf{succ} : \mathsf{T}]$. We know that $a@k$ occurs somewhere in $\langle V{:}\mathsf{T}\rangle$; let $x@z$ be the corresponding sub-pattern in X, and now consider the following code, B, designed to run at h, which tests the data matching the sub-pattern $x@z$ and produces a barb at succ@h′ only if this is the required $a@k$:

$$\mathsf{succ?}(X)\ \mathsf{goto}\ z.\mathsf{if}\ z = k\ \mathsf{then}\ (\mathsf{if}\ x = a\ \mathsf{then}\ x?(Y)\ \mathsf{goto}\ \mathsf{h}'.\mathsf{succ!}\langle X\rangle\ \mathsf{else}\ 0)$$
$$\mathsf{else}\ 0$$

It is easy to see that $\mathcal{I}_{\mathsf{h},\mathsf{h}'} \vdash_{\mathsf{h}} B$ and therefore by *pcontextuality*

$$\mathcal{I}_{\mathsf{h},\mathsf{h}'} \models (\mathsf{new}\,\tilde{e} : \tilde{\mathsf{D}})(M \mid \mathsf{h}[\![\mathsf{succ}!\langle V\rangle]\!]) \;\mid\; \mathsf{h}[\![B]\!]$$
$$\approxeq_p (\mathsf{new}\,\tilde{e} : \tilde{\mathsf{D}}')(N \mid \mathsf{h}[\![\mathsf{succ}!\langle V\rangle]\!]) \;\mid\; \mathsf{h}[\![B]\!]$$

Because of the design of B, one can check that

$$((\mathsf{new}\,\tilde{e} : \tilde{\mathsf{D}})(M \mid \mathsf{h}[\![\mathsf{succ}!\langle V\rangle]\!]) \;\mid\; \mathsf{h}[\![B]\!]) \Downarrow^{\mathsf{barb}}_{\mathcal{I}_{\mathsf{h},\mathsf{h}'}} \mathsf{h}'.\mathsf{succ}$$

and since $\approxeq_p$ preserves barbs we have

$$((\mathsf{new}\,\tilde{e} : \tilde{\mathsf{D}}')(N \mid \mathsf{h}[\![\mathsf{succ}!\langle V\rangle]\!]) \;\mid\; \mathsf{h}[\![B]\!]) \Downarrow^{\mathsf{barb}}_{\mathcal{I}_{\mathsf{h},\mathsf{h}'}} \mathsf{h}'.\mathsf{succ}$$

But, again because of the design of B, this can only happen if M can produce an output on a at k, that is $M \Downarrow^{\mathsf{barb}}_{\mathcal{J}} k.a$.

So let us turn our attention to proving that $\mathcal{R}$ is pcontextual. First let us consider (fresh location weakening). Suppose $\mathcal{J} \models M \;\mathcal{R}\; N$. We have to show

$$\mathcal{J}, \langle l{:}\mathsf{L}\rangle \models M \;\mathcal{R}\; N \tag{6.20}$$

for some l fresh to $\mathcal{J}$; it is convenient to pick one different from the special name h. This assumption enables us to assert that

$$(\mathcal{I}, \langle l{:}\mathsf{L}\rangle)_{\mathsf{h}} \equiv \mathcal{I}_{\mathsf{h}}, \langle l{:}\mathsf{L}\rangle$$

But we know, from Question 10 at the end of the chapter, that $\approxeq_p$ is by preserved by weakening with respect to *any* fresh location; by applying this to (ii) we obtain

$$(\mathcal{I}, \langle l{:}\mathsf{L}\rangle)_{\mathsf{h}} \models (\mathsf{new}\,\tilde{e} : \tilde{\mathsf{D}})(M \mid \mathsf{h}[\![\mathsf{succ}!\langle V\rangle]\!]) \approxeq_p (\mathsf{new}\,\tilde{e} : \tilde{\mathsf{D}}')(N \mid \mathsf{h}[\![\mathsf{succ}!\langle V\rangle]\!])$$

From (i) we can also show $\mathcal{J}, \langle l{:}\mathsf{L}\rangle \equiv (\mathcal{I}, \langle l{:}\mathsf{L}\rangle), \langle V{:}\mathsf{T}\rangle$, which by the definition of $\mathcal{R}$ gives the required (6.20).

Now let us consider (parallel). From $\mathcal{J} \models M \;\mathcal{R}\; N$ we have to establish

$$\mathcal{J} \models k[\![P]\!] \mid M \quad \mathcal{R} \quad k[\![P]\!] \mid N$$

whenever $\mathcal{J} \vdash k[\![P]\!]$.

We know $\mathcal{J} \equiv \mathcal{I}, \langle V{:}\mathsf{T}\rangle$, and

$$\mathcal{I}_{\mathsf{h}} \models (\mathsf{new}\,\tilde{e} : \tilde{\mathsf{D}})(M \mid \mathsf{h}[\![\mathsf{succ}!\langle V\rangle]\!]) \approxeq_p (\mathsf{new}\,\tilde{e} : \tilde{\mathsf{D}}')(N \mid \mathsf{h}[\![\mathsf{succ}!\langle V\rangle]\!]) \tag{6.21}$$

and we will show that

$$\mathcal{I}_{\mathsf{h}'} \models (\mathsf{new}\,\tilde{e} : \tilde{\mathsf{D}})(M \mid k[\![P]\!] \mid \mathsf{h}'[\![\mathsf{succ}!\langle V\rangle]\!]) \approxeq_p (\mathsf{new}\,\tilde{e} : \tilde{\mathsf{D}}')$$
$$(N \mid k[\![P]\!] \mid \mathsf{h}'[\![\mathsf{succ}!\langle V\rangle]\!]) \tag{6.22}$$

for some fresh h'. The hypothesis also says that

$$\mathcal{I}, \langle V{:}\mathsf{T}\rangle \vdash k[\![P]\!] \tag{6.23}$$

and so in (6.22) $k[\![P]\!]$ may use the data V to interact with M and N, although the hypothesis (6.21) a priori does not compare the behaviour of M and N in the presence of the knowledge of V. But this knowledge is available on succ at h. We proceed as in the untyped version of the extrusion lemma, Lemma 2.38. Let F_{hk} denote the following system, which delivers the value V from h to the site k:

$$\mathsf{h}[\![\mathsf{succ}?(X)\,(\mathsf{goto}\,k.P_X \mid \mathsf{goto}\,\mathsf{h}'.\mathsf{succ}!\langle X\rangle)]\!]$$

where X is a pattern that matches V and P_X is designed so that $P_X\{\!|^V\!/\!_X|\!\}$ behaves just like P running at k. Unfortunately the design of P_X is not completely straightforward. There may be more than one variable in the pattern X that is matched to a given name; and the capabilities used by a name in P may partially come from $\mathcal{I}$, and partially from $\langle V\!:\!\mathsf{T}\rangle$. For these reasons, when defining P_X we need to repeatedly use the construct $\mathsf{if}\ v_1 = v_2\ \mathsf{then}\ \ldots\ \mathsf{else}\ \mathbf{0}$ in order to collect these dispersed capabilities. For example if $\mathcal{I}$ consists of k : loc, $b@k : \mathsf{r}\langle\mathsf{A}\rangle$ then $\mathcal{I}, \langle b@k\!:\!\mathsf{w}\langle\mathsf{A}\rangle@\mathsf{loc}\rangle \vdash_k P$ where P denotes $(\mathsf{new}\,a : \mathsf{A})\ b!\langle a\rangle \mid b?(x)\,\mathbf{0}$, and a required P_X, such that $\mathcal{I}, \langle x@z\!:\!\mathsf{r}\langle\mathsf{A}\rangle@\mathsf{loc}\rangle \vdash_k P_X$, is $(\mathsf{new}\,a : \mathsf{A})$ $\mathsf{if}\ k = z\ \mathsf{then}\ x!\langle a\rangle \mid b?(y)\ \mathsf{else}\ \mathbf{0}$.

In this fashion, because $\mathcal{I}, \langle V\!:\!\mathsf{T}\rangle$ is a standard extension, we can design P_X so that

(a) $\mathcal{I}, \langle X\!:\!\mathsf{T}\rangle \vdash_k P_X$
(b) $\mathcal{I}, \langle V\!:\!\mathsf{T}\rangle \models P \approx_{bis} P_X\{\!|^V\!/\!_X|\!\}$.

In (a) the use of the typing rule (TY-MATCH) is essential, as we have just explained. The term $P_X\{\!|^V\!/\!_X|\!\}$ does not correspond precisely with P, because of the required insertions of matchings. But (b) follows because the behaviour of $P_X\{\!|^V\!/\!_X|\!\}$ does mimic that of P precisely except that periodically it has to perform some β-moves of the form $\mathsf{if}\ n = n\ \mathsf{then}\ Q\ \mathsf{else}\ \mathbf{0} \longrightarrow Q$.

From (a) above it is now straightforward to see that $\mathcal{I}_\mathsf{h} \vdash F_{hk}$ and so we can apply *pcontextuality* to (6.21) to obtain

$$\mathcal{I}_{\mathsf{h},\mathsf{h}'} \models (\mathsf{new}\,\tilde{e} : \tilde{\mathsf{D}})(M \mid \mathsf{h}[\![\mathsf{succ}!\langle V\rangle]\!]) \mid F_{hk}$$

$$\eqsim_p$$

$$(\mathsf{new}\,\tilde{e} : \tilde{\mathsf{D}}')(N \mid \mathsf{h}[\![\mathsf{succ}!\langle V\rangle]\!]) \mid F_{hk}$$

Since $\eqsim_p$ is preserved by (environment strengthening), from Question 11, the same identity is also true for the more restricted environment $\mathcal{I}_{\mathsf{h}'}$.

Now it is a simple matter of rewriting these system terms in a semantics preserving manner, to obtain the required result. Exhibiting an explicit bisimulation-up-to-β

moves we can show

$$\mathcal{I}_{\mathsf{h}'} \models (\mathsf{new}\,\tilde{e} : \tilde{\mathsf{D}})(M \mid \mathsf{h}[\![\mathsf{succ}!\langle V\rangle]\!]) \mid F_{hk}$$
$$\approx_{bis}$$
$$(\mathsf{new}\,\tilde{e} : \tilde{\mathsf{D}})(M \mid k[\![P]\!] \mid \mathsf{h}'[\![\mathsf{succ}!\langle V\rangle]\!])$$

Note that this is true because the location h is not available to the environment; it does not occur in $\mathcal{I}_{\mathsf{h}'}$. Since $\mathcal{I} \models M_1 \approx_{bis} M_2$ implies $\mathcal{I} \models M_1 \eqsim_p M_2$, the required (6.22) follows, since the same identity holds for N. ■

These two proofs enable us to derive the essential result:

Corollary 6.39 Suppose that both $\mathcal{I} \triangleright M$ and $\mathcal{I} \triangleright N$ are strict configurations. Then $\mathcal{I} \models M \eqsim N$ implies $\mathcal{I} \models M \approx_a N$.

Proof: We show that the more restricted relation $\eqsim_p$, viewed as a relation over strict configurations, is an asynchronous bisimulation. The result will then follow, as $\mathcal{I} \models M \eqsim N$ obviously implies $\mathcal{I} \models M \eqsim_p N$.

So suppose $\mathcal{I} \models M \eqsim_p N$ and $\mathcal{I} \triangleright M \xrightarrow{\mu}_a M'$. We have to find a corresponding move $\mathcal{I} \triangleright N \xRightarrow{\hat{\mu}'}_a N'$, such that

$$(\mathcal{I}\ \mathsf{after}\ \mu) \models M' \eqsim_p N' \tag{6.24}$$

In fact we do the matching up to structural equivalence.

If μ is the internal action τ, then this follows immediately, since by definition $\eqsim_p$ is reduction closed; note that here we are implicitly using the coincidence of reduction with τ-moves, up to structural induction. So suppose μ is an external action α, of the form $(\tilde{e} : \tilde{\mathsf{D}})k.a!V$ or $(\tilde{e} : \tilde{\mathsf{D}})k.a?V$. Then $\mathcal{I} \triangleright M \xrightarrow{\alpha}_a M'$ ensures, by definability (Theorem 6.36), that

$$T(\alpha) \mid M \longrightarrow^* (\mathsf{new}\,\tilde{e} : \tilde{\mathsf{D}})(\mathsf{h}[\![\mathsf{succ}!\langle \mathsf{v}_{\mathcal{I}}(\alpha)\rangle]\!] \mid M') \tag{6.25}$$

Since $\eqsim_p$ is closed with respect to arbitrary fresh location weakening, we have

$$\mathcal{I}_{\mathsf{h}} \models M \eqsim_p N$$

The definability result also ensures that $\mathcal{I}_{\mathsf{h}} \vdash T(\alpha)$. So the *pcontextuality* of $\eqsim_p$ (and the particular form of the actual system $T(\alpha)$) ensures that

$$\mathcal{I}_{\mathsf{h}} \models T(\alpha) \mid M \eqsim_p T(\alpha) \mid N$$

At this stage the fact that $\eqsim_p$ is reduction-closed ensures that (6.25) must be matched by some reduction

$$T(\alpha) \mid N \longrightarrow^* R$$

where

$$\mathcal{I}_\mathsf{h} \models R \mathrel{\approxeq_p} (\mathsf{new}\,\tilde{e} : \tilde{\mathsf{D}})(\mathsf{h}[\![\mathsf{succ}!\langle \mathsf{v}_\mathcal{I}(\alpha)\rangle]\!] \mid M')$$

But $\approxeq_p$ also preserves barbs and so we must have $R \Downarrow^{\mathsf{barb}}$ h.succ and $R \not\Downarrow^{\mathsf{barb}}$ h.fail. So applying definability again we know that R must be structurally equivalent to a system of the form $(\mathsf{new}\,\tilde{e} : \tilde{\mathsf{D}}')(\mathsf{h}[\![\mathsf{succ}!\langle \mathsf{v}_\mathcal{I}(\alpha)\rangle]\!] \mid N')$, for some N' such that $\mathcal{I} \triangleright N \overset{\alpha'}{\Longrightarrow}_a N'$, for some $\alpha' \sim \alpha$.

Now we can apply extrusion, Lemma 6.38, to obtain

$$\mathcal{I}, \langle \mathsf{v}_\mathcal{I}(\alpha){:}\mathsf{ty}_\mathcal{I}(\alpha)\rangle \models M' \mathrel{\approxeq_p} N' \tag{6.26}$$

But this is enough to establish (6.24) above as $\mathcal{I}, \langle \mathsf{v}_\mathcal{I}(\alpha){:}\mathsf{ty}_\mathcal{I}(\alpha)\rangle$ is by definition $\mathcal{I}$ after α. ■

This concludes our exposition of the theory underlying contextual equivalences for ADPI. The results may be summarised as follows:

Theorem 6.40 (full-abstraction) Suppose $\Gamma \vdash M, N$. *Then*

- $\Gamma \models M \approx_{bis} N$ *implies* $\Gamma \models M \approxeq N$
- $\Gamma \models M \approx_a N$ *if and only if* $\Gamma \models M \approxeq N$. ■

6.8 Questions

1. Suppose $\mathcal{I} \triangleright M \xrightarrow{\mu} \mathcal{I}' \triangleright M'$.
   (i) If μ is the input label $(\tilde{e} : \tilde{\mathsf{D}})k.a?V$, prove
   - each e_i appears in the domain of $\langle V{:}\mathcal{I}^w(a@k)\rangle@k$
   - $\mathsf{fn}(M') \subseteq \mathsf{fn}(M) \cup \mathsf{n}(V)$.

   (ii) If μ is the output label $(\tilde{e} : \tilde{\mathsf{D}})k.a!V$, prove
   - each e_i appears in the domain of $\langle V{:}\mathcal{I}^r(a@k)\rangle@k$
   - $\mathsf{fn}(M') \subseteq \mathsf{fn}(M) \cup \mathsf{bn}(\tilde{e})$
   - $\mathsf{n}(V) \subseteq \mathsf{fn}(M) \cup \mathsf{bn}(\tilde{e})$.

   (iii) If μ is τ then $\mathsf{fn}(M') \subseteq \mathsf{fn}(M)$.
2. Suppose $\mathcal{I} \triangleright M \xrightarrow{\mu} \mathcal{I}' \triangleright M'$, where μ is the label $(c@l : \mathsf{C})k.a!c$. Show that l and k must coincide.
3. Use Question 5 from Chapter 5 to prove that whenever the rule (L-OUT) is applied to a valid configuration, the result, $\mathcal{I}\langle V{:}\mathcal{I}^r(a@k)\rangle@k \triangleright k[\![\mathsf{stop}]\!]$, is also a valid configuration.
4. (Weakening) Suppose $\mathcal{I} \triangleright M \xrightarrow{\mu} M'$ is an action-in-context for ADPI. Let $\mathcal{I}_m \triangleright M$ be a configuration such that $\mathcal{I}_m <: \mathcal{I}$. Prove that $\mathcal{I}_m \triangleright M \xrightarrow{\mu} M'$ is also a valid action-in-context.
   (See Lemma 4.11.)
5. (Fresh strengthening). State and prove a suitable generalisation of (fresh strengthening) from Lemma 4.11 to the actions in context of ADPI.

6. Prove that $\approx_a$, viewed as a typed relation is contextual. That is
   (i) $\mathcal{I} \models M \approx_a N$ and $\mathcal{I} \vdash O$ implies $\mathcal{I} \models M \mid O \approx_a N \mid O$ and $\mathcal{I} \models O \mid M \approx_a O \mid M$
   (ii) $\mathcal{I}, \langle e{:}\mathsf{D}\rangle \models M \approx_a N$ implies $\mathcal{I} \models (\mathsf{new}\, e : \mathsf{D})\, M \approx_a (\mathsf{new}\, e : \mathsf{D})\, N$
   (iii) if $\mathcal{I} \triangleright (\mathsf{new}\, e : \mathsf{D})\, M$ and $\mathcal{I} \triangleright (\mathsf{new}\, e : \mathsf{D})\, N$ are both valid configurations, then $\mathcal{I}, \langle e{:}\mathsf{D}\rangle \models M \,\mathcal{R}\, N$ implies $\mathcal{I} \models (\mathsf{new}\, e : \mathsf{D})\, M \;\mathcal{R}\; (\mathsf{new}\, e : \mathsf{D})\, N$.
7. (i) Referring to Example 6.26, prove $\mathcal{I}_a \models k[\![a?a!]\!] \approx_a k[\![\mathsf{stop}]\!]$.
   (ii) Without using the completeness theorem, Theorem 6.40, prove $\mathcal{I}_a \models k[\![a?a!]\!] \eqsim k[\![\mathsf{stop}]\!]$.
8. Let $\equiv_p$ be the least contextual equivalence relation between ADPI processes that satisfies the appropriate typed version of the axioms in Figure 2.3. Suppose $P \equiv_p Q$. Prove
   (i) $\Gamma \vdash k[P]$ if and only if $\Gamma \vdash k[Q]$.
   (ii) $P \equiv_p Q$ implies $\Gamma \models k[P] \approx_{bis} k[Q]$ for any Γ such that $\Gamma \vdash k[P]$.
9. Prove the assertion (6.18) from Example 6.31.
10. See Question 10 in Chapter 2 for the definition of when a name substitution σ is injective for a set of names.
    - Suppose σ is injective for all (simple) names used in $\mathcal{I}$, M, N. Prove $\mathcal{I} \models M \eqsim N$ implies $\mathcal{I}\sigma \models M\sigma \eqsim N\sigma$.
    - Show that the same property holds for $\eqsim_p$.
    - Use this to show that $\eqsim_p$ is preserved by *arbitrary* fresh location weakening; that is $\mathcal{I} \models M \eqsim_p N$ implies $\mathcal{I}, \langle l{:}\mathsf{L}\rangle \models M \eqsim_p N$ for *any* l fresh to $\mathcal{I}$.
11. Prove that both $\eqsim$ and $\eqsim_p$ are closed under environment strengthening; that is $\mathcal{I} \models M \eqsim_p N$ and $\mathcal{I} <: \mathcal{I}_l$ implies $\mathcal{I}_l \models M \eqsim_p N$.

Sources

Chapter 1: Proofs by induction permeate the theoretical foundations of computer science; [41] is a particularly good source, oriented towards computer scientists. The standard reference for bisimulation theory is [28], although the first part of [29] also covers much of this material. References to a number of introductory papers may be found at the website `http://lampwww.epfl.ch/mobility/`.

Chapter 2: The PI-CALCULUS has its origin in the label passing calculus of [9]; see [10] for a more recent perspective on this work. This led to the actual development of the PI-CALCULUS, reported originally in [30, 31]. However [29] is an excellent introduction, while [39] is now the standard, and encyclopaedic, reference text. When consulting the large research literature on the PI-CALCULUS, the reader should bear in mind that there is considerable variation in the actual syntax used. For example there may be no distinction made between names and variables, the match operator $\mathsf{if}\ v_1 = v_2\ \mathsf{then}\ R_1\ \mathsf{else}\ R_2$ may be absent, or may be replaced by a partial operator $\mathsf{if}\ v_1 = v_2\ \mathsf{then}\ R$, and instead of the recursion operator $\mathsf{rec}\ x.\ R$ there may be an iteration operator $!P$, or some mechanism for defining constants using recursive definitions.

The version of the PI-CALCULUS presented in Chapter 2 is usually referred to as the *asynchronous* PI-CALCULUS. It was originally proposed in [5], and independently in [20, 21], as a simplified language, in which the output action of the original language, $c!\langle V\rangle.P$, is replaced by $c!\langle V\rangle$; see Question 13 at the end of Chapter 2. Our asynchronous lts semantics, in Figure 2.6 and Figure 2.5, is based on the theory developed in [21, 19]. An alternative lts semantics is used in [40], which is based on [2]; see Question 16 at the end of Chapter 2.

Our touchstone behavioural equivalence, *reduction barbed congruence* Definition 2.25, is taken from [21]. A variation, called *barbed congruence* was proposed in [32], and is used extensively in [39]. Briefly *barbed bisimilarity* is first defined as the largest relation that is reduction-closed and preserves observations.

Then *barbed congruence* is defined to be the largest contextual relation contained in *barbed bisimilarity*. In contrast our relation, *reduction barbed congruence*, is simply taken to be the largest one satisfying all three properties simultaneously.

It is difficult to give rational arguments as to why one of these relations is more reasonable than the other. We have chosen *reduction barbed congruence* because it has a simpler definition – we want a behavioural equivalence that has such and such properties, and nothing more – and it is marginally more easy to apply technically.

Chapter 3: An excellent introduction to the theory of types is given in [36], although it is oriented towards their application in sequential programming languages. The first system of types for the PI-CALCULUS appeared in [33], where it was called a *sorting system*. This is more or less equivalent to our simple types, discussed in Sections 3.1 and 3.2, augmented by a mechanism for defining recursive types. Type systems with separate input and output capabilities on channels were first introduced in [34], although our version, in Section 3.4, is based on [16]. The latter is more general in that it allows types of the form $\mathsf{rw}\langle \mathsf{T}_r, \mathsf{T}_w \rangle$, where the types at which values can be read and written, T_r and T_r, need not be the same; in the former these types must be identical. This restricted set of types is not in general partially complete, see Question 13, a property that we use extensively. This idea of allowing different read and write capabilities in channel types was originally introduced in [18].

Part III of [39] discusses numerous other type systems for the PI-CALCULUS, and variations thereof.

Chapter 4: The first treatment of the effect of types on behavioural equivalences appeared in [34], and this line of research was further developed in [35] and [24]; it is discussed at length in Part IV of [39]. Our treatment is simply a variation on this, using the more general capability types. It is based entirely on [16], although there are some technical differences in both the set of types used, and some of the typing rules.

Chapter 5: ADPI is the *asynchronous* version of the language Dπ originally presented in [18]. The type system for ADPI is also taken from there; it is essentially the type system given in section 5 of that paper. The *registered resource* types $\mathsf{rc}\langle \mathsf{C} \rangle$ discussed in Section 5.5 were first introduced in [15]. The approach to type safety for ADPI, in Section 5.4, using tagged agents, is also taken directly from [18]. An alternative approach, in which occurrences of resource names are tagged, was given in [34], and is reported in [39].

Work on ADPI has been developed further in various directions. As presented in Chapter 5, the control of behaviour offered by types depends on a global type environment, and the assurance that all players in a system are well-typed. This is relaxed in [37], where each domain maintains its own type environment, recording its current knowledge of the network; this is periodically updated, with the arrival of new agents. A notion of trust is added to the type of domains, and it is shown how dynamic typing can protect trusted sites from untyped agents. In [17] ADPI is extended with the ability to transfer parameterised higher-order code between domains, which can be instantiated with local parameters by the receiving site. Within this framework both host and agent security can be maintained by the use of dependent and existential types. Finally in [23] recursive types have been added; to appreciate the usefulness of recursive types see Question 4 at the end of Chapter 5.

Chapter 6: The behavioural theory was originally presented in [15], while the example proofs come from [1]. This behavioural theory, parameterised with respect to type environments, should be widely applicable. For example, it has been extended to the higher-order version of ADPI, already referred to above, in [17]. Finally in [11] it has been extended to a version of the language in which locations, and the connectivity links between them, may fail.

General methods for reducing the size of witness bisimulation relations were studied in [38] for *CCS* and the PI-CALCULUS, and are reported in [39]. Many of these transfer to ADPI, but care must be taken in the presence of types. Our technique based on β-moves, in Section 6.3, was influenced by [25], although similar techniques are widely used in the literature; see for example [14, 13].

ADPI represents only one of the many attempts to add notions of *location* or *domain* to the PI-CALCULUS. The website `http://lampwww.epfl.ch/mobility/` maintains an up-to-date account of research activities in the area. Here we mention only briefly a sample of the more obviously related approaches. *Nomadic Pict* [42, 40] is conceptually closely related to ADPI, in that the space of domains is flat, and agents migrate between these domains of their own volition. However, unlike ADPI, agents are explicitly named and these names are used in inter-agent communication. Nevertheless all communication is still channel-based and local to particular domains.

On the other hand in *Klaim* [3, 4], communication is global, in the sense that agents at different domains may nevertheless communicate. In addition the underlying communication mechanism is quite different from that in ADPI. Here every domain maintains a data-set, often called a *tuple-space* and agents communicate indirectly by performing a set of pre-defined look-up and update operations on these spaces.

In the *Seal calculus* [8], domains are hierarchically organised computational sites in which inter-seal communication, which is channel-based, is only allowed among siblings, or between parents and siblings. Seals themselves may be communicated;

in effect this represents a sophisticated form of higher-order communication, in which *active* code is transmitted between domains.

Finally *Ambients* [7, 6, 27] is radically different from ADPI. Here domains, called ambients, are hierarchically nested as in the *Seal calculus*; but in ambients the notion of process as we have been using it more or less disappears. Instead these domains play the primary computational role. In fact computations consist solely of movements of these domains, in or out of their parent domain, or sibling domains. Then more standard notions of communication, such as the local communication channels, are implemented in terms of these mobile domains.

List of figures

Notation

Meta-variables:

n, m, a, b, c, l, k	Names	
x, y, z	Vars	
bv	basic values, integers, etc.	Figure 2.2
u, w	*identifiers*, Names ∪ Vars	
v	*simple values*	Figure 2.2
V	*values*, $(v_1, \ldots, v_n)$	Figure 2.2, Figure 5.3
e	*compound values*	Figure 5.3
R, S, B	terms in aPi	Figure 2.1
	agent terms in aDpi	Figure 5.2
P, Q	processes, *closed* terms in aPi	Notation 2.1
	agents, *closed* process terms in aDpi	page 131
M, N, O	systems in aDpi	Figure 5.2
M_t, N_t	tagged systems in tagged-aDpi	Figure 5.13
$\mu, \alpha, \alpha_o, \alpha_i, \tau$	action labels	aPi page 27
		typed aPi page 99
T	transmission types	aDpi page 195
		typed aPi Figure 3.2, Figure 3.6
		aDpi Figure 5.6
A	value types	typed aPi Figure 3.2, Figure 3.6
		aDpi Figure 5.6
C	channel types in typed aPi	Figure 3.2, Figure 3.6
	local channel types in aDpi	Figure 5.6

D	declaration types	TYPED API Figure 3.2, Figure 3.6
		ADPI Figure 5.6
E	(environment) entry types	TYPED API page 59
		ADPI page 143
Γ, Δ, $\mathcal{I}$	type environments	TYPED API page 59
		ADPI page 143
		ADPI with registered channels page 187

Types

$a \downarrow b$	$\{a, b\}$ has a lower bound	Definition 3.19
$a \uparrow b$	$\{a, b\}$ has an upper bound	Definition 3.19
$S\downarrow$		page 77
$\mathsf{T}_1 \downarrow \mathsf{T}_2$		API Proposition 3.20
		ADPI Proposition 5.9
$a \sqcap b$, $a \sqcup b$	lower/upper bounds	Definition 3.19
$\mathsf{T}_1 \sqcap \mathsf{T}_2$, $\mathsf{T}_1 \sqcup \mathsf{T}_2$		API Proposition 3.20
		ADPI Proposition 5.9
$\mathsf{ty}_{\mathcal{I}}(\alpha)$		ADPI page 236
$\mathsf{v}_{\mathcal{I}}(\alpha)$		ADPI page 236

Type environments

$\langle V{:}\mathsf{T}\rangle$	API Definition 3.2
$\langle V{:}\mathsf{T}\rangle_{@k}$	ADPI Definition 5.12
$\langle e{:}\mathsf{T}\rangle$	ADPI page 146
$\mathcal{I}$ after μ	API Definition 4.6
	ADPI Notation 6.2
$\mathcal{I}$ allows μ	API Definition 4.9
	ADPI Notation 6.2
$\Gamma(u)$, $\Gamma^r(u)$, $\Gamma^w(u)$, $\Gamma(u)\downarrow_{\mathsf{def}}$	API Definition 3.25
$\Gamma(e)$, $\Gamma^r(e)$, $\Gamma^w(e)$, $\Gamma(e)\downarrow_{\mathsf{def}}$	ADPI Definition 5.22
$\Gamma_1 <: \Gamma_2$, $\Gamma_1 \equiv \Gamma_2$	API Definition 3.27
	page 88
	ADPI Definition 5.24
	ADPI with registered names Definition 5.55

$\Gamma \downarrow u : \mathsf{E}$	API page 79, also used for ADPI
$\Gamma \downarrow_w u : \mathsf{E}$	ADPI Definition 5.10
$\Gamma\{u\}$	API page 86
$\Gamma\{e\}$	ADPI page 160

Typing:

$\mathsf{T} <: \mathsf{U}$	TYPED API Figure 3.7 ADPI Figure 5.7
$\Gamma \vdash \mathsf{T} <: \mathsf{U}$	ADPI with registered names Figure 5.15
$\vdash^{s} \mathsf{T} : \mathbf{ty}$	API Notation 3.1
$\vdash \mathsf{T} : \mathbf{ty}$	API Definition 3.16 ADPI Definition 5.8
$\Gamma \vdash^{rc} \mathsf{T} : \mathbf{ty}$	ADPI page 187
$\Gamma \vdash^{s} \mathbf{env}$	TYPED API Figure 3.3
$\Gamma \vdash \mathbf{env}$	TYPED API Figure 3.8 ADPI Figure 5.8 ADPI with registered resources Figure 5.15
$\Gamma \vdash^{s} V : \mathsf{T}$	TYPED API Figure 3.4
$\Gamma \vdash V : \mathsf{T}$	TYPED API Figure 3.9
$\Gamma \vdash_w V : \mathsf{T}$	ADPI Figure 5.9
$\Gamma \vdash^{s} R : \mathsf{proc}$	TYPED API Figure 3.5
$\Gamma \vdash R : \mathsf{proc}$	TYPED API Figure 3.10
$\Gamma \vdash_w R : \mathsf{proc}$	ADPI Figure 5.11
$\Gamma \vdash^{s} M$	ADPI Figure 5.10

Operational semantics:

$P \equiv Q$	structural equivalence	API Figure 2.3
$M \equiv N$		ADPI Figure 5.5
$M_t \equiv N_t$		TAGGED-ADPI Figure 5.13
$P \longrightarrow Q$	reduction semantics	API Figure 2.4
$M \longrightarrow N$		ADPI Figure 5.4
$M_t \longrightarrow_t N_t$		TAGGED-ADPI Figure 5.13
$P \longrightarrow^{err}$	runtime errors	API Figure 3.1
$M \longrightarrow^{err}_{\Gamma}$		ADPI Figure 5.12
$M_t \longrightarrow^{err}$		TAGGED-ADPI Figure 5.14

$P \Downarrow^{\mathsf{barb}} c$	observations	aPi Definition 2.22
$M \Downarrow^{\mathsf{barb}}_{\mathcal{I}} k.c$		aDpi Definition 6.20
$P \xrightarrow{\mu} Q$	actions	aPi Figure 2.5
$\mathcal{I} \triangleright P \xrightarrow{\mu} \mathcal{I} \triangleright Q$	actions-in-context	typed aPi Figure 4.1, Figure 4.2
$\mathcal{I} \triangleright P \xrightarrow{\mu} Q$		shorthand, Notation 4.8
$P \xrightarrow{\mu} Q$		shorthand, Notation 4.8
$\mathcal{I} \triangleright M \xrightarrow{\mu} \mathcal{I}' \triangleright N$		aDpi Figure 6.1, Figure 6.2
$\mathcal{I} \triangleright M \xrightarrow{\mu} N$		shorthand page 199
$M \xrightarrow{\mu} N$		shorthand, Notation 6.2
$\mathcal{I} \triangleright M \xrightarrow{\mu}_a \mathcal{I} \triangleright N$	asynchronous actions-in-context	aDpi Figure 6.3
$\mathcal{I} \triangleright M \xrightarrow{\tau_\beta} N$	β-moves	aDpi page 203

Semantic equivalences

$\mathsf{un}(\mu)$	output type omission	aPi page 113 aDpi page 199
$\mu \sim \mu'$	action equivalence	aPi page 199 aDpi page 199
$P \sim_{bis} Q$	strong bisimulation equivalence	page 5
$P \approx_{bis} Q$	bisimulation equivalence	Definition 1.5, Definition 1.6 aPi page 34
$P \approx_a Q$	asynchronous bisimulation equivalence	aPi Definition 2.31
$P \cong Q$	reduction barbed congruence	aPi Definition 2.25
$\mathcal{I} \models P \approx_{bis} Q$	typed bisimulation equivalence	aPi page 114
$\mathcal{I} \models M \approx_{bis} N$		aDpi page 201
$\mathcal{I} \models M \approx_a N$	typed asynchronous bisimulation	aDpi Definition 6.28
$\mathcal{I} \models M \cong N$	typed reduction barbed congruence	aDpi Definition 6.23

Bibliography

[1] Julian Rathke, Alberto Ciaffaglione, and Matthew Hennessy. Proof methodologies for behavioural equivalence in distributed pi-calculus. Computer Science Report 3:2005, University of Sussex, 2005.

[2] R. Amadio, I. Castellani, and D. Sangiorgi. On bisimulations for the asynchronous π-calculus. *Theoretical Computer Science*, **195**:291–324, 1998.

[3] Lorenzo Bettini, Viviana Bono, Rocco De Nicola, Gian Luigi Ferrari, Daniele Gorla, Michele Loreti, Eugenio Moggi, Rosario Pugliese, Emilio Tuosto, and Betti Venneri. The klaim project: Theory and practice. In Corrado Priami, ed., *Global Computing*, volume 2874 of *Lecture Notes in Computer Science*, pp. 88–150. Springer, 2003.

[4] Lorenzo Bettini and Rocco De Nicola. Mobile distributed programming in x-klaim. In Marco Bernardo and Alessandro Bogliolo, eds, *SFM*, volume 3465 of *Lecture Notes in Computer Science*, pp. 29–68. Springer, 2005.

[5] G. Boudol. Asynchrony and the π-calculus. Technical Report 1702, INRIA-Sophia Antipolis, 1992.

[6] Luca Cardelli and Andrew D. Gordon. Types for mobile ambients. In *POPL '99: Proceedings of the 26th ACM SIGPLAN-SIGACT symposium on principles of programming languages*, pp. 79–92, New York, NY, USA, 1999. ACM Press.

[7] Luca Cardelli and Andrew D. Gordon. Mobile ambients. *Theoretical Computer Science*, **240**(1):177–213, 2000.

[8] G. Castagna, J. Vitek, and F. Zappa Nardelli. The seal calculus. *Information and Computation*, **201**(1):1–54, 2005.

[9] U. Engberg and M. Nielsen. A calculus of communicating systems with label-passing. Technical Report, Arhus University, 1986.

[10] Uffe H. Engberg and Mogens Nielsen. A calculus of communicating systems with label passing-ten years after. In Gordon Plotkin, Colin Stirling and Mads Tofte, eds, *Proof, Language, and Interaction; Essays in Honour of Robin Milner*, Foundations of Computing, chapter V, Mobility, pp. 599–622. MIT Press, 2000.

[11] Adrian Francalanza and Matthew Hennessy. A theory of system behaviour in the presence of node and link failures. In *Conference on Concurrency Theory*, pp. 368–382, 2005.

[12] A.D. Gordon and A.S.A. Jeffrey. Types and effects for asymmetric cryptographic protocols. *Journal of Computer Security*, **12**(3/4):435–484, 2004.

[13] J.F. Groote and M.P.A. Sellink. Confluence for process verification. *Theoretical Computer Science*, **170**(1–2):47–81, 1996.

[14] Jan Friso Groote and Jaco van de Pol. State space reduction using partial tau-confluence. In *Mathematical Foundations of Computer Science*, pp. 383–393, 2000.

[15] Matthew Hennessy, Massimo Merro, and Julian Rathke. Towards a behavioural theory of access and mobility control in distributed systems. *Theoretical Computer Science*, **322**:615–669, 2003.

[16] Matthew Hennessy and Julian Rathke. Typed behavioural equivalences for processes in the presence of subtyping. *Mathematical Structures in Computer Science*, **14**:651–684, 2004.

[17] Matthew Hennessy, Julian Rathke, and Nobuko Yoshida. Safedpi: A language for controlling mobile code. *Acta Informatica*, **42**(4-5):227–290, 2005.

[18] Matthew Hennessy and James Riely. Resource access control in systems of mobile agents. *Information and Computation*, **173**:82–120, 2002.

[19] K. Honda and N. Yoshida. On reduction-based process semantics. *Theoretical Computer Science*, **152**(2):437–486, 1995.

[20] Kohei Honda and Mario Tokoro. An object calculus for asynchronous communication. In *ECOOP '91: Proceedings of the European Conference on Object-Oriented Programming*, pp. 133–147, London, UK, 1991. Springer-Verlag.

[21] Kohei Honda and Mario Tokoro. On asynchronous communication semantics. In P. Wegner, M. Tokoro, and O. Nierstrasz, eds, *Proceedings of the ECOOP '91 Workshop on Object-Based Concurrent Computing*, volume 612 of *LNCS 612*. Springer-Verlag, 1992.

[22] Kohei Honda and Nobuko Yoshida. A uniform type structure for secure information flow. In *Symposium on Principles of Programming Languages*, pp. 81–92, 2002.

[23] Samuel Hym and Matthew Hennessy. Adding recursion to dpi. In Peter D. Mosses and Irek Ulidowski, eds, *Preliminary Proceedings of the Second Workshop on Structural Operational Semantics*, pp. 50–67, 2005. Full version available as Computer Science Report 2005:06, University of Sussex.

[24] A.S.A. Jeffrey and J. Rathke. Full abstraction for polymorphic pi-calculus. In *Proceedings of Foundations of Software Science and Computation Structures*, volume 3441 of *Lecture Notes in Computer Science*, pp. 266–281. Springer-Verlag, 2005.

[25] Alan Jeffrey and Julian Rathke. A theory of bisimulation for a fragment of concurrent ml with local names. *Theoretical Computer Science*, **323**:1–48, 2004.

[26] Naoki Kobayashi. Type systems for concurrent processes: From deadlock-freedom to livelock-freedom, time-boundedness. In Jan van Leeuwen, Osamu Watanabe, Masami Hagiya, Peter D. Mosses, and Takayasu Ito, eds, *IFIP TCS*, volume 1872 of *Lecture Notes in Computer Science*, pp. 365–389. Springer, 2000.

[27] Massimo Merro and Francesco Zappa Nardelli. Behavioural theory for mobile ambients. In Jean-Jacques Lévy, Ernst W. Mayr, and John C. Mitchell, eds, *IFIP TCS*, pp. 549–562. Kluwer, 2004.

[28] R. Milner. *Communication and Concurrency*. Prentice-Hall, 1989.

[29] R. Milner. *Comunicating and mobile systems: the π-calculus*. Cambridge University Press, 1999.

[30] R. Milner, J. Parrow, and D. Walker. A calculus of mobile processes, Part I. *Information and Computation*, **100**(1):1–40, 1992.

[31] R. Milner, J. Parrow, and D. Walker. A calculus of mobile processes, Part II. *Information and Computation*, **100**(1):41–77, 1992.

[32] R. Milner and D. Sangiorgi. Barbed bisimulation. In W. Kuich, ed., *Proceedings 19th ICALP*, volume 623 of *Lecture Notes in Computer Science*, pp. 685–695. Springer-Verlag, 1992.

[33] Robin Milner. The polyadic π-calculus: a tutorial. In *Proceedings International Summer School on Logic and Algebra of Specification*, Marktoberdorf, 1991.

[34] B. Pierce and D. Sangiorgi. Typing and subtyping for mobile processes. *Journal of Mathematical Structures in Computer Science*, **6**(5):409–454, 1996. An extended abstract in *Proceedings LICS 93*, IEEE Computer Society Press.

[35] B. Pierce and D. Sangiorgi. Behavioral equivalence in the polymorphic pi-calculus. *Journal of the ACM*, **47**(3):531–584, 2000.

[36] B.C. Pierce. *Types and programming languages*. The MIT Press, 2002.

[37] James Riely and Matthew Hennessy. Trust and partial typing in open systems of mobile agents. *Journal of Automated Reasoning*, **31**:335–370, 2003.

[38] D. Sangiorgi. On the bisimulation proof method. *Mathematical Structures in Computer Science*, **8**:447–479, 1998.

[39] D. Sangiorgi and D. Walker. *The π-calculus: a Theory of Mobile Processes*. Cambridge University Press, 2001.

[40] Peter Sewell, Paweł T. Wojciechowski, and Benjamin C. Pierce. Location-independent communication for mobile agents: a two-level architecture. In *Internet Programming Languages, LNCS 1686*, pp. 1–31. Springer-Verlag, October 1999.

[41] G. Winskel. *The Formal Semantics of Programming Languages*. The MIT Press, 1992.

[42] Paweł T. Wojciechowski and Peter Sewell. Nomadic Pict: Language and infrastructure design for mobile agents. In *Proceedings of ASA/MA 99: Agent Systems and Applications/Mobile Agents (Palm Springs)*, pp. 2–12, October 1999.

Index

Printed in the United States
by Baker & Taylor Publisher Services